Business
Studies
Today

Business Studies Today

John Ryan
Head of Economics and Business Studies
Bedford Modern School
and
John Richards
Head of Careers
Bedford Modern School

CAMBRIDGE
UNIVERSITY PRESS

Published by the Press Syndicate
of the University of Cambridge
The Pitt Building, Trumpington Street, Cambridge CB2 1RP
40 West 20th Street, New York, NY 10011-4211, USA
10 Stamford Road, Oakleigh, Melbourne 3166, Australia

First published 1991
Third printing 1994

Printed in Great Britain by Scotprint Ltd, Musselburgh

British Library cataloguing in publication data

Ryan, John
Business studies today.
1. Business studies
1. Title   II. Richard, John
658

ISBN 0 521 37632 7

Contents

Acknowledgements

The author and publisher would like to thank the following for their kind permission to reproduce material in this book:

Tick Ahearn for Figures 1.1, 1.4 (milling photo by Tick Ahearn with kind permission of Foster Mills of Cambridge; bakery photo by Tick Ahearn with kind permission of Tesco, Bar Hill, Cambridge), 1.5, 1.6, 5.2, 5.3, 6.5, 10.1, 10.2, 15.3a,b,c,e and 22.2; Association of British Travel Agents for Figure 22.5.; Association of Consumer Research for Figure 22.6.; Barclays Bank PLC for the Barclays Bank job application form on page 72; Basil Blackwell for Tables 7.1, 9.5, 9.6 and 9.7; Beecham Health care for Figure 15.4; British Standards Institution for Figure 22.7; *Cambridge Evening News* for advertisement in Figure 6.6; Club Twenty Four for Figure 22.3; *The Financial Times* for the articles on pages 84 and 242, and for Tables 13.3. and 14.1; Glass and Glazing Federation for Figure 22.5; Grafton Books, part of HarperCollins Publishers, for Figure 5.4 on job satisfaction, from Frederick Herzberg, *Work and the Nature of Man*; The Guardian News Service Ltd for the article on pages 111–12 by Steven Percy and Harriet Lamb, © *The Guardian*; The Controller of Her Majesty's Stationery Office for Table 7.3 (taken from the Department of Employment Labour Force Survey), Figures 7.5, 7.6 and 7.7 and Table 7.4 (taken from *Labour Market Quarterly*, January 1989); Table 8.1 (taken from New Earnings Survey, Department of Employment, 1986), Table 9.1 (Department of Employment), Figure 9.1 and Table 9.2 (taken from *Annual Abstract of Statistics*, 1988 edition), Table 9.3 (taken from the Annual Report of the Certification Officer, 1988), Table 9.4 (taken from the Annual Report of the Certification Officer, 1988), Tables 9.8 and Table 9.9 (taken from the *Department of Employment Gazette*), the table on page 226 (Department of Employment); Hoover PLC for Figure 15.3d; International Stock Exchange Photo Library for Figures 2.2 and 18.1; Tick Ahearn and Marks & Spencer PLC for the collage of document covers on page 71; Milton Keynes Development Corporation for Table A on page 127; Office of Fair Trading for Figure 22.4; Philip Allan Publishers for Table 10.1 and the table on page 227; Retail Motor Industry Federation for Figure 22.5; Mr G. Williams and *Teachers' Weekly* for the article on pages 62–3; and Professor Roger Vickerman and Philip Allan Publishers for Figure 19.2 (from 'The Economic Implications of the Channel Tunnel' in *Economic review* vol. 3, no. 5, May 1986); Ford Motor Co. Ltd for Fig. 5.3.

Every effort has been made to reach all the copyright holders; the publishers would be glad to hear from anyone whose rights they have unknowingly infringed.

SECTION A

The Structure and Organisation of Business

CHAPTER 1

The Background to Business Activity

All business activity is essentially concerned with the satisfying of human wants. The term **business** describes any organisation which exists to provide the goods and services which people wish to consume. However, the satisfying of wants requires the utilisation of **resources**. The nature of all business activity, therefore, is the using, combining and organisation of resources in order to satisfy wants. To understand more fully the nature of business activity it is necessary to investigate what is meant by the terms **wants** and **resources**.

Wants

People want many things. First, they need the basic essentials of life – food, shelter, clothing, warmth and so on. Once these essentials have been provided, people want more luxury items, usually called **consumer goods**. These are such things as furniture, cars, televisions and microwave cookers. The more developed the society becomes the more diverse the wants – dishwashers, video recorders, foreign holidays.

In addition to consumer goods there are **capital goods**, also called **producer goods**. These are the goods which are produced not to satisfy our immediate wants but which add to our long-term ability to produce more consumer goods. Capital goods include factories, machines, tools, transport systems and so on. Therefore many businesses are involved in the production of capital goods to meet the requirements of other businesses which in turn produce consumer goods.

The most important characteristic of all wants is that they are unlimited. As soon as certain wants are satisfied new wants appear. People in Britain today want many things which were not even dreamed of

Figure 1.1 Consumer Goods

20 years ago – home computers, cordless telephones, compact disc players and much more. However, the resources available to produce the goods and services people want are limited.

Resources

Resources are usually called the **factors of production** and can be divided into four broad groups.

1. **Land**: this factor consists of all naturally occurring non-human resources. It therefore includes the land itself, the oceans, minerals and timber. Even the climate can be considered as a natural resource.
2. **Labour**: this is the use of human skills, both physical and mental. It is not only the number of workers available which is important when considering the factor labour but also their skill, health, education and so on.

3. **Capital Goods**: capital goods are not naturally occurring resources. As mentioned above, they consist of everything which is manufactured in order to assist future production, and therefore include everything from simple tools to factories and industrial complexes.

4. **Enterprise**: enterprise is the term used to describe the organizing of resources in order to produce the goods and services people want. The person undertaking this role is called an **entrepreneur**. The functions of the entrepreneur are first to hire and combine the other factors of production and secondly to take the risk that the resulting output may or may not be sold at a profit.

It is the combination of the above factors which enables the country to produce the things people want. However, because resources are limited in supply it is not possible to produce everything people want to consume. It is this relationship between unlimited wants and limited resources which gives rise to the central problem of all societies – **scarcity**.

QUICK QUESTIONS 1

1. *Explain the central purpose of business activity.*
2. *Explain the difference between consumer goods and capital goods. Give an example of each.*
3. *Name the four factors of production and write a sentence about each.*

Scarcity

To say something is scarce does not necessarily mean that there is only a small amount of it. The important point about scarcity is that there is less of something available than people want. Therefore a resource is scarce if the total amount available is not sufficient to produce all the things people want. However, such things as rotten eggs are not scarce because no one wants them. The existence of scarcity gives rise to the necessity to make choices.

Choice

If it is not possible to produce everything people want from the available resources, we must choose which wants are to be satisfied. If more capital goods are produced there will be fewer consumer goods in the short term. These types of economic choices are usually explained in terms of how people spend their money. More spent on clothes means less spent on records. Do we have a foreign holiday or new car? These choices also occur in the satisfying of national wants: more hospitals means fewer schools, better roads means less spent on defence, and so on. Having to make choices about which wants are to be satisfied and which wants will remain unsatisfied gives rise to a very important concept: **opportunity cost**.

Opportunity Cost

Opportunity cost is simply the cost of satisfying any want in terms of what opportunities must be forgone in order to do so. It is the true value of satisfying any want. Here are two examples:

1. Assume you are given £20 as a birthday present. There are a great many possibilities as to how you spend the money. In the end you bring the choice down to either a new pair of shoes or a personal stereo. If you buy one you will not be able to buy the other. Therefore the opportunity cost of the shoes is the stereo and the opportunity cost of the stereo is the shoes.
2. A Japanese car manufacturer has decided to build a new factory in Britain. There are three possible sites for the factory. After careful consideration it is decided that site A is just more suitable than site B, which is just better than site C. The opportunity cost of the chosen site is site B because this is the **next-best alternative**.

Therefore the process of satisfying wants can be expressed as:

$$\text{Finite resources} \atop \text{Infinite wants} \rightarrow {\text{Scarce} \atop \text{Resources}} \rightarrow {\text{Choice of} \atop \text{Resource} \atop \text{allocation}} \rightarrow {\text{Opportunity} \atop \text{cost}}$$

Finally, it is important to note that not all goods have an opportunity cost. If there is more of something available than people want, then nothing has to be given up in order to possess it. This means the item has no opportunity cost and therefore, in an economic sense, no value. Such items, e.g. fresh air, are known as **free goods**. Goods which have an opportunity cost are known as **economic goods**.

The concepts of scarcity and opportunity cost lead to the necessity of making choices. The principal choices facing all societies can be summarised as:

What   to produce
How much   to produce
For whom   to produce

How different societies organise themselves to answer these questions will be dealt with later in the chapter. However, one factor common to all societies is that they are concerned to use their resources as efficiently as possible in order to satisfy the largest number of wants. The efficient use of resources involves **specialisation**.

Specialisation

The best way to use the factors of production is to specialise in what people can do best. Even very primitive societies operate some form of basic specialisation, e.g. in prehistoric tribes some people concentrated on hunting, some on fishing, some on making basic tools and weapons, and so on. In this way they were able to improve the provision of the basic essentials they needed. The alternative would have been for each member of the tribe to try and provide for all of their needs themselves, which would have been very inefficient. This specialisation is the basis of all economic organisation and has become more and more complex as society has developed. There are a number of obvious advantages associated with specialisation. Not only do

people perform tasks for which they have a special aptitude but also, because the tasks are repeated many times, people become skilled in them. Time and resources are saved in not moving from one job to another. This process can be carried further than just concentrating on one or more selected tasks. It is possible to divide up the the processes involved in most tasks into a series of very much smaller tasks, with one worker concentrating on each of these smaller activities. This further extension of specialisation is known as the **division of labour**. In some industries, e.g. the motor industry, such division of labour breaks the activity of making a motor vehicle down into very small operations. Inserting and tightening a screw may be in two or more stages. Once each task can be broken down into a number of simple operations workers can be trained more easily and cheaply. It also makes possible the introduction of machinery, which adds precision and power to the job.

Figure 1.2 Specialisation

STUDENT TASK

The first person to undertake a detailed study of the benefits of specialisation was the economist Adam Smith in his famous work *An Inquiry into the Nature and Causes of the Wealth of Nations*. He used the example of the production of pins to illustrate the gains resulting from breaking down the manufacture of a simple item into a number of separate operations. He explained how this was done in the following way:

> One man draws out the wire, another straights it, a third cuts it, a fourth points it, a fifth grinds it at the top (for receiving the head). To make the head requires two or three distinct operations. To put it on is a peculiar business, to whiten the pins is another. It is even a trade by itself to put them into the paper, and the important business of making a pin is divided in this way into eighteen different processes, which in some manufactories are all performed by distinct hands.

Smith showed that the result of this specialisation was to dramatically increase the number of pins which could be produced. He continued:

> Each person, therefore, could make one-tenth of 48,000 pins in a day. But if they had wrought separately without having been educated to this peculiar business, they certainly could not have each made twenty, and possibly not even one.

Smith's example shows how the division of labour has led to the ability to mass produce all manner of items, from a simple pin to extremely complex items such as cars and aeroplanes.

1. List 4 reasons why the division of labour described by Smith resulted in such a large increase in the number of pins produced.
2. Can you think of any disadvantages which may result from workers concentrating on only a very small part of the production process?
3. Select a simple household item, e.g. a pair of scissors or a toothbrush, and list the major operations involved in its manufacture.

However, when workers specialise in a product or one part of a product they cannot live from what they themselves produce. The blacksmith cannot eat the horseshoes he makes and the baker will need something more than bread to live on. Both have to **exchange** their produce for the items they want. Also, goods are not often bought directly from the manufacturer. They are made available at convenient times and places, and in the form people want them, by a chain of individuals and organisations involved in the **distribution** of goods and services.

Therefore the use of resources to satisfy wants involves both production and distribution. In addition there is one other group of activities which must be mentioned. This is the group of services which make the other activities in the productive process easier to perform. Such services as banking, insurance, transport and communications are in this group. They help both production and consumption, and taken together with distribution they are collectively known as **commerce**. It is usual to distinguish distribution, which links production and consumption, from the other commercial activities which surround this process and make it more efficient. This can be shown in Figure 1.3.

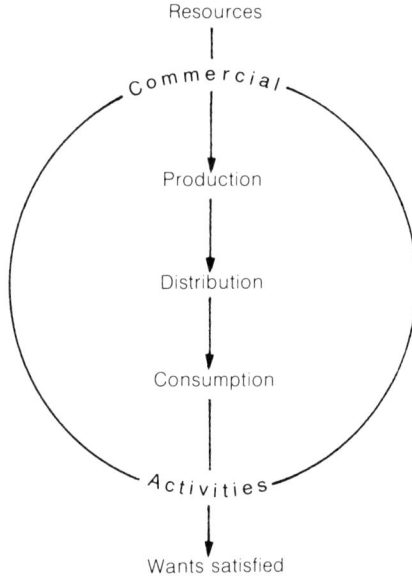

Figure 1.3 The Flow of Economic Activity

The existence of specialisation and the division of labour in the production process means that everything which is produced will pass through a number of stages. These stages will now be studied in more detail.

The Stages of Production

All of the many processes involved in the using of resources to produce different goods and services can be grouped into three distinct stages. These are **primary**, **secondary** and **tertiary** – meaning simply first second and third.

The Primary Stage

This is the **extraction** stage in the production process. All natural resources come from the Earth, and the first task is to extract the materials required for production. Therefore, the primary stage includes **agriculture** and **fisheries**, which are concerned with using the Earth's natural resources to produce food, **forestry**, which is concerned with obtaining timber, and **mining** and **quarrying**, which are concerned with obtaining minerals, fossil fuels, building materials and so on from the earth.

The primary stage uses both **renewable** and **non-renewable** resources. Using the earth to grow wheat with the aid of the sun and rain is making use of renewable resources because the process can be repeated year after year. However, drilling for North Sea oil removes part of a natural resource for ever as it will not be replaced by the Earth's natural forces.

The Secondary Stage

This is the **manufacturing** stage. At this stage the resources obtained in the primary stage are used to produce the goods which people want. Most of the output of the primary sector of the economy will enter the secondary sector. Most food will need some form of preparation. Wheat, for example, is milled to obtain flour, which is used to make bread. Other foodstuffs are processed, tinned, frozen and packaged.

Other resources, e.g. wood, metals, oil, are used to produce the huge variety of goods people want, e.g. cars, houses, personal and household goods, via the process of manufacture. Thus the secondary sector includes engineering, chemical industries, electrical and electronic industries and many others. Secondary production is concerned with both capital goods and consumer goods. Factories, machines, and industrial equipment must also be manufactured from natural resources.

The Tertiary Stage

This is the **distribution** and **services** stage. Once goods have been produced there is the problem of distributing them to the people who want them. Thus, the economy requires transport systems – road, rail, sea and air – and wholesaling and retailing chains to distribute production.

Also, this stage includes the various **aids to trade**, which ensure the whole production process works smoothly and efficiently. These include financial services, e.g. banking and insurance, as well as other specialist services such as agents, brokers and consultants. The tertiary stage is not directly productive in the sense that nothing is physically produced. However, without the tertiary services the ability efficiently to manufacture goods at the secondary stage would not be possible.

Therefore, the process of production from obtaining the raw materials to delivering the final goods to the consumer consists of three distinct stages, as shown in Figure 1.4. on page 8.

The relative sizes of each of the 3 sectors of the economy will vary from one country to another, depending upon the state of development of the economy. As countries develop and become industrialised there is a shift from primary activities – particularly agriculture – to secondary activities such as manufacturing industry. In Britain this was most marked during the period of the Industrial Revolution. Continued development leads to a growth in the tertiary sector as services and such things as leisure facilities become more in demand. A country where the tertiary stage is the largest sector of the economy is known as a **post-industrial society**.

The changes in the relative sizes of the three sectors in the United Kingdom over recent years is shown in Table 1.1. The figures in the table relate to the percentage contribution to gross domestic product (GDP). GDP means the total value of all goods and services produced in the country during the year. Notice that over the period the secondary sector has declined in importance whilst the tertiary sector has grown in importance. The trend in

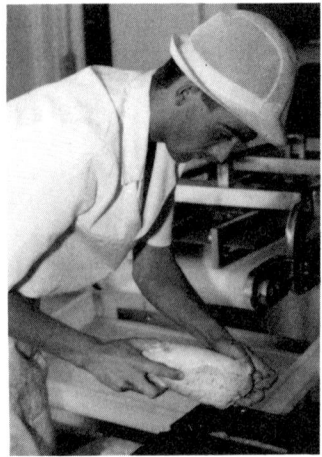

Figure 1.4 The Stages of Production

primary production is surprising because it shows a significant increase between 1977 and 1982 and then a subsequent decline. In fact the primary sector steadily declined in importance during this century until the mid-1970s. The trend was reversed with the discovery of North Sea oil and gas, which has contributed a significant amount to the value of the country's production in recent years. However, North Sea oil production peaked in 1985 and is now declining.

Table 1.1. *Relative Sizes of Sectors of the Economy*

Sector	Percentage Share of GDP*		
	1977	1982	1987
Primary	9.3	13.2	8.5
Secondary	35.6	30.8	30.2
Tertiary	55.2	56.0	61.3

* Gross domestic product

The above shows how production is organised, broken down into stages, occupations and small operations efficiently to utilise limited resources to produce the goods and services people want. However, so far nothing has been said about **what** is being produced. Earlier it was explained that unlimited wants and scarce resources give rise to the necessity to make choices. The economic choices facing any society were mentioned above. These are:

1. What goods and services are to be produced?
2. How much should be produced?
3. For whom will these goods and services be produced?

All societies must address these questions. How they do so determines the country's economic system.

Economic Systems

An economic system, or, to put it more simply, an **economy**, is the framework in which production is organised and distributed. There are broadly two types of economic system, and they approach the problems of deciding what, how much and for whom to produce in completely different ways. These are the **planned economy** and the **market economy**.

The Planned Economy

In a planned economy all the economic decisions are taken by the state. The state (government) owns all the means of production. Therefore, all workers from labourers to managers are employees of the state; all land, factories and machines are owned by the state; and all goods are distributed through state-owned shops. In this way the state can direct production and decide what is produced, how much is produced and who will benefit from this produc-

tion. For this reason planned economies are also known as **command economies** because the state dictates all economic activity.

Of course, it is not an easy task to decide what goods should be produced and how much of each. The government has to employ officials to find out what is needed and what resources are available to produce it. A consideration of just one product, steel, shows how difficult the problems are. The government will need to know the capacity of the steel industry and the amount of iron ore which is available to be mined and converted into iron. Will some iron have to be imported? How many blast furnaces are there? How much can they produce? Where are they located in relation to the iron ore? What transport facilities are available to carry the raw materials and the finished product? A great many products use steel, e.g. cars, ships, planes, trains, railway lines, washing machines, fridges. The officials will want to know how many of each of these products can be, and will be, produced. They will want to know what proportion of these goods are made of steel and thus how much steel will be needed.

Thus the system is extremely complex. The plans have to be co-ordinated, e.g. it is no good setting too high a target for output from the furniture industry if the timber industry is unable to supply enough wood. Also, decisions regarding the quantities of products cannot be made for just one year. It takes a long time for certain planning decisions to work through to affect final outputs, e.g. a decision to build a new steel works. Therefore decisions need to be made now about what will be required in a few years' time. The usual procedure is to organise production within the framework of a five-year plan. To construct the plan, targets are set for each sector of the economy and for all enterprises within each sector. The most difficult aspect of the plan is to ensure that all the hundreds of thousands of different targets match each other and that there are as few discrepancies as possible in the targets set. However, circumstances change during the 5-year period and adjustments to the plan and the targets have to be made continually.

There are 2 major problems associated with the operation of a planned economy. The first is actually meeting the output targets. Some targets may have been based on too little information and may be unrealistic, some may be frustrated by the under-fulfilment of other targets. Unforeseen circumstances may make targets impossible, e.g. poor weather conditions may affect grain targets. The second problem is getting the targets right in the first place. If the targets are wrong, which is very common, then too much of certain goods will be produced and not enough of other goods. This can lead to massive unsold stocks in some shops and queues for other goods.

The Soviet Union and other Communist-Bloc countries, e.g. Poland, Czechoslovakia, Romania, all have economies which have been organised along these lines. However, *perestroika* (restructuring) in the Soviet Union and the changes which occurred in the political systems of other Communist countries in the late 1980s have resulted in a movement away from state planning and towards a market economy.

STUDENT TASK

Read the following extract from a newspaper article about the Soviet economy and answer the questions which follow.

Soviet wholesale and retail prices are established by the State Committee for Prices, based theoretically on the cost of production and not on demand. They are a system of rationing developed in conditions of scarcity of almost all goods in the 50 years before 1970. The key relationship for any enterprise is not with its customers or other enterprises but vertically with the top, with Moscow. Suppliers and clients are not free to choose each other. They must make requests to the State Supply Committee (Gosnab), which then allocates supplies. Today, there is no trade in industrial products between enterprises, but a system of rationing administered from the top.

Retail prices are also determined centrally, and change in these is politically sensitive. Essentials such as bread are very cheap; shop prices of bakery products, sugar and vegetable oil were last changed in 1955. The price of meat and milk products were last raised in 1962 and have been

static ever since. Anything more than the essentials of life, such as furniture and many articles of clothing, are very expensive and often in short supply. Goods not considered necessary, such as cars, are sold at whatever the market will bear. The 12 million Soviet private car owners have each paid 7,000–8,000 roubles (£14,000–£16,000) for their cars and on average saved for eight years.

This system of pricing and procuring goods, rough and ready at the best of times, was devised after the 1917 Revolution and has remained unchanged despite growing disadvantages. The result today is that manufactured goods are generally too expensive and food prices are too cheap. The most serious problems in the retail sector include:
– Long queues and often poor quality goods as a result of low prices. This leads to large secondary and black markets. In the legal peasant markets, a kilo of meat costs 8 roubles and there are no queues. Many quality goods miss out on legal retail trade entirely. People in Moscow and Leningrad are increasingly well-dressed but the cloth for their garments is often imported. Many of their clothes are bought at great expense from private tailors and dressmakers who operate illegally.
– Overproduction of some items as a result of putting emphasis on the output of quantity rather than quality. For instance, in 1984 the Soviet Union, with a population of 275 million, produced 740 million shoes – more than the US, Britain, France and West Germany combined. Yet many of these are unsaleable and the preference of people for sports shoes or sandals is evident in the streets of Moscow.

1. What organisation decides prices in Russia? Who makes these decisions in Britain?
2. What possible disadvantages could arise from prices not changing since 1955?
3. Why do you think essential items, e.g. bread, are very cheap while clothing is expensive?
4. What are black markets and why do they operate? Do you find black markets in Britain?
5. What problems arise as a result of prices being set centrally by the state?

The Market Economy

The market economy organises economic decision-making in a completely different way from the planned economy. In a pure market economy the state has no or very little role to play in the directing of resources. A market is simply a place where buyers and sellers meet. The buyers are **consumers**, who come to the market to satisfy their wants. The sellers are **producers** (businesses), who own the resources and produce goods and services to sell at a profit. For a market economy to operate efficiently there must be complete freedom of economic activity. Consumers must be free to choose between different goods and services and free to spend their income as they wish. Producers must be free to organise resources as they wish in the pursuit of profit; this means the freedom to hire and fire labour, employ capital and switch from producing one type of good or service to another. In other words, in a market economy resources must be completely mobile. Government interference must be kept to a minimum to ensure the efficiency of the market system.

Central to the market system is the **price mechanism**. Prices move continually within markets to ensure that the decisions on how consumers wish to spend their incomes – known as **demand** – will always equal the amount producers are willing to produce – known as **supply**. Thus a market is concerned with matching demand and supply. This is often described as the operation of **market forces**. It is through this process of consumers voting for the goods and services they wish to consume via the way they spend their income that resources are directed towards the satisfying of those wants. The operation of a market is best illustrated by an example.

Figure 1.5 Buying and Selling

Assume a particular product, e.g. compact disc players, becomes very popular with consumers. Increasing demand will soon outstrip supply at the existing market price and a shortage will develop as shops run out of stocks. This will cause the price to rise, which will prevent some of the consumers who would have wished to purchase a compact disc player at the old price from being able to satisfy their want. At the same time the higher price acts as a signal to producers that it is worthwhile increasing production of compact disc players because higher prices mean higher profits. Thus existing businesses will produce more output and new businesses will enter the compact disc player market (from markets where the opportunity to make profits is lower) and supply will increase. The increased availability of compact disc players will reduce the price and enable more people to satisfy their want for the product. Therefore, the result of the increased popularity of compact disc players is that more resources – land, labour and capital – have been employed in their production, with price acting as a signal as to where resources can be profitably employed.

In the same way the price mechanism indicates those areas where resources are being inefficiently utilised. Products which become less popular, e.g. conventional record players, will not all be sold at the existing price and surpluses will build up. To remove the surplus the price will be lowered, which will induce more consumers to purchase the product and at the same time act as a signal to producers to produce less as profits fall. Resources will be released from this market and become available to be employed in other markets where demand is expanding.

The results of a change in people's wants can be summarised as follows:

> Increase in demand → rise in price → more produced
> Result: more resources now directed towards satisfying this want.
>
> Decrease in demand → fall in price → less produced
> Result: less resources now directed towards satisfying this want.

Thus a market economy is based upon individual consumer choices, with the government playing no part in the direction of resources. Therefore, this type of system is also known as **consumer sovereignty** or a **laissez-faire** system (from the French *laisser faire*, 'to leave alone').

QUICK QUESTIONS 4

1. Explain in one sentence what is meant by a market.

2. How does a market ensure that the demand for goods and the supply of goods are always in balance?

3. Explain why package holidays are more expensive at certain times of the year than at others.

4. Why is a market economy said to be based upon consumer sovereignty?

These 2 approaches to economic organisation are extreme systems at opposite ends of a spectrum. Most countries have systems which are mixtures of both the planned and market systems. An economic system which combines elements of both state direction of resources and free market choice is known as a **mixed economy**. The diagram below gives an approximate picture of where some countries' economic systems lie within the spectrum.

FREE MARKET ECONOMY	← MIXED → ECONOMIES	PLANNED/COMMAND ECONOMY
USA, Japan	W. Germany, France UK, Yugoslavia	USSR/Communist Bloc

Most countries, including the UK, have mixed economic systems. It is to the organisation of a mixed economy that we now turn.

The Mixed Economy

As stated above, a mixed economy uses elements of both the planned and market systems to allocate resources. There is a **private sector**, which allocates resources according to the market mechanism, and a **public sector**, which is under the control of the government.

In Britain since the Industrial Revolution an increasing amount of government intervention has been accepted in a basically private enterprise system, although this trend has been reversed by the Conservative government elected in 1979. At present just under half of all economic activity is directed in some way by the state. This is shown by the fact that in 1986 expenditure by 'general government' – central and local government combined – accounted for 48.7% of the gross domestic product.

(a) The Private Sector

The private sector accounts for marginally the largest proportion of all goods and services produced in Britain. There are hundreds of thousands of private businesses, from large multinational companies such as ICI and British Petroleum to small family businesses and individual traders. These businesses exist to operate at a profit by selling goods and services to the general public. They therefore operate according to market forces.

However, there are certain problems associated with leaving economic activity entirely to the private sector. The profit motive does not always lead to the best use of resources. The principal problems which occur in the market system are as follows:

1. There are certain goods and services which cannot be provided by a free market because it is not possible to ensure that only those who pay for them benefit from their provision. These goods are known as **public goods** as they have to be provided to all consumers or not at all. Examples of public goods are national defence, the police force, street lighting and so on. Therefore these goods are provided by the state, which has the power to charge all consumers through the taxation system.

2. In addition to public goods there are goods which the government believes should be available to all but which not everyone would pay for if they were given the choice. These are known as **merit goods** because of the high value placed upon such goods. Examples include the National Health Service, education, Social Service provision and so on. In Britain many of these merit goods are provided by the state and financed by taxation.

3. Some industries may be seen as too important to be left entirely in private hands because of their relationship to the whole economy. The government has always exercised some involvement in agriculture to prevent violent price fluctuations and to ensure long-term continuation of supply. Similarly, areas such as transport and basic industries, e.g. coal and steel, have always been regarded as too important to be left completely to the free market. Some of these industries have been taken under direct state control and others are carefully regulated.

4. The provision of certain goods or services may be a situation of a **natural monopoly**. This means that it is economically most efficient to

organise the industry as one enterprise. Competition would be wasteful and lead to expensive duplication of resources. This can be seen, for example, in the case of railways, the postal service and the electricity supply industry. Having more than one national electricity grid or several railway lines between London and Edinburgh would obviously be very wasteful. However, markets do not work efficiently in the interests of the consumer if there is only one monopoly supplier. The result is often higher prices and a poorer service as lack of competition removes the necessity to keep prices down and improve quality in order to attract customers. In such circumstances it has been common for the government to take control of these industries and operate them in the public interest. However, during the 1980s there was a move to return many of these natural mono-polies to the private sector and try to inject some degree of competition into the industries. Examples of this policy are British Telecom, British Gas and the electricity supply industry. It should be noted that where this has happened the government has retained a degree of control over the operation of the industries via specifically instituted regulatory bodies, e.g. the Office of Fair Telecommunications (OFTEL).

5. The provision of certain goods may be strategic to the national interest or there may be concern regarding the safety of the industry, e.g. atomic energy. In these circumstances it is common for the government to operate the industry to ensure these factors are taken into account.

These and other considerations have gradually led to a significant proportion of economic activity being undertaken by the state. It is this economic activity which constitutes the public sector of the economy.

Figure 1.6 A Comparison of Public and Private Provision

(b) The Public Sector

The public sector consists of all economic activity under the control of the state, at both national and local level. Government economic activity can be divided into 2 broad types:

1. The direct provision of services. The government levies taxes on the private sector and uses the revenue to provide certain national services. These are mainly public goods, e.g. defence, police, the legal system, and merit goods, e.g. the National Health Service, schools and universities, Social Services. These services are provided by the various departments of government at both national and local level, e.g. by the Ministry of Defence, the Departments of Health and Social Security and Local Education Authorities. This means that these services are under the direct political control of ministers and local councillors.

2. The indirect provision of goods and services. The government can set up bodies to undertake various aspects of economic activity on behalf of the public. The nationalised industries have been set up to run certain key industries, e.g. railways, postal services. These organisations are at arm's length from the government but are still under indirect political control. One of the main reasons for the establishment of such organisations is to take natural monopolies under state control, although, as mentioned above, government policy has changed in this respect during the 1980s. These industries charge for their services but do not always make a profit. In the case of losses, the difference is made up from the government's taxation revenue.

It is important to realise that both the above types of economic provision constitute business activity as they are concerned with the utilisation of the country's resources to satisfy people's wants. In fact there are many similarities between the management structures of central government, local authority departments and nationalised industries and those of private enterprises.

QUICK QUESTIONS 5

1. *Distinguish between the private sector and the public sector of the economy.*
2. *Explain what is meant by a public good and a merit good. Give an example of each.*
3. *Briefly explain the difference between the direct and indirect state provision of goods and services.*

Finally, it should be noted that the government's attitude to the size and composition of the public sector changes as the political colour of the government changes. It has already been mentioned that the Conservative government elected in 1979 favoured regulation of large industries rather than nationalisation. Many previously state-owned enterprises, such as British Telecom, British Gas, British Airways, the British Airports Authority, British Aerospace, and a number of other smaller enterprises, were **privatised**, i.e. returned to the private sector of the economy.

PROJECT AND ASSIGNMENT SUGGESTIONS

1. Undertake a local business survey in your area. Your survey could consider the following types of questions:
   (a) What is the proportion of primary, secondary and tertiary activity in your area?
   (b) Is there one type of business activity which is particularly important to your local economy?
   (c) Is your area experiencing the growth or decline of a particular type of business activity? If so, what are the reasons for this?
   (d) What type of business activity is privately owned? What examples are there of public sector business organisations?
   (e) Which businesses are concerned with the production of consumer goods and which with producing capital goods?

2. Find out as much as you can about an important manufacturing business in your area. If possible try to visit the business and speak to the people who work there. Write a report on the business based upon the answers to the following questions.
   (a) What processes occur within the business to convert the raw materials into the finished product or products?

(b) What is the extent of the division of labour within the business?

(c) Are the people employed by the business mainly skilled workers or can the work be undertaken by unskilled workers?

(d) Is the finished product sold to the final consumer or is it part of another manufacturing process?

3. Choose a primary product and make a study of all the different ways it can be used. You can make use of library reference books or even write for information to businesses involved in using the product. Examples you could consider are coal, oil, diamonds, iron and chalk. Your study should include a diagram showing all the various applications of your product.

CHAPTER 2

The Structure of
Business in the UK

It was explained in the last chapter that Britain is a mixed economy. This means that business activity can be divided into 2 different types. These are **private enterprise**, which are the businesses which operate in the private sector, and **public enterprise**, which is business activity in the public sector. However, within each of the 2 sectors of the economy, businesses differ in relation to the type of ownership, number of owners, the type of management structure and so on. The essential differences between private and public enterprise and the various different types of business units which operate in each sector of the economy are summarised in Table 2.1.

In this chapter the different types of businesses which operate in both the private and the public sectors of the economy will be examined in detail.

Private Enterprise

Table 2.1 lists 4 different types of business structure which occur in the private sector. It is important to understand the essential differences in the legal structure of each type of business unit and how they differ with respect to ownership and control. The simplest form of business unit is the sole trader.

Table 2.1. *Private and Public Enterprise*

	Private Enterprise	Public Enterprise
Owned and operated by	Private individuals	The state – in the form of (a) local government (b) central government departments (c) public bodies established by government
Objectives	To operate at a profit	To operate in the public interest. There may be a requirement to make profits (or at least cover costs) in the case of some organisations
Risk (i.e. responsibility for losses) is borne by	The private individuals concerned	The government, either local or national. Losses are ultimately borne by the public via the payment of taxes
Types of business unit	(a) Sole trader (b) Partnerships (c) Companies (d) Co-operatives	(a) Local undertakings (b) Central government organised services, e.g. the NHS (c) Public corporations

The Sole Trader

The most important characteristic of a sole trader business, or more correctly a **sole proprietorship**, is that it is legally owned and controlled by one person. However, even though it is commonly called a 'one-man business' it does not mean that only one person is necessarily involved in the business. There are often employees who work for the firm. However, these employees have no legal responsibility for the conduct of the business.

In order to establish such a business the owner will require finance – known as the **capital** of the business. Capital in this sense means the money required to set up the business and purchase the necessary items to start trading, e.g. premises, machinery and so on. The source of financial capital available to establish and expand a sole trader business are quite limited, which means that most tend to be rather small. The principal sources of finance are set out below.

1. The sole trader's own savings. These are very important because other people and institutions are likely to be much more willing to lend money to the business if the owner has committed a significant sum himself or herself.
2. Borrowing from friends and relatives. The amount of money contributed by the owner's family is often considerable in the case of sole traders because of the difficulties of obtaining money elsewhere.
3. Borrowing from banks and building societies. These sources are rather limited because of the risks involved in lending to this type of business. However, building societies are very important in providing the finance for the purchase of premises.
4. Trade credit. This means obtaining stock without having to pay until the goods have been sold and the business has had time to generate some cash. This is a very important source of finance for businesses involved in the retail trade.
5. Investing past profits is an important source of finance for small businesses which are trying to expand. However, by definition small businesses tend to generate small profits and this makes growth difficult.

In spite of the difficulties of raising capital, sole trader businesses are a very common type of business unit. They tend to be concentrated in certain areas of the economy, e.g. retailing, especially in the case of village and neighbourhood shops. Also, many tradesmen, e.g. small building firms, plumbers, window cleaners, gardeners and so on are sole traders. The large number of sole traders in any area can be seen by looking at the advertisements in local papers for such services as washing machine and lawn mower repairs, fencing and turfing, painting and decorating and so on. In the 1980s the government actively tried to encourage the establishment of such businesses as a way of trying to reduce the level of unemployment. The government has set up a number of schemes to help the unemployed establish new businesses. These provide help in the form of initial capital and allowances payable during the first year of trading. However, the survival rate of such businesses is not very high because of the problems of making a success of these small concerns.

Notwithstanding the problems, many people do make a success of a sole trader business, and this type of business unit does have certain advantages over larger organisations. The main advantages are set out below.

1. They are easy to establish in the sense that no formal procedures are required to set up such a business.
2. The complete unity of ownership and control is in the hands of one person. This not only makes management easier to organise and the legal position easier to state and control but it also gives the owner an independence which he or she often sees as the greatest reward from running the business. There is considerable self-interest and a complete and simple link between successful management and the owner's income.
3. Generally there is a better understanding between the owner and the business's employees because the business is smaller and more personal.
4. Often there is a more personal service offered to the consumer, e.g. people often prefer to shop locally because of the friendly atmosphere.

There are of course a number of problems associated with this type of business unit, some of which have already been referred to. The major drawbacks are as follows:

1. As stated above, the sources of finance available to the business are very limited. This makes expansion and growth difficult and the business can become locked into a vicious circle of small profits meaning little opportunity to expand and so profits remain low.
2. The owner is entirely responsible personally for the debts of the business. This is known as **unlimited liability**. If the firm incurs debts which cannot be paid from the assets of the business, the owner can be declared bankrupt. This means all the owner's personal assets, e.g. house, car, furniture, can be taken to settle the debts. This obviously means the sole trader is unlikely to want to take risks and hence enterprise is stifled.
3. The owner is unlikely to be a specialist in all aspects of managing the business. It is also rare that a sole trader can afford to employ specialists to work for him or her.
4. It is often necessary for the sole trader to work long and unsocial hours.
5. There is no continuity of the business. Since the business is personal to the owner it has no existence outside the owner. Therefore, if the owner dies or becomes ill the business is unlikely to be able to continue.

The above problems often lead the sole trader to consider ways of expanding the firm which will involve changing the legal structure of the business. The first form of organisation the owner is likely to consider is changing the business into a partnership. It is this form of business organisation which will be looked at next.

QUICK QUESTIONS 1

1. *Distinguish between private enterprise and public enterprise.*
2. *What is the most important characteristic of a sole trader business?*
3. *Give 3 sources of capital which may be available to a person starting a sole trader business.*
4. *One of the major drawbacks of a sole trader business is unlimited personal liability. Explain what this means.*

Partnerships

A partnership occurs when a business is jointly owned by 2 or more people. The legal rights and responsibilities of partners in this type of business have been laid down by Acts of Parliament. These have given rise to 2 different types of partnership.

(a) The Ordinary Partnership

An ordinary partnership is regulated by the Partnership Act 1870. The most important characteristic of this type of partnership is that all the partners have unlimited personal liability for the debts of the business. This means that all partners can be declared bankrupt if the business fails. It is common for the partners to draw up a legal document called a **Deed of Partnership** outlining the rights and duties of each partner. In the absence of such a signed agreement the law states that the following rules will apply to the partnership:

1. Partners have the right to share equally in both the capital and profits (or losses) of the business.
2. They only have the right to receive payment for working on partnership business if there is an actual agreement to this effect. For example, it is common to appoint one of the partners as a 'managing partner' and to pay him or her a salary from the proceeds of the business for doing so. This will be in addition to his or her rights to a share of the profits.
3. Disputes between partners will be settled by majority decision. There will, however, be some major issues which they will have to be unanimous about, e.g. the introduction of a new partner. This rule often makes it difficult for the partnership to grow and develop.
4. Every ordinary partner has the right to participate in the management of the firm and to take decisions which the others are bound to accept.

(b) The Limited Partnership

Limited partnerships were allowed by the Limited Partnership Act 1907, which modified the 1870 Act. The major change this made was to allow some partners to join the business who would contribute money only. They take no part in the management of the business and have no right to be consulted about decisions. However, these partners can enjoy limited liability, i.e. they are not liable for the debts of the business beyond the amount they have already contributed. These partners are of course entitled to receive a return on the amount of money they contribute.

The Act therefore made it possible for those with savings but who do not wish to be involved in the management of the business to invest in the partnership in reasonable safety. However, the Act does stipulate that at least one partner shall be an ordinary partner, i.e. there must be at least one (there can be more) partner with unlimited liability. This partner (or partners) is known as the general partner. Limited partners who contribute money only are often known as **sleeping partners** because they are not actively involved in the running of the business.

Partnerships have certain advantages over sole proprietorships as a type of business organisation.

1. There are more sources of capital available to the business. However, the amount of finance available is still not likely to be very large.
2. There are more people involved in the business and therefore more ideas and initiative to make the business a success.
3. Decision-making can be shared so that the burden of management is reduced. Also it is common for specialisation to occur in partnerships, with partners concentrating on different aspects of the business.

Partnerships are quite common in certain fields of business activity, particularly in the professions, e.g. doctors, dentists, solicitors, accountants. However, the drawbacks of this type of business unit do not make it suitable for all types of businesses. The main problems associated with partnerships are as follows:

1. Each partner is capable of making decisions on behalf of all the partners. Although decisions will normally be discussed, one partner's decisions will be legally binding on the others. This is true regardless of whether there is a formal agreement or not.
2. Some or all of the partners will have unlimited liability. They thus risk their personal assets if the business is not a success.
3. There can be disputes between the partners which in extreme cases may lead to the dissolution of the partnership.
4. The continuity of the business is uncertain. If

one of the partners dies the partnership may have to be dissolved.

QUICK QUESTIONS 2

1. *Distinguish between an ordinary partnership and a limited partnership.*
2. *Give one reason why 2 independent traders might consider going into partnership.*
3. *What reservations might they have about going into partnership?*
4. *What is the attraction of joining a partnership as a sleeping partner?*
5. *Give 3 types of business which are commonly organised as a partnership.*

STUDENT TASK

Peter Brewster has worked for a local building firm for a number of years. He is quite happy with his job but the pay is fairly low and he feels he could do better by striking out on his own. He is considering setting up a small roofing and guttering business but is not sure how to go about it.

He consults the small-business advisor at the local branch of his bank to find out the problems of becoming self-employed. They discuss how he could raise the finance he needs to start the business, keeping accurate accounts, tax liability, personal pensions, the legal implications, insurance and advertising.

1. What type of business is Peter considering setting up?
2. What sources of finance will the business advisor have suggested to Peter?
3. Why do you think the business advisor discussed insurance with Peter?
4. What problems could Peter encounter in his first year of trading?

After careful consideration Peter decides to go ahead and become self-employed. He finds there is a steady demand for this type of work and his business gradually becomes established. The success of the business means he eventually has to turn customers away as he cannot meet the demand. He therefore considers ways of expanding the business. However, most of his capital is tied up in equipment and materials and he has already borrowed a significant sum from the bank. He wonders whether he should look for an equal partner who could bring new capital into the business.

1. As well as providing capital for the expansion of the business, what other benefits are there from going into partnership?
2. What other factors should Peter seriously consider before he decides to find a partner?

The disadvantages of partnerships, particularly in terms of limited capital and unlimited liability, mean that the majority of businesses which are looking to expand are more likely to seek **incorporation** rather than partnership.

Incorporation and Legal Personality

The important point about both sole proprietorships and partnerships is that there is no legal distinction between the business and the person or persons who own it. Therefore commitments entered into by the business must be honoured by the owner(s). However, it is possible to establish a business which has a completely separate legal existence from the people who own and manage it. If we are going to have a system of business organisation which protects its owners by making them independent of the business they create and run, then it is necessary to give to the business the rights of people and the duties and responsibilities of people at least in as far as it is necessary to allow the business to work for itself and be responsible for itself. This process is known as incorporation, and it creates a separate legal or judicial (i.e. in the eyes of the law) personality.

The process of incorporation is explained below. Once complete, the business is in effect a 'legal entity' in its own right. It can sue and be sued in the courts and, most importantly, it can make contracts in its own name, separate from its owners.

Incorporation gives the owners of such a business a number of benefits, including the following:

1. The business is able to own and dispose of property and capital assets in its own name and can make contracts on its own behalf.
2. It is able to protect itself at law and can also be sued in law in its own name. This protects not only the business but also the people who work for it.
3. The owners of the business have limited personal liability.
4. The existence of the business is not affected by the death of the owners. In fact the business has a continuing existence until it is **liquidated**. This means selling all the items owned by the business, i.e. changing assets into cash. This can occur voluntarily by agreement between the owners or it may be forced upon the business if the creditors (people to whom the business owes money) get together and force the business to sell its assets to pay off its debts. However, this process cannot involve the personal assets of people involved with the business.

The most common type of business unit established by the process of incorporation is the **limited company**.

The Limited Company

As outlined above, the most important feature of a limited company is that it has a legal identity separate from the people who own and manage it. A limited company is owned by shareholders. These are people who are prepared to buy part of the business in return for part of the profits each year. It is then the shareholders who collectively determine how the business shall be run.

There are 2 types of limited company, the **private limited company** and the **public limited company**. The principal differences are in the size of the company and in how the shares are bought and sold (see below). However, common to both types of limited company is that they are established as businesses with an independent legal status. A company may be established by changing the legal status of an existing sole proprietorship or partnership but not all companies start life in this way. Where large-scale operations are involved the limited company is the normal type of business unit and many businesses are initially started as a limited company.

The rules regarding the establishment of a limited company are laid down in the Companies Acts 1948 to 1989. The company has to be registered with the **Registrar of Companies**. To do this the promoters of the company must provide certain documents setting out the important information regarding the company. The types of documents which must be provided are explained below.

(a) The Memorandum of Association

This governs the company's relationship with the outside world. The main contents are as follows:

1. The company's name, which must contain the word limited. This is a warning to anyone dealing with the company that they cannot look beyond the company for the redress of any grievance.
2. The address of the company's registered office.
3. The objectives of the company. Prospective shareholders then know what they are committing their funds to, and have a legitimate claim against the company if their money is used for anything else.
4. A statement of the limited liability of shareholders (for the benefit of potential creditors as well as shareholders).
5. The amount of capital to be raised by issuing shares, and the type of shares issued.
6. The agreement of the founder members that they wish to form a limited company and that they will purchase the stated number of shares.

(b) The Articles of Association

These control the internal running of the company. They will usually follow the model articles set out in the Companies Act 1948, rather than being a tailor-made set of articles. These cover the following information.

1. The procedure for calling a general meeting of shareholders.
2. The rights and obligations of directors.
3. The election of directors.
4. The borrowing powers of the company.

(c) The Statutory Declaration

This is simply a signed statement by the promoters of the company that they have complied with all the requirements of the Companies Acts.

These 3 documents are presented to the Registrar and if all is in order he will issue a **Certificate of Incorporation**, which establishes the business as a separate legal entity. In law the business can now do anything that an individual can do, in particular it can enter into contracts and be sued through the courts.

The procedure for setting up a company is the same for both private and public companies although the latter also requires one further document. This is a **Certificate of Trading**, which is issued by the Registrar when he is satisfied the company has raised the necessary amount of capital. Other differences between the 2 types of company are set out below.

The Public Limited Company

The largest and most important businesses in the private sector are public limited companies. Some are very large, e.g. in 1986 Imperial Chemical Industries (ICI) employed 119,000 people and sold goods to the value of £10.7 billion. Currently about 2% of all companies are public. The basic requirements to form a public company are listed below.

1. The minimum number of persons necessary to form a public limited company is 2. There is no limit on the number of shareholders.
2. There is a minimum authorised share capital (£50,000 as at 1 January 1990).
3. Clause 2 of the company's Memorandum of Association must state that the company is a public limited company.
4. The name of the company must end with the words **Public Limited Company** or PLC.

The Private Limited Company

Any registered company which does not comply with the regulations above is by definition a private company. As can be seen from the number of public companies, the vast majority of companies are private. The essential features of a private company are:

1. There is no longer a limit on the number of shareholders. (Until 1981 this was the major difference between private and public companies.)
2. The name of the company must contain the words **Company Limited**.
3. The company is not allowed to sell shares or debentures (see below) to the general public.

Although the legal requirements seem complicated, the major difference which you should remember is that anyone can buy shares in a public limited company, hence the name. Whereas the shares in a private limited company are only available privately, i.e. with the consent of the existing shareholders. This means that the formalities for establishing a PLC are more complex because the shares have to be made available to the public through the Stock Market. This process is called **floatation** and is explained in more detail in Chapter 18.

Important Note

It is very important not to confuse private and public limited **companies** with private and public **enterprise**. Remember, a public limited company is a private enterprise and its shares are available to the general public.

QUICK QUESTIONS 3

1. *What is the purpose of incorporation?*
2. *What is the principal benefit of this process to the owners of a business?*
3. *What documents are necessary to establish a limited company?*
4. *Give 2 differences between a private limited company and a public limited company.*
5. *In what way does the distinction between private and public enterprise differ from the distinction between private and public limited companies?*

STUDENT TASK

Judy Ferris set up a Health Food Shop in her local town in 1980. The increasing interest in natural products ensured the business was quite successful. She extended her range of product and entered into an agreement with a local organic farmer to obtain additive-free yoghurts and cheese. However, buying small amounts of these products meant she could not negotiate for more favourable prices. She therefore decided to expand the business and she opened another shop in a neighbouring town.

It soon became clear that the present structure of the business would make any further expansion difficult and so Judy decided to convert the business into a limited company. The company, called 'Healthy Eating Ltd', was established with 3 directors: Judy, her husband and Paul Weston, a family friend who works as a solicitor.

1. What are the major advantages of converting the business into a limited company?
2. Explain the procedure for converting the business into a company.
3. Why do you think Judy asked Paul Weston to become a director of the company?

The Ownership and Control of Limited Companies

If a business is run by a sole proprietor it is quite clear that he or she contributes the capital, takes the decisions and enjoys the profits. However, in a limited company these functions are divided between different groups of people. A company is owned by **shareholders**, and in a large public limited company there may be several thousand of them. Their rights vary according to the type of shares they own (see below), but it is quite clear that they cannot all be consulted about every decision that needs to be made in the running of the business. If this was to happen nothing would ever get done. Therefore, in all public limited companies and some private limited companies there is a **divorce of ownership and control**, i.e. the people who own the business are not responsible for the day-to-day decisions on how the business is run. Instead arrangements are made to delegate the control of the company to a small group of shareholders.

Each year the company must hold its **annual general meeting** (AGM), to which all the shareholders are invited. One of the purposes of the meeting is to elect a **board of directors**, which will be responsible for managing the business over the coming year. The size of the board will be laid down in the Articles of Association and will depend upon the size of the company. Each ordinary shareholder has one vote for each share they own. Hence if someone owns 51% of the ordinary shares they can control the business. However, general meetings are characterised by sparse attendance and it is common for the same board to continue unopposed. Many shareholders in large companies are content to receive their share of the profits each year. However, if shareholders are not satisfied with how the business is being run they can call an **extraordinary general meeting** and vote in a new board, but this is very rare.

Once the board has been elected it will elect one of its members to be the Managing Director. It is the Managing Director who is the principal decision-maker with regard to how the business is run on a day-to-day basis.

The pattern of internal organisation within most limited companies can be illustrated by the simple diagram in Figure 2.1.

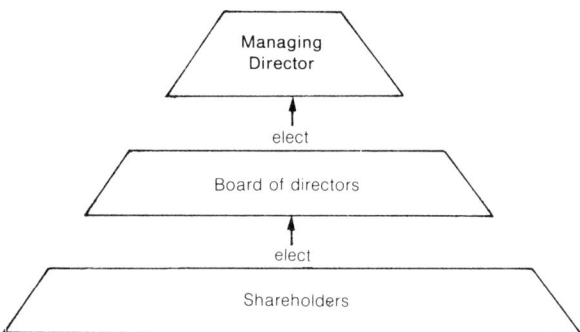

Figure 2.1 The Structure of a Limited Company

The exception to the structure shown in Figure 2.1 is in the case of small private limited companies with only a few shareholders. In these businesses it is not uncommon for all the shareholders to constitute the board of directors. This is particularly true of small family companies.

The Shares of a Limited Company

So far the general term 'shareholder' has been used. However, there are different types of shareholders because there are several different kinds of shares that a company can issue. Some shares carry a fixed rate of return and guarantee payment, while others have no fixed return and no guarantee of payment.

(a) Ordinary Shares

These represent the risk capital of the business. The holders of such shares are not guaranteed a **dividend** (share of the profits) at the end of the year, this will depend on the size of the company's profits. However, they do have voting rights, which allows these shareholders to elect the board of directors. When a dividend is paid on ordinary shares each share will be paid the same; hence these shares are also known as **equities**. Ordinary shares in first-class sound public companies are sometimes called **blue chips**.

(b) Preference Shares

These shares carry a fixed dividend, e.g. 8% per annum. This means that the shareholder is entitled to a sum equal to 8% of his or her capital invested at the end of the trading year providing the company has made sufficient profit. The dividend on these shares must be paid first before the ordinary shareholders receive a dividend, hence the name. There are a number of different types of preference share.

1. **Basic Preference Share**: these will receive their fixed dividend if the firm makes a profit. If there is no profit in a particular year then the dividend is lost.
2. **Cumulative Preference Share**: if the holders of these shares fail to receive a dividend one year because of poor profitability the dividend will be carried over to the next year.
3. **Participating Preference Share**: these carry a fixed dividend but also entitle the holder to a further share of the profits if the dividend paid to ordinary shareholders exceeds a certain amount.

Whilst all preference shares entitle the holder to first call on the company's profits, they do not carry voting rights. Therefore preference shareholders have no say in the control of the company.

(c) Deferred Ordinary Shares

These shares are usually held by the promoters of the company as a way of keeping control with very little capital outlay. They are worth very little but carry voting rights. They do not receive a dividend until the dividend on ordinary shares has reached a certain level. Because of their function they are also known as founders' shares.

Therefore, if a large company had issued all types of shares the profits will be distributed in the following way. Preference shareholders must be paid first, including any previous dividends owed to cumulative preference shareholders. Ordinary shareholders receive their dividend next. If this

Figure 2.2 Example of a Share Certificate

exceeds a certain level (as laid down in the company's memorandum of association), then the holders of participating preference shares will receive a further dividend. Finally, a dividend may be paid to holders of deferred shares if the profit is sufficient to do so, and if the dividend to ordinary shareholders has exceeded the required amount.

In addition to shares, companies can also issue **debentures**.

Debentures

A debenture is not a share although it can be bought and sold in the same way as a share. A debenture is a loan to the company which will receive a fixed interest payment every year. People who buy debentures in a company do not become shareholders, they are creditors of the company. The interest on debentures is a necessary and unavoidable payment. It constitutes a cost to the business and must therefore be paid before a profit for the year can be declared. Debentures are a secure form of investment because they are usually issued on the value of the company's property. This means that if the company fails debenture holders are assured of the return of their capital through the sale of the property. If the debenture holders do not receive their annual interest payment they can force the company into liquidation.

QUICK QUESTIONS 4

1. *Explain the term 'divorce of ownership and control'.*
2. *What name is given to the group of people responsible for the management of a limited company?*
3. *Briefly explain the difference between an ordinary share and a preference share.*
4. *What is a debenture? How does a debenture differ from a share?*

It can be seen from the above information that a business which is organised as a limited company has a number of advantages over a partnership or sole trader business. The main ones are:

1. A limited company has an independent legal status, which allows its shareholders to enjoy limited liability.
2. The security of limited liability means the company is able to attract capital from people who otherwise would not be prepared to invest.
3. The ability to attract capital means the business

can expand and possibly reap the benefits of **economies of scale** (greater efficiency brought about by increasing the size of the business).

4. It allows the risks of business activity to be spread amongst a wider number of people and gives the opportunity for many people to become involved in economic life.

The major problems associated with this type of business unit are also worth noting. The principal disadvantages are:

1. The formalities of establishing a limited company are quite involved.
2. In the case of public companies, raising capital can be very expensive.
3. Sometimes a company grows so large that it becomes difficult to manage, although this problem can also occur in other forms of businesses.
4. The accounts of a company must be published, so there can be no secrecy about its affairs. If the company does not file its annual accounts with the Registrar of Companies it can be fined.
5. There is the problem in larger public companies that the owners – the shareholders – cannot exercise very much control over the running of the business.

In spite of the drawbacks associated with limited companies, they are the most important businesses in the private sector.

The final type of business unit which exists in the private sector is the **co-operative**.

Co-operative Organisation

The term co-operative is used basically to describe a situation in which people jointly undertake some form of business activity and share in the proceeds. There are 3 main areas where co-operatives may occur.

(a) Co-operatives in Distribution

Co-operatives started in the area of retailing in Rochdale in 1844 (the Rochdale Pioneers). A group of workers collectively formed a shop to sell the goods they all required so as to free them from being dependent on the shops operated by their employers. The profit of the shop was then distributed amongst themselves according to how much each had spent in the shop. Modern day co-operative stores are descended from these early ventures.

Co-operative stores today are essentially local organisations which consist of members. Membership is open to anyone prepared to buy a share in the society. A share normally costs £1. Each member may subscribe up to £1,000 and will receive interest on their capital. It is not, of course, necessary to be a member of the society to buy goods from the co-operative. This type of co-operative society is controlled by a management committee. Each member of the co-operative has one vote in the election of the management committee however much capital they have contributed and however much they purchase from the society. The profits of these societies used to be divided between members half-yearly in proportion to their purchases from the society. This led to a considerable amount of book-keeping, and in most societies it is now the practice to give stamps with purchases instead. Under this system dividends are no longer restricted to members.

(b) Co-operatives in Production

These are generally worker co-operatives. Here the workers collectively own the business and share the profits between them. One of the most famous examples in Britain was the establishment of the Meriden Motorcycle Co-operative in 1973. This was set up by the workers at the Norton Villiers Triumph Company after it collapsed. The government helped to finance the project in order to allow the workers to try and save the business by running it themselves. This type of co-operative organisation has never achieved much success in Britain. However, it is only usually tried as a form of business organisation when more traditional methods have already failed.

This type of business organisation is more popular in parts of Africa and Asia. Co-operatives are encouraged by governments in many developing countries as a way of establishing small-scale businesses.

(c) Co-operative Joint Ventures

This is quite a common feature of modern business. It refers to a situation where separate business concerns join together for specific purposes for their mutual benefit. It is particularly common in agriculture, where individual farmers combine to purchase expensive machinery and share its use. The co-operation may extend to sharing transport to take their produce to market and so on. Another area where this type of co-operation is quite common is retailing. Individual retailers often combine into buying groups to achieve savings from manufacturers on larger orders. Some of these buying groups have become well-known national names, e.g. Mace, Spar.

It can be seen from the above that the term 'co-operative' covers a wide range of different types of business venture. Sometimes the term refers to a simple pooling of resources by other types of business units and sometimes it means a totally different type of organisation and management structure.

QUICK QUESTIONS 5

1. *What was the original reason for the setting up of retail co-operatives?*
2. *Briefly describe the structure of a retail co-operative society.*
3. *Can you think of any advantages which could result from organising a factory as a workers' co-operative?*
4. *Why might a group of farmers decide to co-operate in the purchase and use of farm machinery?*

Public Enterprise

As explained in the last chapter, public enterprise refers to economic activity under the control of the state. There is a wide range of public provision of goods and services in Britain but it is usual to distinguish three broad types.

Local Authority Undertakings

Local councils in Britain undertake the provision of many public services. Some of these services the local authority is under an obligation to provide by laws laid down by central government, e.g. the provision of schools and Social Services, but other services will vary from council to council. Some services are financed entirely from the local authority's resources, i.e. central government grants

and money raised from the community charge and the business rate. There is, therefore, no direct charge for these services, e.g. street lighting, refuse collection, provision of parks and open spaces. In addition, most local authorities undertake a variety of trading activities for which people pay directly. Examples include swimming pools, bus services, golf courses, dance halls and theatres. Although the authorities make a charge for the use of these services, many do not break even and are therefore subsidised from the council's other sources of income.

Central Government Undertakings

These are activities which are operated directly by central government departments. They include the public goods mentioned in the previous chapter, e.g. national defence and the legal system, and also merit goods, e.g. the National Health Service. However, in addition to these directly provided services, central government also operates a number of trading activities. These are generally important undertakings associated with the work of government which for various reasons cannot be provided by private enterprise. Examples include the Royal Mint and Her Majesty's Stationery Office. However, the majority of commercial activities which are found in the public sector are not operated directly by government departments but are organised as public corporations.

Public Corporations

The most important institutions under public ownership are organised as public corporations. A public corporation is an organisation established by the government through an Act of Parliament to operate and manage a particular industry or public service. Examples include such organisations as the BBC and the ITC. However, the majority of public corporations are responsible for the operation of the nationalised industries. The nationalised industries sector has traditionally included the important basic industries of the economy, e.g. gas, electricity, coal, steel and railways. However, during the 1980s the government has been implementing a policy of systematically returning these industries to private ownership – a policy called **privatisation**. Therefore the size of this sector of the economy has been substantially reduced. Examples of important institutions organised as nationalised industries are British Coal, British Rail and the Post Office. However, the government has already announced plans to **privatise** the coal industry to follow the previous privatisations of telecommuncations, gas and electricity.

The Structure of a Public Corporation

No hard-and-fast rules have been laid down about the organisation and control of these enterprises since each corporation is controlled by its own Act of Parliament. Each act aims at devising the organisation most suited to the particular industry. However, the general features of public corporations are as follows.

The industries have been set up to operate as commercial businesses without direct day-to-day interference by the government. Each industry is managed by a **board** headed by a **Chairman**. The Chairman is appointed by the government and the board is composed of several interest groups, e.g. users, workers, managers and some outside experts. The Chairman and the board are left free to operate the industry within the guidelines laid down by parliament.

Parliamentary control is exercised in a number of ways. Each industry is the responsibility of a **government department**, e.g. British Rail is the responsibility of the Department of Transport and British Coal is the responsibility of the Department of Energy. Each department has a minister who is responsible to parliament for the conduct of the industry. In addition, each industry's accounts are scrutinised by a **select committee of parliament** and there is a debate every year on the performance of the industry. Also, in the last event it is parliament which must underwrite the losses of those industries which are not profitable.

These industries cannot apply directly to the public for funds as public limited companies can. All capital investment is provided via the Treasury, which borrows on behalf of the industries. This gives the government an indirect control over the operation of the industries through the purse strings.

In the case of certain industries, e.g. the railways, the Post Office, parliament has set up **consumer councils**. These are watchdog bodies which look after the interests of the consumer and through which the consumer can comment on the performance of the industry.

The structure of a public corporation is illustrated in Figure 2.3.

Reasons in Support of Nationalisation

The arguments which have been put forward for the nationalisation of the basic industries of the economy are outlined below.

1. Many nationalised industries are natural monopolies, i.e. competition within these industries would mean wasteful duplication of resources. It is therefore argued that it is better that these industries be organised as public services rather than as private monopolies.

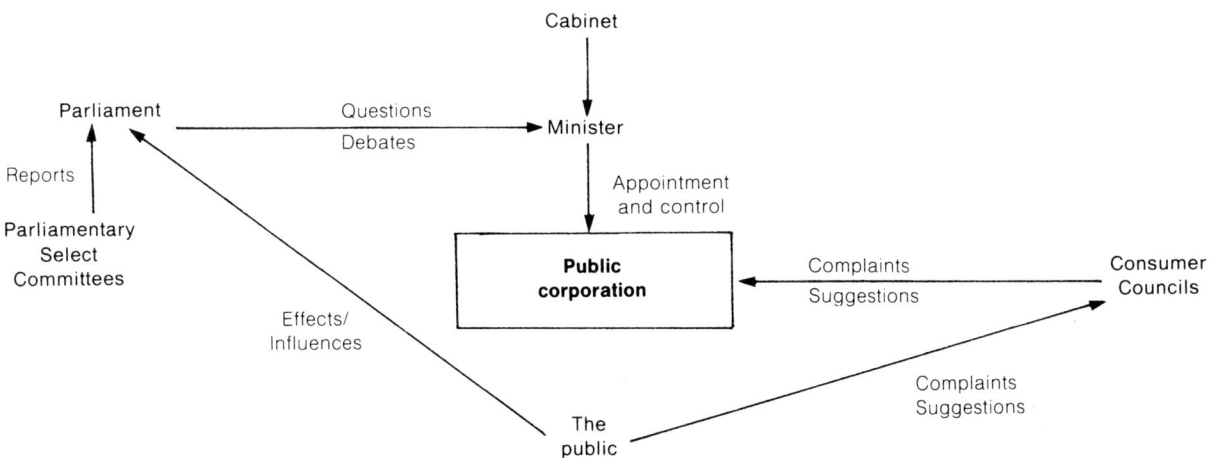

Figure 2.3 The Structure of a Public Corporation

2. The fact that these industries are organised on a national basis means that they can take advantage of economies of scale. This means greater efficiency brought about by increased size.

3. Nationalised industries can provide important national services which might not be provided by private enterprise because of the emphasis on profit, e.g. rural transport services, postal deliveries to remote areas.

4. Some private industries cannot attract enough private capital to finance research and development. A nationalised industry is in a better position to obtain government funds. This was particularly true in the case of coal and railways, which needed vast sums for investment after the second world war.

From Nationalisation to Privatisation

The Conservative government elected in 1979 believed that these large state enterprises were over-bureaucratic, inefficiently run and not properly accountable to the public. They believed there were a number of benefits which would result from returning these industries to the private sector. The principal reasons behind this policy of privatisation are outlined below.

1. Placing these industries in the private sector opens up the possibility of more competition. This should result in improved efficiency and lower prices for the consumer.

2. In addition, the profit motive is the best way of ensuring costs are kept as low as possible and resources are efficiently employed.

3. The industries are able to raise the finance they require for investment by attracting private sector finance rather than being dependent upon the government for capital investment.

4. Private individuals are able to buy shares in the industries. This makes these industries truly accountable to the general public. Wider share ownership is seen as the best way of allowing individuals to benefit from successful business activity.

5. In some cases the taxpayer is freed from subsidising loss-making industries. Also, the income from privatisation can be used to increase government expenditure in other areas, or to cut taxes.

Figure 2.4 Advertisement for Shares in a Privatised Industry

The extent of the government's privatisation programme can be seen in Table 2.2. The government's long-term aim is to return all publicly owned industries to the private sector.

Table 2.2. *Major Sales of State Industries*

Date of Sale	Company and Percentage Sold
1981 (Feb)	British Aerospace (50%)
1981 (Oct)	Cable and Wireless (49%)
1982 (Feb)	Amersham International (100%)
1982 (Nov)	Britoil (51%)
1983 (Feb)	Associated British Ports (51.5%)
1983 (Dec)	Cable and Wireless (further 22%)
1984 (April)	Associated British Ports (remaining 48.5)
1984 (June)	Enterprise Oil (100%)
1984 (July)	Jaguar (100%)
1984 (Nov)	British Telecom (50.2%)
1985 (May)	British Aerospace (remaining 50%)
1985 (Aug)	Britoil (remaining 49%)
1985 (Dec)	Cable and Wireless (remaining 29%)
1986 (Dec)	British Gas (100%)
1987 (Feb)	British Airways (100%)
1987 (May)	Rolls-Royce (100%)
1987 (July)	British Airports Authority (100%)
1987 (Oct)	British Petroleum (all 31.5% shareholding)

In conclusion it should be noted that full nationalisation is not the only way of bringing an industry under state control. An alternative method is for the government to take a majority shareholding in a public limited company. This allows the government to appoint the directors and hence control the enterprise. This method has been used in the past to save ailing industries and prevent them going out of business, e.g. Rolls Royce in 1971. This method of public ownership is usually seen as a temporary measure to sort out the business's problems, with the long-term aim of returning it back to private ownership. In the 1980s the government disposed of most of its interests of this type as part of its privatisation policy.

QUICK QUESTIONS 6

1. *What is the person who heads the management team of a public corporation called?*
2. *To whom is the board of a nationalised industry responsible?*
3. *What is the role of a nationalised industry consumer council?*
4. *Explain the meaning of the term 'privatisation'.*
5. *Give 3 benefits which may result from the privatisation of an enterprise.*

STUDENT TASK

Read the following extract adapted from a newspaper article about the privatisation of the electricity industry.

The National Grid Company was formed yesterday as the first of three new companies to be carved out of the Central Electricity Generating Board ready for privatisation next year.

Meanwhile, the Department of Energy has begun discussions on how independent generators and suppliers of electricity should be licensed after privatisation.

"For the first time they will be able to compete on an equal footing with the successor companies to the CEGB and the area boards," said a spokesman for the department.

"Already the Government is aware of some 20 new electricity generation projects as a result of the opportunities created by privatisation."

Under the 1989 Electricity Act anyone who makes or supplies electricity will need a licence unless exempted. "Licensing is designed to achieve a balance between ensuring a secure and reliable supply for consumers and the creation of a flourishing competitive market," the spokesman added.

National Grid will be owned by the 12 regional electricity boards when they are also converted to independent companies and sold. The generating side of the CEGB is being split into two independent companies, one to be called PowerGen and the other National Power.

1. What major objective of privatisation is referred to in the article?
2. According to the Department spokesman, how will the achievement of this objective benefit electricity consumers?
3. How will the structure of the 2 new companies, PowerGen PLC and National Power PLC, differ from the public corporation they replace?

The Multinational Company

Finally, any discussion of business structures should make mention of the multinational company. A multinational is a business which has operating units in more than one country. Although multinationals have existed since before the turn of the century, their development has expanded greatly since the end of the second world war. The trend towards expansion on an international scale started with American businesses but in the last 20 years more multinationals have had non-American bases. Some multinational companies are medium-sized businesses with operations in a few countries and others are very large multibillion organisations which operate all over the world.

A multinational company aims to produce on a global scale with plants in many countries. Often each plant specialises in part of the firm's product range or in specific components for the product range. The company then aims to sell its products in the countries in which it operates, giving it a much larger market for its products. The Ford Motor company is an example of an American company which has plants in many countries. Many Ford cars have components assembled from Ford factories all over the world. The same is true of the General Motor Corporation, which operates in Britain under the name of Vauxhall Motors. Many British businesses are multinational companies, e.g. British Petroleum and ICI.

The existence of multinational companies means it is often difficult to determine the nationality of a product. Many 'British' products contain components which are manufactured overseas, and many 'foreign' products contain British parts.

Multinational companies often prove difficult to control and manage as they are so diverse and, by definition, decentralised. There is also the problem of decisions affecting important economic institutions in one country being taken by managers in another country, e.g. the decision by Chrysler, based in America, to close its UK car plant at Coventry in the 1970s. Notwithstanding these problems, businesses are becoming increasingly concerned with producing for a world rather than a national market. Therefore multinational companies are a very important form of economic organisation.

QUICK QUESTIONS 7

1. *What is a multinational company?*
2. *Why is it sometimes difficult to establish the nationality of the products of a multinational company?*
3. *Name 3 non-British multinational companies which have plants in this country.*

PROJECT AND ASSIGNMENT SUGGESTIONS

1. Find out as much as you can about the type of sole trader businesses which exist in your area. You can use your local business directory or go around a particular area and make a note of the types of business you find. Your local Chamber of Commerce may also be able to help you with your survey. Try to find answers to the following questions:

   (a) Is there a particular type of business activity which is commonly undertaken by a sole trader?
   (b) What reasons can you find for certain types of activity being organised as a sole proprietorship?

   Select a sole trader business and try and find out information from the owner.

   (c) Why has the owner remained as a sole trader? Has he or she ever considered taking on a partner?
   (d) What are the problems of managing this type of business?
   (e) What are the major attractions of being your own boss?

2. Choose a large public limited company which operates in your area, or one which interests you, and find out as much as you can about it. Most companies will send you a copy of their annual report if you write to their head office, and many have other types of publicity material which they will be happy to give you. Try and find out the following:

   (a) The history of the company. How long has it been established? Did the business start as a company or did it grow from a smaller business?

(b) How large is the company? This can be expressed in a number of ways, e.g. the value of the company's assets, its income over the last year, the number of people it employs and so on.

(c) What are the main activities of the company? What products does it make? What services does it offer?

(d) What type of shares has the company issued? Does the company have debenture holders?

(e) What is the management structure of the company? How many directors does it have? What was the attendance at its last annual general meeting?

(f) Is the company based in Britain alone or does it have plants or offices in other countries? If so, what percentage of its business is conducted overseas?

In addition you can follow the company's share price movements in one of the financial newspapers. You could plot the share price changes over a given period on a graph. If it changes significantly, you could try and find out why.

3. Contact your local authority and ask for a list of the services it provides. You can usually get this information from leaflets produced to accompany the annual Community Charge demand. You may have to contact two types of local authority to find out about the full range of services provided by local government, but in London and other Metroplitan areas there is only one type of authority. Write a report about local government provision in your area showing:

(a) The total amount of money spent on local services.

(b) The services which absorb the largest percentage of this expenditure.

(c) Which services are provided with no direct charge to the recipient and which are directly paid for.

(d) The extent to which the services are paid for through the Community Charge. Where the rest of the money comes from.

(e) Whether all the services are provided by people directly employed by the council or if some services are contracted out to private sector businesses.

You could conclude your report with a table summarising your findings.

4. Collect as much information as you can about the most recent privatisation of a large industry. You could build up a scrapbook of newspaper cuttings about the privatisation or write to the industry for information. The following are questions you could consider:

(a) What benefits does the government say will result from the privatisation?

(b) What are the arguments put forward by those opposed to the industry being sold?

(c) What is the value of the industry concerned?

(d) What price per share will you have to pay if you want to invest in the industry?

(e) Are there any special inducements being offered to attract investors?

(f) How do you go about buying shares in the industry?

CHAPTER 3

The Organisation and Management of Business

The Objectives of Business Organisations

Business organisations are established to meet wants in society. Private businesses are formed mainly to provide for material wants (i.e. goods and services) and commercial wants (e.g. banking, insurance) in society. Government organisations, on the other hand, tend to satisfy society's desire for defence, law and order, education and social welfare.

Organisations are thus established to meet wants in society. In meeting these, organisations will set very definite and clear aims, e.g. a manufacturing firm will want to stay in business and make a profit. The aims of an organisation are normally decided by the board of directors, or in the case of public organisations by government ministers.

Aims of Private Organisations

Profitability is the main aim of private organisations but it is important to realise that a business will have other aims. These include:

1. **Survival**: most of the time firms will not be worried about this. However, particularly in times of economic difficulty – such as recession – surviving will become an important short-term aim of the firm. In order to survive, the firm may have to make workers redundant and close some of its factories.
2. **Growth**: not all firms want to grow continually but growth is closely associated with survival. Very often, particularly for firms in highly competitive situations, e.g. computing and electronics, growth and development are the only way to ensure survival. Furthermore, shareholders and employees alike may benefit from the growth of the company.
3. **Image**: how the public at large views a company can be particularly important, and to this end a number of companies have public relations departments that have specific responsibility to improve the image of the company. A tarnished image can very often lose the company business.

Aims of Public Corporations

The aims of public corporations are decided by the government. Basically the nationalised industries have 2 broad obligations:

1. **Economic obligations**: each nationalised industry has to manage its resources and adopt pricing policies such that it meets its target rate of return on capital. This target is reviewed annually and differs from industry to industry, e.g. the water authorities were set a target return of 1.6% in 1986–7 while that for the electricity industry was 2.75%.
2. **Social obligations**: the economic obligations of public corporations are tempered by their social obligations, e.g. British Rail may continue to provide a rail service in a rural area even though that service may be unprofitable. Similarly, the Post Office may provide unprofitable postal services in isolated communities, e.g. the Shetland Isles.

QUICK QUESTIONS 1

1. *Name some government organisations and identify what needs these organisations satisfy.*
2. *What are the aims of private organisations? How successful are they at achieving these?*
3. *Suggest ways in which a company can improve its 'public image'.*

Formal Organisation

Any group of people with a task to do or an objective to fulfil – win a cricket match, build a house, run a school or a profitable business – will form or organise themselves into a team. If the team is a small one, then the leader or captain will be able to influence all members personally and will be able to make all the necessary decisions, e.g. a cricket captain has a comparatively small team of 10 other players. However, if the team is a large one, e.g. a multinational company, it will have to be divided into manageable sections or departments.

In order to enable the organisation to fulfil its aims policy decisions have to be carried out, and most large businesses have departments which specialise in certain functions, e.g. production, marketing, distribution and personnel. Imposing a formal organisation structure on a business allows each department to be set its own target or objective, e.g. the production department may be set a target of so many units of output per week. It allows each department to have a well-defined role within the organisation so that functions are not duplicated or repeated. And it means that the functions of each department can be easily co-ordinated with others in the organisation so that the business runs smoothly.

Emphasis on teamwork and co-ordination are important, and the following examples may illustrate the point:

1. There would be little point in the Production Department producing a product as efficiently as it could if the Marketing Department could not sell it. On the other hand, it would be silly if the sales force was attempting to sell more products than the company could produce.
2. The firm must keep levels of stocks which ensure that components and materials are available in the right quantities when the production team wants them.

3. The Finance Department must ensure that cash is flowing into the business as it is needed, e.g. to pay the workforce or suppliers of materials to the firm.

These 3 examples highlight the close association between organisational structure, co-ordination and communication. Most companies' organisational structure can be presented in simple diagrammatic form. The formal relationships between departments is shown by a hierarchical organisational chart.

A very simple organisation chart showing the 4 main functions – production, marketing, personnel and finance – which exist in most large businesses is shown in Figure 3.1.

Organisation charts are like the family trees of the organisation. More detailed ones can be used to show:

1. The levels of authority and responsibility from the top to the bottom of the organisation.
2. Interdepartmental relationships within the organisation.
3. The lines of formal communication channels.
4. The relative status and prestige of employees.

A more complex organisation chart showing the separate functions of the Marketing Department is given in Figure 3.2.

The form of organisation chart illustrated in Figure 3.1 is known as functional – for obvious reasons. Such charts are found in all kinds of organisations, from the army to ICI. The lines of communication are both upwards, downwards and horizontal, though communication is normally downwards.

In this particular case, where instructions are passed down lines in the hierarchy, the functions in the chart are called **line functions**, and the system is referred to as **line management**. Figure 3.2 highlights the Marketing Department's line management system. However, there are some functions – normally consultative or advisory – within a firm whose

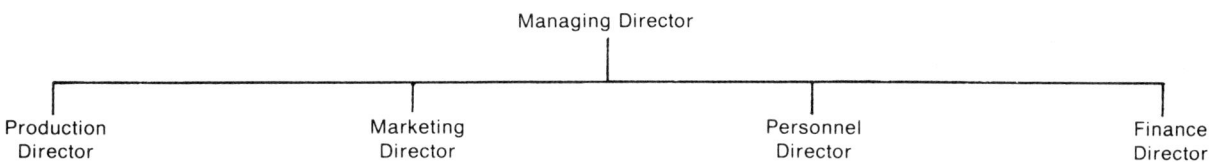

Figure 3.1 Organisation Chart of a Typical Business

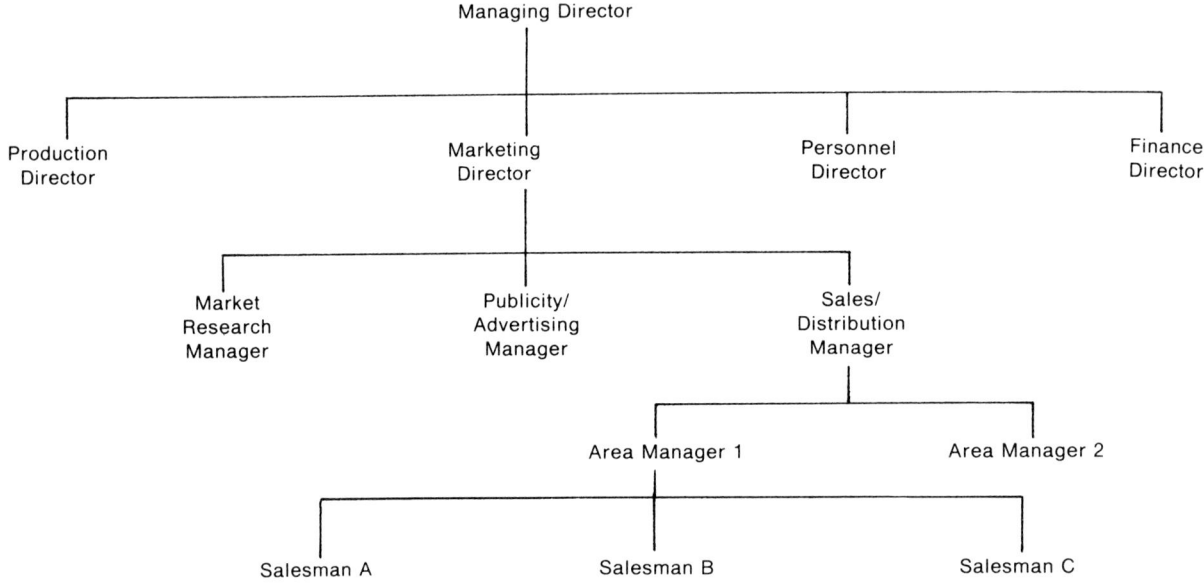

Figure 3.2 An Organisation Chart Showing the Line Management of the Marketing Department

role it is to move into other departments and provide a service. This frequently happens with the Personnel Department in most firms. All recruitment and training could be undertaken by this department. People who offer this kind of specialist service will belong to their own line (or department) but when working in other departments, or for them, they are not part of that line. These advisory or specialist support services are called **staff posts**.

There can be cases of conflict between line and staff because line managers sometimes see the work that the staff people do as interference in their departments. For example, the Area Manager 1 may have problems with Salesman B, who is arriving at work late, leaving early and not selling very much. Personnel may intervene and may give Salesman B a caution or warning. Area Manager 1 may interpret this as interference in his department and a challenge to his authority to discipline and manage.

The Organisation chart of Mercedez-Benz Parts Department is shown in Figure 3.3. The Parts Department has 4 lines: Administration; Warehouse Operations; Parts Marketing and Field Operations.

So far the organisation chart of a business has been examined by **function**. However, some organisations have their structure divided not by function but by their **market(s)** or **product(s)**. One example is Lloyds Bank PLC. In 1985 they reorganised their structure into one integrated, international bank, with 5 main operating units, focussed on specific **market** segments. Their particular organisation chart is shown in Figure 3.4.

QUICK QUESTIONS 2

1. *What do you understand by the term 'organisation chart' and what purposes do organisation charts serve?*

2. *Explain the term 'line management'. Give an example of this situation from your school or college.*

3. *What are 'staff posts' and how do they differ from 'line functions'?*

4. *Suggest 3 ways in which a company could organise itself.*

STUDENT TASK

Think about how your institution is organised and the functions that are carried out within it. For example, year groups, forms and subject departments may be the principal units of organisation, with teaching, maintenance, cleaning and meal provision the prime functions. Try to draw an organisation chart of your school or college that shows this information.

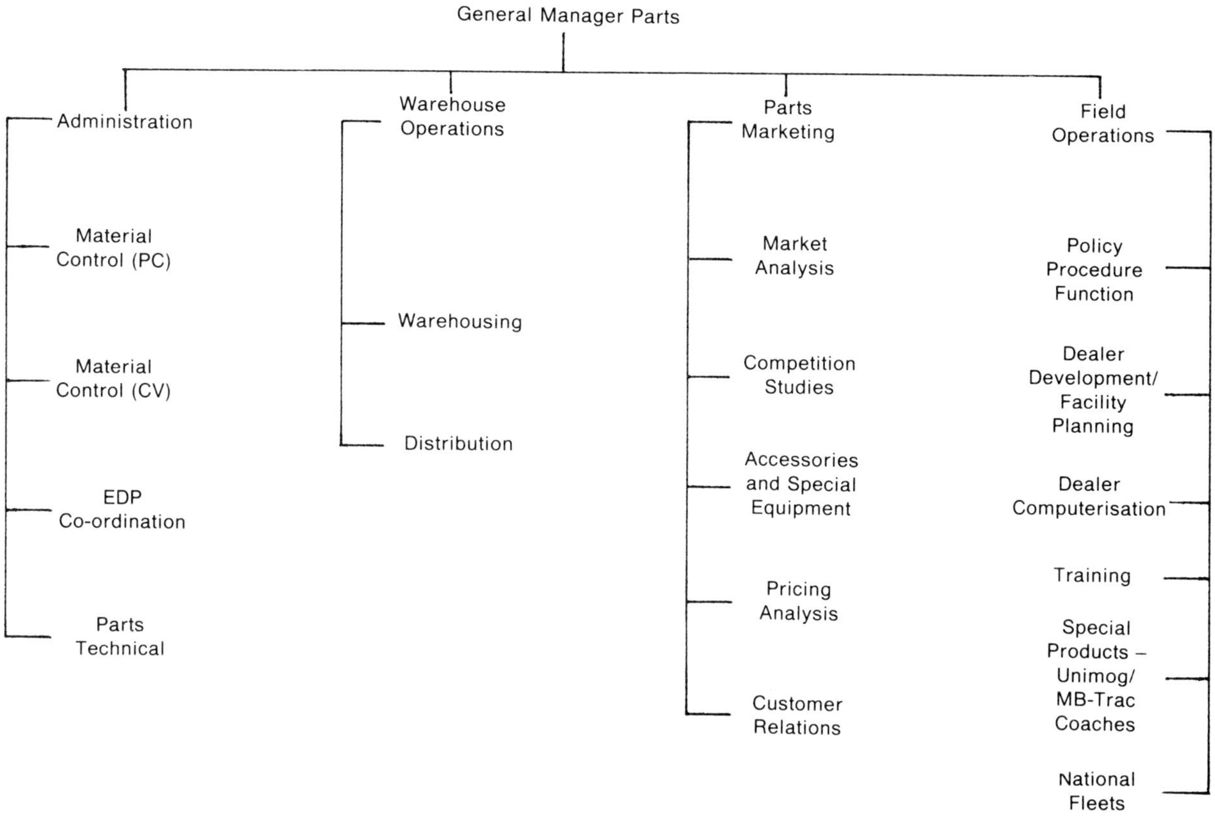

General Manager Parts
Administration
Material Control (PC)
Material Control (CV)
EDP Co-ordination
Parts Technical
Warehouse Operations
Warehousing
Distribution
Parts Marketing
Market Analysis
Competition Studies
Accessories and Special Equipment
Pricing Analysis
Customer Relations
Field Operations
Policy Procedure Function
Dealer Development/ Facility Planning
Dealer Computerisation
Training
Special Products – Unimog/ MB-Trac Coaches
National Fleets

Figure 3.3 The Organisation of Mercedes-Benz Parts Department

Finance Division
Risk-Management Division
Strategic Planning
Chief Executive
Deputy Chief Executive
Support Services
Corporate Communications
UK Retail Banking
International Banking
Corporate Banking
Merchant Banking
Treasury

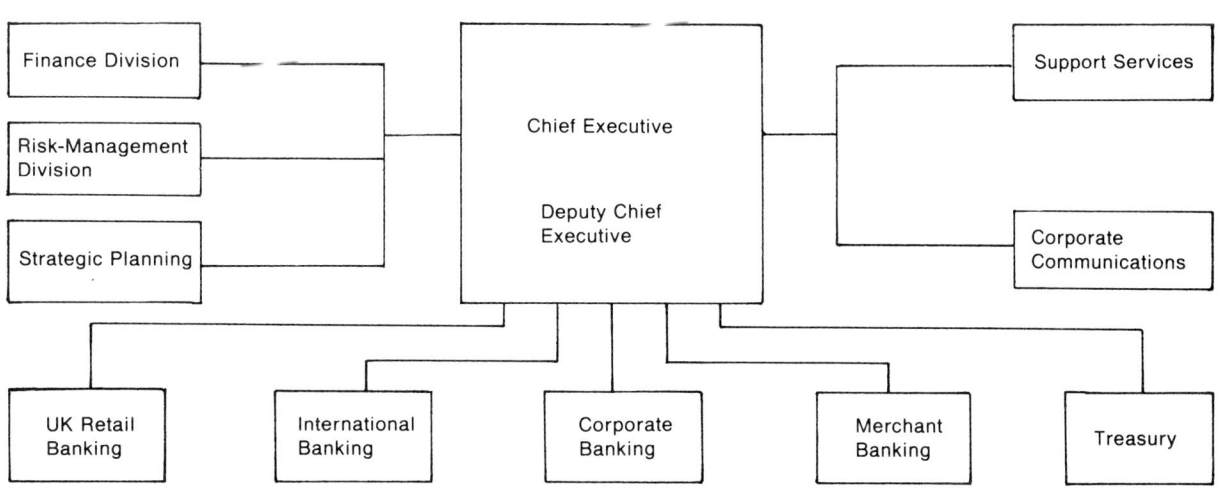

Figure 3.4 The Organisation Structure of Lloyds Bank PLC

Firm A

Manager

Works Manager

Foremen

Workforce

Firm B

General Manager
Deputy General Manager
Product Manager
Works Manager
Supervisor
Foremen
Chargehands
Workforce

Figure 3.5 Levels of Authority in Two Firms

Authority and Levels of Authority

Authority can be defined as the **right to use** or **exercise power**, and in a formal organisation chart this right is defined by the hierarchy. Figure 3.2 showed that in the Marketing Department's line management system there are 5 levels of authority, from the Managing Director down to the salesman. In practice the number of levels of authority within a firm varies enormously. In Figure 3.5 firm A has 4 levels of authority and firm B has 8.

Each of the two structures in Figure 3.5 has advantages and disadvantages. Each level of authority may mean additional communication has to be made and it may take considerable time to communicate from top to bottom and vice-versa. In firm A, communication is theoretically much quicker because there are only half the levels of authority compared with firm B, but in practice the people at each level may be so overwhelmed with work that communication between each level is inadequate.

Chain of Command

This refers to the number of levels of authority from the top to the bottom of a firm. In Figure 3.5 the chain of command in firm A is 4 levels long while in firm B it is 8.

Span of Control

This is the number of people or relationships for which a person is **directly** responsible. Figure 3.2

shows that the Managing Director has a span of control of 4 – Production, Marketing, Personnel and Finance Directors – while the Marketing Director has a span of control of 3. The Sales/Distribution Manager has a span of control of 2 and Area Manager 1 has a span of control of 3.

Many people have argued about span of control and have attempted to suggest general principles about it. Henri Fayol (1841–1925), who was one of the pioneers of management thought and organisation theory, recommended that the span of control or the number of subordinates reporting to any one manager should not normally exceed 7 or 8. Otherwise, this could lead to problems.

If the manager is to get the best from his or her employees, he or she must communicate with them, and communication is a time-consuming process. The number of subordinates any one manager can supervise is therefore limited by the need to communicate and the nature of the communication. If the relationship between manager and staff is to be effective, the span of control needs to be quite small. However, in some circumstances where individuals can work alone for long periods unsupervised, such as research projects, then one manager or project leader can look after perhaps 15 or 20 staff. Some managers may claim to have a very large number of subordinates, e.g. the manager of a large shopping store may have more than 100 staff. In reality, the only way in which a manager can control such large number of people is by **delegating** to another level of managers or supervisors. It is important to mention here the 'unit of command' principle, which states that subordinates should at best report to only one supervisor, and that the command over one individual should not be shared between different managers – 'a dog cannot serve two masters'.

QUICK QUESTIONS 3

1. *What is authority? Give examples of (i) how it is used in your school and (ii) how you would expect it to be used in a firm.*
2. *What do you understand by the term 'chain of command'? What problems arise if this chain is too long?*
3. *Give a definition of 'span of control'. What is the span of control of your parents at home? What is the span of control of (a) the Head of Maths; (b) the Head of Economics or Business Studies at your school? Are these spans of control too large? If so, why?*

Delegation and Centralisation

Delegation is the act of designing tasks and objectives for subordinates and getting the subordinates to do those tasks. The work of a business organisation, as we have seen, can be divided by function – production, marketing, personnel and finance – and by level. At the top of any organisation there is a Managing Director or Chief Executive who operates by making the head of each department responsible for everything relating to that department. Similarly, the head of department will pass tasks down to his subordinates. In a typical school, for example, the Headmaster is similar to the Chief Executive; each subject department will have its head, and members of that department are directly answerable to him or her.

One of the most difficult decisions for a medium- or large-scale organisation to make is how much decentralisation to allow. This is rarely a problem for small firms since they are too small to decentralise. Decentralisation simply means that management decisions are not taken centrally within the organisation. Some functions, however, are the preserve of head office, e.g. financial control. When a company increases in size it becomes impossible for one person, or group of persons, to make each and every decision about all aspects of the business. It would be impossible, inefficient and time-consuming for all decisions to be

made centrally. Further, there will always be some decisions which need to be made there and then, or 'on the spot'. In such cases it will be more efficient for the organisation to decentralise its decision-making process as too much centralisation can make for ineffective communication and poor control.

Large organisations can overcome these 2 problems by decentralisation or greater delegation. In a decentralised organisation the firm is divided into several autonomous (independent) units and each unit is responsible for its own performance. In Miss Selfridge, which is part of the larger Sears empire, each shop has its own manager who is responsible to a regional manager, and the performance of each shop is judged in relation both to one another as well as to outside competitors. Each shop is given a set objective to achieve and its operating results, e.g. sales, can guide the decisions of top management since they have indicators of good or bad performance by each retail unit.

Peter Drucker, one of the leading modern authors on management, argues that decentralisation best suits the firm that has distinct product lines which can be separated into different establishments, like shops. It brings with it 3 principal advantages. First, it allows for flexibility of policy. In retailing, for example, firms that own several shops in different areas allow managers to order their own stock and be responsible for the layout of their own store. This allows each individual shop to adapt to and reflect the peculiar needs of its own locality. For example, certain product ranges sell well in particular areas and only individual managers have this specialist knowledge. So they are better qualified to make decisions about the items which they decide to stock. Such a decision would be very difficult to make centrally. Secondly, it tends to strengthen rather than weaken management. The decentralisation of decision-making means that important decisions are made in all establishments of a business at different levels, and this makes for a much more effective training ground than if all decisions were made centrally. Encouraging people to stand on their own 2 feet thus makes for effective and strong management. Thirdly, it allows the firm to respond quickly and effectively to changing local circumstances. If all decisions were taken centrally, the business would be sluggish in responding to situations.

Decentralisation, however, is not without its

problems. The principal difficulty is that communication between each division tends to be generally poor. Co-ordination is essential if the left hand is to know what the right hand is doing.

Informal Organisation

A formal organisation structure defines roles and relationships for people but organisation charts show only the basic and official relationships within the workplace. They reflect the intentions of the firm in terms of the chain of command and who reports to whom but they omit all the informal contacts which must have an influence upon the way in which the firm operates. The formal organisation chart does not and cannot show all the relationships that exist. In particular it completely ignores the role of informal groups and informal relationships.

An informal group is one which arises naturally in a work situation because members of the group have one or more interests in common. They exist for a number of reasons and come about because each individual does many things in life apart from work, and will meet colleagues in settings away from the workplace, e.g. at the pub or down the gym. The existence and importance of informal groups was first pointed out by Elton Mayo at the Western Electric Company factory at Hawthorne, near Chicago, between 1924 and 1932. The 'Hawthorne Studies' suggested that informal groups had a very important role to play in the organisation, as will be seen in Chapter 5.

QUICK QUESTIONS 4

1. *What do you understand by the term 'delegation'? Give examples of delegation within the school.*
2. *What are the advantages of 'delegation'?*
3. *What is an 'informal group'? Give examples of informal groups that you belong to within the school or college. Why are they important to you?*

STUDENT EXERCISE: BUSINESS ORGANISATION AND STRUCTURE

In 1980 I. Fittem, a carpenter, set up in business by himself building and fitting kitchen units. In 1985 he took on a former workmate, A. Bolt, as a partner to provide extra capital in order to expand production. Shortly after this time Fittem and Bolt became a private limited company as they had been advised that this would give them certain advantages.

When home improvement grants of 100% were offered by the government, demand for the services of Fittem and Bolt increased sharply. In order to make the most of this opportunity the company 'went public' and was thus able to move to a bigger factory and employ more people. At this time Mrs Fittem left her job in a bank to become Administration Director, in overall charge of personnel, accounting and general office functions, while Mr Bolt sold his shares but stayed on as Production Manager.

In addition to those mentioned above, the present workforce is as follows:

7 clerks – 2 in the Accounts Department, 2 in the General Office, 2 in the Purchasing Department and 1 in the Personnel Department
3 sales representatives
1 Purchase Manager
1 General Office Manager
1 Accountant
1 Sales Manager
1 Personnel Manager
20 production workers
2 YT trainees – 1 clerical trainee in the General Office and 1 trainee learning the production process

1. From the information given above, draw up an organisation chart for the company as it is at the present time.
2. What is Mrs Fittem's 'span of control'?
3. What is the 'span of control' of the Sales Manager?
4. How many levels of authority are there from the Managing Director to the sales representatives?

PROJECT AND ASSIGNMENT SUGGESTIONS

1. Select 2 businesses which operate in your local area and compare their organisational structures. If possible try to make a comparison between a small local business which operates from one establishment and a larger national company which operates in different parts of the country. Your study of each business should try and answer the following questions:

   (a) Is the business organised according to functions, products or markets?
   (b) Is a distinction made between line and staff organisation?
   (c) How many levels of authority are there in the organisational structure?
   (d) What are the various spans of control of the senior management in the business?
   (e) To what extent is authority delegated within the business?

   Write up your findings in the form of a report which includes a diagram showing the organisational structure of each business.

2. Assume that you and a group of friends have decided to organise a live music concert at your school or college. It is your responsibility to devise an efficient organisational structure to ensure the event runs smoothly.

   (a) Make a list of your objectives in organising and staging the concert.
   (b) Draw up a list of all the tasks which will have to be completed both before the concert and during the concert.
   (c) Devise an organisation chart which you think would be best suited to ensuring all the tasks are completed and your objectives achieved.
   (d) What is the best way of delegating the tasks to different members of the group?
   (e) What do you think will be the major problems you will face in trying to make the concert a success? How would you try and overcome these problems?

3. Find out what you can about the Young Enterprise Organisation or the Mini Enterprise Scheme. These are designed to involve young people in the organising and managing of business activity. Write a short account showing how the type of activities members of these schemes undertake are similar to organising a real business. What do you think you could learn about business organisation and management by being involved in one of these schemes?

CHAPTER 4

Communication in Business

Communication, and particularly effective communication, is very important within an organisation. It should be obvious that every day we are being continually bombarded with communication messages from parents, teachers, friends and companies. What these people have to say, the way in which they say it (their manner) and how they choose to say it (their choice of language) can vary enormously. When people talk about 'communication' they usually have in mind verbal or oral communication. However, there are other means of communicating a message, e.g. visual communication such as the school noticeboard, or the advertising hoarding in the bus shelter; written communication such as an essay, assignment or letter; and body language – which is a form of non-verbal communication. Figure 4.1 shows the process of communication and emphasises the four components of all communication: the **message**, the **sender**, the **medium** and the receiver. The speaker (or sender) is shown to be thinking about what he or she wants to say (the message). He or she can say it in a variety of ways and styles (the medium) so that the listener (or receiver) can understand it.

The messages that businesses wish to communicate vary enormously. They range from simple signs such as 'Exit' or 'Fire Escape' inside an office or factory, an advertising slogan such as 'Persil washes whiter', to financial or technical information as contained in an annual report or operating manual. Within the organisation itself, employees will be receiving instructions, orders and requests which have to be acted upon. If these are misunderstood or misinterpreted the wrong action, or even inaction, may occur. This emphasises the need for effective communication within the business.

In order for communication to be effective it is important to select the most suitable method (or

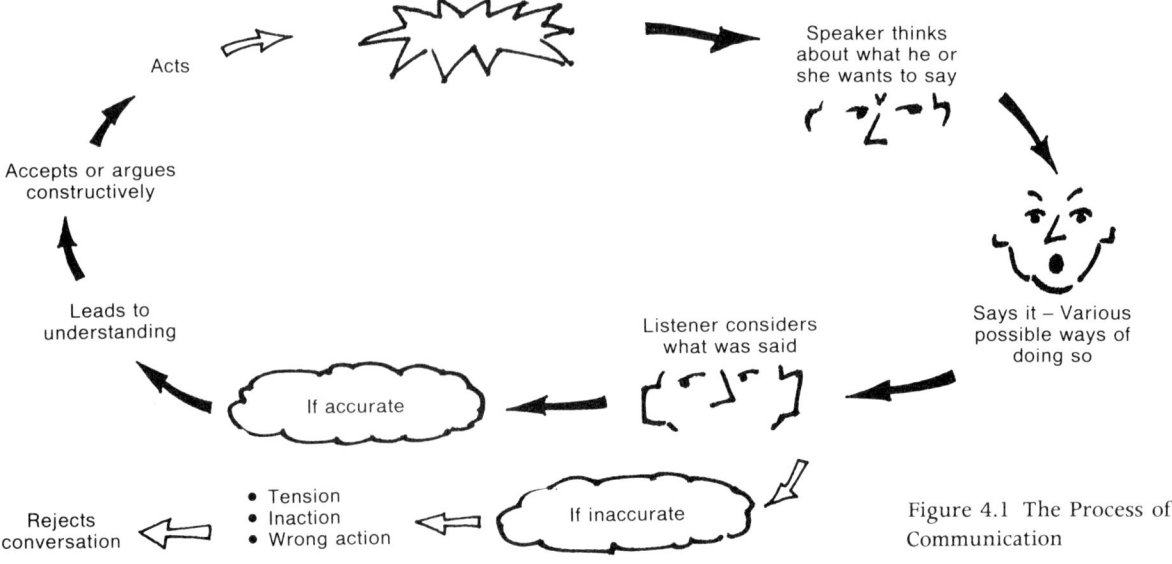

Figure 4.1 The Process of Communication

medium) of communication. Methods of communicating within the company can be divided into 3 categories: 1. written communication; 2. spoken/oral communication; 3. non-verbal communication or body language. Each of these is examined in turn below.

1. Written Communication

Information which is to be used more than once is usually kept in written form, e.g. reports, financial information, invoice and purchase records and stock control forms. Legal obligations will require other internal records, such as staff pay and pension details, accident reports and attendance registers at school, to be kept. The main forms of written communication are:

(a) **Letters**: these tend to be used by a business when it is communicating with clients or prospective employees. For example, when you apply for a job the company will usually write to inform you as to whether you have been successful or not in securing an interview. It will also give you information about the next stage of the recruitment process, such as the time of an interview and the name of the interviewer. Companies sometimes send letters to their employees concerning promotion and pay increases. However, it is unlikely that letters will form the bulk of internal written communication – far more common will be memoranda (memos).

(b) **Memoranda**: internal memos are internal written correspondence. The paper on which they are written or typed is usually pre-printed, and it is often of A5 size to encourage staff to keep memos short. If a memo is to be sent to several people, two alternative means of sending it are available. First, several copies could be made and sent to each person. This could be time-consuming and expensive, although you are sure that everyone concerned receives it. Second, a 'circulation list' could be attached; each reader will tick their name on the list to indicate that he or she has read it. Two problems arise with this method: one person may forget to pass the memo onto the next person on the circulation list, or they may hang on to it for so long that the intended receivers do not get the message on time.

Sometimes memos are used as notices for display on a board, e.g. quite a few households nowadays have a 'memo-board' hung in the kitchen to remind them of shopping to get, times of doctor's appointments and important telephone numbers. Information on a memo-board should be clearly displayed and very easy to read, and out-of-date notices should be removed regularly.

(c) **Handbooks and manuals**: companies produce a variety of short handbooks for potential employees and existing staff. There may well be one that gives the history of the company, particularly if it is celebrating a centenary or marking an important occasion. Another may set out rules and regulations for each member of staff, together with the facilities the company offers. All such booklets attempt to provide information in a permanent, neat and concise form to which staff may refer quickly and easily. Companies also provide handbooks or operating manuals with instructions on how to use a particular piece of equipment such as a lathe or a word processor. They are essential in order for employees to get to know how a piece of equipment works. It is important therefore that they are written clearly with no ambiguities.

(d) **Reports**: a business report is a formal document that analyses a situation or problem. Such reports are a common feature in most companies and they vary in length, degree of formality, and format. Business reports can cover areas such as finance, marketing, personnel and research. Most will examine a problem – using factual information – and then make recommendations or suggestions as to how the problem can be overcome.

(e) **Noticeboards**: all organisations will make use of this method of communication. Internal memos, safety posters, internal job vacancies and more general notices can all be found on a typical company noticeboard. In schools, noticeboards are used for posting sports teams and travel arrangements, changes to the timetable, forthcoming events such as a careers evening or a jumble sale, and dates and times of examinations.

Noticeboards need to be strategically placed so that people can see them easily – in a recreation area or near the main exit or clock-cards. This encourages people to use them. Notices should be well displayed and the board should be regularly cleared of out-of-date information so that new items are clearly visible. The board can also be divided into sections for different types of information, and there may even be an 'Urgent' or 'Today' section. It is important that notices are carefully phrased so as to avoid misunderstanding.

(f) **House magazines and newsletters**: one means of giving detailed information to staff is the company magazine or newsletter. This can be a simple A4 duplicated sheet or, in very large organisations, a glossy magazine or full-size newspaper. It may contain general information about the company, e.g. new products and company performance, and also information about specific employees in the company, e.g. retirements, new recruits and achievements of company teams in local/national events. Schools and colleges will have their own form of house magazine or newsletter.

(g) **Circulars**: these can be given to employees in their pay packets or pay slips. Important information, such as notification of a pay rise or redundancy, is often communicated in this way because virtually all employees will take notice of what is contained in their pay packet.

(h) **Minutes**: these are formal written records of meetings. A record should be made of almost every formal meeting and circulated among those who attended to ensure that this was an accurate description of what took place. This record can also be given to those who were not present to inform them of what took place. Minutes are always taken at formal meetings and sometimes this is a legal requirement, e.g. at board of directors meetings. Minutes would also be taken at the annual general meeting of a local sports club. This job is done by the Club Secretary, an officer elected by the members of the club.

QUICK QUESTIONS 1

1. *What is the difference between a letter and a memo? Give examples of situations where a memo is more likely to be used as a method of communication.*

2. *What sorts of information are displayed on (i) school noticeboards and (ii) company noticeboards? Why do you think the noticeboards in your school are positioned where they are? Do you think they could be positioned better? If so, give reasons why.*

3. *Why do companies place important pieces of information in pay packets?*

STUDENT TASK

Go round your institution and note where the noticeboards are placed. Does their position make sense or are there other places that would be better? Examine the noticeboard and see if it is up-to-date. How is it laid out? Is it organised? Are the notices clear?

---

2. Oral Communication

(a) **Conversation**: individuals talk to one another in the work environment. The topics of conversation can range enormously, e.g. a group of friends may talk about what happened over the weekend while a supervisor at work is more likely to pass down instructions to subordinates. It is important that such instructions, e.g. those given to candidates at the start of an examination, are clear and not open to misinterpretation.

(b) **Interviews**: these are mainly used when a candidate is being assessed for a job or when somebody is being considered for promotion. They can be conducted for disciplinary reasons too. Interview formats vary enormously – from a one-to-one situation, to where the interviewee is confronted by a panel of up to a dozen. Interviewing is an important skill and the interviewer must give the interviewee the opportunity to explain his or her points of view. Asking searching and probing questions is part of the interviewer's job. Very often the way the interviewee 'performs' during the conversation will determine whether they get the job. Does the interviewee appear relaxed or do they keep rubbing their hands nervously? Does the interviewee have anything interesting to say? The interview obviously provides the opportunity for two-way communication, unlike the spoken instruction, where communication is a one-way process.

(c) **Meetings**: these are often divided into two types – formal and informal. A formal meeting usually involves one or all of the following elements:

(i) a Chairman

(ii) a set of rules which govern how the meeting is convened, the topics of the meeting and how the business of the meeting is recorded

(iii) conventions applied to the way in which the business of the meeting is discussed.

When the procedure adopted for calling a meeting, conducting its business and recording it is determined by rules, these rules may or may not be legally binding. For example, company law states certain requirements about the conduct of company business which affect the meetings of shareholders and boards of directors. In the UK these rules are specified in the Memorandum and Articles of Association of each individual company.

There are several procedures to be followed in the calling and conduct of most properly organised meetings. Some of the more important are:

(i) **Agenda**: it is sensible to have a written agenda and distribute it to those who are expected to attend the meeting, together with any relevant papers. It is important to have a clear agenda if meetings are to be effective. This allows the orderly conduct of the business of the meeting.

(ii) **The Chair:** One person should control the meeting and this could be either an elected chairman or the most senior manager. This person is responsible for the control and direction of the meeting. The chair has a number of important responsibilities and duties.

(iii) **The minutes and the Secretary**: it is desirable to keep a written record of what is discussed in a meeting. The Company Secretary, an elected officer, is usually responsible for this. The record – the minutes – can then be circulated to confirm what was discussed.

(iv) **Motions**: in some cases motions need to be submitted in writing before a specified date prior to the meeting. Sometimes these motions have to be proposed and seconded. For example, prior to an annual general meeting some shareholders may propose a motion that they have no confidence in the board of directors (a 'no confidence motion'). This will then be voted on at the AGM. Motions can be amended before being voted upon.

(v) **Debate:** motions in a meeting are debated and each person should be given the chance to put across their point of view.

(vi) **The ballot**: at many formal meetings, a motion is decided by means of a vote, either by a show of hands or a secret ballot. A simple majority usually means the motion will be carried (approved).

(vii) **The casting vote**: if there is a tie in the vote, the chair may have the casting vote in order to break the deadlock.

(d) **Telephone calls**: telephones have the advantage of speed. Most large organisations have their own internal telephone system, together with extension numbers, and a separate external system. Companies now equip some of their executives and reps with carphones. This is designed to encourage communication, to improve co-ordination and to save the reps' time.

STUDENT TASK

You must organise a committee, e.g. a local residents' association. This requires the appointment of a chairperson and a secretary. The committee wants to hold a meeting because, for example, it is angry at the council's decision to turn a recreational facility, such as tennis courts, into new houses. Try to devise an agenda for the meeting. Conduct the meeting and have the secretary make notes as to what points were raised.

---

3. Non-Verbal Communication

Not all communication has to be verbal or written – a shrug, frown or wink can mean something. This is frequently called 'body language', and it is communicated by posture or facial expression. The ability to interpret such signs is an important social skill.

QUICK QUESTIONS 2

The 4 basic elements of communication are the message, the source, the medium and the receiver.

Explain carefully, with examples, what is meant by each of these terms.

Choice of Communication Medium

No communication will be effective unless it is presented through the best or most suitable medium. Selection of the best medium will depend on a whole host of factors, including the following:

1. The nature of the message: if the message is private or confidential then it should not be announced in front of a large group of staff. It should instead be delivered through a letter or a private conversation. However, if you need to tell all members of staff, it may be best to announce the message at a meeting or over the work's tannoy.

2. The urgency of the message: if the message is urgent then it may need to be given orally, e.g. by telephone, since a letter or memo may be delayed.

3. The receiver(s): if there is only one receiver then oral communication may be appropriate. If a large number of people is to receive the message then memos or the noticeboard could be more appropriate.

4. The timing of the communication: people doing urgent work should not be interrupted for non-urgent messages, nor can a busy manager be expected to listen on the telephone to personal problems in the middle of an important conference.

5. The place of communication: this will affect the method used. Sign or body language might be necessary in a noisy workshop while a written message might be used in a library where silence is expected.

6. The length and importance of the message: if there is a large amount of important information to be transmitted then written communication may be more sensible than spoken words. Teachers often discuss something in class first and then use the blackboard to note the important ideas.

QUICK QUESTIONS 3

Malcolm Hinton is the owner of a small engineering business employing 15 people. In the course of the next week he has the following tasks to perform:

(i) Discuss with his advertising company the style of advertising campaign for a new product.

(ii) Inform certain employees of the changes in their overtime rates that were agreed with the union last week.

(iii) Let the Bank Manager know that an increase in the business's overdraft facility will not after all be required.

(iv) Choose, among 4 possible production workers, who should be promoted to foreman.

(v) Place details of a vacancy for a machine operator with the local job centre.

(vi) Inform the office staff of the holiday arrangements for next summer.

Each of these tasks requires some form of communication. In each case select the channel of communication you think is appropriate and explain why you think it is suitable.

Styles and Structure of Communication

There is an undeniable link between the organisation structure and the communication structure. By and large, vertical communication follows the chain of command, whether upward or downward, but even the organisation chart does not show all lines of communication. The communication structure is far more complex. Look at Figure 4.2 which focusses on the production line management team. The chart illustrates the downward flow of formal information. This is known as one-way communication. Commands are issued from the top and foremen have to see that these are executed. However, the big drawback with one-way communication is that there is no guarantee that the message has been understood and acted upon properly. To avoid misunderstanding and encourage a response to the message, the firm could allow feedback to the message, in which case communication would travel upward and back to the top.

Some firms have developed formal systems such as staff development interviews and joint consultative committees in order to encourage the upward flow of ideas and opinions. Such systems also motivate the employees since they give them the opportunity to air grievances and discuss career prospects with a senior member of the management team.

One disadvantage of the organisation chart is that it does not show horizontal/lateral communication between departments or even between members of the same department. Co-ordination between depart-

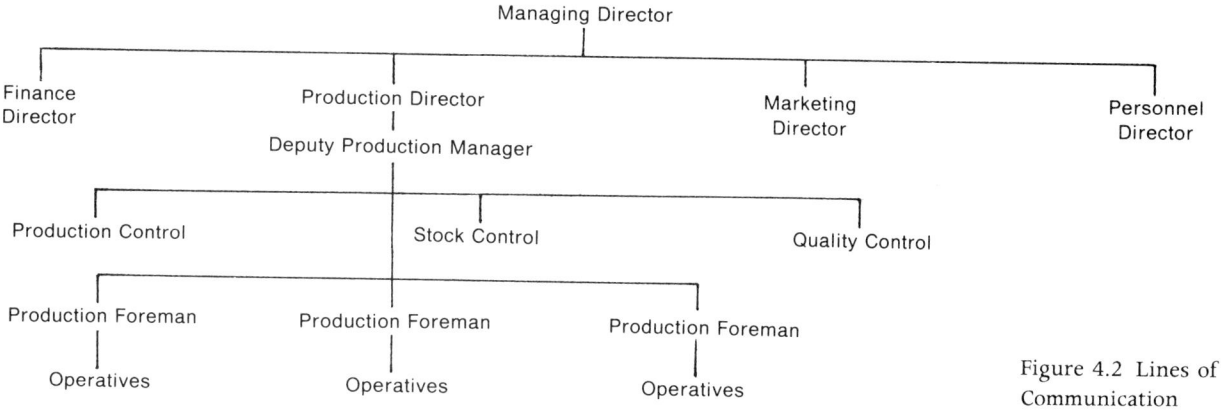

Figure 4.2 Lines of Communication

ments is essential and so communication between people at the same level in an organisation's hierarchy is common, e.g. between heads of departments in a school.

Finally, the organisation chart does not show the multidirectional communication that takes place in any organisation. The so-called 'grapevine' – the unofficial network of information channels – is important in any organisation. Where such informal methods are in operation a message can often circulate quickly and cheaply and so help or supplement the formal communication system. One disadvantage of the grapevine is that messages can be distorted leading to misunderstanding.

STUDENT TASK

Look at the process of communication diagram in Figure 4.1. Pay particular attention to the bottom left-hand part of the diagram concerning inaccurate information/communication. To highlight the inaction/tension/wrong action response, organise the class as described below.

1. Pick 6–7 pupils.
2. Each of these pupils and the teacher should be given the following Lego pieces: (i) three 8-dimple white blocks; (ii) two 6-dimple blue blocks; (iii) one 4-dimple red block; (iv) one 12-dimple yellow block; and (v) one 2-dimple white block.
3. The teacher then uses his or her pieces to make a shape that cannot be seen by other members of the class.
4. Choose one member of the class to come to the front and sit down with his or her back to the group which has the Lego pieces. The teacher then passes the model to this pupil and asks him or her to give a description of the model to the other participants.
5. Communication must be one-way only and no questions are allowed.
6. Two points are worth making: the information given should be in terms of colours and numbers of dimples, and instructions need to be clear.
7. After the object has been described, the teacher's model is then compared with the models that have been constructed from the instructions. Note how many are right and how many are wrong. What are the impressions of the group? Were they satisfied with the instructions? Was the information accurate?
8. Select another member of the class and go through the same procedure with a different shape. The second time around more models should be correct – particularly if the pitfalls from round one have been noted and acted upon.
9. The exercise should highlight the drawbacks of one-way communication and the difficulty of conveying technical information using oral communication. To emphasise how two-way communication is (generally) better, pick a spokesperson from the group of 'constructors'. He or she is allowed to interrupt/stop/talk to the person describing the model. There should be a certain amount of feedback and the number of correct models should increase.
10. Next allow complete communication: each member of the group is allowed to communicate with the person at the front. This will be more time-consuming, people will be constantly interrupting, and some may change their models on the basis of misinterpretation of information.

Communication Nets

Since the organisation chart does not show all possible lines of communication in an organisation (except upward or downward), an analysis of communication channels can be made by examining communication networks (or nets). The most common of these nets are illustrated and described below. The arrows show lines of communication.

Common Communication Network

Persons A,B,C,D and E are equal in terms of the communication channels available to them. For example, A can communicate with B,C,D or E. Similarly, B can communicate with A,C,D or E. Each person has 4 lines of communication.

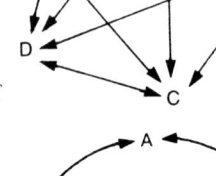

Circular Communication Network

Each person communicates with the person on the left or right, e.g. C can communicate with B or D but not with A or E. Each person has 2 communication lines.

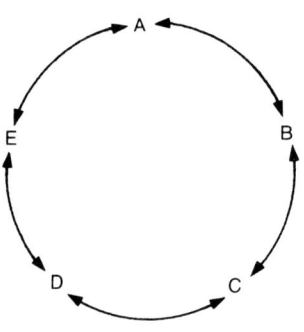

Chain Communication Network

A can only communicate with B. B can communicate with A or C, and E can communicate with D only. A and E have 1 line of communication, while B,C and D have 2.

Y Communication Network

A,B and E have 1 line of communication, D has 2, and C has 3.

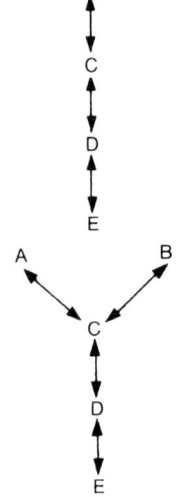

Wheel Communication Network

A,B,C and D have only one channel of communication and that is with person E. Person E has 4 channels of communication.

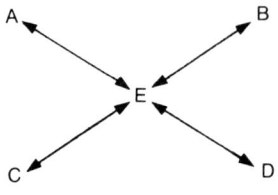

STUDENT TASK

1. Divide the pupils into 5 groups of 5.
2. Arrange the seating in the room so as to give the communication nets as presented in the diagrams.
3. Each group member should have a pencil and several pieces of scrap paper. Information received by each individual must be recorded.
4. Communication must be by written note only. The original pieces of information must be returned to the sender.
5. To avoid the possibility of cheating, a messenger should be used to transfer notes from one member of the net to another (as in an office situation). The messenger must not be a member of the group.
6. The exercise is complete when all members of the group have the relevant information.

Problem 1

Each member of the group is given a list of 5 numbers. The object of the exercise is to find the common number and pass this information to each member of the group. The initial information given to each person is as follows:

A	B	C	D	E
100	96	85	112	96
85	79	112	73	79
73	85	34	28	85
27	44	28	41	77
64	62	14	85	19

The time it takes each particular network to complete the exercise should be recorded. From this a discussion should follow regarding the best/worst network (in terms of time taken) and the reasons for the result.

Problem 2

Each member of each network is given the following separate pieces of information:

A	B	C	D	E
N	T	K	W	O
K	S	R	O	W
L	R	Z	N	P
E	Q	E	V	X
Y	C	T	A	E

Each person must hold onto the original piece of paper that contains this information. Each member of the group must find any letters which appear twice and record them on a piece of paper. It is possible to make a word from the letters that appear twice and all members of the group must know the answer before the exercise is complete.

The answer is NETWORK.

External Communication of a Business Organisation

A business needs to communicate with many different types of people, including suppliers, customers, shareholders and possibly the general public. The medium of communication is determined by the type of receiver. The most important media are listed below.

1. **The mass media**: communication with the press, radio and television has become an important aspect of a company's public relations. A company can use the mass media to improve its image, e.g. in 1988 the British Steel Corporation started to advertise how successful it had become – prior to its privatisation – given that it had made spectacular losses in the 1970s and early 1980s. Relations with the press are usually handled in a large firm by the public relations or publicity department.

2. **Annual reports and accounts**: to comply with the legislation laid down in the Companies Acts 1948–1988 all companies must send a directors's report to its shareholders. This report includes: the profit and loss account; the balance sheet; source and applications of funds statement and the report of the auditors. These documents are examined in considerable detail in Chapter 16. They basically contain all the information regarding the financial position of the company throughout the preceding trading year. This is an effective method of communicating with those who have an interest in the company and larger companies (PLCs), as a matter of routine, send such reports to the press e.g. to *The Financial Times, The Guardian, The Times, The Daily Telegraph* and *The Independent*. These newspapers very often publish the material in their business sections.

3. **Trade exhibitions and conferences**: this is a very specialised form of communication, mainly aimed at customers but also useful for keeping in touch with one's competitors. Famous examples include the Motor Show and the Ideal Home Exhibition, both of which attract a large audience and are given a lot of publicity on television and in the newspapers.

4. **Local activities**: there are many opportunities for companies to enhance their public image in the local community. Some of the major companies hold 'open days' for employees and the general public in order to give a greater understanding of the firm, its products, policies and premises. The Sizewell Exhibition has tried very hard to allay people's fears about nuclear power.

   Participation in local community affairs can take many forms – company teams sometimes take part in local leagues and competitions; or a company might sponsor local events and donate prizes, grants and occasional gifts to the community.

5. **Company letters**: most companies write letters to customers, clients and suppliers. Headed paper, giving the company's address, and possibly the company logo, is usually used. A company that answers complaints with a prompt and courteous reply often gains a good reputation. It is important to keep letters brief and to the point not only so that they can be understood but also because writing letters is an expensive activity. It has been suggested that a business letter can cost at least £10 when account is taken of the time taken by the manager to compose and dictate it, by the secretary to type it, and other overheads, of which the stamp is probably the least.

   Usually the first form of contact with a firm is via a letter and so it is important for the company to give a good impression. This will be determined by the way the words are arranged on paper (margins on both sides), by the quality of the typing (it is important to check spelling), the quality of the paper and the design of the letterhead. In fact there is a standard format in writing a business letter in terms of how you address the person you are writing to, how the paragraphs are arranged and how you should close the letter. Often there is a reference number quoted at the top of the page which the receiver must use in reply. This helps the administration of the company to deal with replies more efficiently.

Communication Failure

There are a number of reasons why communication (both internal and external) can be distorted or break down. These can be examined from the point of view of the 4 elements of communication – the sender, the message, the medium and the receiver.

Very often the message can be phrased in such a way that it is impossible for the receiver to understand it. The use of jargon, abbreviations and technical terms often causes confusion. Few people bother to read a notice on a board if the phrasing makes the message unintelligible, and a contract may be left unread if the complex legal terminology makes it incomprehensible. Government departments are notorious for their very cryptic letters, and the BBC programme *That's Life* has drawn attention to unfathomable communications. Having said this, some companies – particularly in advertising campaigns – have built the image of their products on rather cryptic messages.

Not only may the message be difficult to understand but the sender may choose the wrong medium. The choice of medium depends on the type of information, how quickly it needs to be sent and the number of intended recipients. Written messages can take longer than oral messages but spoken messages may not get passed on – somebody may forget. The distance the message has to travel and the number of receivers involved can also create problems. In large organisations there may be very long lines of communication, which slows down the message, or it could be the sheer geographic distance between the sender and receiver that makes communication difficult, e.g. it is more difficult to communicate with people overseas and with travelling sales personnel,

who may spend much of their time out of the office. Modern technology is improving such situations.

The Impact of Modern Technology on Communication

Offices throughout the world now contain very sophisticated equipment. There are cordless phones, telexes, electronic typewriters, micro-computers, word processors and viewdata systems.

Word processing is the use of a computer to prepare and edit text. It has revolutionised the sending of letters and has led to the growth of electronic mail – companies can store names and addresses on disk and can print letters and labels of thousands of clients at the touch of a button. The amount of so-called 'junk mail' that is now delivered is a direct result of the word-processing revolution. Both word processors and computers can be linked between offices and countries via the telephone. This has made unnecessary the printing and posting of letters since the information can be sent electronically from one computer terminal to another. Computer technology has also meant that newspapers can be transmitted electronically from, say, the U.K. to France, and printed so that copies of foreign newspapers are available in other countries on the day of publication.

Pictures and data can also be sent – by a series of digital impulses – through facsimile transmission (FAX), and it is possible to hold business meetings without people having to be in the same location, thanks to closed-circuit and satellite television. Computer transmission of data and facsimile transmission of diagrams and data have reduced the need for business executives to travel back to head office. This has speeded up communication procedure.

Viewdata (teletex) systems, now available to the general public, are very widely used by business. Information systems, such as BBC Ceefax and ITV Oracle, which present constantly updated information on a wide variety of topics, are available on special television sets. Prestel is another national information system that links the television via the telephone with computer-stored information, but it is also an interactive system, e.g. it is possible to book an air flight or order goods from retail outlets. Businesses find the system very useful for their financial information, and travel agencies also use it.

Finally, mobile communication methods should also be mentioned. These include carphones and paging systems. In addition, many firms use public address systems to make announcements, call a member of staff to the telephone and even to play music.

One of the likely consequences of the communications revolution is an increase in the volume of information being transmitted. It is even more likely to speed up information flows: management will have up-to-date statistics at their fingertips and will therefore be able to react more quickly to any situation. The advent of the carphone means that sales personnel out on the road no longer have to stop and make calls back to the office. With the growing emphasis on the written word there is likely to be a reduction in personal contact. This may be unattractive for those who value direct contact with people in their working lives.

QUICK QUESTIONS 4

1. *From the 5 possibilities listed below, select the form of communication that you would choose in situations (i–v).*

   A. *Telephone*
   B. *Trade magazine*
   C. *Notes in pay packets*
   D. *House magazine*
   E. *Tannoy*

   (i) *A firm announcing redundancies to its employees.*
   (ii) *The discussion of a business problem with a colleague at a branch in another town.*
   (iii) *A firm announcing an urgent message to all its employees.*
   (iv) *A firm announcing the new product range it has launched.*
   (v) *A firm reporting its activities of the last 3 months to employees.*

2. *What are the essential differences between telex and telephone as a method of communication?*
3. *What is a FAX machine?*
4. *What are the causes of communication failure? Give examples of communication failure from your own experience. Why do you think this happened?*

STUDENT TASK

Think about the ways in which your school communicates with you as pupils and also with your parents. Why do you think they choose the methods they do, and what are the advantages/disadvantages of each method? Could you suggest any other method of improved communication?

PROJECT AND ASSIGNMENT SUGGESTIONS

1. Arrange a visit to a local business in order to study the methods of communication it employs. Your research should distinguish between internal communication among the employees of the business and external communication between the business and outside groups. Make a list of all the communication channels within the business, e.g. telephones, letters, memos, noticeboards and so on, and write a short account on the function of each of these methods of communication. You could summarise your findings in the form of a table of results.

2. As mentioned above, new technology has revolutionised both the speed and efficiency of business communication in recent years. This has extended to other organisations, and some schools now make use of computer-based systems, including 'electronic noticeboards' which can be continually updated from a central location. Undertake an investigation as to how this type of technology could benefit your school or college. Start by considering how such a system could be designed and installed. Then make a list of the advantages of such a system and discuss how it may open up possibilities for the communication of information that do not exist at present. In addition you will have to investigate the cost of the system and how the money could be raised. Your report should take the form of a feasibility study which concludes with your recommendation regarding whether the system should be introduced.

SECTION B

Working in Business

CHAPTER 5

Motivation and Fulfilment at Work

Organisations employ 3 main factors of production: land, labour and capital. Most people suggest that labour – the human input – is the most important asset to any firm.

Individuals perform various tasks or do different jobs within a company but all work has three elements:

1. **Mechanical**: this describes what tasks an employee performs during the course of a working day/week. It could be called the person's 'job description', and it outlines the function or duties an employee must fulfil in carrying out his or her job.
2. **Psychological**: this is the employee's reaction to work and the effect it has upon him or her as an individual. Some workers find their work challenging, exciting and stimulating, and this has a beneficial impact upon their performance. If employees find work boring and uninteresting, this is likely to have a negative impact on their performance.
3. **Economic**: this is the rewards that people get from working. This is generally expressed in terms of money, e.g. the wage or salary that a person earns for working, but economic rewards could also include company cars, free coal, cheap loans and subsidised living accommodation.

If a person was asked to draw up a list of the most important reasons for working, money would undoubtedly occur somewhere in the list. But how important is money as a motivating factor? Does it automatically follow that if an employee is paid more money to do a job, he or she will work harder and be better motivated? Some people believe it does while others disagree. One argument is that 'money isn't everything' and employees get far more out of work than a simple economic reward. Other factors which employees take into consideration include: achievement, promotion, interesting work, personal relationships; recognition, responsibility, job security and working conditions.

These factors suggest that people have different **needs** which they have to satisfy. These needs vary according to the personal characteristics of the individual, such as abilities, skills, training, emotions and attitudes. Companies have to be aware of their employees' needs if they want to try and increase the commitment of people to their work. The psychologist A. Maslow developed a simple classification of people's needs to explain motivation which he illustrated in a pyramid form, as shown in Figure 5.1. It is referred to as the **hierarchy of needs**.

Maslow's Hierarchy of Needs

Maslow's theory is that the needs of employees are very complex and that they occur at five different levels. The levels are in ascending or hierarchical order because, according to Maslow, the second level of needs (safety) cannot be satisfied until the first level (basic) is satisfied. Similarly, the third level (social) cannot be satisfied until the second one is, and so on. This idea is illustrated in Figure 5.1 by the steps or ladders from the bottom of the pyramid to the top.

1. Physiological Needs

These are at the very bottom of the pyramid and are sometimes called the basic or 'animal' needs. These are the needs that we share with animals for food, drink, warmth, shelter and survival.

Figure 5.1 Maslow's Hierarchy of Needs

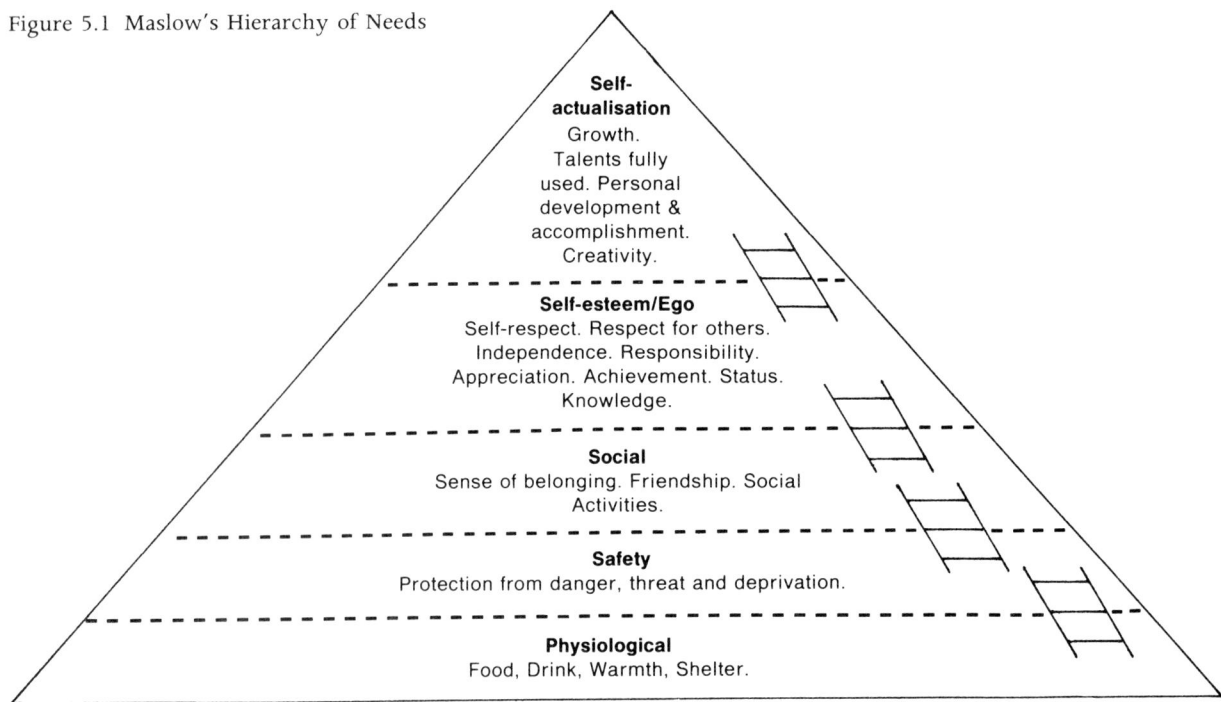

2. Safety Needs

These go beyond the need to survive and include comfort, security and protection from danger.

3. Social Needs

Most animals tend to congregate or herd. Man, likewise, is a social animal. The development of close personal relationships and group relationships is important. Family, friends and social activities provide us with our social needs.

4. Self Esteem/Ego Needs

There are 2 types of ego needs:

(a) **Personal**: this is the need to like oneself — sometimes called self-respect. Most people hold ambitions and have expectations about themselves that they try to live up to.

(b) **Inter-personal**: this is the need to have the respect of others.

5. Self-Actualisation

This is at the very top of the pyramid. It is sometimes called self-fulfilment or self-realisation, and it could be expressed in terms of achieving all that one is capable of achieving. This is particularly relevant in jobs where there is an opportunity to create, e.g. art, craft and music. However, the need to use our talents fully occurs in almost everything we do.

Maslow grouped these needs as a hierarchy because the aim is to move upwards to the top of the pyramid. People who reach the top achieve self-actualisation. It is not possible to move to a higher level unless the needs of the lower level have been satisfied. For example, a hungry person will have very little concern for safety.

QUICK QUESTIONS 1

1. *What are the 5 needs of employees according to Maslow? Give 3 examples of each.*
2. *Apart from money, what other benefits do people get from work?*

3. *All jobs have 3 elements – mechanical, psychological and economic. Draw up a table like the one below and conduct a small survey of your family and friends about the elements of their work.*

Job Title	Mechanical	Psychological	Economic

What conclusions do you draw from this survey?

Does Work Satisfy Needs?

The money that people earn from working may be used to satisfy the physiological and safety needs but it may not satisfy the higher needs. Money alone cannot bring this satisfaction. It is important to examine how companies can attempt to satisfy these higher needs. If they don't attempt to do this, the workforce may become dissatisfied and demotivated. It is the job of a manager to try and make sure that his subordinates feel fulfilled at work. In situations where this is difficult to achieve, as in dull, repetitive work, higher pay is very important and workers may be forced to find satisfaction outside their work. The part played by work in satisfying/frustrating human needs is considered below.

Physiological Needs

These are satisfied by turning the money that is earned at work into food, drink and housing. However, if workers are low-paid, the government tries to ensure that they are entitled to state benefits to supplement their incomes. In 1971 the government introduced Family Income Supplement to help offset poverty caused by low pay. This was abolished in 1988 and replaced by the Family Credit Scheme.

For those people out of work the state provides Unemployment and Supplementary Benefit; for those who are sick, Sickness Benefit; for those whose job no longer exists, redundancy payments; for those who retire, retirement pensions; and those who are placed on short-time work, guarantee payments. The state also offers rent and rate rebates and free school meals to families with little or no income.

Safety Needs

The satisfaction of safety needs – the protection from threat and danger and the need for security – is a complicated issue. It is possible for these needs to be overlooked in the work enriv,ment and so various governments have passed a whole series of Factories Acts and Offices and Shops Acts in order to promote safety. Some workplaces, e.g. those where there are poisonous gases, electrical machinery, toxic chemicals and cutting machines such as lathes and saws, are particularly dangerous. In the 1980s there was a number of headline cases where consumers and workers died because of dangers in the workplace, e.g. Piper Alpha, King's Cross and the *Herald of Free Enterprise*. In the construction industry 110 workers were killed in 1987–8. The Health and Safety at Work Act 1974 requires that all workplaces are to be safe and healthy places to work, e.g. goggles to be worn when welding, guards to be fitted on moving parts of machines, ear muffs to be worn when driving tractors, hard hats to be worn on building sites, and clean and sterilised clothing to be worn in food-processing industries.

Figure 5.2 Safety Precautions in the Workplace

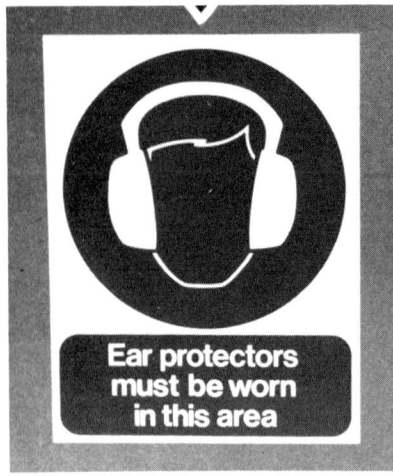  

Firms have a duty to educate their workforce in the promotion of health and safety. This includes involving members of the workforce in a Health and Safety Committee so that they may contribute their own suggestions and assist in the enforcement of precautions. Typically, these committees would meet once a month in most large firms. The government's Health and Safety Executive, which in 1988 had 562 inspectors, is responsible for giving advice and inspecting workplaces to make sure companies obey the law. It has the power to prosecute and can close factories if necessary.

Social Needs

The need for social relations – friendship – is important for people at work. Such relations offer a sense of belonging or group identity, perhaps making an otherwise boring job bearable.

The type of work a person does sometimes helps the growth of friendship, particularly if the whole process requires teamwork. In other circumstances, e.g. assembly-line work or individual machine operation in a noisy factory, the work may get in the way of relationship development. A noisy factory floor is not ideal for holding conversations. Some workers may even be wearing ear muffs! Jobs that are performed alone tend also to discourage social relationships. However, long-distance lorry drivers with their CB radios prove that social relations can still exist in such circumstances.

In recent years firms have begun to realise the importance of social needs and have taken a number of steps to assist their satisfaction. These have included measures to promote relationships away from the job, such as rest rooms, subsidised canteen facilities, social and recreational facilities at work, e.g. dartboards, pool tables, table-tennis tables, and also clubs and activities that are partly financed by the company. A lot of firms encourage employees to organise clubs and societies and many of these compete in local sports leagues. Other sports facilities may include bowls, tennis, swimming and fishing. Many employees now regard such facilities as commonplace.

In addition to these 'formal' activities which promote social needs within the firm, there are **informal** relationships. These are important both to employees and to management.

Informal groups: an informal group is one that arises naturally in the work situation because members share one or more common interests. It is a quite natural thing for workers to be drawn together by type of work, seniority, age and interests. Such groups may be seen together in the works' canteen and also down the pub after work.

The importance of informal groups was discovered by Elton Mayo at the Hawthorne factory of the Western Electric Company near Chicago between 1927 and 1932. He found that enthusiasm for work was far greater where there was group friendship. Such groups were of great benefit to the firm because of the higher morale of employees. Individuals had a sense of belonging and the group helped to reduce absenteeism and lateness. The new or inexperienced worker could be helped through the advice of the informal group – by being taken 'under someone's wing' and 'shown the ropes'. Additionally, the informal group could provide an extra channel of communication between management and employees and so improve any weakness in its lines of communication.

However, Mayo also discovered drawbacks for the company as a result of informal groups. He found that groups of workers set their own output norms, standards of behaviour and the pace at which a job was done. The self-appointed leaders of the group could be different from the ones chosen by management, sometimes resulting in a conflict of interest and split loyalties. For example, should an employee follow the instructions of the foreman or the 'leader' of the group?

Informal groups are very important to the successful operation of the firm since they help to satisfy workers' social needs. However, the informal group's own objectives may run against those of the firm.

QUICK QUESTIONS 2

1. *How do companies attempt to satisfy a worker's social needs? Do you think these methods are successful?*
2. *How does the government try to promote Health and Safety at work?*
3. *What are informal groups? Suggest why they are important to the workings of a firm.*

Ego Needs

Nowadays many employees are asked to perform tasks which are becoming more mechanical, offering less scope for creativity, initiative and individuality. To examine ego needs in more detail it is helpful to examine the problems faced by one group of employees – **assembly-line workers** – and the initiatives that have been taken to try and improve their working lives.

Mass production to increase output was introduced in the United States during the first world war. Each job was broken down into a simple operation, with each worker performing repetitive tasks. By doing the same job over and over again the workers became very quick at their work, enabling more goods to be produced. There was little skill involved,

the process was boring and employees had no real idea as to how their job fitted into the making of the completed product.

The greater use of machinery and the introduction of production-line methods led employees to feel they had very little control over their work. They gained less satisfaction from it as a result. The employees in this situation are said to be **alienated**.

Various factors can lead to this feeling of alienation. The most important are: work is controlled by the pace of the machine or the 'pace of the line'; the 'job cycle' is short, so the task performed by the worker is very quick indeed; the job is repetitive; little or no training is required; and the worker only performs a small part of the whole process.

In situations like these employees may find it difficult to satisfy their ego needs. These centre around the job that a person is doing. To derive satisfaction a worker must be given greater control over the task being performed and be made to feel that the work being done is important.

In an effort to satisfy ego needs some companies have attempted to arrange jobs so that they are more satisfying. Four examples are offered below.

(i) **Job rotation**: this is where each person in the team moves from one job to another. Doing other people's jobs as well as one's own is less monotonous and less repetitive than performing your own over and over again.

(ii) **Longer job cycles**: another solution is to arrange work so that each employee has a number of different things to do. A vacuum cleaner was originally made on a production line with short job cycles. An alternative would be to allow the worker to sit at a bench with the trays of the various parts revolving around the bench. This allows the employee to build up a complete vacuum cleaner step by step. The repetition is part of a longer job cycle and the worker builds the complete product.

(iii) **Robots**: replacing assembly-line workers with robots.

(iv) **Job enlargement**: this allows workers to rotate on jobs and also build a complete end product in small teams. The Swedish motor car manufacturer Volvo has introduced a scheme of this type with impressive results.

Volvo is attempting to return the manufacture of cars

back to the made-by-hand-in-teams approach that existed before Henry Ford's assembly-line method began in 1914. Roger Holtback, the President of Volvo's car division, has said:

> Before 1914 auto workers were all-round, skilful mechanics who worked in small groups of six or seven and together they built an entire car in one and the same place. Most of them were well-trained and experienced craftsmen, who felt professional pride and dignity and identified deeply with their work.

At Volvo's Uddevalla plant, workers are grouped in teams of 8–10. They are independent groups responsible for the complete assembly of the car, for the volume of output as well as quality control. The team members, 40% of whom are women, assemble the car in a stationary position, not on a moving line. The number of cars assembled each day is decided by the team at the start of the working week. Each worker, after a 16-month training programme, is expected to be able to perform about 25% of the tasks required for car assembly. The plant itself is characterised by low decibel noise levels, sophisticated ventilation, lack of dirt and smells, the use of natural light, and stress-free colour designs on the walls. In fact it is completely unlike a traditional car assembly plant.

By organising workers into teams the company is attempting to make a limited job into a more creative one through the stimulus of team spirit and delegation of power. (This information is based on an article by R. Taylor in *The Financial Times*, 9 June 1989.)

Ego needs not only embrace individuality and achievement but also include respect for others. This requires that other people realise the importance of a worker's job. In some cases this is quite easy, e.g. the craftsman, surgeon or nurse, or those jobs that involve responsibility, e.g. Managing Director or Headmaster. For other tasks, e.g. the job of an office cleaner or possibly the assembly-line worker described above, it is quite difficult to offer status and respect.

Self-Actualisation (Self-Fulfilment)

If a worker is going to achieve all that he or she is capable of, then the management must know a

Figure 5.3 Contrasting Production Methods

worker's true capabilities. Very few employees reach self-actualisation because a worker's true talents may go unnoticed.

Promotion offers great scope for the satisfaction of this kind of need but the structure of many firms may often hinder promotion. This is sometimes referred to as 'dead man's shoes', or 'Buggins turn' in British Rail, where promotion depends on seniority and age rather than capability. Some companies do recognise the need for self-actualisation and have specially designed 'career paths' for their employees. The banks, for example, have 'accelerated training programmes' for their graduates. This allows them to climb both the company hierarchy and the Maslow hierarchy as quickly as their ability allows them to.

QUICK QUESTIONS 3

1. *What is mass production and how has it led to the frustration of a worker's ego needs?*
2. *What is 'alienation'? What factors have led workers to feel alienated from their work?*
3. *Give examples of how companies can try to satisfy the ego needs of their employees.*
4. *Outline the major features of Volvo's attempts to satisfy their workers' ego needs. Could their approach work in any type of job? If not, give reasons.*
5. *What is self-actualisation and how can companies let their workers achieve it?*

Herzberg's model of Job Satisfaction and Dissatisfaction

In addition to Maslow, other researchers have examined factors that lead to job satisfaction/dissatisfaction and fulfilment at work. For example, Frederick Herzberg asked many people in different jobs at different levels the following 2 questions:

1. What factors lead you to experience extreme dissatisfaction with your job?
2. What factors lead you to experience extreme satisfaction with your job?

The results are displayed in Figure 5.4 (a form of horizontal bar chart), showing the order and the number of times in which 'factors' were mentioned.

Herzberg argued that the factors on the right-hand side of Figure 5.4. can make people very dissatisfied but do not motivate them to work harder. He called them 'maintenance' factors because they either maintain or prevent job satisfaction. The factors on the left-hand side of Figure 5.4 Herzberg referred to as 'motivators'. They have very little to do with money or status but are concerned with achievement and responsibility. He suggested that they play a very important role in increasing people's commitment to their work and their company. Table 5.1 offers a short summary of these 2 sets of factors.

Table 5.1. *Herzberg's Model of Job Satisfaction/ Dissatisfaction*

Motivators	Maintenance Factors
1. **Achievement**: a feeling of personal accomplishment; meeting success in solving a problem; seeing good results from one's work or completing a challenging job.	1. **Salary**: anything involving compensation and fringe benefits.
2. **Recognition**: being recognised for doing one's work well; receiving praise from supervisors, fellow workers and the public.	2. **Working conditions**: tools; lighting; heating; parking facilities.
3. **The work itself**: performing creative or challenging work; liking the work one does.	3. **Security**: feeling certainty about the future.
4. **Responsibility**: having some control over one's work; being permitted to work without close supervision.	4. **Company policy and administration**: confidence in the competence of top management and their policies.
5. **Growth**: the opportunity to learn new skills; personal development.	5. **Behaviour of supervisors**: the competence of supervisors; ability to give guidance and offer fairness.
6. **Advancement**: opportunity for promotion.	6. **Inter-personal relationships**: social interaction with fellow workers and managers.

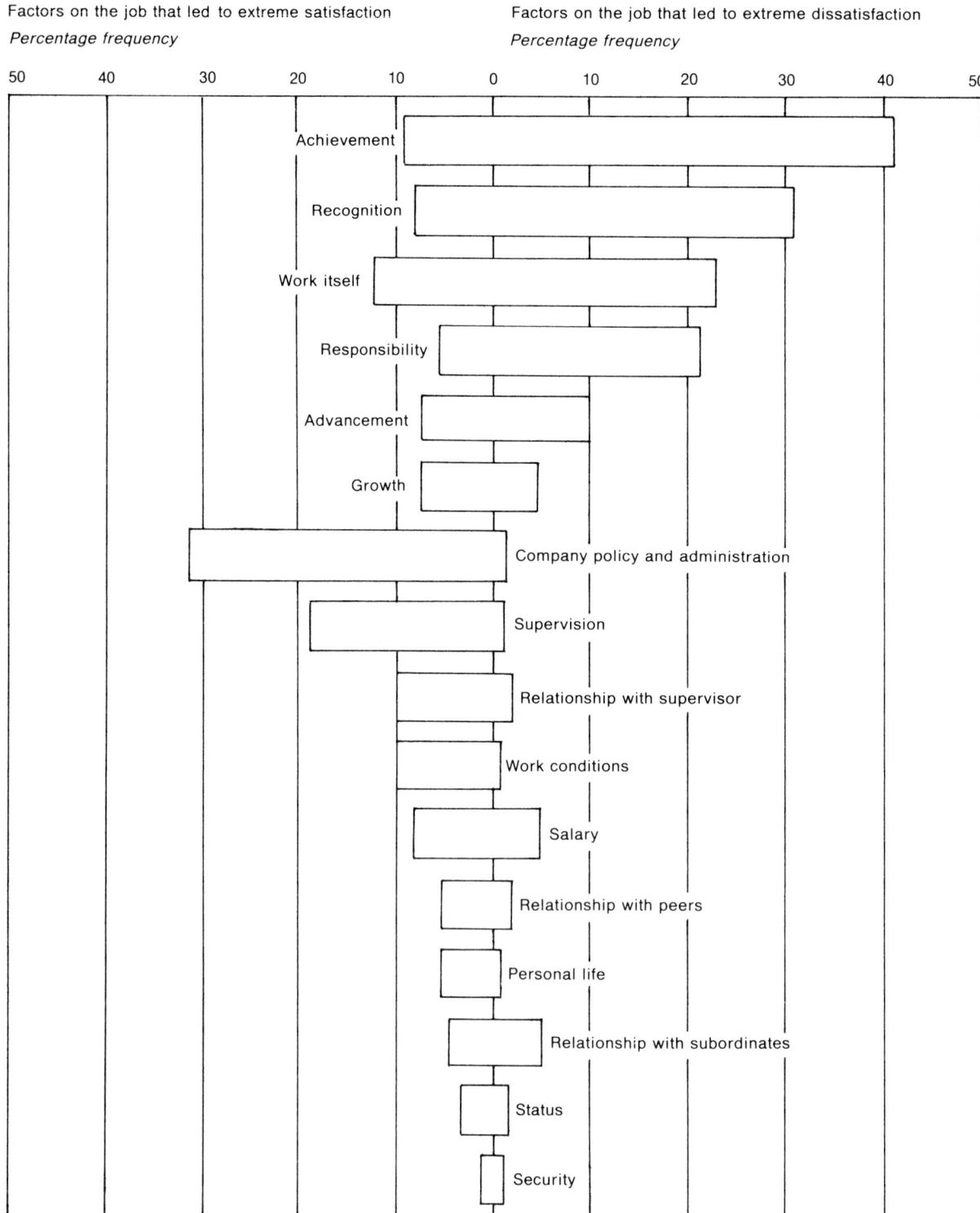

Figure 5.4 Bar Chart Showing factors leading to job satisfaction/dissatisfaction

Figure 5.5 Job satisfaction

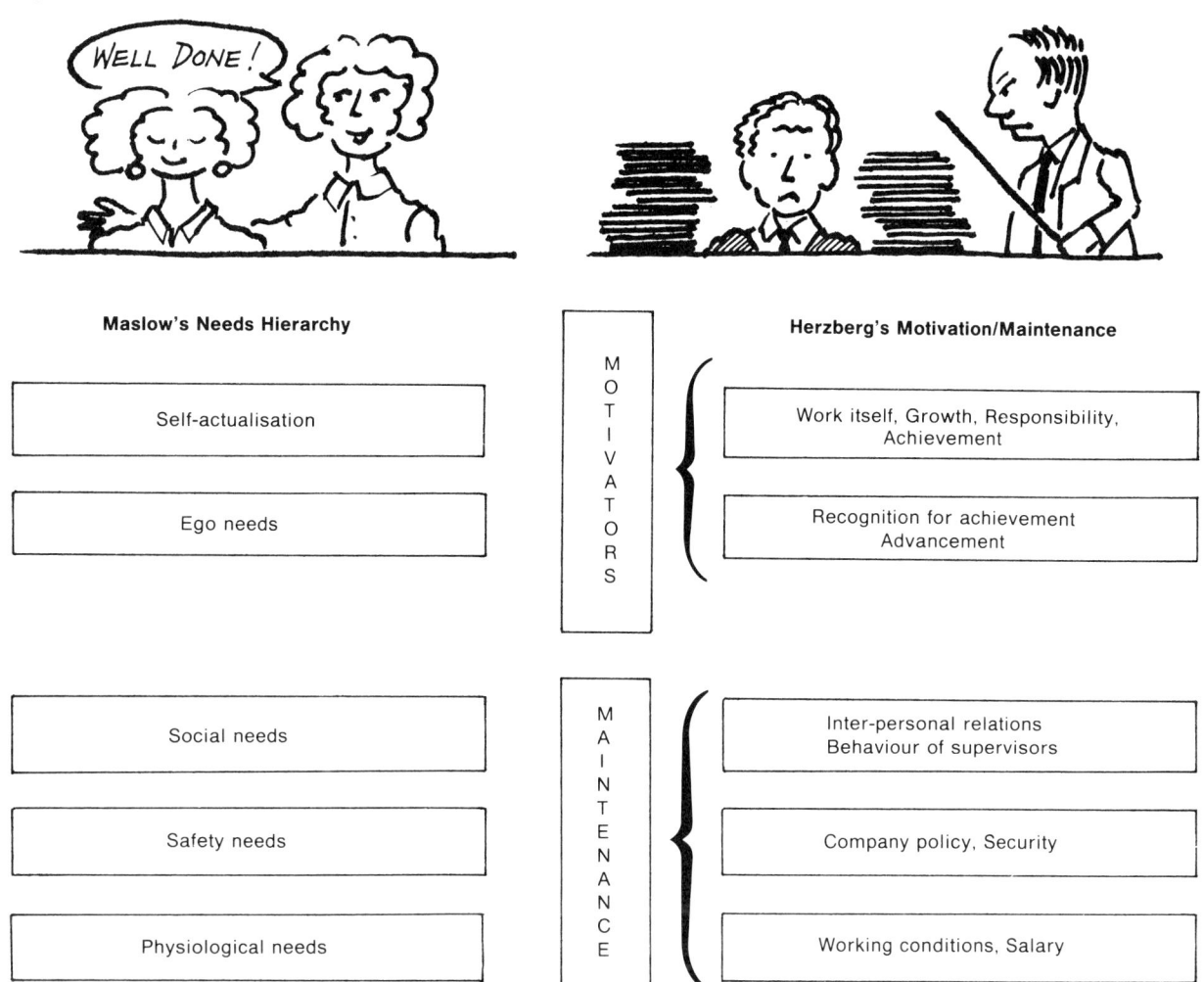

Figure 5.6 A Comparison of Maslow and Herzberg

The Herzberg 'motivators' match – very approximately – the top 2 levels of Maslow's hierarchy and are concerned with job content. The 'maintenance' factors match – very approximately – the bottom 3 levels of Maslow's hierarchy. Figure 5.6 shows how the 2 theories can be related.

QUICK QUESTIONS 4

1. *What do you understand by 'motivators' and 'maintenance' factors in the Herzberg model? Give examples to illustrate your answer.*
2. *Evaluate the Maslow and Herzberg models. How do they compare with one another?*

Recent Work on Motivation

Two examples of recent research evidence on human needs at work and motivation are examined below.

An opinion survey of 1,063 adult private sector workers carried out for the Industrial Society in June 1988 reported the following:

1. 50% of unskilled workers said they could do more work in their current job (increase productivity) without too much effort.
2. Just under one third found they had no opportunity to express ideas and said that no-one listens to them when they do.

3. Workers rated having an interesting and enjoyable job, security and a feeling of doing something worthwhile higher than basic pay as a motivator.
4. Compared with other managers, supervisors of manual workers felt relatively little involvement in the company, and felt they had little control over changes.
5. Only 25% of manual supervisors were very happy with their job.

The report recommended that managers should consider a series of strategies for improving employee involvement and raising morale. These included share-ownership schemes, profit-related pay, team briefings and better training. An attitude survey amongst British Rail staff confirms this lack of involvement – only 30% of workers received any feedback on their performance (recognition) in the form of praise or blame.

The second piece of more detailed research concerns the teaching profession. Mr Geoffrey Williams, a member of Bede Comprehensive School in Sunderland, completed a survey of 82 teaching staff. This took the form of a written questionnaire on causes of job satisfaction and dissatisfaction, and was followed up with more detailed interviews with a cross-section of staff.

In the questionnaire teachers were asked to rank, in order of importance (1,2,3 etc.), various factors associated with job satisfaction and dissatisfaction. These rankings were used to arrive at a league table of motivators and demotivators. This is shown in Table 5.2.

Table 5.2 *A League Table of Motivators and Demotivators amongst Bede Staff*

Motivators	Demotivators
1. Recognition at work	1. Poor working conditions
2. Challenge at work	2. Limited promotion prospects
3. Control over work	3. Low pay
4. Interesting job	4. Management structure
5. Working with compatible people	5. Poor communication

Williams found the following general results:

(a) Over 50% had considered leaving teaching.
(b) 16 of the 82 (19.5%) said they would encourage their children to enter teaching.
(c) 34 of the 82 (42.5%) had held jobs outside of teaching, only 2 of these said job security was the main reason for entering teaching.
(d) The attraction to teaching for 18 women teachers was the convenience of hours and holidays for those with children.
(e) Just over 50% said they would teach again. This is lower than a previous study by Blauner in 1960, which found that 91% of mathematicians, 83% of lawyers and 82% of journalists would choose the same job again. This may not augur well for future teacher recruitment.

Williams discovered a number of differences in the replies of various age- and sex-groups. Looking at the male–female replies for the motivators he found:

- Both men and women ranked recognition first.
- Females ranked challenge at work second while control over work was placed second for men.
- An interesting job came third for women.
- Promotion was fourth in the female list but did not get in the male top 5. This could be related to the greater difficulty experienced by women in gaining promotion.
- Job security was fifth for males but was placed lower by females. This may be related to the traditional role of males acting as the 'breadwinner'.

Between the age-groups for motivators he found:

- For the 55 + age-group, challenge at work was not among the top 5 motivators. This could be explained by the fact that members of this group were nearing the end of their career and therefore seeking motivation through interesting work.
- The 35–44 age-group ranked job security highly. This could be due to this age-group having teenage children, which is a notoriously expensive claim on the family budget.

Amongst the demotivators Williams found 2 significant differences between age-groups:

- Low pay was ranked fifth by teachers in the

25–34 age-group (it was third in the whole sample). This may be because the members of the younger group have the rest of their working lives ahead of them to climb the pay scale.

- Dissatisfaction with the formal management structure was the greatest demotivator for the 45–54 age-group. These people may hold more senior posts in the school and have a greater wish to carry out their own plans – which could conflict with the existing management structure.

It is not just low pay that demotivates teachers. Poor promotion prospects, ineffective communication, lack of recognition, discontent with management policy and poorly maintained buildings are causing concern. The nature of the job allows most teachers considerable flexibility in their daily work. However, the new GCSE, A/S levels and the National Curriculum may increase bureaucracy and reduce individual control. This poor motivation has been reflected in a very high absenteeism, applications for early retirement and a shortage in particular subjects.

Source: adapted from the *Teachers' Weekly*, April 1989.

STUDENT EXERCISE

Angela Crawford has recently been appointed General Manager of the shoe-making company Lost Soles Ltd. She was determined to improve the performance of the company. Management consultants were brought in and suggested the following changes:

- Better payments for employees.
- Improvement in canteen facilities.
- Stricter supervision of workers.

These changes took place but performance did not improve. She discussed the problem with her Personnel Manager, Peter Ward, who felt that Angela was on the wrong track. He said:

More and more companies are discovering that higher wages are not persuading people to work more effectively. The motivation appears to come from satisfaction from the job itself.

An experimental reorganisation of the factory took place. It involved the following changes:

- Dividing the workforce into teams headed by a team leader who was responsible for the work of the group.
- Each team was responsible for its own work: ordering stock, inspection of its own work, and job rotation.
- Consultation on the design and method of assembly of the shoes.
- Regular meetings between the team leader and the team to discuss targets and performance.

The workforce accepted these changes and performance improved.

1. Outline the main changes that were made and say how each contributed to job satisfaction.
2. Why do you think these changes improved performance?
3. Can these sort of changes be made with all jobs?
4. Why did the stricter supervision of workers not improve performance?

PROJECT AND ASSIGNMENT SUGGESTIONS

1. You wish to discover those factors which motivate workers and those which lead to dissatisfaction with their jobs.
   (a) With the aid of the information given in Chapter 5, design a questionnaire which will help you to find out the information you need. This will have to be done carefully as people are generally unwilling to give information they feel is personal and confidential.
   (b) Select 3 or 4 employees known to you who do different types of jobs and ask them to complete your questionnaire.
   (c) Write up the results of your survey by comparing the factors which seem most important to each type of worker.
   (d) Include a table summarising your results and see if there is a pattern in the answers to the questionnaire.
   (e) How do your findings compare with the research of Maslow and Herzberg?

2. Investigate the various informal groups which exist in your school or college. How do these informal groups relate to the formal organisation of the institution? Write an account showing how the existence of these informal groups helps the efficient management of the institution. In what ways do informal groups make the management of the school or college more difficult?

3. With the help of a medium-sized or large manufacturing business in your area, find out how firms try to motivate their workers. Your investigation should pay attention to the following factors:

   (a) The organisation of the work itself: Does the business try to reduce the boredom involved in repetitive jobs? Has it introduced any forms of job enlargement schemes?

   (b) The facilities available to workers: Does the business provide any form of social or sporting facilities?

   (c) Career development: What policy has the business adopted with respect to the advancement and promotion of workers?

   (d) Worker participation: In what ways, if any, does the business try to involve the workforce in management decisions? Are there any management/worker committees? Is there a profit-sharing scheme?

Write up your findings in the form of a report. Suggest ways in which you think the business could improve the motivation of its workers.

CHAPTER 6

The Personnel Function: Selection and Recruitment

Personnel management is concerned with selecting the people who are to work in an organisation and developing them into an effective, trained workforce so that they can make their best contribution to its success, both as individuals and as members of a team.

In a small company there may only be one person responsible for all the various aspects of personnel work, but most large firms employ a number of specialists who form a structured Personnel Department. The organisation chart of a typical Personnel Department is shown in Figure 6.1.

Selection and recruitment are examined in this chapter, training and development in Chapter 7, wages and salaries in Chapter 8 and industrial relations in Chapter 9. Aspects of employee welfare, health and safety are dealt with in Chapter 21.

Types of Labour Market

A company, whether large or small, is made up of a group of people with different skills and talents who work together to achieve the aims of the firm. The range of skills that a large organisation may employ is very wide. A simple classification is given in Figure 6.2.

Figure 6.1 The Work of a Typical Personnel Department

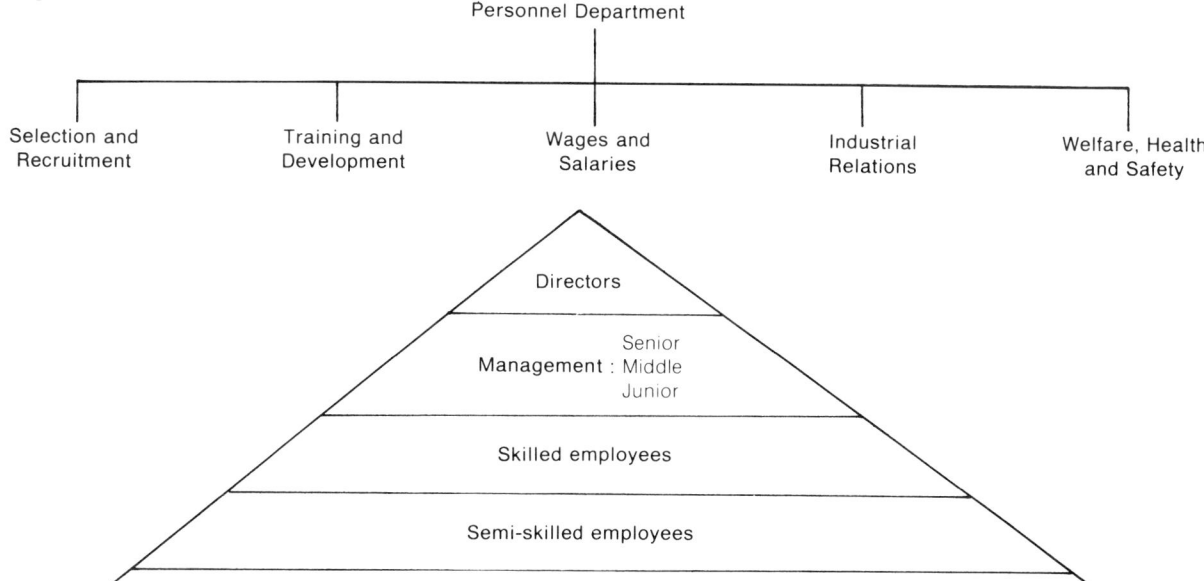

Figure 6.2 Different Types of Labour Used in the Firm

The differences between these 5 categories of labour is emphasised in a number of ways. First, there are different methods/channels of recruitment for each of these employees. Secondly, each type of labour performs different tasks within the business and possesses different abilities. Thirdly, each type of labour will receive different forms of training. Finally, each type of employee will receive a different wage payment from the company unless the business is organised as a worker co-operative (see Chapter 2). In fact, the way in which their pay is calculated may differ too.

Selection and Recruitment

The recruitment and selection of employees lies at the heart of the personnel function. It is the job of the Personnel Department to ensure that the company has the right people for the correct job at the right time.

It is important to realise that the UK labour market is constantly changing. Organisations need a continuous flow of new employees to replace those lost through death, retirement, resignation, promotion or dismissal. In addition to people moving jobs within the same company, it is estimated that there are some 10 million job changes in the UK each year. Further, over half a million school-leavers enter the labour market annually, and women may leave employment temporarily to have children.

All these changes create job vacancies – this is ignoring the demand for new types of workers – which must be filled if the firm is to function effectively. If a vacancy is not filled quickly it may be costly for the firm. Delay could lose the firm valuable production and sales and it may place a greater strain on people who are expected to cover the vacant job – a process that could lead to demotivation.

As soon as a vacancy has been notified to the Personnel Department, it must undertake a **job analysis** in order to draw up two documents, the **job description** and the **job specification**.

Job Analysis

This is the process by which the Personnel Department identifies and records all features and facts relating to a job. The purpose of a job analysis is

to produce both a job description and a job specification. A firm can use a number of methods to analyse a job and what it involves. The most popular include:

1. **Observation**: the task the employee does is observed and recorded as it is performed by the average employee. This method tends to apply to manual jobs. One disadvantage is that it does not show how much thought goes into doing a particular job, e.g. observing a teacher in the classroom demonstrates what he or she does but does not show the thought or preparation that is involved in a particular lesson.
2. **Interview**: an existing job holder is interviewed and questions are asked about what the job involves.
3. **Diary**: this is where the employee keeps a written record of the tasks undertaken over a given period.
4. **Questionnaire**: the business asks workers to complete a set of questions concerning the nature of their job.

Job Description

The information obtained from the job analysis is then used to write up a job description. Very simply this outlines or describes the content of a job. Items contained in a typical job description would include the following:

1. **Basic details**: the title and grade of the job in the departments concerned.
2. **Job summary**: the purpose of the job, identifying main tasks and the standards to be maintained. Information on the social and work environment may also be provided.
3. **Responsibilities**: this identifies the position of the job in the organisation structure. It gives details of subordinates and immediate superiors.
4. **Conditions of employment**: salary, hours of work, pension scheme, welfare and social facilities.
5. **Training**: the training that will be offered.
6. **Promotion**: opportunities for promotion and the career structure within the firm.

Two examples of job descriptions are given in Table 6.1 and Figure 6.3. As can be seen, they are very detailed.

Table 6.1. *Job Description for Personal Assistant to Personnel Manager*

Title	Personal Assistant to the Personnel Manager.
Department	Personnel
Function	To assist the Personnel Manager in the discharge of her duties by providing administrative support; to maintain effective communication with the Personnel Manager and all members of staff and people in contact with her office; to supervise the work of 3 junior/clerical staff.
Hours of work	8.50 a.m. – 5.20 p.m., Mondays to Fridays (1 hour lunch). 37.5 hours weekly plus overtime as necessary.
Accountable to	Personnel Manager.
Responsible for	3 members of staff as indicated above.
Duties/Responsibilities	Work within company rules, regulations and procedures. Assist the Personnel Manager in all aspects of her work, using appropriate administrative skills. Maintain the efficient operation of Personnel Manager's office and its systems. Act on behalf of the Personnel Manager in her absence as required. Supervise the work of 3 junior staff so as to maintain efficient standards of work and productive staff relations. Co-ordinate and attend meetings and conferences and take minutes/notes as required. Receive visitors and company personnel and maintain a favourable company image.

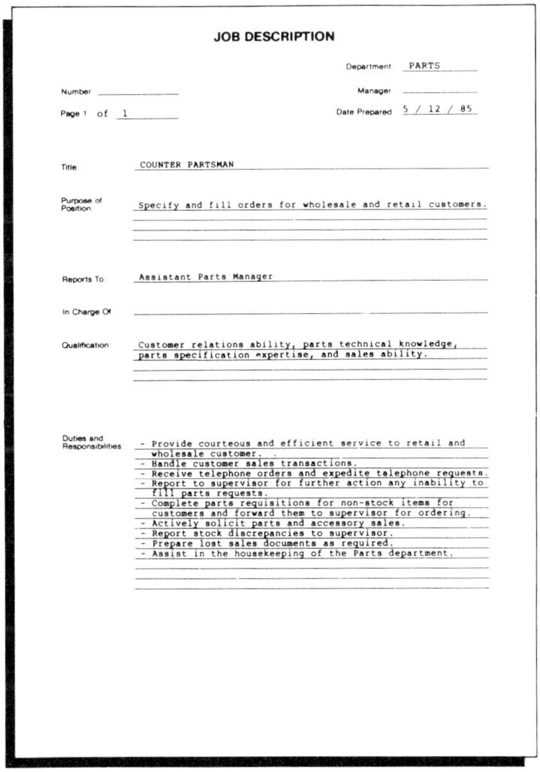
JOB DESCRIPTION

Department PARTS
Number
Manager
Page 1 of 1
Date Prepared 5 / 12 / 85

Title: COUNTER PARTSMAN

Purpose of Position: Specify and fill orders for wholesale and retail customers.

Reports To: Assistant Parts Manager

In Charge Of:

Qualification: Customer relations ability, parts technical knowledge, parts specification expertise, and sales ability.

Duties and Responsibilities:
- Provide courteous and efficient service to retail and wholesale customer.
- Handle customer sales transactions.
- Receive telephone orders and expedite telephone requests.
- Report to supervisor for further action any inability to fill parts requests.
- Complete parts requisitions for non-stock items for customers and forward them to supervisor for ordering.
- Actively solicit parts and accessory sales.
- Report stock discrepancies to supervisor.
- Prepare lost sales documents as required.
- Assist in the housekeeping of the Parts department.

Figure 6.3 Job Description for a Counter Partsman

Once a job description has been drawn up, the company can use the information for a variety of purposes. It could be used for wage and salary administration, measuring each job's level of difficulty and responsibility. This helps the firm decide on the pay to be given for doing a certain job (this is called 'job evaluation'). Job descriptions also give the company information on the skills, abilities and knowledge required of a person and so it allows the firm to design training programmes for employees. Finally, the job description could be used as the basis for a recruitment advertisement. The job description forms the basis of the job specification, which in turn identifies the likely qualities and qualifications a person should possess in order to do the job.

QUICK QUESTIONS 1

1. *Name 3 functions of the Personnel Department.*
2. *It is estimated that there are 10 million job changes in Britain each year. Give 3 reasons why job vacancies may occur.*
3. *In order to fill a job vacancy it is first necessary to find all the relevant details regarding the job. What is this process called? State one way in which this information can be found out.*
4. *List 4 important items which should be included in a job description.*

Job Specification

Job specifications differ considerably. This reflects the different requirements of various jobs, e.g. in some types of work physical strength may be important while in others numeracy or the ability to speak a foreign language may be emphasised. Job specifications can also distinguish between what are considered to be **essential** or **desirable** qualities.

Characteristics which are commonly specified include:

1. **Physical characteristics**: age, health and appearance.
2. **Attainments**: academic education, professional qualifications and training.
3. **Experience/Knowledge**: background of the person, positions held and knowledge gained.
4. **Aptitudes**: mechanical, verbal, ability to work alone, self-motivation and ability to work under pressure.
5. **Domestic circumstance**: ability to move for the job and to spend time away from home.

Figure 6.4 provides a summary of the suggested qualities to look for in job applicants.

To help the firm decide who to appoint to a vacancy the firm must know what the job involves and what skills and characteristics the applicants should possess. This is the purpose of the job specification. It gives details of the job itself, the necessary skills, qualifications and experience. An example of a job specification for a Regional Sales Manager is given in Table 6.2.

SUGGESTED QUALITIES TO LOOK FOR IN STAFF

Aptitude

Keen & Eager

Appearance

Ability To Communicate

Numeric

Honest

Loyal

Self Confident

Qualifications

Age

Background (Local Lad)

Punctuality

Health

Mechanical Aptitude

Hobbies

Figure 6.4 Qualities to Look for in Staff

Table 6.2. *A Job Specification*

Title	Regional Sales Manager.
Accountable to	Marketing Director.
Responsible for	A sales force of 10 people in the East Midlands Region.
Duties	Supervise work of sales force, maintain good relations with clients. Write reports. Liaise with the Production Department. Carry out duties required by MD.
Age	30–35
Qualifications/Experience	Honours graduate in Economics or related discipline, e.g. Marketing. At least 5 years experience with some managerial or supervisory content.
Personal qualities	Self-reliant and self-motivated. Ability to lead and motivate people, initiative, ability to work under pressure. Must be a good communicator. Smart appearance is essential.
Salary	£20,000–£30,000 according to experience and qualifications.
Conditions of work	Minimum of 40 hours per week. 25 days holiday. Non-contributory pension scheme. Health insurance. Company car.

The Process of Selection and Recruitment

When a vacancy arises the Personnel Department has to consider the best way to fill it. There are 2 possibilities: recruit the candidate from inside the firm (an **internal appointment**) or bring in a new employee from outside the firm (an **external appointment**).

Internal Recruitment

When jobs are to be filled by internal applicants the posts are advertised on the company noticeboard and in its internal circulars. Appointing internally has several advantages. First, it may improve the morale and motivation of employees within the firm. Secondly, an existing employee is known to management and may have demonstrated the right qualities. Finally, it may be quicker and cheaper to fill the job from inside. Set against these advantages of internal promotion are the following potential disadvantages: it may create jealousy and rivalry; it creates a vacancy elsewhere; and a new employee from outside the firm might have brought new ideas and methods – 'a new broom sweeps clean'.

External Recruitment

If a company is recruiting externally, it has a number of possible sources:

1. **Government agencies, job centres**: vacancies in many occupations, but particularly in unskilled and semi-skilled areas, are posted to job centres.
2. **Local careers offices**.
3. **Private agencies**: these are private firms that are in business to provide companies with new employees. They charge a fee which is related to the starting salary of the new employee. Examples include Brook Street Bureau, Reeds Employment Agency and PER (Personnel and Executive Recruitment). Some agencies specialise in certain types of labour, e.g. the recruitment of nannies, au pairs and nurses.
4. **Universities, polytechnics and schools**: many employers visit the universities and polytechnics to recruit graduates on the so-called 'milk round'. The Services, e.g. the Army, Navy and RAF, recruit directly in schools and also use 'careers fairs' to recruit school-leavers.
5. **Advertisements**: many newspapers and journals display columns of 'Situations Vacant', and this is the most popular means of trying to find new employees. Some firms may advertise jobs over local commercial radio and on or outside their own premises, e.g. a pub might place an advert in its own window stating 'Bar Staff Wanted – Apply Within'. Other firms may use the local post office window or they may have a board outside their premises headed 'Vacancies'.

Figure 6.5 Recruitment Opportunities

Job Advertising

Before a firm decides to advertise a job vacancy, it needs to ask itself 3 important questions. First, what should be included in the advert? Secondly, where should the advert be placed? And thirdly, how much will the advertising cost and can we afford to spend that amount?

The answer to the first question is straightforward. Most of what needs to be included in the advert – information about the job, its duties, qualifications required, salary, conditions of employment – can be drawn from the job specification. The company needs to provide information about itself and about the **method of application**.

There is no standard method of application to a business for a job. This can be done in a number of ways: telephone, letter, application form and curriculum vitae (C.V.).

1. **By telephone**: the firm may ask people to telephone a particular person on a certain number in order to find out further details and ask for an application form.

2. **By letter**: if the firm does not have a suitable application form for the job, or if it feels that it could learn more about the candidate from a handwritten letter, this is the best method. Some companies even employ handwriting specialists – graphologists – to determine a person's personality from their writing.

3. **Application form**: the advantage of an application form is that all candidates have to answer all the relevant questions, to a standard format, which makes it easier for the personnel department to process.

4. **Curriculum vitae**: sometimes, particularly for more senior posts, candidates may be asked to submit a curriculum vitae. A C.V. contains almost the same information as asked for by an application form except it has been composed by the candidates themselves.

Examples of various job advertisements are shown in Figure 6.6. They emphasise the different means of application required by particular jobs.

Figure 6.6 Examples of Job Advertisements

Table 6.3. *National Daily Papers with Specialist Job Pages*

Paper	Monday	Tuesday	Wednesday	Thursday	Friday
Guardian	Media Creative Marketing Secretarial	Education	Public appointments	Computing Technology Science	Environmental
The Independent	Science Technology Computing	Accountancy Management	Sales & marketing Media Creative	Education Public General Graduate	Legal
The Financial Times	Legal		Financial Managerial	Accountancy	
The Daily Telegraph	Public	Finance Business	Sales & marketing	Special pull-out	
The Times	Educational Secretarial	Computing Legal	Special pull-out	General Banking Accountancy	

Having decided **what** to put in the advert, the firm then needs to decide **where** to place the advert. This depends on 2 factors: the type of job being advertised and how much money the firm has got to spend on recruitment. These 2 issues are connected. The type of job being advertised will determine where the advert should be placed. For example, it would be inappropriate for a pub to advertise for bar staff in *The Financial Times*! It is unlikely that a small, local business would have a large amount of money to spend on advertising, and someone looking for part-time bar work is not likely to look in *The Financial Times*. The firm would do far better advertising in the local press where such adverts are typically found. The national papers run adverts for particular types of jobs on different days, as shown in Table 6.3. Table 6.4 shows the cost of using the different sorts of advertising media.

In addition to newspapers, specialist magazines can also be used, e.g. *Farmers' Weekly*, *The Economist* and *New Scientist*. Schools with vacant teaching posts will often use *The Times Educational Supplement*.

Table 6.4. *The Cost of Using Different Advertising Media 1987*

The Independent	Full display only. £55 per single column cm.
The Financial Times	Full display only. £75 for 3×1 cm up to 40 words (excluding address). Then £25 per single column cm.
The Times	£5 per line (20 characters). Minimum 3 lines. Boxed display £327 per single column cm.
The Sunday Times	Minimum size 5×2 cm = £860. Then £66 per single column cm (semi-display) or £86 for full display. Repeat in following Thursday's *Times*.
The Daily Telegraph	Rates vary per day. Thursday Appointments: display £86 per column cm; semi-display £60 per single column cm or £12 per line (average 5 words per line).
Guardian	£125 for first 3×1 cm. Then £45 per cm.
Commercial radio	Chiltern Radio offers 2 packages. Ten 30-second spots over 3 days at peak times costs £263. Fifteen 30-second spots costs £382.
Careers offices	Free.
Job centres	Free.
Factory gates	Free.

QUICK QUESTIONS 2

1. *When a vacancy arises it is possible to recruit either internally or externally. Give one advantage and one disadvantage of these methods.*
2. *If a firm decides to appoint externally it is necessary to advertise the vacancy to attract suitable applicants. Give 4 possible methods of advertising job vacancies.*
3. *Suggest 2 ways in which people can apply for jobs.*
4. *Which would be the most suitable method of advertising the following vacancies: (i) an unskilled machine operator; (ii) a Master Chef at a London hotel; (iii) a company Finance Director. Give reasons for your choice.*

Design of the Job Application Form

Once the advert has been placed, applicants will write or phone for details and the firm may want them to complete an application form. The design of a job application form is very important and tends to follow a similar format. The following basic information is normally required:

1. Name and sex of applicant
2. Address/Telephone number
3. Date of birth
4. Marital status
5. Dependants
6. Education and qualifications
7. Employment details and experience
8. Interests and hobbies
9. Medical history
10. Name and address of referees

Part of a specimen application form for Barclays Bank is illustrated in Figure 6.7.

BARCLAYS

Please tick relevant boxes ✓

Full Time		Part Time	
Clerical – STD		Clerical	
Clerical – ATP		Secretarial	
Secretarial			
Other (specify)			
Are you prepared to work in Central London?	YES/NO		

APPLICATION FOR EMPLOYMENT

PLEASE COMPLETE THIS FORM IN YOUR OWN HANDWRITING

SURNAME (Mr/Mrs/Miss/Ms) ____ *(In Block Letters)* FIRST NAME(S) ____

HOME ADDRESS ____

DO YOU NEED A WORK PERMIT TO TAKE UP EMPLOYMENT IN THE UK? ____

TELEPHONE NUMBER ____ NATIONAL INSURANCE NUMBER ____

DATE OF BIRTH ____ MARITAL STATUS ____

MAIDEN NAME ____ *(To be used for school references only)*

Please complete each section of this form as fully and as carefully as possible. We shall use the information you provide to decide whether we can offer you an interview and if so, as a basis for discussion during interview.

EDUCATION – Secondary Schools and Colleges attended

NAME OF SCHOOL OR COLLEGE	FOSTAL ADDRESS	Dates (Month/Year) From	To

All Examinations taken (Please indicate also Examinations which you are sitting, or awaiting results)

G.C.S.E./'O' Level/C.S.E.	Month/ Year	Grade	'A' Level	Month/ Year	Grade	Any other qualifications	Month/ Year	Result

SECRETARIAL QUALIFICATIONS If you are applying for a Copy/Audio/Typing position please complete the following

Copy Typing W.P.M.	Audio Typing W.P.M.	Shorthand W.P.M.
Can you operate a Word Processor **YES/NO**	If **YES**, State type(s)	

DS380 (8/88)

The Bank is an equal opportunity employer. All applications will receive equal treatment regardless of sex, race, marital status or disability. To help us ensure that our Policy is being carried out would you please indicate your ethnic origins by ticking the appropriate box. The categories used are those recommended by the Commission for Racial Equality. This information plays no part in selection. It is required only for monitoring purposes.

BLACK		WHITE	
Afro-Caribbean origin		European origin *(including UK origin)*	
African origin		Other: Please specify	
Asian origin			
Other: Please specify			

HEALTH DECLARATION

The following questions do not form part of the selection procedure. Medicals, if necessary, will only be held after interviews take place.

The Bank welcomes applications from disabled people.

Before answering these questions, please read carefully the declaration that follows them.
Delete YES or NO where appropriate leaving a clear answer to each question which should be considered carefully.

1. How much school/work time have you lost from illness/disability in the past two years? ____ WEEKS
2. Do you enjoy good health and the ability to participate in a normal social and business life? YES/NO
3. Are you aware of any medical condition, disability or inherited disorder which may prevent you from fulfilling your contract of employment without reservation now or in the foreseeable future? YES/NO
4. Do you have any disability in any of the following areas?
   Use of Limbs .... YES/NO — Impediment of vision (despite corrective lenses) .... YES/NO
   Writing .... YES/NO — Bending and Lifting .... YES/NO
   Speech .... YES/NO — Working in any particular environment .... YES/NO
   Hearing .... YES/NO — Use of stairs and public transport .... YES/NO
5. Have you, during the past two years, used/required treatment or counselling for any form of chemical substance abuse (e.g. tranquilisers, solvents, alcohol, heroin or any illegal substance)? YES/NO
6. Are you taking any form of prescribed medication on a continuous or regular basis? (Other than oral contraceptives or a course of antibiotics or antihystamines). YES/NO
7. Are you registered as a disabled person? YES/NO
8. Please give your doctor's name, address and telephone number: ____

Please give further details of any disability if you wish, attaching a separate sheet if necessary.

Declaration

I have read carefully the instructions and questions above and declare the statements I have given are true and that I have not knowingly withheld any material fact. I am prepared to submit to a medical examination by an independent Doctor instructed by the Bank. Should I accept employment with Barclays Bank PLC, I understand that it will be on the basis that the truthful completion of this form constitutes part of the terms of contract for my employment.

SIGNATURE OF APPLICANT ____ DATE ____

SIGNATURE OF PARENT/GUARDIAN ____ DATE ____
(If applicant is under age 18)

Have you ever previously made application to enter the service of this or any other Bank or any Company within the Barclays Group? YES/NO*

If YES, give date(s) and particulars ____

Please return this application form to: (unless an alternative address is indicated here):
Recruitment Manager
BARCLAYS BANK PLC
Personnel Department
P.O. Box No. 256
Fleetway House
25 Farringdon Street
London EC4A 4LP

BARCLAYS BANK PLC
CAMBRIDGE
REGIONAL OFFICE
MORTLOCK HOUSE
P.O BOX 90
HISTON
CAMBRIDGE
CB4 4ZX

Please leave this area blank for official use.

Figure 6.7 Barclays Bank Application Form

The application form is important to the firm because it helps to build up a picture of the applicant. Once the firm receives the forms a process of **shortlisting** begins. Normally the firm will sort the application forms into 3 groups: suitable, unsuitable and marginal. This means that the firm does not have to interview all applicants, which would be too costly and time-consuming. Exactly how the firm decides – on paper – which applicants are suitable or unsuitable is very difficult to define, but it would normally take into account the following factors:

a. The way the form has been completed. Is it messy? Does it contain spelling mistakes?
b. The applicant's age. Is it suitable for the job?
c. The applicant's qualifications. Are they relevant?
d. The applicant's work-experience. Is it relevant?
e. The applicant's medical history. Is it likely to cause problems in the future?

When the vetting of applications has been completed, unsuccessful and successful candidates are informed, usually by letter. The successful candidates are invited for interview and their references will also be taken up. This means writing to the referees named on the application form. They are expected to provide information concerning the applicant's qualities, character and experience.

Writing a Letter of Application

Setting out a letter of application for a job requires a certain technique. It is important to bear in mind that it is the first form of contact that a company has with the applicant and it is important to make a good impression. A letter of application can be typed but companies often prefer handwritten applications. This means the candidate needs to write clearly, using plain paper, pen and ink or ballpoint pen (preferably black). Corrections should be avoided. Spelling, punctuation and grammar need to be checked carefully. It is a good idea to draft out in rough what you want to say. As far as content is concerned, the employer may wish to know a number of things, including the following:

1. The job which the candidate is applying for and where he or she saw it advertised.
2. Candidate's name, address, age and nationality.
3. Educational qualifications and schools/colleges attended, with dates.
4. Job experience and how it applies to the job being applied for. It may be worthwhile for the candidate to explain why he or she is interested in the job.
5. Previous employers and the length of time spent with each one.
6. Personal interests, hobbies and achievements.
7. Names and addresses of 2 people to provide references or testimonials.

QUICK QUESTIONS 3

1. *What do you understand by the term 'shortlisting'. Why does the firm shortlist candidates?*
2. *Suggest 3 factors a firm will consider when deciding whether to accept or reject a candidate's application for a job.*
3. *How does a letter of application differ from an application form?*

STUDENT EXERCISE

You are the Personnel Manager of Just Looking Ltd, a high-class department store. Recently a vacancy has arisen in the Men's Fashion Department. You place the following advert in the local job centre.

COMPANY:	Just Looking Ltd.
JOB:	Full-Time Sales Assistant (male or female).
SALARY:	£3 per hour. Annual staff bonus. Fringe benefits.
HOURS:	40 per week, 6-day flexible pattern.
DETAILS:	Men's Fashion Dept. Age 25–45. Experience essential.

1. The advertisement was not successful. Only 3 people applied and none of them had experience of working in a shop. By what other means might Just Looking Ltd find the staff it needs?
2. Having tried these other means, there are a flood of applicants. You need to design an application form to send to them. Your form should ask for at least 10 pieces of information that you require. Set the form out neatly and clearly.
3. Explain briefly why you have asked for any 6 of the 10 pieces of information.

4. When recruiting staff, a firm often uses a job description which states exactly what the job involves. Write a job description that you think would be appropriate for this job at Just Looking Ltd.

5. What other 2 uses may the firm have for the job description?

6. As the Personnel Manager you draw up the following list of qualities which you are looking for in the ideal applicant:

Helpful	Reliable
Physically strong	Honest
Humorous	Ambitious
Serious	Imaginative
Highly intelligent	Responsible
Well-motivated	Numerate
Clean driving licence	Punctual
	Well-groomed

Group these 15 qualities under the following headings: Essential, Desirable and Not applicable.

7. Briefly explain why you have chosen at least 3 of the qualities as essential.

8. Give another desirable quality not listed above which should be included. Give reasons for your choice.

Interviews

An interview is simply a conversation with a purpose. The aim is to get the maximum information from the applicant in the shortest possible time. The interview begins as soon as the candidate walks through the door. The interviewer notices how the candidate is dressed, walks and shakes hands. A good interviewer tries to put the candidate at their ease by starting with a few simple questions, e.g. 'Did you have a good journey?' or 'Did you get here OK?' After these opening remarks, the interviewer starts to ask more probing questions about either the letter of application or what is written on the application form.

The role of the interviewer is to listen and make an assessment of the candidate. The questions need to be kept open, e.g. 'why' and 'how' questions rather than ones that can be answered 'yes' and 'no'. The type of questions that are likely to be asked may include:

- Tell me about yourself.
- Why have you applied for the job?
- What are your leisure interests?
- What qualities do you have to offer us?
- What is your career ambition?
- What kind of books or newspapers do you read?

In answering the questions it is important for the candidate to be relaxed. Answers must be clear, detailed and precise. Towards the end of the interview the candidate may be asked if they have any questions. These could refer to the firm, the job itself, the pay, the hours, career prospects and training.

There are no rules and regulations about the style and structure of an interview. They can vary in length from half an hour to a 3-day selection procedure. The number of interviewers and who they are differs from firm to firm. Companies with specialist Personnel Departments may use somebody who is trained in interview techniques, and the manager of the relevant department may also be present. For some jobs a panel interview may be used – the panel could consist of as many as ten or a dozen people.

Some companies may use an interview assessment form to compare candidates. This sets out a number of features that are relevant for the job vacancy and the candidate scores points/marks according to the interviewer's assessment of the candidate. The advantage of using such a form is that it permits the interviewer to listen without having to do much writing, and it makes it easier to compare applicants – especially if the interviews have been taking place all day.

As a supplement to the interview, some firms ask the candidates to sit aptitude tests. This could be a series of tests related to verbal and numerical reasoning, mechanical reasoning, spatial awareness and language usage. Although such tests are proving more and more popular, a company is only likely to use them as a back-up to the interview. Where the company has difficulty in deciding between applicants then it could use these test scores.

The process that a firm goes through to fill a job vacancy is shown in Figure 6.8.

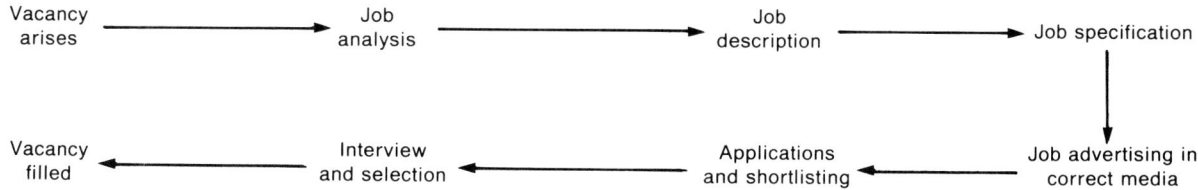

Figure 6.8 The Process of Filling a Vacancy

QUICK QUESTIONS 4

1. *What is the purpose of a job interview?*
2. *Write down 3 things an interviewer may notice about a candidate when they first meet.*
3. *What is an interview assessment form and why is it important?*
4. *Why do some firms use aptitude tests at interview?*

STUDENT TASK

Imagine you are applying for a particular job with Barclays Bank. Complete the application form and submit it to your teacher. The teacher then selects an interview panel of, say, 4 people and 2 candidates to be interviewed. The rest of the class watch the interview (it could be recorded on video) and take notes on what happens. A discussion based on the mock interviews then takes place.

STUDENT EXERCISE

You are the owner of a firm which supplies office equipment to companies in the Midlands. The firm has a vacancy for a sales representative.

1. Design an advert on a sheet of A4 paper to be inserted in the local newspaper.
2. Draw up a job description for the post of sales representative.
3. Write a letter of application for this vacancy.
4. Imagine you receive a flood of applicants. List 5 essential qualities that you are looking for in the applicants.
5. Draw up a list of 10 questions that you would ask candidates at the selection interview.

PROJECT AND ASSIGNMENT SUGGESTIONS

1. Contact the Personnel Manager of a local firm and ask if you can investigate the selection and recruitment procedures of the business. If possible arrange an interview with a member of the Personnel Department and find out the answers to the following questions:
   (a) What are the main types of workers the firm employs?
   (b) Approximately how many job vacancies does the firm have to fill each year?
   (c) Does the Personnel Department draw up a job description when a vacancy arises? If so, how is this done?
   (d) What are the main qualities the firm is seeking when selecting each type of worker?
   (e) What is the firm's policy with regard to recruiting candidates internally?
   (f) In what ways does the firm advertise its job vacancies?
   (g) Does the firm use an application form or does it require a letter and/or curriculum vitae from applicants?
   (h) What are the main problems the firm experiences in recruiting suitable employees?
   Write up your findings in the form of a report which follows the firm's selection and recruitment procedure from the point when the vacancy arises to the appointment of the employee.
2. Undertake a survey of newspaper job advertisements. Over a given period make a collection of advertisements from selected local and national newspapers. Divide up the advertisements according to the type of jobs to which they refer, e.g. unskilled workers, skilled workers, management posts. Is there a pattern concerning which types of jobs are advertised in which papers? Compare the cost of advertising in each paper and see if there is a relationship between cost of advertising and the job advertised.

3. Assume you are the Personnel Director of a medium-sized business and your Personnel Manager is about to retire. Design a job description for the position of Personnel Manager listing the qualifications you would expect an applicant to possess and the duties and responsibilities of the post. Devise an advertisement for the vacancy and suggest which form of advertising would be most appropriate in order to fill the post.

CHAPTER 7

The Personnel Function: Training and Development

Labour – the human input – is the organisation's most important resource. It is in the interests of a company to try and develop the skills and knowledge of its employees. This can be described as **training**. The aim of a training programme is to develop or improve a person's skill and performance. If training is effective it should increase the production of the firm and also increase employees' motivation.

Training is not confined just to new or inexperienced workers. It also applies to the experienced and long-serving employees. There are 6 types of training activity that take place within a firm. These are examined below.

Forms of Training

The types of training offered by firms include:

1. Induction Training

This is the initial training that employees receive when they first join a firm. Most new entrants to a firm know very little about the organisation they have joined – it is all very new and confusing. Induction training tries to provide some of the background information, e.g. the company's history, its objectives, the structure of the company, the products made and the services supplied. Some firms issue new employees with company brochures and give tours of the factory or office. Marks and Spencer plc issue a wallet of information to new employees that includes a letter from the Chairman, the organisation chart of the particular store, a job description, a training index, fire and bomb precautions, health services, a fact sheet, a pension guide and a book of M & S 'jargon'.

Induction training is not really concerned with the specific tasks or skills that the new employee will perform but it allows the new entrant to become familiar with the firm. A company will usually offer a tour of the workplace, together with the chance to meet workers from certain departments. It may also explain the work of the department in which the employee is to work. Many organisations neglect

Figure 7.1 Examples of Information Given by Marks and Spencer PLC to New Employees

induction training. Perhaps this is why such a high proportion of new employees leave within 6 months of joining the organisation. The new employee may have difficulty in understanding and adapting to the firm's methods and procedures. Some companies have highly structured induction programmes where new employees are given the chance to experience the work of different departments before deciding which department they would like to work for.

2. Operative Training

Most of the tasks performed by operatives involve little previous knowledge and a relatively low level of skill. The training of operatives tends to take place 'on the job'. Here, the trainee is placed in the work environment and uses the same machinery, tools and materials as the experienced worker. The trainee learns the job while he or she performs it or by watching while others perform it. It is frequently called 'learning by doing' or 'hands-on experience'. The major advantages of this form of training are that it is cheap, the trainee is placed in the actual workplace and is using the equipment and machinery. The disadvantages of this form of training might include a lack of supervision and instruction, resulting in a large amount of scrapped work, damage to machinery and faulty goods. The trainee may also pick up the bad habits of the instructor.

QUICK QUESTIONS 1

1. *What is training and what are the aims of a training programme?*
2. *What is 'induction training' and who receives it?*
3. *What is 'operative training' and where does it take place?*
4. *What are (a) the advantages and (b) the disadvantages of operative training?*

3. Apprentice Training

The apprenticeship system dates back a long way. It is a formal and highly structured training programme lasting between 3 and 5 years. To qualify for an apprenticeship a person will have had to reach a given standard in stated examinations, e.g. for an apprentice electrician this may be 5 GCSEs at grade C or above, including English, maths and physics.

Apprenticeships normally consist of both 'on-the-job' and 'off-the-job' training. The theoretical education takes place at a local college on a **day-release** or **block-release** basis (or even at night school) where students are prepared for professional qualifications. These are normally organised by the Business Technician Education Council (BTEC) or the City and Guilds of London Institute. In order to move onto the next stage of the apprenticeship each set of professional examinations has to be passed. The practical knowledge is gained 'on the job' and in the work environment. This may take the form of **module training**, which is controlled through instruction manuals and tests.

Apprentice training is generally associated with the craft professions. Manufacturing industry has by far the largest number of apprentices, with a marked concentration in the engineering trades. Hairdressing and catering also recruit a large number of apprentices. Training an apprentice is not a cheap activity. For example, in 1984 it was estimated that the average cost of apprentice training was £23,200. This cost was based on the figures in Table 7.1.

Table 7.1. *The Cost of an Apprenticeship in 1984*

Expense	Explanation	£
1. Trainee's wages	The pay received by apprentices is generally low because they are not as valuable to the firm as experienced workers. In 1984 engineering apprentices earned about £50 per week. Wages are the main component of training costs.	16,800
2. Off-the-job training, further education and administration	Examination fees and tuition costs	2,400
3. Training supervision	Instructor's time, materials and power	4,000
TOTAL		23,200

Source: I. S. Jones, *British Journal of Industrial Relations*, Vol. XXIV, No. 3, November 1986, pp. 333–62.

The apprentice may also contribute towards the output of the firm, e.g. trainee hairdressers wash hair, sweep up and make tea, but it is recognised that this is not as valuable as the contribution of the experienced worker. However, once the apprenticeship has been served, the person will receive full craftsman's wages because their contribution to output is greater than when they were apprentices.

4. Simulated Training

Some jobs are dangerous or expensive to learn by performing the task itself. For example, simply to get into an aircraft and fly it would be both dangerous and expensive, but aircraft pilots need to be trained. This problem is solved by offering simulation training whereby trainee pilots will use flight simulators to learn.

5. Supervisor Training

Achieving a position in an organisation which involves the supervision of people at work is normally attained by promotion. People who are good at their job are often promoted to the position of supervisor. However, although they may have technical expertise and know the so-called 'ins and outs' of the job, they may not have the ability to control, motivate and lead the people who are under their supervision. The training of supervisors consists of both 'on-' and 'off-the-job' training. The 'on-the-job' element may consist of watching other supervisors at work (**job shadowing**) and discussing with them what they do. There is also scope for simulated training here, e.g. presenting a situation to supervisors and asking them how they would deal with it and why. The 'off-the-job' element could consist of attending courses at local colleges where the work and role of supervisors is examined. This may involve case studies and role-playing exercises to simulate 'real-life' work situations.

QUICK QUESTIONS 2

1. *Give examples of jobs where apprentice training takes place.*
2. *What do you understand by (a) 'on-the-job' training and (b) 'off-the-job' training?*
3. *What are the costs associated with apprentice training?*

4. *Why do apprentices receive lower wages than fully skilled workers?*
5. *Give other examples of simulated training.*

---

6. Management Training

The training and development of managerial staff follows a less well-defined pattern compared with, say, the training of operatives or apprentices. The reason for this is that there are a whole host of courses aimed at developing management skills. There is no one particular route to becoming a manager. Some managers may have worked their way up through the company's ranks via promotion, while others could have been appointed from outside the company. Although there are no specific routes to becoming a manager, the training of managerial talent may include the following three elements:

(a) **A long period of formal training**: this may take place before employment – in the form of a degree (Bachelor of Arts or Science), other formal qualifications (BTEC Higher National Diploma) or even postgraduate study, e.g. a Masters Degree or a Ph.D. On the other hand, the formal training may involve periods of work experience with a company whilst a student is still studying for a degree. These are called **sandwich courses**. The training of an architect, for example, involves academic study at a school of architecture together with time spent in an architect's office.

(b) **Professional/technical qualifications**: most managers begin with a general qualification such as a degree or an HND and then study for professional qualifications. This could be as a Chartered Accountant, as an engineer or a Personnel Manager. Most of these qualifications require students to pass professional examinations and do further work experience. Such training is available either at a college on a day-release or block-release basis or via a correspondence course. This type of qualification often leads to a management position.

(c) **Management development courses**: formal qualifications in management are provided by business schools, polytechnics, universities and private management centres. These courses are aimed at developing managerial skills such as

Table 7.2. *Types of Training Offered to Different Employees*

Work Type	Training	Place of Training	Method of Training	Other Training	Remarks
Machine operating (e.g. textiles, cars)	Operative	Workplace	On the job, 'learning by doing'	Very little	Starts at any age. Quick and cheap
Craftsman (e.g. printer, electrician, carpenter)	Apprentice	Workplace	Practice under guidance	Day/block release at college	Structured. Lasts 3–5 years. Starting age 16–19
Foreman electrician	Supervisor	Workplace	On the job	Internal/external courses	May occur at any age. It is the first step on the management ladder
Professional (e.g. architect, engineer, accountant)	Technical then management	College, university, polytechnic	Theoretical followed by professional examinations	On the job, internal/external courses	Firm can train own employees once degree complete. Training is long and expensive

planning, decision-making, leadership, motivation and communication.

Table 7.2 provides a summary of the types of training offered to different types of employees.

The Effect of Training

It is important that employers train their existing workers in order to increase productivity. The effect of training on the productivity of an employee can be shown through the use of a **training profile**. This shows, in graph form, how quickly a previously untrained worker reaches **experienced worker standard** (EWS), i.e. produces as much as the experienced worker. During the course of training productivity is often lower because some of the output does not reach the required standard and therefore has to be scrapped. Two examples of training profiles are shown in Figures 7.2 and 7.3. The percentage of experienced worker standard is measured along the vertical axis and training time is measured on the horizontal axis.

As can be seen in Figure 7.2, it only takes 6 weeks to reach experienced worker standard – a relatively short time. Even without training, the untrained worker is 50% of EWS. This could be the training profile of an operative.

In Figure 7.3 it takes 6 years to reach full experienced worker standard. This could be the training profile of a professional worker such as an accountant. The normal route to becoming an accountant is to study for a degree (lasting 3–4 years) and then take professional examinations while working for a firm (over a period of 3 years). The overall training period is thus very long indeed.

The Amount of Training

Every spring the Department of Employment conducts an annual survey on training. The number and percentage of employees receiving training has increased steadily since 1984, as shown in Table 7.3. In the spring of 1984, 9.1% of employees were receiving job-related training. In 1988 this stood at 13.3% of employees.

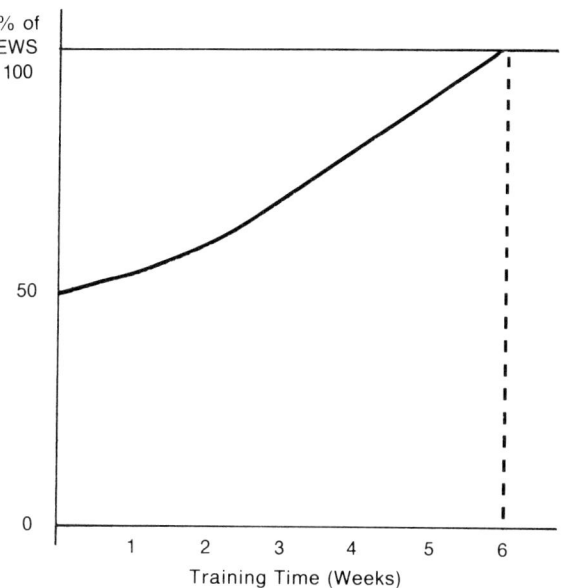

Figure 7.2 Training Profile of an Operative

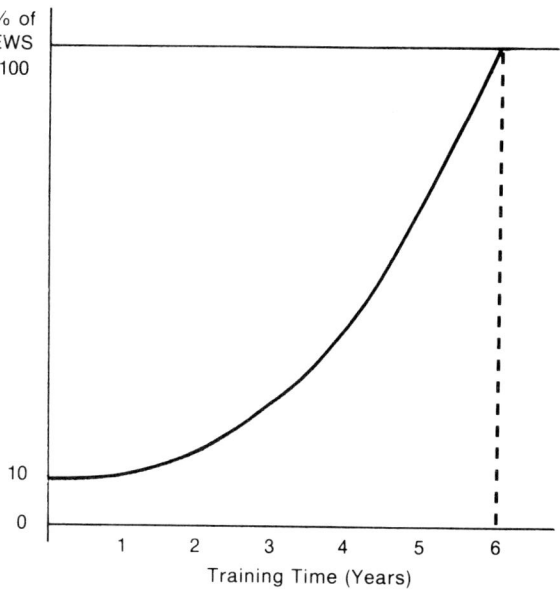

Figure 7.3 Training Profile of a Professional Worker

Table 7.3. *Number and Percentage of Employees Receiving Training in the Spring of Each Year*

	Number of Employees Receiving Training (000s)	% of All in Employment
1984	1,806	9.1
1985	2,088	10.4
1986	2,176	10.8
1987	2,380	11.7
1988	2,776	13.3

Source: Department of Employment Labour Force Survey.

The amount of job-related training an employee receives is generally determined by an employee's age, the industry worked in and the occupation. This information is shown in Figures 7.4, 7.5 and 7.6.

Figure 7.4 shows that job-related training declines with age. The largest amount of training is given to 16–19 year olds: 23.1% were receiving some form of training in spring 1988. This compares with 11.8% of the 35–49 year olds and 5.5.% of the 50–64 year olds. This is not surprising. It coud be that the older age-groups have already received training earlier in their working lives. Furthermore, as training is an investment by the firm in its workers, an older person is

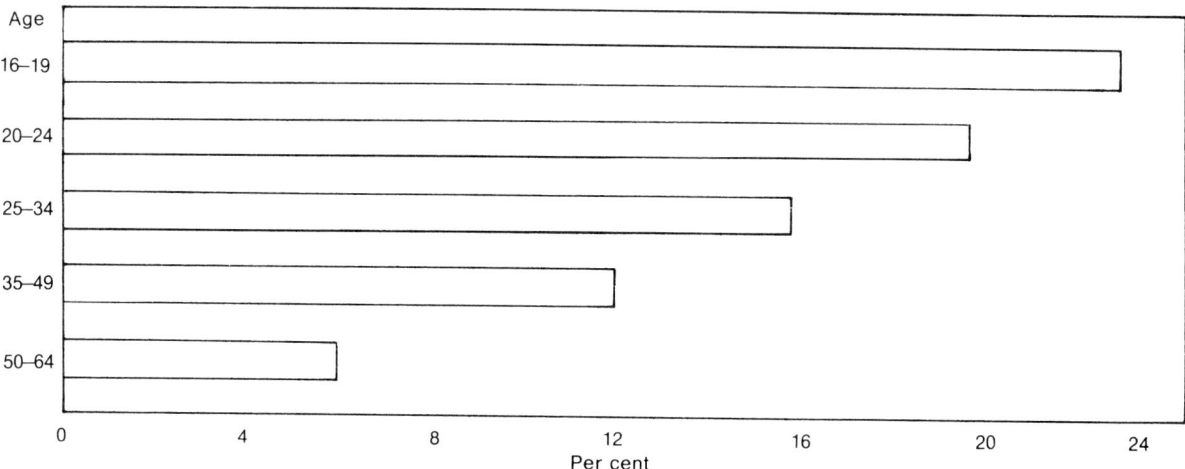

Figure 7.4 Percentage of Employees Receiving Job-Related Training by Age

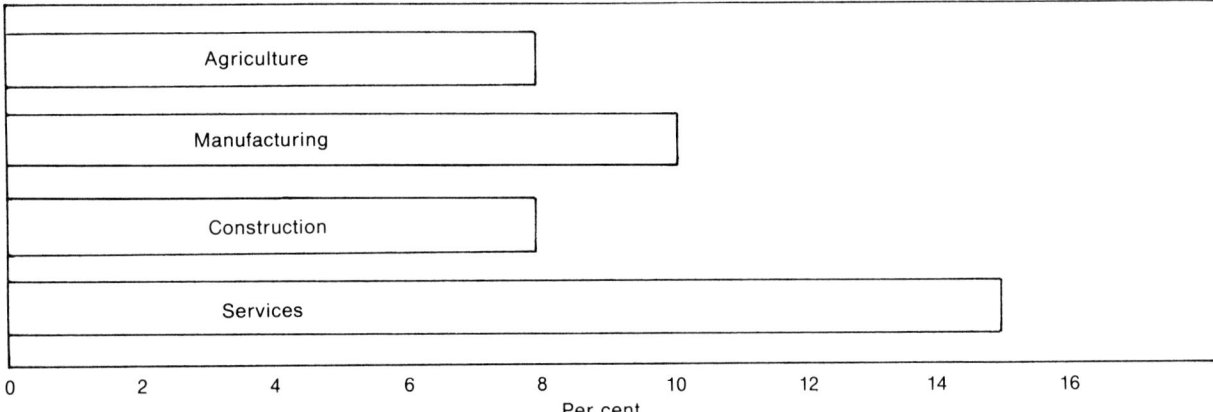

Figure 7.5 Percentage of Employees Receiving Job-Related Training in the Four Weeks before the Survey, by Industry, GB, Spring 1988

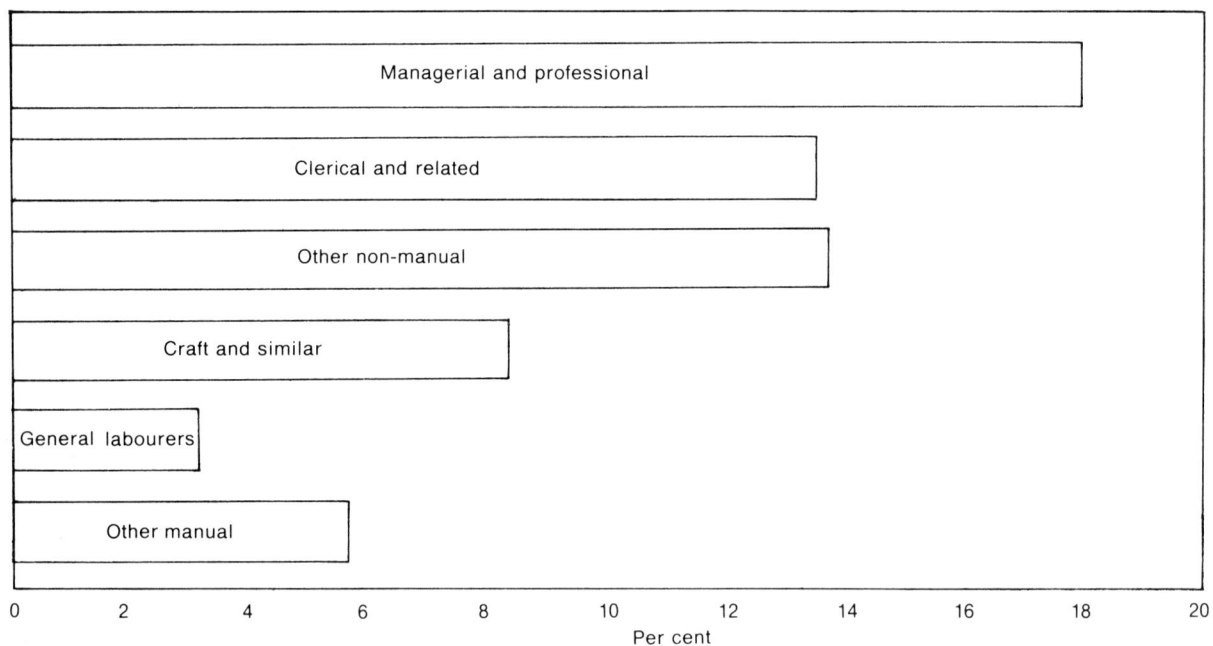

Figure 7.6 Percentage of Employees Receiving Job-Related Training in the Four Weeks before the Survey, by Occupation, GB, Spring 1988

likely to get less training because the firm will have fewer years benefit from that investment.

Figure 7.5 shows that a greater proportion of service sector workers were getting training than those in agriculture, manufacturing and construction, and Figure 7.6 shows that non-manual workers, particularly managerial and professional workers, get more training than manual workers.

A study by the Training Agency has found that national training costs are just over £25 billion a year, with employers' costs amounting to £18 billion. The largest element of this was the wages of trainees (85%), while training-course fees amounted to 5%. Figure 7.7 shows a breakdown of employers' training costs.

The survey found a number of interesting results. Half of the employees surveyed had received no training at all in 1986–7, while the other half had

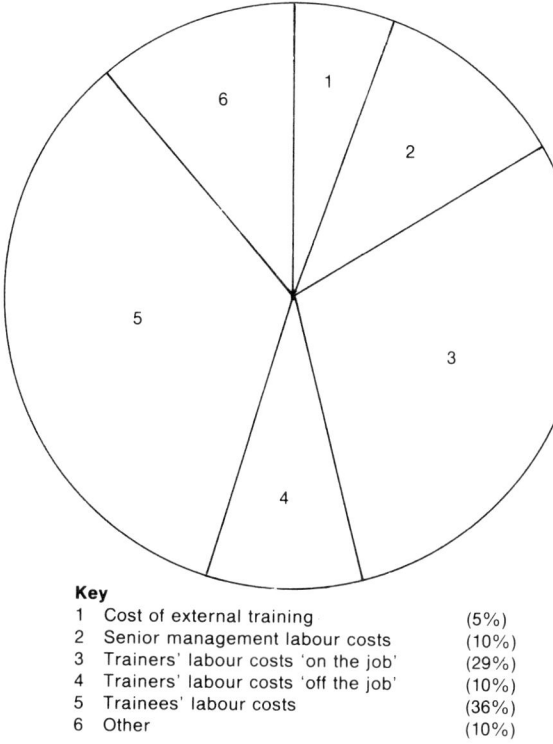

Key

1	Cost of external training	(5%)
2	Senior management labour costs	(10%)
3	Trainers' labour costs 'on the job'	(29%)
4	Trainers' labour costs 'off the job'	(10%)
5	Trainees' labour costs	(36%)
6	Other	(10%)

Source: *Labour Market Quarterly*, January 1989

Figure 7.7 Breakdown of Employers' Training Costs

received an average of only three weeks training. A third of the individuals said they had never received any training. About 1 in 5 companies said they provided no training. These companies presumably get their skilled labour by 'poaching' it from other firms. This has given rise to something called 'head-hunting' for very highly qualified labour, where firms try to lure skilled labour away from other firms by offering high salaries and other rewards.

QUICK QUESTIONS 3

1. *What are the typical elements in management training?*
2. *What effect does training have (a) for the firm and (b) for the employee?*
3. *Why does the amount of training vary with the age of employees?*
4. *What is the largest component of employers' training costs?*
5. *What do you understand by the term 'poaching of skilled labour'?*

Training and the Youth Labour Market

Young people are one of the largest sources of labour supply to the British labour market, but since 1983 their numbers have been falling and the rate of decline is expected to increase sharply up to 1992. The post-war baby boom produced the first swell in the number of school-leavers in the early 1960s. The second surge occurred in 1983, when there were 3.7 million 16–19 year olds. Between 1987 and 1995 the number of 16–19 year olds is projected to fall by 850,000 – a fall of 25%. The British teenager will become an increasingly rare commodity.

There are 2 striking features in the development of youth training in the UK over the last decade. First, the decline in the traditional apprenticeship system and secondly, the widening spread of the government's **Youth Training Scheme** (YTS). In 1979, before YTS had started, there were 22,752 first-year registered apprentices in the engineering indus-try. By 1984–5 the number had fallen to 6,042.

YTS was launched in April 1983 and became operational in September of that year. Its predecessor – the **Youth Opportunities Programme** (YOP) – had been introduced against the background of high and rising youth unemployment.

YTS is a permanent basic training scheme organ-ised on a national scale. All 16 year olds entering the labour market are guaranteed a place on YTS for 2 years – prior to April 1986 it had been 1 year – and in 1987/8 there were some 327,600 first time entrants to YTS.

Many industries such as construction, agriculture, hairdressing, travel and clothing, recruit almost all their young entrants through YTS. Many other industries, such as retailing, catering, engineering, business and clerical and transport, are also involved.

A YTS programme contains the following elements:

- A period of induction training covering the course content, an understanding of safe work-ing practices and off-the-job training arrangements.
- Experience of different types of work in a real work environment in order to learn and practise skills and to discover what they like and dislike

about the tasks they undertake.

- A period of 20 weeks' off-the-job training which takes place in a college of further education, a private training college, a training centre or a workshop.
- A chance to learn about computers, new technology and information technology.
- An opportunity to gain a vocational qualification or a credit towards a qualification, e.g. City and Guilds of London Institute (CGLI).

At the end of YTS each trainee receives a record of achievement – a YTS certificate which describes the training programme, how well he or she did and any qualifications obtained.

Table 7.4. *Destination of YTS Leavers, Great Britain*

Destination	%
In a job with a different employer	37.2
In a job with YTS employer	22.7
Unemployed	20.5
On another YTS scheme	12.3
On a full-time course/other	7.3

Source: Labour Market Quarterly, May 1989.

The evidence suggests that almost 60% of YTS trainees are in jobs after completing the scheme.

QUICK QUESTIONS 4

1. *Why are teenagers likely to become a 'rare commodity' in the mid-1990s?*
2. *Which industries make significant use of YTS?*
3. *What are the advantages to a firm of recruiting school-leavers under YTS?*

STUDENT EXERCISE: WOOLWORTH'S STAFF TRAINING PROGRAMME

David Rose, Woolworth's Personnel Director, was faced with problems in the company's 817 stores. Many Woolworth's assistants are young, the average age is 27 and new employees tend to be in their mid to late teens. A staff survey in 1985 found that the sales force was petrified of customers, so afraid they did not want to talk to them. Rose's wife attempted to buy a pair of shoes from a Woolworth's store. She was first met by a young assistant who said she was going to lunch, and then by another who said that if the shoes were not on display they were not in stock.

To tackle the problem Woolworth devised a training programme – 'Excellence'. This is divided into 2 halves of 5 sections each. The first half covers basic skills: induction; feelings; till training, secondary selling and product knowledge. The second covers the five departments within a Woolworth's store.

The ideas behind 'Excellence' come from 2 people – Walt Disney, who believed that work was meant to be fun, and Lord Baden Powell (founder of the Scout movement), who devised the idea of badges for passing proficiency tests.

When the new recruit receives his or her letter of appointment to the company, with it comes a glossy magazine – *Woolworth's Scene* – that contains information on matters like how to put on make-up and how to look after customers. The magazine uses language aimed at a young audience, e.g. 'ciggies', 'naff', 'brill' and 'wally'.

On joining the store, new assistants are sent to a regional centre for a 2-day induction programme. Here, the trainee learns about the background of the company and is also introduced to the 'Warm Fuzzy' – a creature like a red, furry football with arms and legs. This is meant to be a symbol of the correct way for an assistant to behave towards customers. The 'Fuzzy' is part of the feelings section of the training programme and is taught in groups, with lessons in the skills of giving customers Warm Fuzzies, by complimenting them or smiling at them. For example, in the feelings section of the training booklet it says 'Customers shop where they feel most welcome. Warm fuzzies create that welcome. Discourtesy, indifference, slow service, ignorance, errors and negative are cold pricklies, and customers hate cold pricklies.'

All assistants receive a training pack with a booklet covering each section of the 'Excellence' programme. They are expected to teach themselves from the booklets and be tested by their head of department when they think they are ready. If they pass, they gain a star to put on their badges. Five stars and a cash bonus of £110 is given. After a year, assistants are retested and they may lose stars if they fail to pass each section again. If successful, there is another £110 bonus.

The scheme may sound simple but it is practised

elsewhere, e.g. in McDonalds restaurants. It has also been successful. Woolworth has invested £4.5 million in retraining staff and in the 4 stores at which the feelings part of the 'Excellence' programme was tested sales increased by 18%. A survey of customers about the helpfulness of Woolworth's 19,066 assistants showed a 15–20% improvement between starting in July 1987 and November 1987.

Source: J. Gapper, 'Why Woolworth's Staff Are Having a Brill Time', *The Financial Times*, 30 November 1987.

Answer the following questions based on the case study:

1. What were the problems faced by David Rose, the Personnel Director of Woolworth?
2. What are the elements of the 'Excellence' training programme?
3. Why does the glossy magazine *Woolworth's Scene* use words such as 'naff' and 'brill'?
4. Where are the new assistants sent when they first join the company and what happens when they get there?
5. What is the 'Warm Fuzzy' meant to represent?
6. What factors, according to the case study, may have put customers off a Woolworth's store?
7. Why do you think the 'badge system' at Woolworth works?

PROJECT AND ASSIGNMENT SUGGESTIONS

1. Compare the type of training given to an unskilled worker with that given to a professional worker. If possible, contact a firm which employs both types of employee and ask them about the training they provide. Draw up a table showing the differences in training with respect to the time taken, the skills learned, the cost, and so on. Your table should clearly distinguish between training received at the place of employment and training completed outside the firm.

2. Find out more about the operation of the Youth Training Scheme in your local area. Your local careers office should be able to provide you with some information, including a list of which local businesses are actively involved in the scheme. Investigate the types of occupations where YTS trainees are most common. If you know someone who is involved with the scheme, ask them what type of skills they are learning and what their views are on the operation of the scheme.

CHAPTER 8

The Personnel Function: Wages and Salaries Administration

Labour supply to a firm is the amount of human resources, both physical and mental effort, used in the production process. An individual works for many reasons but the satisfaction of needs and wants, as shown in earlier chapters, is an important motivating factor. The money earned by a worker, in the form of **wages** or **salaries**, is one means of satisfying these needs and wants.

Wages are normally paid weekly in notes and coins in a pay packet. Salaries are normally paid monthly by cheque or directly into the bank account of the employee. Salaries are normally paid to so-called 'white-collar' workers, such as office and supervisory staff, e.g. managers and teachers. Wages are normally paid to so-called 'blue-collar' or manual workers, e.g. assembly-line workers, refuse collectors and bus drivers.

Methods of Wage Payment

It is important to distinguish between 2 methods of paying the workforce: **time rates** and **piece rates**. A worker who is paid on a time-rate basis earns the rate per hour multiplied by the number of hours worked. So, for example, a worker who is paid at the rate of £3.50 per hour and who works 40 hours in a week receives £3.50 × 40 = £140 as their earnings for the week. Piece rates (or **payments by results**, PBR) differ from time rates in that workers are paid according to their output. A fruit picker who is paid 30p per pound of strawberries picked earns 250 × 30p = £75 in a week if he or she picks 250 lbs of strawberries in that week. The choice of payment system – time or piece rate – depends on many different factors.

Time Rates

Time rates tend to be used in jobs where it is difficult to measure the output of the worker, e.g. teaching, police work and nursing, or where the quality of the product might be seriously affected if workers rushed their jobs simply to earn more money. For example, if train or bus drivers were paid according to the number of miles they drove, or according to the number of passengers picked up, this might encourage high speed and lead to safety problems.

Paying wages on the basis of time rates has a number of disadvantages.

1. No distinction is made between the hard-working and the lazy workers. The energetic and enthusiastic employees receive nothing extra for making greater work effort than the lazy workers.
2. As there is no incentive to work hard there may be a temptation to 'take it easy' during the normal working day so that overtime has to be worked. This is more costly to the firm.
3. To counteract this temptation to work slowly the supervision of employees by foremen or managers may be necessary to ensure that work is being done. Again, this is more costly to the firm.

Piece Rates

Under piece rates the worker is paid according to output – the number of units produced, items assembled or processes performed. Piece-rate systems come in many different forms: some relate to individuals, others to groups or even whole factories. The piece-rate principle can be applied to bonus systems which reward employees for exceeding a standard target of output or finishing within a standard time allowed for the job. Piece rates can only be applied where it is possible to measure the output produced by an individual or team. For this reason this method of wage payment is commonly found in assembly-line work, e.g. car production, agriculture, e.g. fruit picking, selling, where agents work on a commission basis, and mining.

All piece-rate systems are designed to solve the problem of supervision by giving the worker incentives to work. The harder the employee works the larger the reward. The lazy employee is punished under this system by lower earnings. However, there are disadvantages:

1. The employee could produce fast but faulty work, and so this means quality inspection and control are necessary.
2. The reputation of the company may be damaged by shoddy or faulty goods, e.g. the so-called 'Friday car' (car workers might rush assembly on a Friday to make sure they produced enough cars to earn the production bonus for the week).
3. Individual differences in performance may lead to friction and unrest among the workforce. Where an item is assembled on a production line the pace of work could be governed by the pace of the slowest worker. This may hinder production.
4. The breakdown of machinery or the stopping of the line may affect output and hence earnings. For this reason many firms have a system of **guarantee pay**, where workers are guaranteed a basic wage if production cannot be carried on.

QUICK QUESTIONS 1

1. *What is the difference between a 'wage' and a 'salary'?*
2. *What do you understand by the terms 'white-collar' and 'blue-collar' workers? Give examples of each.*
3. *What are the differences between time rates and piece rates as methods of wage payment?*
4. *What are the advantages and disadvantages of piece rates?*

Working Hours

The meaning of 'full-time' work has changed considerably over the last 90 years. At the turn of the century, full-time employees were typically working 10 hours a day, 6 days a week – 60 hours per week.

However, normal or standard working hours have been reduced substantially since then and currently most full-time workers work a 40- or 39-hour week. For many people the standard working week is 5 days (Monday to Friday) from 9 a.m. to 5 p.m. In some manufacturing firms it is from 7.30 a.m. to 3.30 p.m. However, for other people, e.g. shop workers, the working week may be spread over 6 days. Most shops are open on Saturdays (some also open on Sundays) and so the shop worker normally has a day off in the week to compensate for working on Saturdays. Alternatively, these Saturdays may be worked in rotation – 1 in 2 or 1 in 3.

Flexitime

A number of firms, particularly those in the service sector, have introduced **flexitime**. This was a response to 2 forces: (a) the growth in the number of married women in the labour force who had family commitments, and (b) the desire to see the rush-hour problem spread more evenly. Flexitime does not affect the number of hours worked but it allows workers to be flexible – within reason – in choosing their working hours. Employees generally have to work **core time**, e.g. between 9.30 a.m. and 3.30 p.m., but are allowed to come into work early, e.g. 7.30 a.m., or leave work late, e.g. 6 p.m. It is possible for employees to accumulate 'credit hours' over a monthly cycle, and these can then be taken as days off. Alternatively, an employee who has not worked enough hours usually has to make up such 'debit hours' later in the month.

Overtime

In addition to working a normal basic work-week, a considerable number of employees have the opportunity to work overtime hours. These are defined as hours above the basic workweek. To encourage employees to work overtime, such hours are paid at 'premium' rates, i.e. above the normal hourly rate of pay. This could be time and a third, time and a half, double time or triple time. Double time simply means each hour of overtime is paid at double the normal hourly rate. So if a person's normal hourly rate is £3 per hour, overtime would be paid at £6 per hour. A large number of maintenance workers in manufacturing industry, e.g. electricians, plumbers and fitters, work overtime on Saturday and Sunday since this is the only time when the factory machines are switched off and repairs can be carried out.

Shifts

Many employees work under a shift system, particularly in continuous process industries such as chemicals and steel manufacture, where the machinery has to be kept running for 24 hours a day, 7 days a week. Also, a number of workers in the service industries, e.g. nurses, firemen, policemen and security guards, work shifts. Patterns of shiftwork vary enormously but a common one is the treble shift system where the day is split into 3 segments: 6 a.m.–2 p.m. 2 p.m.–10 p.m. and 10 p.m.–6 a.m. Each worker usually rotates in this system on a monthly cycle, working combinations of mornings, afternoons and nights. Shift **premia** are paid to employees to compensate for working antisocial hours.

Part-Time Working

In the 1970s and 1980s there has been a massive growth of part-time work. A part-time worker is defined by the Department of Employment as somebody who works less than 30 hours per week. In June 1984 Britain had 4.9 million part-time employees, of whom almost 90% were in the service sector. Moreover, 84% of all part-time employees are women, with part-time work accounting for 46% of all female employment.

Table 8.1 shows the structure of earnings for manual workers in selected industries for 1986.

The figures are percentages of average gross weekly earnings (see below) accounted for by the various methods of wage payment – overtime, payments by results and shift pay. The figures in brackets show the percentage of employees receiving the various pay elements. It can be seen that an employee's earnings are made up of different elements. In the baking industry, for example, overtime pay accounts for 31% of gross weekly earnings, and 82.8% of employees received this payment. Piece-rate payment is relatively unimportant – it accounted for only 2% of earnings and only just over 10% of employees received it. Shiftwork is important in the baking industry, as it is in the chemical industry. In the other 3 industries, shiftwork is unimportant, as one would expect – very few garages repair cars on a night shift although on 1 August some garages open at midnight to start selling new cars. In the building and construction industries piece-rate systems are important. Here, it is relatively easy to measure the output of the workers, and the use of penalty clauses (a system of fines) when building work is not completed on schedule means firms have to give incentives to employees to complete the contract on time.

Table 8.1. *The Make-Up of Weekly Earnings of British Manual Workers 1986*

Industry	Overtime	PBR	Shift Premia	All Other Pay
	%	%	%	%
Baking	31.0	2.0	7.3	59.7
	(82.8)	(10.1)	(34.3)	
Chemical and allied	15.6	4.1	8.5	71.9
	(53.0)	(49.4)	(56.0)	
Civil engineering construction	19.9	16.8	0.2	63.1
	(77.0)	(74.7)	(2.5)	
Building trade	12.7	15.3	0.2	71.8
	(56.7)	(59.1)	(1.8)	
Motor vehicle retail and repair	9.7	9.0	0.3	81.0
	(52.6)	(36.2)	(2.9)	

Source: New Earnings Survey, Department of Employment, 1986.

Different Wage Terms

An employee's **basic earnings** refers to the hourly wage multiplied by the normal number of hours that are worked per week. This information can be shown on a diagram, as in Figure 8.1. Plotted along the vertical axis are the employee's basic earnings, and along the horizontal axis are the employee's hours of work. It can be seen that the employee receives £100 for working 40 hours. This means the hourly rate of pay is £2.50. The straight line shows the relationship between basic earnings and hours worked, e.g. for working 5 hours the employee receives £12.50, for 10 hours £25, and so on.

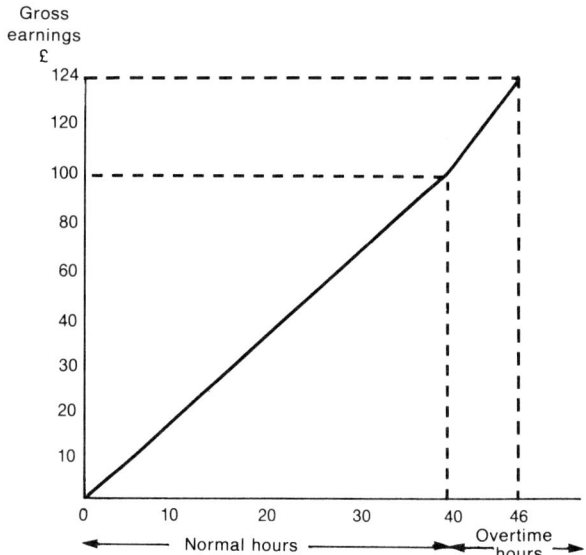

Figure 8.2 The Effect of Overtime on Earnings

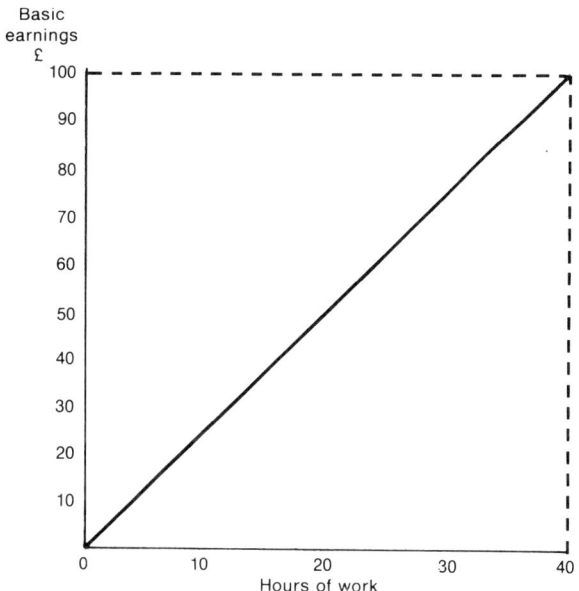

Figure 8.1 Basic Earnings for Working Normal Hours

An employee's **gross earnings** are often higher than basic earnings because they are boosted by overtime, bonuses and shift pay. In fact, the basic earnings of some workers can be a small part of total earnings. The tendency for gross earnings to rise above basic earnings is referred to as **wages drift**. Figure 8.2 illustrates the way overtime causes gross earnings to drift above basic earnings.

Imagine that overtime is paid at a rate of £4 per hour up to a maximum of 6 hours overtime. The gross weekly earnings of an employee who works overtime will be made up of 2 elements: the basic weekly wage and overtime earnings. The person's gross weekly earnings can be calculated using the following formula:

Gross weekly earnings = Basic earnings + overtime payments

where

Basic earnings = Hourly wage rate × normal hours
= £2.50 × 40 hours
= £100

and

Overtime payments = Overtime rate × overtime hours
= £4 × 6 hours
= £24

so

Gross weekly earnings = £100 + £24
= £124

In Figure 8.2 it can be seen that the earnings/hours line gets steeper after 40 hours. This is because the

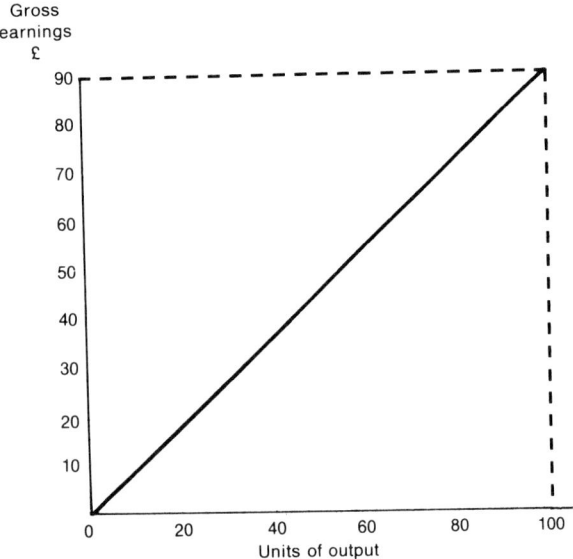

Figure 8.3 The Payments by Results Wage System

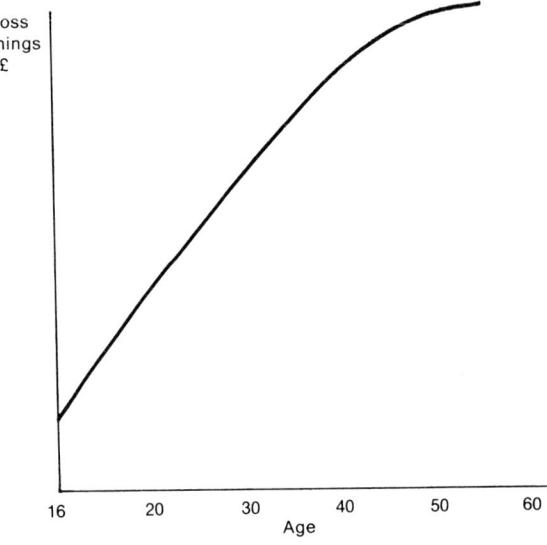

Figure 8.4 An Age-Earnings Profile

hourly rate of pay for overtime (£4) is higher than the basic hourly rate (£2.50).

Figures 8.1 and 8.2 illustrate the earnings of a time-rate worker. In the case of piece-rate workers, earnings are still plotted along the vertical axis but the amount of output (not hours) is plotted along the horizontal axis. This is shown in Figure 8.3. In this case the employee receives £90 for producing 100 units of output. From Figure 8.3 it is straightforward to calculate how much the employee earns for producing each unit of output. It is simply earnings divided by units of output produced.

Earnings per unit of output
= Earnings ÷ output produced
Earnings per unit of output = £90 ÷ 100
= £0.90

Figures 8.1–8.3 show the weekly earnings of a worker. Figure 8.4 is an example of how a graph can be used to show the way a person's earnings are related to age and/or experience. This is called an **age/earnings profile**.

In Figure 8.4 the employee's earnings rise according to age/experience. This payment system, where pay goes up with each year of experience or at each birthday, is used by many organisations. There are good reasons for this: a person who has been with the company a long time has more experience and so is more valuable to the firm. It is also designed to encourage loyalty and to reduce labour turnover – many people stay with a firm because their pay is related to age/experience.

QUICK QUESTIONS 2

1. What do you understand by the term 'flexitime' and why has it been introduced?
2. What is overtime and what incentive does an employee have to work overtime?
3. What is shiftwork? Name some industries that are likely to adopt this work pattern. Give reasons for your choice.
4. What is the difference between basic and gross earnings?

An employee's gross earnings are different from **take-home pay** or **net earnings** because employees have certain items deducted from their gross earnings. When these items have been deducted, the employee is left with net pay or take-home pay. This literally means what it says, the pay the employee has to take home. The monthly pay slip in Figure 8.5 will help to explain these deductions.

PAY DATE: 30 July 1989		BASIC PAY	950.00		GROSS PAY
		OVERTIME	150.00		
		BONUS	100.00		1200.00

NAME: J. Fielding	STATUTORY DEDUCTIONS		OTHER DEDUCTIONS		TOTAL DEDUCTIONS
PAY NUMBER: 075990	Income Tax	208.86	BUPA	12.80	
LOCATION: 543	National Insurance	95.96	Union	4.00	
NATIONAL INSURANCE NUMBER: WL 13 93 11 C	Superann-uation	72.00			

TAX CODE	GROSS PAY TO DATE	INCOME TAX TO DATE	N.INSURANCE TO DATE	PENSION TO DATE	NET PAY
437H	5114.00	843.50	372.94	279.84	806.38

Figure 8.5 An Employee's Itemised Pay Slip

An Itemised Pay Slip

An employee is entitled to an itemised pay slip which gives the details of how gross pay has been calculated, the deductions which have been made, and net pay. The employer is required to make certain deductions from the gross pay of the employee and the employee must be notified of the amount and nature of these deductions on each pay slip.

The pay slip in Figure 8.5 contains the following important features:

The Employee's Pay Number

All employees are allocated a pay number by the company. In this case it is 075990.

National Insurance Number

A National Insurance number is given to all employees when they first start work. It remains with them for the whole of their working life. Here it is WL 13 93 11 C.

Tax Code

All employees are given a tax code. This can change when a person's circumstances change. In this case the tax code is 437H. In order to understand the specific meaning of this code, it is necessary to look briefly at how income tax operates in the UK.

In the UK income tax is collected by the Inland Revenue through what is known as the **PAYE** (pay-as-you-earn) system. Different rates of income tax apply to what are known as **taxable income bands**. The income tax rates and bands for 1989–90 are shown in Table 8.2. These rates mean that for every £1 a person earns between £0 and £20,700, he or she must pay 25p in income tax. For every £1 earned above £20,700, he or she pays 40p in income tax. Before the tax on a person's income can be calculated, a number of **personal allowances** have to be deducted. These are shown in Table 8.3.

Table 8.2. *Income Tax Rates and Bands 1989/90*

Income Tax Band (£)	Income Tax Rate (%)
0–20,700	25
20,700–	40

Table 8.3. *Income Tax Personal Allowance 1989/90*

	£
Personal Allowances	
Married	4,375
Single/Wife's income	2,785
Age Allowances	
Married (65–74)	5,385 (over 80s 5,205)
Married (75–9)	5,565 (over 80s 5,565)
Single (65–74)	3,400 (over 80s 3,540)
Single (75–9)	3,540
Mortgage Allowance	30,000 per property (Mortgage Interest Relief at Source, MIRAS)

Payments of Certain Subscriptions
e.g. charitable donations and subscriptions to
professional associations

A married man is entitled to a basic tax-free personal allowance of £4,375 per year. This means he can earn this much in a year before paying tax. Alternatively, he is allowed to earn £364.58 per month (£84.13 per week) before paying income tax. These income tax allowances determine the person's tax code. In Figure 8.5, J. Fielding's tax code was 437H. If a 5 is added on the end of this number – giving 4375 – this tells us the tax free allowance. If the tax code was 278, then the tax-free allowance would be £2,785 per year.

Gross Pay

In this case Fielding earns £1,200 in the month of July. This is made up of £950 basic pay, £150 overtime and £100 bonus.

Statutory Deductions

These are made up of 3 elements:

1. Income tax
2. National Insurance
3. Superannuation (pension fund).

1. **Income tax**: the calculation of Fielding's income tax is as follows. His tax code is 437 so he is allowed to earn £4,375 per year or £364.58 per month tax free. Anything earned over this amount is liable to income tax. In this example he will pay tax at the rate of 25%. To calculate his income tax payments the

following formulae are used:

Gross pay − income tax allowance = taxable income

Taxable income × income tax rate = income tax paid

In this case we have:

Gross pay = £1,200
Income tax allowance = £364.58 per month
Taxable income = £1,200 − £364.58 = £835.42
Income tax rate = 0.25

Putting these numbers into the formula gives:

Income tax paid = £835.42 × 0.25
= £208.86

2. **National Insurance**: National Insurance is a tax on earnings paid by both the employer and the employee. Contributions provide funds for unemployment, sickness and other Social Security benefits. In 1989/90 the National Insurance contributions were structured as shown in Table 8.4.

Table 8.4. *Weekly Rates of National Insurance Contributions*

Total Weekly Earnings £	Employer's Contributions %	Employee's Contributions %
Below 43	0	0
43–74.99	5	2% on the first £43 each week, i.e. 86p, and 9% on the rest up to an earnings limit of £325
75–114.99	7	
115–164.99	9	
165–325	10.45	
Above 325	10.46	

In Figure 8.5 it can be seen that Fielding pays £95.96 in National Insurance. This amount is arrived at as follows: he pays 2% on £43 each week (0.02 × £43 × 4 = £3.44) for the four weeks in the month and then 9% on his earnings above the £43 per week. In monthly terms we have 0.09 × (£1,200−£172) = £92.52. The total paid is therefore £95.96.

3. **Superannuation**: this is the employee's own contribution to a pension scheme/fund. It is a form of compulsory saving for when a person retires. All

employees have to belong to either a company's own pension scheme or the state pension scheme. In our example, Fielding pays 6% of his gross pay into the pension scheme i.e. $0.06 \times £1,200 = £72$. The employer also makes a contribution. This money is then invested in unit trusts, bonds and other financial assets.

Other Deductions

These can vary but the typical ones are contributions to private medical insurance (BUPA for example) and trade union subscriptions. Fielding subscribes £12.80 to BUPA and £4 to his union.

Net Pay

This is what the employee is left with to 'take home'. It is calculated by subtracting all deductions from gross pay. In Fielding's case net pay is £806.38 ($£1,200 - £393.62$).

The Cumulative Figures

In Figure 8.5 along the bottom part of the pay slip is a series of cumulative totals. This shows how much Fielding has earned in the current financial year (each financial year runs from April to March), how much tax and National Insurance he has paid and total contributions to the pension scheme.

QUICK QUESTIONS 3

1. *What items are included on an employee's pay slip?*
2. *What is the difference between gross and net pay?*
3. *Give examples of the deductions that are made from an employee's gross pay.*
4. *What do the initials PAYE stand for? What is PAYE?*

Other Forms of Reward/Remuneration

A considerable number of employees receive other types of remuneration in addition to a wage or salary. These are sometimes called **perquisites** (**perks**) or **fringe benefits**. These are some of the more typical ones:

Company Cars

These are enjoyed by professional, managerial and executive workers. It is an obvious financial benefit since the cost of buying and running a car is often the largest item of household expenditure after mortgages and holidays. For many employees it is also a sign of status. If a company car is not provided, some companies offer petrol allowances.

Accommodation

Some employers, e.g. the Services and farm-owners, provide permanent accommodation for their employees. Others offer temporary accommodation, e.g. hotels, for relocation purposes, i.e. when an employee has to move to a new town because of a job change and is unable to find somewhere to live before moving.

Health/Sports Clubs

Some companies finance or subsidise membership of health and sports clubs.

Canteen/Meal Facilities

Many companies now offer subsidised in-house catering facilities. The 25th annual survey of the catering industry published by the Industrial Society in 1986 suggested that 58 out of every 100 employees bought meals at work during their main break. This can be a benefit to employees (if such meals are subsidised). Menus can be designed for nutritional value for example. The alternative to in-house catering facilities has traditionally been luncheon vouchers. 14,000 British companies give luncheon vouchers to 400,000 employees, with an average value of 56p per day.

Occupational Health Schemes

The provision of medical insurance as part of a benefit package for managerial/executive workers is familiar in a lot of large organisations, e.g. IBM offers all its 16,000 employees both medical insurance and medical screening through BUPA. At Marks & Spencer, doctors, chiropodists, dentists and hairdressers attend most stores for the benefit of staff.

Non-Contributory Pension Scheme

Some companies, e.g. Marks & Spencer, offer their employees a non-contributory pension scheme. This means that the company pays the whole pension contribution and the employee does not have money deducted from salary.

Discounts on Company Products

Many firms offer this perk, e.g. miners get cheap coal and bank employees get subsidised loans. Shop employees may be allowed to buy goods at a discount of perhaps 5% or 10%. Marks & Spencer offers cheap food to staff at the end of the day if it has reached its sell-by date.

Profit-Related Pay

A profit-related bonus can be paid to employees either in cash (as a percentage of profits) or shares. This has been an important trend in the late 1980s, prompted by the desire to give employees the chance to participate in the profits of the company. This generally motivates them to work harder and improve company performance. The largest company with an employee share distribution scheme is ICI.

Real Wages and Money Wages

A person's money wage is expressed in money terms, e.g. £120 per week. A person's **real wage** is the actual **purchasing power**, in goods and services, of the money wage. Purchasing power refers to the command over goods and services given the person's money income and the prices of those goods and services. The real wage depends on two things – the money wage and the price of goods and services that the worker buys. If money wages rise faster than prices then real wages will rise, and vice versa. This relationship is illustrated in Table 8.5. In 1985 the money wage is £100 and the price of the items bought by the employee is £10 each. This allows 10 units of the item to be bought. By 1990 the money wage has doubled to £200 but prices have risen by 300%. This means the employee can now only buy 5 units of the item and so the real wage has halved even though the money wage has doubled.

Table 8.5. *Real Wages, Money Wages and Prices*

	1985	1990
Money wage	£100	£200
Prices	£10	£40
Real wage	10 units	5 units

Pay Determination

The determination of pay – the price of labour – can be explained by the operation of the economic laws of **supply** and **demand** in the labour market. Very simply these state that the greater the demand for a particular type of labour the higher that labour will be paid, other things being equal. Similarly, the lower the supply of labour the greater will be labour's reward. (For a more detailed analysis of supply and demand see Chapter 12.)

The demand for labour is said to be a **derived demand**. The word 'derived' is used because labour is not employed for its own sake but for what it can produce, e.g. the demand for double glazing will determine the number of people who are employed as double-glazing salesmen. Similarly, the lower the demand for housing the lower will be the demand for estate agents.

The supply of labour to a particular job will depend not only on the wage that is offered – the higher the wage the greater the number of people willing to do that job – but also on the relative attractiveness of the job. People get higher pay if they work in dangerous or unpleasant occupations. Pay will also be determined by the characteristics of the individual, the geographical position of the industry and the characteristics associated with the industry. These factors are summarised in Table 8.6.

The characteristics of an individual employee will influence the rate of pay. Older workers with more experience get paid more than younger workers with less experience. Greater education, formal qualifications and training result in higher pay. On average, people with degrees (graduates) earn more than non-graduates. Similarly, trained or skilled workers, e.g. bricklayers, earn more than general labourers. Higher pay also goes to exceptional workers with natural ability, such as professional sportsmen and women and entertainers. Membership of a trade union also increases pay. Evidence suggests that union members receive 8–10% more than non-union members. This may be due to restrictions placed by unions on who is allowed to do certain jobs, which limits the supply of labour. Sex and race are also factors that determine pay – an example of discrimination in the labour market. However, legislation is reducing this undesirable aspect of pay differentials.

The characteristics of a job are important in

Table 8.6. *Factors Determining Pay*

Individual Characteristics	Job Characteristics	Industry Conditions	Geographical Location
Age	Job security	Size of firm	Region
Experience	Physical danger	Profits	Town
Education	Dirt/Noise	Competition	
Qualifications	Antisocial hours		
Training	Holidays		
Sex	Stress		
Race	Responsibility		
Union member			
Natural ability			
Marital status			

determining pay. Such factors may include:

1. **Job security**: some jobs are very insecure, e.g. construction workers run the risk of being laid off during the winter months when weather conditions mean that work cannot take place. A low level of job security may lead to higher pay.
2. **Physical danger**: certain jobs carry a higher risk of injury or death than others. For this reason such workers are compensated in the form of higher pay, e.g. in the construction industry employees who work at heights get a higher rate of pay than those who work on the ground. Similarly, divers get paid danger money for working at depths.
3. **Dirtiness/Noise**: employers who work in dirty or noisy working environments tend to get paid more than employees who work in comfortable surroundings. Miners working underground in dirty conditions get paid more than 'surface workers'.
4. **Anti-social hours**: people who work nights or on shifts have their family and personal lives disrupted because of the hours that they are expected to work. They usually receive higher pay to compensate them for this.
5. **Holidays**: one attractive feature of the teaching profession is the length of holidays. These are far longer than those of, say, a manual worker, who may be entitled to 20–5 days per year plus public holidays such as Christmas and Easter.
6. **Stress/Responsibility**: the more stressful a job is, or the greater the responsibility it involves,

the higher will be the rate of pay, e.g. foremen and supervisors are paid more than their charges.

7. **Industrial and geographical conditions**: these also play a role in pay determination. Larger firms with bigger profits who face little competition from rival firms tend to pay more, on average. People who live in the South East or who work in London receive higher pay than similar workers in the North or Midlands. The payment of a 'London Weighting' allowance is designed to compensate for higher costs of living for workers who live in London. Also, higher pay in the South East generally reflects the difficulty that some firms have in recruiting labour in that particular region.

QUICK QUESTIONS 4

1. *In addition to earnings, how can firms reward their workers? Give examples.*
2. *What is the difference between money and real wages?*
3. *What factors determine an employee's pay?*
4. *Why do firms based in the South East pay more for the same type of labour than firms in the Midlands?*
5. *Why does the curve in Figure 8.4 flatten out after the age of 50?*

STUDENT EXERCISE

Flexible Working Hours and Pay

A building construction firm, Bates and Company Ltd, has introduced flexible working hours for its head office staff. All 200 employees must work for the whole of the 'core time' period from 10 a.m. to 4 p.m., less a 45-minute lunch break. Each employee is allowed to choose arrival/departure times from 8 a.m. to 10 a.m. and from 4 p.m. to 5.45 p.m. During each 4-week period a total of 148 hours (which excludes lunch breaks) must be worked. 'Debit' or 'credit' time up to 8 hours can be carried forward to the next 4-week period. An employee need not choose the same working hours every day.

In the first 4-week period of the scheme, an employee who has worked a total of 73 hours in the first 2 weeks records the following hours in the third week:

Day	Arrival	Departure	Lunch
Monday	8.30 (a.m.)	4.30 (p.m.)	45 (minutes)
Tuesday	8.30	5.00	45
Wednesday	8.30	4.45	45
Thursday	8.30	4.30	45
Friday	8.30	4.30	45

1. Calculate how many hours the employee has worked each day and hence find the total for the week.
2. Show how many hours the employee will need to work in the fourth week assuming that she wishes to reach the 148-hour figure. Draw up a table of these hours (similar to the one above) from Monday to Friday of the fourth week, including times for lunch breaks.

At the end of the 4-week period, the employee receives the following pay slip:

Gross pay	£444
Income tax	£XXX
National Insurance	£XXX
Superannuation	£XXX
Net pay	£XXX

Due to a computer error there are a number of omissions (marked XXX). You are given the following information: income tax is payable at the rate of 25%; tax-free income is £232 per month; National Insurance is 9% of gross pay; superannuation is 6% of gross pay. Using this information, answer the following:

3. What is the employee's hourly rate of pay?
4. How much is paid in income tax?
5. What are the employee's National Insurance contributions?
6. How much did the employee pay in pension contributions?
7. Calculate the employee's net pay for the month.
8. What important information is missing?

PROJECT AND ASSIGNMENT SUGGESTIONS

1. Select 4 different types of occupation and using local and national newspaper advertisements investigate the range of wages or salaries paid in each case. Try to discover the factors that are important in determining the rates of pay for each one. Present your results in the form of a table comparing each type of occupation. If, for a particular occupation, different businesses seem to pay widely differing rates of pay, investigate why this might be so.
2. Contact a local business which has both waged and salaried employees. See if you can find answers to the following questions:
   (a) Which types of workers receive a weekly wage and which a monthly salary?
   (b) What are the reasons for paying different types of employees in different ways?
   (c) Are wage earners paid by results or are they on time rates?
   (d) If overtime is paid, how are the overtime rates calculated?
   (e) If the business operates a flexitime system, how does this work? Does it involve all employees in the business? If no such system exists, has the business ever considered introducing one?
   (f) What other forms of reward or remuneration do employees receive apart from their wage or salary?

Write up your findings in the form of a report.

CHAPTER 9

The Personnel Function: Industrial Relations

In order to produce goods and services profitably a firm needs efficient and effective manpower. The objective of firms in the private sector is to make a profit, while those in the public sector are under pressure to use resources – including labour – efficiently. This could be interpreted as keeping costs as low as possible. The labour force in the public and private sectors – the employees – will have their own objectives apart from making sure the firm runs profitably. A major concern of employees is to maintain and improve their own living standards. The principal means of achieving this is through improvements in pay, but increased leisure time, shorter working hours, improved working conditions, security of employment, training and promotion opportunities and job satisfaction all contribute to an employee's standard of living.

It is quite possible for the aims of the firm and the aims of its employees to conflict. This is most clearly seen in the pay relationship. The firm seeks to maximise its profit while employees seek satisfaction of their needs – including higher pay. This may increase the costs of the firm and hence reduce profit. There are other potential sources of conflict, including: the pay differences that exist between workers (**pay differentials**); which group of workers should perform which jobs (**demarcation**); how many workers should perform a particular job (**manning**); the time it takes to perform a given job (**job speed**) and the nature of the work and the working environment (**health, safety and welfare**).

This potential conflict of interests gives rise to the process of industrial relations, which aims to settle these differences. Both the employer and the employee must recognise that they are dependent on each other. Without labour the firm cannot provide goods and services, and similarly labour relies on the firm to provide employment and the means to satisfy its demands for goods and services. Industrial relations is thus concerned with the way in which these two parties – the employer and employee – interact. The way in which employers and employees are organised and the process by which industrial relations are carried out in Britain is the focus of this chapter.

The Organisation of Employees: Trade Unions

Trade unions are groups of working people who have something in common – they are all employees rather than employers. They may also have in common a skill, a trade, an industry, an employer or an occupation. They are formed, financed and run by their members in their own interests, and several have existed for over 100 years. Combinations of workers have existed since medieval times but modern trade unions were born out of the Industrial Revolution and the factory system of the nineteenth century. This was a period of appalling working conditions and low wages for the working population. A single worker was found to be powerless against the strength of the employer. By combining together and collectively withdrawing their labour services workers were far more powerful and managed to gain concessions from employers.

Trade Union Membership

Membership of trade unions at the end of 1987 stood at 10,480,150. This is around 49% of all employees in employment. These union members belonged to 367 different unions. Table 9.1 shows the changes in union membership and the percentage of employees unionised (union density) since 1960. Figure 9.1 illustrates the behaviour of union membership.

Table 9.1. *Union Membership and Union Density, 1960–87*

Year	Union Membership 000s	Employees in Employment 000s	Union Density %
1960	9,835	21,452	45.8
1961	9,897	21,783	45.4
1962	9,887	21,993	45.0
1963	9,934	22,045	45.1
1964	10,079	22,344	45.1
1965	10,181	22,603	45.0
1966	10,259	22,775	45.0
1967	10,188	22,339	45.6
1968	10,191	22,175	45.6
1969	10,470	22,135	47.3
1970	11,178	21,999	50.9
1971	11,126	21,640	51.4
1972	11,351	21,644	52.4
1973	11,447	22,128	51.6
1974	11,755	22,297	52.7
1975	12,184	22,213	54.9
1976	12,376	22,028	56.2
1977	12,846	22,114	58.1
1978	13,112	22,246	58.9
1979	13,289	22,611	58.8
1980	12,947	22,432	57.7
1981	12,106	21,362	56.7
1982	11,593	20,896	55.5
1983	11,236	20,556	54.6
1984	10,994	20,728	53.0
1985	10,716	21,010	51.0
1986	10,598	21,059	50.3
1987	10,480	21,310	49.2

Source: Department of Employment.

Both Table 9.1 and Figure 9.1 demonstrate that union membership was increasing steadily from 1967 to 1979, when membership reached a peak of almost 13.3 million belonging to 453 unions. Both the number of unions and union membership have declined consecutively since 1979. In fact, membership has fallen by 2.81 million in this 8-year period. This decline is partially blamed on the massive loss of

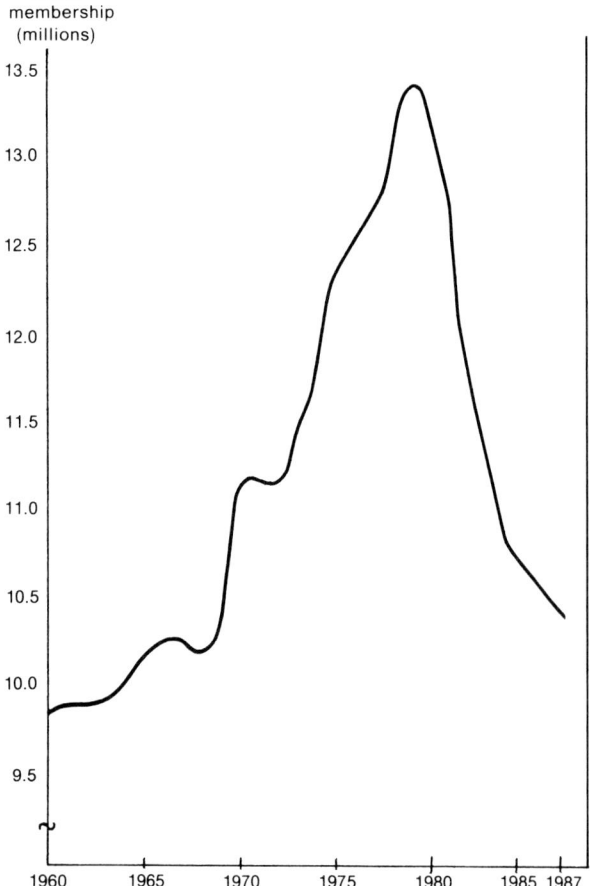

Figure 9.1 The Behaviour of Union Membership, 1960–87

jobs in the manufacturing sector – the traditional stronghold of trade unionism.

Table 9.2 suggests that many trade unions are very small, e.g. 168 of the 373 (45%) unions in 1985 had fewer than 1,000 members but these only accounted for a very small percentage of total union membership (less than half a percent). By contrast, there were 24 unions each with 100,000 or more members, which together accounted for 80% of all trade union membership. In fact the 10 largest unions (those with more than 250,000 members each) accounted for 59% of all union members. Table 9.3 gives details of those unions which had more than 100,000 members in 1987.

Size of Union (Number of Members)	Number of Unions	Union Membership
Under 100	74	10,716
100–499	94	21,432
500–999	37	32,148
1,000–2,499	57	96,444
2,500–4,999	26	107,160
5,000–9,999	14	85,728
10,000–14,999	4	42,864
15,000–24,999	11	203,604
25,000–49,999	23	803,700
50,000–99,999	9	653,676
100,000–249,999	14	2,346,804
250,000 +	10	6,311,724
ALL	373	10,716,000

Source: Annual Abstract of Statistics, 1988 Edition.

Table 9.2. *Trade Unions: Numbers and Membership, 1985*

The largest union – TGWU – had a membership of almost 1.4 million workers. At the other extreme, the Sheffield Wool Shear Workers' Trade Union has a membership of just 17. However, the vast majority of union membership is accounted for by the 24 trade unions listed in Table 9.3. The tendency towards bigger and bigger unions is increasing with trade union mergers, i.e. when two or more unions join together. For example, in January 1988 an amalgamation took place between the ASTMS and TASS to form the Manufacturing Science and Finance Union (MSF), which has a combined membership of 653,000. In March 1989 the GMB amalgamated with the Association of Professional Executive Clerical

Table 9.3. *Unions with 100,000 + Members in 1987*

Union	Membership
Transport & General Workers Union (TGWU)	1,348,712
Amalgamated Engineering Union (AEU)	815,072
General Municipal Boilermakers & Allied Trade Union (GMBU)	803,319
National & Local Government Officers Association (NALGO)	758,780
National Union of Public Employees (NUPE)	650,930
Association of Scientific, Technical & Managerial Staffs (ASTMS)	400,000
Union of Shop Distributive & Allied Workers (USDAW)	387,207
Electrical Electronic Telecommunication and Plumbing Union (EETPU)	369,244
Royal College of Nursing (RCN)	270,053
Union of Construction Allied Trades & Technicians (UCATT)	255,883
Amalgamated Union of Engineering Workers-Technical Administrative & Supervisory Section (TASS)	253,000
National Union of Teachers (NUT)	224,538
Confederation of Health Service Employees (COHSE)	207,841
Union of Communication Workers (UCW)	197,798
Society of Graphical & Allied Trades 1982 (SOGAT 1982)	196,231
National Union of Mineworkers (NUM)	186,753
Banking Insurance & Finance Union (BIFU)	165,939
National Association of Schoolmasters & Union of Women Teachers (NASUWT)	163,051
National Communications Union (Engineering & Clerical) (NCU)	151,407
Civil & Public Services Associations (CPSA)	149,484
National Graphical Association 1982 (NGA 1982)	130,992
Assistant Masters & Mistresses Association (AMMA)	129,392
National Union of Railwaymen (NUR)	117,622
Clearing Bank Union (CBU)	113,108
TOTAL OF ABOVE UNIONS WITH 100,000 MEMBERS OR MORE	8,446,216

Source: Annual Report of the Certification Officer, 1988.

and Computer Staff (APEX), giving the new union a combined strength of almost 900,000 workers.

QUICK QUESTIONS 1

1. *How can employees bring about improvements in their own living standards?*
2. *Why may the aims of a firm and its employees conflict? Give examples to illustrate your answer.*
3. *What do you understand by the term 'industrial relations'?*
4. *What are trade unions and why were they formed?*
5. *Why has trade union membership declined since 1979?*

Types of Unions

The British trade union movement is a mixture of different types of unions, as Table 9.3 suggests. They may be crudely classified into 4 categories: 'craft', 'industrial', 'general', and 'non-manual' (white-collar) unions.

Craft Unions

British trade unionism was founded on the craft unions which developed during the 1850s. To make sure that the standards of work, the supply of labour and the pay of craftsmen were maintained, the craft unions restricted membership to craftsmen who had served a proper apprenticeship to the trade, and they also limited the number of apprentices. Very few wholly craft unions exist today, and where they do they tend to be small, e.g. Society of Shuttlemakers and National Union of Scalemakers.

General Unions

Changes in the method of manufacturing around the turn of the century led to the disappearance of many traditional skills and the growth of industries employing semi-skilled and unskilled workers. Employees in these industries were not catered for by the traditional craft unions and were in a weak position. The general unions began to organise employees in the docks, transport services and gas industry. The GMB, currently the third-largest union, began life in 1889 as the National Union of Gasworkers and General Labourers. After the first world war many unions amalgamated and

the large general unions were formed. Today, the 3 largest trade unions are 'general' unions. The TGWU has members in most industries, e.g. docks, transport, motor manufacturing and engineering. The AEU is regarded as a 'general' engineering union and the GMB represents workers in gas, local government, engineering and boilermaking.

Industrial Unions

These were formed in the early part of the twentieth century with the aim of attempting to represent all the workers in a single industry regardless of the occupation or craft of the individual workers in the industry. There are very few, if any, unions that have achieved the aim of organising an entire industry. In part this is because it is difficult to define the limits of a particular industry, e.g. engineers exist in most industries. Examples of industrial unions are the National Union of Railwaymen (NUR), the National Union of Mineworkers (NUM), the Union Of Communication Workers (UCW), the National Union of Footwear, Leather and Allied Trades (NUFLAT) and the Iron and Steel Trades Confederation (ISTC). In the case of the NUM and NUR, neither have been completely successful in organising the whole industry. By tradition most of the engine drivers and firemen on the railways belong to the Associated Society of Locomotive Engineers and Firemen (ASLEF) and most railway clerks belong to the Transport Salaried Staffs Association (TSSA). In coal mining the National Association of Colliery Overmen Deputies and Shotfirers (NACODS) recruits the mining deputies, and there was a breakaway union formed in Nottinghamshire following the miners' strike in 1984/5 – the Union of Democratic Mineworkers (UDM).

Non-Manual (White-Collar) Unions

These are sometimes called 'occupational' unions and are, as their name suggests, mainly for non-manual workers. Members tend to work in clerical, professional and administrative occupations. They tend to recruit in a particular occupation regardless of the industry the employee works in. Examples of white-collar unions include the Manufacturing Science and Finance Union (MSF), the National Union of Teachers (NUT) and the National Association of Local Government Employees (NALGO). While trade union membership has been declining generally, non-manual unions are the most rapidly expanding, a trend which reflects the growth of non-manual occupations since the war.

The Internal Organisation of a Trade Union

Trade unions have laid down certain rules and regulations which determine the way they run their internal affairs. Every union has a slightly different structure and organisation, although there are characteristics that are common to most unions. A typical union structure is illustrated in Figure 9.2.

Unions are run on a democratic basis with members voting in elections for their representatives at local and national level. The first point of contact between a member and his or her union occurs at the workplace through the **shop steward**. The shop steward is elected by the workers from his or her place of work, and it is the shop steward's duty to represent the workforce on the shopfloor. In the printing industry the shop steward is called the 'Father of the Chapel' (most printing was originally done by monks). The shop steward is a full-time

employee of the firm and is not paid by the union for performing union duties. These include recruiting new members, collecting union dues (subscriptions), negotiating with management over conditions of work, e.g. pay, overtime, health and safety, and distributing union information to its members.

The **branch** of the union is often organised on a local/area basis and generally covers a number of workplaces rather than one factory. This often means that branch meetings are poorly attended, and consequently union officials find it difficult to find out the wishes of the branch membership. In most of the larger unions the branches elect a representative to sit on a district, regional or area committee. These control the running of the branches in the area.

The branches also elect delegates to represent them at the annual or biennial conference. The number of delegates sent to the national conference is determined by the size of the branch. In theory, the conference is the main policy-making body of the union but as it meets infrequently this job tends to be performed by the **National Executive Committee** (NEC). The members of the NEC are usually full-time officials of the union and are elected by the conference or by a vote of all union members. Its duties include administration, finance, wage negotiation and the authorisation of industrial action.

The **General Secretary** of the union is a full-time paid official of the union who is elected by the membership. He or she is responsible for the day-to-day running of the union and for national negotiations with employers. Supporting the General Secretary will be a number of other full-time paid officials working at head office.

The Trades Union Congress (TUC)

The TUC was formed in 1868 in Manchester as a permanent association of trade unions. It is not a union itself and only 90% of trade unions belong to it. The TUC acts as a mouthpiece for the union movement. It holds an annual conference in September each year and each union is entitled to send one delegate per 5,000 members. The conference debates the report of the General Council, and resolutions are passed which form the economic and social policy of the TUC. The membership of the General Council usually consists of the secretaries or presidents of the different unions. It meets for half a day each month.

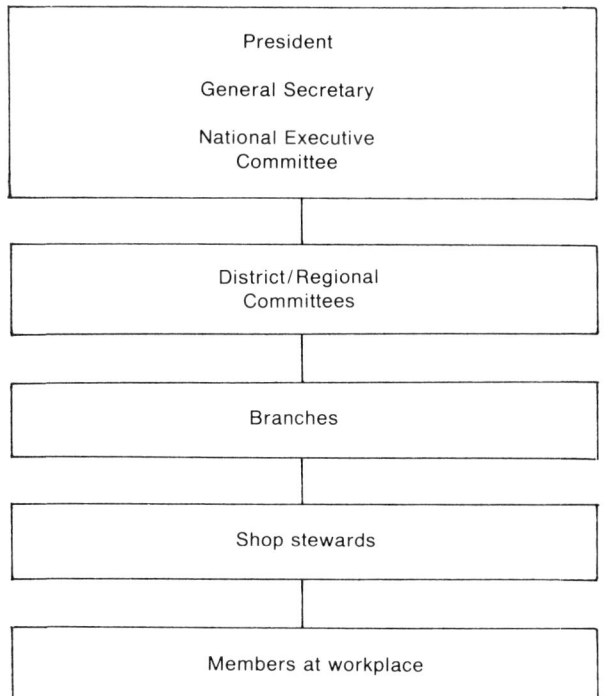

Figure 9.2 A Typical Union Structure

Most of the work of the Council is done in committees, e.g. Economic Affairs, International Affairs, Finance and General Purpose, and Education. The head of the TUC bureaucracy is the General Secretary. The TUC has 6 major departments: Economic, International, Finance, Education, Health and Safety, Organisation and Industrial Relations. These carry out research and provide information for the committees of the General Council.

The Aims and Objectives of Trade Unions

The common function of every trade union is to represent, further and protect its members' interests in every aspect of the work situation. The more specific objectives of trade unions are normally:

1. **Improved conditions of employment**: this covers better pay, shorter working hours and longer holidays.
2. **Improved physical working conditions**: this embraces heating, lighting, ventilation, and health and safety. Unions have been successful in influencing governments to pass legislation on health and industrial diseases, safety, accident prevention and industrial compensation.
3. **Job security**: unions will try to ensure job security for their members. They have sought to protect employees from unfair dismissal, and redundancy. Unions provide legal services to their members, e.g. if they need to be represented before the tribunals which deal with appeals over redundancy, breach of contract and unfair dismissal. They can also offer advice on pension rights, social security benefits and industrial accident compensation.
4. **Income security**: this involves the protection of income when work is interrupted by illness, accident, redundancy or unemployment.
5. **Job satisfaction**: this involves training, retraining and education of employees.
6. **Full employment**: unions try to bring pressure to bear on governments to increase the level of employment or reduce the level of unemployment through calls for increased public expenditure by the government.
7. **Redistribution of income and wealth**: here the unions are concerned with altering the

shares of income that goes to labour and those who provide capital.
8. **A share in the planning and control of industry**: trade unions will try to influence management decisions in favour of their members.
9. **Influence government decisions**: a number of trade unions sponsor MPs in parliament and charge a political levy on their members to pay for this.

QUICK QUESTIONS 2

1. *What are the different types of trade unions that exist in the UK?*
2. *What are general unions and which groups of workers do they represent?*
3. *Why has there been a growth in the membership of white-collar trade unions?*
4. *What is a shop steward and what role does he or she perform?*
5. *Give some examples of the aims of trade unions.*

The Organisation of Employers: Employers' Associations

Just as workers belong to trade unions, employers can also organise themselves into federations or associations. A list of the larger associations is given in Table 9.4.

There was a total of 291 Employers' Associations in 1987, with a membership of 308,027. Some of these associations are large, e.g. the National Farmers Union, while others are small, e.g. the Test and County Cricket Board. They carry out a number of functions for their members including: national negotiations with trade unions to draw up agreements on basic pay and conditions of work; giving information to members on industrial relations; offering trade and technical information to members; giving advice on the development of training schemes; negotiation with government on behalf of their members; and providing management and consultancy services to their members.

Table 9.4. *Large Employers' Associations, 1987*

Name of Association	Number of Members
Engineering Employers Federation	17
Engineering Employers London Association	666
Engineering Employers West Midlands Association	982
13 Other Engineering Employers Associations	2,910
National Farmers Union	114,375
Freight Transport Association	13,588
Test and County Cricket Board	19
Building Employers Confederation	9,251
Electrical Contractors Association	2,296
Chemical Industries Association	154
Motor Agents Association Limited	13,672
British Printing Industries Federation	3,117
National Federation of Retail Newsagents	31,765
Newspaper Society	251
Heating and Ventilating Contractors Association	1,176
Road Haulage Association Ltd	10,407
Federation of Master Builders	19,651
National Pharmaceutical Association	7,114
Federation of Civil Engineering Contractors	376
Incorporated National Association of British and Irish Millers	50
Publishers Association	238
British Paper and Board Industry Federation Ltd	66
Vehicle Builders and Repairers Association	3,347
TOTAL OF ALL 291 ASSOCIATIONS	308,027

Source: Annual Report of the Certification Officer, 1988.

The Confederation of British Industry (CBI)

The CBI was formed in 1965. Its aim is to act as the spokesperson for British industry, seeking to advise and consult the government on policy that affects British industry at home and abroad. It has a membership of nearly 12,000 companies, and a permanent staff led by a Director General.

Professional Associations

In addition to employers' and employees' federations and unions, there are also certain professional groups or associations which have formed to discuss issues relating to their profession and to act as a voice for their profession. The Institute of Personnel Management (IPM), which has its own examinations, publishes its own journal and organises its own annual conference, the Institute of Directors and the British Institute of Management are examples of such associations.

Pay Negotiations

Collective Bargaining

Collective bargaining can be defined as the process by which workers, through their trade union representatives, negotiate changes in pay and working conditions with their employer or an employers' association. Within the UK, collective bargaining takes place at two different levels: national and local.

At the national level, negotiations typically take place between groups of trade unions and the corresponding employers' federation. For example, the Confederation of Shipbuilding and Engineering Unions negotiates on behalf of almost 2 million workers with the Engineering Employers' Federation. Such 'multi-employer' agreements cover particular industries or regions and tend to deal with issues such as minimum rates of pay, the length of the normal working week, redundancy, holidays, pensions and physical working conditions.

At the local level, the participants in negotiations are the local officials of the union, or shop stewards, representing the employees, and managers (personnel or industrial relations specialists), representing the employer. Negotiations can be carried out at company level, e.g. Ford UK, or at the plant level. Table 9.5 shows the importance of the different levels of bargaining for manual and non-manual workers in manufacturing industry.

Table 9.5. *The Level of Bargaining in British Manufacturing*

Level of Agreement	% of Workers Covered by Type of Agreement	
	Manuals	Non-Manuals
Industry-wide	24.0	8.3
Regional	2.7	0.9
All 'multi-employer'	26.7	9.2
Company	21.1	28.6
Plant	46.5	44.7
All 'single-employer'	67.6	73.3
Other	1.3	2.8
No bargaining	4.4	14.7

Source: W. Brown, *The Changing Contours of Industrial Relations* (1981).

Clearly, local or 'single-employer' bargaining is far more important than national or 'multi-employer' bargaining, with over two-thirds of manual workers and nearly three-quarters of non-manuals being covered by local collective bargaining. Ford UK is a large company that prefers to conduct its own bargaining arrangements. It does not belong to the Engineering Employers' Federation and has up to 16 unions to deal with in negotiations. This is called **multi-unionism**, and it does create problems for a company dealing with so many unions in a single place of work. For this reason there has been a growth in so-called **single-union deals**, where one trade union has the sole negotiating rights for a group of employees in a factory. Such deals are associated with the Japanese system of industrial relations and are found in Japanese companies based in the UK.

A central issue discussed in collective bargaining is pay. Negotiations about pay generally take place annually. This is sometimes referred to as the **annual wage round** because particular groups of employers and employees discuss pay rises at particular times of the year, e.g. Fords UK negotiates each September with its workers. The process of collective bargaining involves the union making a pay demand and the management making a pay offer. Typically the union demand and the management offer are not the same, e.g. one strategy of the union is to ask for a large pay rise (above what they expect to get in the end) while management may make a low offer (below what they expect to pay). Negotiation is then needed to try and agree on a pay settlement.

The factors that determine the **level of pay settlements** – the outcome of pay negotiations – are varied. Two pieces of recent evidence, shown in Tables 9.6 and 9.7, indicate what influences these pay settlements.

One important feature to emerge from Table 9.7 is that the factors that influence pay settlements change from year to year according to economic circumstances.

The most common factors determining pay are:

1. **Cost of living**: if inflation rises (prices go up), then unions will demand higher pay and managers may feel sympathetic to union demands. This is related to the idea of increasing real wages and maintaining living standards. Some pay increases are **index-linked**, which means that they are automatically tied to the rate of inflation.
2. **Profitability/Productivity**: wages demands will depend on workers' efforts (productivity) and on whether the company is financially in a position to offer its employees higher pay.
3. **Wage comparisons**: comparisons with what other groups of workers have been paid are sometimes called **pay differentials**, and if one group of workers, e.g. bricklayers, gets a certain percentage pay rise, another group, e.g. plumb-

Table 9.6. *Factors Influencing the Level of Pay Settlements of Manual Workers*

Factors Affecting Pay Settlements	% of Firms Giving the Reason	
	Union Sector	Non-Union Sector
All establishment could afford	11	5
Increasing cost of living	34	29
Going rate in industry	15	23
Merit/Individual performance	4	20
Published norms	3	2
Internal pay structure	2	3
External pay structure	15	15
Government regulation	6	3
Strikes	1	0
Profitability/Productivity	34	35
Economic climate	9	2
Other*	13	7
Not answered	8	3
Number of plants	488	613

* 'Other' includes union pressure, change in payments system, keeping labour/recruitment and changes in working practices.
Source: *British Journal of Industrial Relations*, Vol. 26, No. 3, 1988.

ers, will try to get a similar increase. This pattern of pay bargaining is sometimes called 'leapfrogging'. These groups are not necessarily similar, e.g. manual workers may look at what their bosses are paying themselves in order to determine their own wage demands.

Wage Councils

Not all workers have their terms of employment set by collective bargaining. Over 2.7 million workers have their wages set by **Wage Councils**. These exist in industries where the power of employees is weak because of low union membership. They are found in industries such as hairdressing, retailing, catering, agriculture and hotels, where there are a large number of small firms, a large proportion of female and part-time workers and the industries are highly competitive. A **Wages Inspec-**

Table 9.7. *The 'Very Important' Factors Determining Manufacturing Pay Settlements in 1979/80 and 1983/84*

	% of Replies Giving the Factor as Very Important	
	1979–80	1983–4
Factors Giving an **Upward** *Push to Pay Settlements*		
(a) Level of company/establishment profits	11	21
(b) Management able to pass on large part of pay increase in prices	6	4
(c) A need to improve ability to recruit/retain labour	22	9
(d) Cost of living increases	60	40
(e) Industrial action threatened	2	3
(f) Industrial action taken	3	2
Factors Giving a **Downward** *Push to Pay Settlements*		
(g) Level of company/establishment profits	45	45
(h) Management unable to pass on a large part of a pay increase in prices	38	51
(i) Risk of redundancy if large pay increase awarded	20	21
(j) Direct tax cuts/Employee involvement policies	2	3
Other Factors Influencing Level of Settlement		
(k) Comparisons with other employees in same company	24	21
(l) Comparisons with other employees in same industry	21	17
(m) Comparisons with other local employees	27	18
(n) Comparisons with general level of pay and/or pay increases nationally	26	19
(o) Effects of national/district agreement negotiated by an employers' organisation to which the company belongs	16	9
(p) Effects of a national/district agreement negotiated by an employers' organisation to which the company does not belong	6	3

Source: *British Journal of Industrial Relations*, Vol. 23, No. 3, 1985.

torate, a government body, has the power to check up on firms which are not paying the Wage Council rate of pay, and may prosecute the firm.

Industrial Action

Not all collective bargaining proceeds smoothly. In fact, sometimes the 2 parties may reach a 'stalemate' or 'deadlock' where neither group can agree on what the other group is demanding or offering. A trade union has many different forms of industrial action at its disposal in order to bring pressure on the employer – before and during collective bargaining and also when collective bargaining has broken down. The main forms of industrial action are:

1. **An overtime ban**: this is where employees refuse to work beyond their normal working hours. It can be particularly damaging when a firm's order books are full and when it has a large amount of work. An overtime ban also hits industries which rely on overtime to maintain services, e.g. transport industries such as British Rail and London Underground, and firms using maintenance workers often require long and irregular hours to maintain production. An overtime ban can cause severe disruption without the loss of workers' basic pay.

2. **A 'go slow'**: this is where workers carry out their duties at a slower rate than normal, or use disruptive tactics to ensure production is reduced.

3. **A work to rule**: this is where employees stick rigidly to the rules and regulations which are supposed to govern the way in which they work. It is a useful weapon in some industries, e.g. the railways, where there is a mass of regulations which are ignored under normal working conditions.

4. **A 'sit-in'**: this is where workers occupy a factory to make sure that no goods can leave the factory and to prevent managers from continu-

ing to run the business. Usually, a 'sit-in' is a reaction by workers to a decision to close the factory and make them redundant.

5. **Strikes**: a strike is a planned withdrawal of labour. The firm is unable to function properly and employees who are on strike will not be paid by the firm. Strike action can take a number of different forms. An 'all-out' strike is where workers refuse to work until the dispute is resolved. A 'token strike' is where employees stage a one-day or half-day strike in support of their claim. A 'selective strike' is when a particular group of workers refuse to work. A 'sympathy strike' occurs when one group of workers stage a strike in sympathy with another group who are on strike. This could also involve 'blacking', where one union may ask another to help it by refusing to work or move the products of a firm with which the union is in dispute. An example of 'blacking' was the refusal of railwaymen to move coal from the pit heads to the power stations during the miners' strike of 1984–5. Picketing is common during strike action. It involves trying to persuade fellow workers not to cross the picket line, i.e. enter the factory or bring goods in or out. Mass picketing and secondary picketing (picketing that takes place away from the company involved in the dispute) were considered to be an unsavoury aspect of British industrial relations, and the government has passed legislation to curb strike action and picketing.

In the UK the number of days lost through industrial action fluctuates from year to year, as illustrated in Table 9.8.

During this period, most working days were lost in 1979 and 1984. However, more detailed figures show that in 1979 well over half the working days lost (17,863,000) were in just one dispute – an engineering strike which took place in summer and early autumn. The figures for 1984 show that 83% of the working days lost (22,483,000) were the result of the miners' strike. The average duration of industrial action tends to be very short, e.g. in 1982 the 5,313,000 working days lost involved 2,103,000 workers, so that each worker who took industrial action lost about 2.5 days work. This is not particularly long, and estimates suggest that for every 1

Table 9.8. *Stoppages of Work in the UK 1970–87*

Year	Number of Disputes	Working Days Lost 000s	Number of Workers Involved 000s
1970	3,906	10,980	1,801
1971	2,228	13,551	1,178
1972	2,497	23,909	1,734
1973	2,873	7,197	1,528
1974	2,922	14,750	1,626
1975	2,282	6,012	809
1976	2,016	3,284	668
1977	2,703	10,142	1,166
1978	2,471	9,405	1,041
1979	2,080	29,474	4,608
1980	1,330	11,964	834
1981	1,338	4,266	1,513
1982	1,528	5,313	2,103
1983	1,352	3,754	574
1984	1,221	27,135	1,464
1985	887	6,402	791
1986	1,053	1,920	720
1987	901	3,525	856

Source: Department of Employment Gazette (various issues).

day lost to industrial action 40–50 are lost through sickness and accident. In 1982, for example, 281 million days were lost through sickness or accident, compared with 5.3 million through strikes.

The Causes of Industrial Action

Workers take industrial action for a number of reasons. Details of the causes of strike action for 1983 are shown in Table 9.9.

The most common cause of strikes in 1983 was pay (40.5% of the total), involving wage rates, earnings and fringe benefits. This was followed by manning and work allocation questions (21.3% of the total), involving the number of employees required to operate a production process and which workers are allowed to perform what jobs. The latter is sometimes called demarcation. In British Rail the idea of one-man-driver-only trains is an example of a manning change. The unions have suggested that driver- and guard-operated trains provide a better quality and safer service although the wages of the guard add to the cost of the company and the price of the tickets. As far as demarcation is concerned, employees will try to hold onto jobs that have traditionally been performed by them. This has the effect of restricting the employer in the use and allocation of labour. To get round this problem more firms have begun to introduce 'multiskilling' agreements where workers are more flexible in the jobs they are expected to perform.

Conciliation and Arbitration

When collective bargaining comes to a stalemate, then one option may be to call on the services of ACAS – the **Advisory, Conciliation and Arbit-**

Table 9.9. *Reasons Given for Industrial Action, 1983*

Reason	Strikes No.	%	Working Days Lost 000s	%	Workers Involved 000s	%
Pay	548	40.5	2,311	58.1	290.1	53.4
Duration and patterns of hours worked	49	3.6	104	2.6	20.3	3.7
Redundancy questions	136	10.0	658	16.5	93.7	17.3
Trade union matters	70	5.2	78	2.0	9.9	1.8
Working conditions and supervision	134	9.9	172	4.3	27.0	5.0
Manning and works allocation	288	21.3	321	8.1	63.0	11.6
Dismissal and other disciplinary measures	127	9.5	336	8.4	38.6	7.2
TOTAL	1,352	100	3,980	100	542.6	100

Source: Department of Employment Gazette, July 1984.

ration Service. This is an independent body, set up by the Employment Protection Act 1975, whose services are provided free to employers and employees. There are 4 aspects to its work:

1. **Conciliation**: this is an attempt to settle an industrial dispute at the request of one or more of the parties to the dispute or on ACAS' own initiative. Use of this facility is voluntary. In 1987 ACAS received 1,302 requests for conciliation, and it completed action in 1,147 of these.
2. **Arbitration and mediation**: ACAS will, if the 2 parties agree, refer a dispute to arbitration. In major disputes a Board of Arbitration is set up, with a Chairman sitting with members of the two sides, appointed from lists of employers and trade unionists. In 1987 there were 10 references to Boards of Arbitration. It is far more common for a dispute to be referred to a single arbitrator – there were 122 cases of this in 1987. The decisions of ACAS are not legally binding although in most cases both parties accept the arbitrator's award. If the parties in a dispute do not feel able to promise to accept the arbitrator's award but want positive suggestions on how to resolve their dispute, then a mediator or a Board of Mediation is appointed to make recommendations to solve the dispute. In 1987 there were 13 mediation references made to ACAS.
3. **Advisory and information services**: ACAS has a series of regional offices that provide information for employers, employees and trade union officials. This covers a whole range of employment and industrial relations matters such as legislation, employment contracts and individual employment rights. Booklets on industrial relations topics are also produced by ACAS.
4. **Individual conciliation**: in 1987 ACAS received 40,817 cases for individual conciliation. The vast majority of these concerned claims for unfair dismissal. Either the employer or employee may ask ACAS for help either before or after a complaint has been made to an Industrial Tribunal. In 1987, 59% of cases were settled by ACAS, 22% went to an Industrial Tribunal and 19% were withdrawn. Such tribunals deal with cases arising from employment legislation, e.g. equal pay, unfair dismissal, discrimination and

safety. They have the power to make compensation awards and insist on reinstatement. Their decisions are legally binding.

Trade Union Legislation

The Conservative government that came to power in 1979 had pledged to pass legislation to curtail the power of the trade unions. It was widely recognised that the power of the trade union movement had become excessive and was being abused. For example, in a General Election opinion poll in 1979 three-quarters of the electorate thought that union power was the most important problem facing the (new) government. By contrast, in the corresponding poll in 1987 only 10% even mentioned unions as an important issue. Similarly, a Market and Opinion Research International (MORI) poll reported in *The Times* (7 September 1987) showed that in 1979 69% thought unions had too much power while in 1987 only 31% thought that this was the case. Clearly, a significant reduction in union power had come about. A large part of this is the result of 4 Acts of Parliament – the Employment Acts of 1980, 1982 and 1988 and the Trade Union Act 1984 – designed to curb the monopoly power of the unions.

The provisions of these Acts were justified as a means of giving a voice to the silent majority of trade union members so that they could show their opposition to closed shop agreements, strikes, militant union leaders and political funds. A **closed shop** can be of two types: **pre-entry**, where in order to get a job the person must be a union member, and **post-entry**, where the person must join the union after taking the job. The number of employees covered by closed shop agreements has been declining and in 1984 only 3.6 million employees were governed by such an arrangement. A closed shop arrangement challenges an individual's right to choose not to join a trade union, and in 1979 an Opinion Research Centre poll found that 58% of trade union members agreed with the statement that people have a right to join or not join a union. New closed shop arrangements now have to be approved by 80% of employees entitled to vote in a secret ballot. Any industrial action in support of the closed shop is automatically unlawful and it is unlawful to dismiss or discipline an employee who refuses to belong to a closed shop even where this has been approved in a secret ballot.

Before organising official industrial action a secret ballot of the workforce must now be held. If the majority approve then the industrial action can be taken. It is now unlawful for a trade union to discipline members for not supporting industrial action even where the action has been approved by a ballot. Legal protection is now offered for workers who wish to work in defiance of a strike ballot. Secondary picketing is also illegal and the number of pickets allowed outside their own place of work is limited to 6. Employers can now also use injunctions – court orders – against unions and their own employees when they think the law on strikes and picketing is being broken. A union can have its actions declared unlawful and can also be fined.

Every member of a union's governing body and its General Secretary and President must now be elected by a secret ballot every 5 years. If unions wish to maintain **political funds** – funds that are used to support a political party – a ballot must be held every 10 years to see if this is the wish of the majority.

QUICK QUESTIONS 4

1. *What do you understand by the following terms:*
   (a) overtime ban
   (b) work to rule
   (c) go slow?
2. *Give examples of the types of strike action taken by employees.*
3. *What does the abbreviation ACAS stand for and what are the functions of the service?*
4. *What is a closed shop?*
5. *Why has the government passed Acts of Parliament on trade unions?*

STUDENT EXERCISE

Background Information: The Role and Responsibility of Managers and Shop Stewards

Managers and shop stewards share a concern for the long-term prosperity of the company but there can be a conflict of interests between the 2 groups. An increase in wages is an increase in the firm's costs. A decision to automate – introduce new capital equipment – may mean redundancy for some of the workforce.

Such conflict has little to do with militancy or personalities; it arises from the fact that the different interests of the 2 groups affect the way they would like the company to spend money. Normally these differences can be resolved through discussions and negotiations without the need to resort to industrial action.

Shop Stewards are workplace representatives. Many people think that they are only concerned with pay but they are also involved in matters such as health and safety, training, hours of work, redundancy, dismissal and holidays. A shop steward is also responsible for recruiting new workers into the union.

Managers are often appointed by the directors of the company. They are concerned with running an efficient business and making the best use of resources, including labour, the human resource. They need to maintain contact with the workforce and keep its morale high. A manager's responsibility is not only to make profits but also to be concerned with the welfare of the workforce.

The Collective Bargaining Simulation Game

1. The aim of the game is to achieve agreement between 2 groups. If no agreement is reached, then stalemate occurs. The 2 parties have different information: the unions have one set of information and the management has another set, although some information is common to both groups.
2. Each round of negotiations must be recorded by an impartial observer. It is up to the observer to note down what the union demands are and what the management offers. This must be done for each round of negotiations
3. Each round of negotiations lasts 10 minutes only and there is a maximum of 5 rounds, by which time a settlement must have been reached. Otherwise a stalemate occurs and industrial action may follow.
4. The issues that have to be resolved are typical of collective bargaining situations: pay, hours of work, redundancy, and what to do with the profits of the firm. The negotiations must address these issues.

Shared Information

The following information is available to both parties.

Electron Ltd has been making micro-chips on a greenfield site for some time. Its factory is one of the few situated in the area. Employment opportunities in manufacturing are limited and those jobs available in the area are concentrated in agriculture, which has recently gone into decline. Besides, wages in the agricultural sector are considered to be low by national standards.

The firm, which employs 1,000 workers, 400 of whom are women, has recently won a big export order. Its machinery is old and often needs to be repaired. This means that production is frequently disrupted. To win this order the company has to buy a lot of new machinery to increase production. The introduction of the new machinery will result in some redundancies. The average wage in the country is £4,000 and inflation is forecast to be 8% next year.

Management Information

The Company Accountant reports that last year the financial position of Electron was as follows:

Profit and Loss Account for 1988

Income		Expenditure	
Sales	9,000,000	Materials	3,240,000
Interest on company investments	50,000	Labour	3,400,000
		Overheads	1,140,000
		Maintenance	120,000
		Depreciation	240,000
		Interest on bank loans	110,000
TOTALS	9,050,000		8,250,000

In 1988 the firm produced 1,000,000 units and employed 1,000 production workers. Half of the company profit was paid to the shareholders. The remainder stays in the company and can be used to invest in new machinery so as to secure the new export order for an extra 20,000 units of the product – making a total of 1,020,000 units for 1989. To win the export order new machines must be installed. The company must make a larger profit this year otherwise it runs the risk of being taken over by a foreign multinational.

The economics involved in buying the new machinery to win the export order are straightforward:

1. After the shareholders have been paid you have

exactly enough money to buy 10 new machines.
2. A machine can do the work of the equivalent of 20 men.
3. Depreciation and maintenance costs are half what they were in 1988 if **all** the new machines are installed. If not, then depreciation and maintenance fall by 2.5% for each machine introduced, e.g. if 8 machines are introduced then depreciation and maintenance costs fall by 20% (2.5% × 8).
4. Any money not invested in the new machinery can be invested. It earns a rate of interest of 10%.
5. Each redundant employee costs the company £2,500.

Questions

1. What is the average wage per employee?
2. What is the selling price of the product?
3. What was the gross profit of the company last year?
4. How much is given to shareholders and how much of this is available to buy new machinery?
5. What is the cost of each new machine?
6. If the firm installs all the new machines how many redundancies will the firm have to make?
7. How much will the company save in wage payments in a year?
8. If you get exactly what you want and assuming that you do not offer a pay increase to your workforce, what will be the profits of the company this year? (Note that materials costs rise in relation to output, so you have to calculate the material cost per unit. Also take into account the savings on depreciation and maintenance.)

On the basis of the above information and your answers to these questions, work out your bargaining strategy for the game.

Union Information

The company accounts presented above show the financial position of Electron in 1988. These figures relate to the firm producing 1,000,000 units and employing 1,000 production employees. Half of the company profit was paid to shareholders. The remainder stays in the company and can be used to invest in new machinery so as to secure the new export order for extra units of the product. To win the export order new machinery must be installed. Rumour has it (and it is no more than a rumour) that each machine can do the work of 25 men. The company needs to make a larger profit this year otherwise it runs the risk of being taken over by a foreign multinational.

You know the following – **for certain** – about the economics involved in buying the new machinery:

1. Depreciation and maintenance costs are half what they were in 1988 if **all** the new machines are installed. If not, then depreciation and maintenance fall by 2.5% for each machine introduced, e.g. if 8 machines are introduced then depreciation and maintenance costs fall by 20% (2.5% × 8)
2. Any money not invested in the new machinery can be invested. It earns a rate of interest of 10%.
3. Each redundant employee costs the company £2,500. You would like to increase this.

Questions

1. What is the average wage per employee?
2. What is the selling price of the product?
3. Calculate the labour productivity of each man.
4. What was the gross profit of the company last year?
5. How much is given to shareholders and how much of this is available to buy new machinery?
6. To bring your union members up to the national average wage, what percentage increase in pay will you ask for?
7. Calculate the effect of this on the company's profits for last year.

On the basis of the above information and your answers to these questions, work out your bargaining strategy for the game.

Use a table like the one below to keep the results at the end of each round of negotiations. Note what happens to the position of each group through each round of negotiations.

Union–Management Bargaining Positions Table

Round	Union Position	Management Position
One		
Two		
Three		
Four		
Final outcome		

STUDENT EXERCISE

Read the following article and answer the questions that follow.

The squalor behind the bright fast food lights

The hamburger economy relies on youngsters who are overworked and underpaid. Steven Percy and Harriet Lamb report on a new exploitation

"CAN I help you, Sir? That will be £1.60 please." The 100-second sale put more in McDonald's computerised till than Clare will earn in an hour.

The hamburger economy has come to town. One in ten young people walk straight from the classroom into hotel and catering. Many go into the multinational fast food chains, where sales are growing by 25 per cent and profits even faster.

"I was desperate for some money and there wasn't much else going," said Clare, who at 17 left Wales looking for work and ended up in the Brighton McDonald's. 'It was awful work and I was rang up on my rest day to go in. But there's nothing at all for 17-year-olds. I don't know how the government expects you to make out."

More than 19,000 people work under a McDonald's cap with 4,000 new "crew members" joining the payroll last year alone. As the haemorrhage in manufacturing jobs continues, Big Mac has become one of London's five largest employers. It's a shining example of the service sector heralded by the government as Britain's new economic saviour.

But behind the neon lights is a slum industry which feeds on those discriminated against in the labour market – women, ethnic minorities, and the young. "No one ever stays more than 6 to 9 months," said one ex-worker. "It's the pressure, heavy hours, awful pay and it's a degrading job – having to clean tables and scrub floors in front of all the customers – and always having to smile."

Working in fast food has never been the same since the Burger Baron hit the British high street 13 years ago. McDonald's revolutionised the industry with a new production process. Each outlet is a factory which combines the old mass standardised production of the assembly line with the new Japanese emphasis on flexibility.

Workers' skills are eliminated by hi-tech computerised machinery which does the cooking for you and regulates your movements to the second. Each task is systematically planned; from Sheffield to Singapore workers follow the identical 19 steps to prepare and bag the identical French fries. No creative chefs, no apprentices wanted on this burgerline where every routine task is learnt in a day. That leaves McDonald's free to follow a cheap, flexible labour policy.

High productivity and tight labour control go hand in hand. Always under-staffed, workers are kept smiling at the customers but at each other's throats. Every four months they fall in line for a gold merit star, bringing 5 to 15p extra. Workers with more stars chase those stationed below to meet production targets – they have to, their next pay rise is at stake.

Three-quarters of McDonald's workers are under 21, many still at school. "We're under pressure from head office," said one store manager, "to hire as many under-18-year-olds as possible and we worry more about them leaving. Even if we give 20p an hour extra to keep them on, we cut costs."

Lakshmi, a McDonald's veteran at six months, has won two gold merit stars taking her pay from £1.58 to £1.74 an hour. Even if she works a 39-hour week – many don't – she'll get £67 at the top which puts her firmly at the bottom of the pay league along with hairdressers, cleaners, shop assistants and agricultural workers. In 1985 some 60 per cent of all women in hotel and catering fell below the DHSS poverty line of £41.40.

Even tougher times are ahead for young workers. Rates in the fast food industry are set by the Wages Council. But the 1986 Wages Act stripped workers under 21 of all legal rights to a minimum rate or holiday pay. According to the Low Pay Unit, young people face cuts of 40 to 50 per cent while the incentive is there to fire them at an age when higher rates become obligatory. Britain is now one of the few industrialised countries in the world with no protection for young workers.

"Flexible labour practices" – the employers' new buzzword – are sweeping the high street. "We don't have full and part-timers here," said one store manager. "Everyone at McDonald's works flexible hours."

Julie knows all about that: "Yesterday I was meant to go home at midnight but they were short-staffed and asked me to clean up till 2.30 in the morning. I didn't want to but there was nothing else I could do! A lot of us are working 12 hours without proper breaks." One woman has done 86 hours over her scheduled time in the past three weeks and John hasn't had a day off for months. They keep ringing him up on his rest day." McDonald's pays no overtime rate.

The Crew Handbook – "Welcome to the McDonald's team" – spells out the motive behind flexibility: "Your hours of work cannot be permanently guaranteed because the number of staff we employ depends on how busy the restaurant is."

Labour costs at any outlet must never exceed 15 per cent of sales. "It is very tight," said one manager. "If sales are down, labour costs must come down: you have to cut the staff and make those remaining work harder." He had hired large numbers of Italian students for the unwrapping of a new London store on Christmas Eve: "But we soon got rid of them once things had settled down."

Fast food workers fill the ranks of those on the so-called "periphery" of the new labour order. Today, one in four British workers are part-time, the vast majority women. Along with temporary workers, they have felt the sharp end of Tory legislation designed to remove any remaining "rigidities" in the labour market.

Unless they clock up five years, those working under 16 hours have none of the basic employment rights – such as redundancy or maternity pay, time off for trade union activities, or to claim for unfair dismissal. And the White Paper – Building Business Not Barriers – proposes to raise that to 20 hours.

"It's the 150,000 kids out there that make us tick. If the unions succeed at McDonald's, then my job has failed" said Jim Kuhn, chief management consultant. He's good at his job, and would go along with the company claim that workers don't need unions – they have "rap sessions" to "get it off their chests" with management.

"The company is totally anti-union," said one store manager. "If you want to start a union they'll hear about it and sack you." At one West London store the crew were so fed up they decided to start their own union. McDonald's closed down the restaurant, sacked the lot and didn't reopen until they'd got new staff. None of the managers belong to the union either. Not a single one."

Less than 10 per cent of workers in hotel and catering are unionised. They are a key target of the TGWU's and GMB's new recruitment campaigns. "At the moment we're a long way from tackling McDonald's," says David Turnbull, TGWU. "The main problem to building any organised base is the massive staff turnover and the part-time nature of the jobs. But there are ways, and the campaign demands – full-time rights for part-time workers – are the correct ones." The first inroads have been made: Casey Jones workers are in the NUR.

Back on the menu: Working for Big Mac. Available for £1.50 including post and packing from Transnationals Information Centre London, 9 Poland Street, London WC 1.
Source: The Guardian.

---

1. What proportion of young people enter the hotel and catering industry from school?
2. How rapidly have fast-food sales been growing and what are the reasons for this growth?
3. Explain the term 'haemorrhage in manufacturing jobs'. Why is the 'service sector heralded by the government as Britain's new economic saviour'?
4. Why is the fast-food industry described as a 'slum industry'?
5. What do you understand by 'discrimination in the labour market'? Give examples to illustrate your answer.
6. What is the average length of a job in the fast-food industry?
7. What are the advantages of the 'gold merit star'

for (a) the employer and (b) the employee?
8. What proportion of McDonald's staff are under 21?
9. What is a typical hourly rate of pay at McDonald's and what other groups of workers in the economy are low-paid?
10. Who or what determines the rate of pay in the fast-food industry?
11. What percentage of workers in Britian are part-time? Who forms the majority of this group?
12. Describe some basic employment rights. How old do you have to be and how long do you have to have worked before you get these?
13. Why doesn't McDonald's want to allow trade unions in its organisation?
14. What percentage of workers in hotel and catering

are unionised? Why is this figure so low?

15. What advantages would employees get from belonging to a trade union?

16. What do the abbreviations TGWU, GMB and NUR stand for?

PROJECT AND ASSIGNMENT SUGGESTIONS

1. Select a well-known national trade union and find out as much as you can about its membership, structure and functions. Write to the union's headquarters and ask for any information they can provide to help you with your investigation. The main points you should consider are:

   (a) How can the union be classified and what types of workers does it represent?

   (b) How does the union describe its aims and policies?

   (c) How many members belong to the union?

   (d) What is the cost of membership?

   (e) How is the union organised? Draw an organisation chart showing the main elements in the union's structure.

   (f) How many full-time officials does the union employ?

   (g) Has the union been recently involved in any industrial disputes? If so, write a short account of the circumstances of the dispute.

2. Using newspaper reports and other news sources, make a study of a topical industrial dispute. Analyse the causes of the dispute and write a short summary of the position taken by both the management and the union. Describe the tactics of the union and say whether you think these are likely to be successful. Make a list of the costs of the dispute to the employees involved and to the firm or firms affected. Describe the steps taken to solve the dispute, including any involvement from outside organisations.

3. Find out more about the work of national organisations concerned with industrial relations. Write an account of the work of the Confederation of British Industry, the Trades Union Congress and the Advisory Conciliation and Arbitration Service. Illustrate your study where possible with recent examples of the involvement of these organisations in the attempt to settle industrial disputes.

Producing and Selling

CHAPTER 10

The Location and Scale of Production

Production: The Organisation of the Manufacturing Process

Production can be defined as the process which converts raw materials into a finished product. In relation to production the company needs to ask itself 4 questions:

1. **Where should we produce?** This is known as the 'location decision'.

2. **What should we produce?** This will depend on whether the firm is **market-orientated** or **production-orientated**. If the firm is market-orientated then the products the company produces will be determined by what the consumer wants. Information about these wants is obtained by a process known as **market research** (examined in more detail in Chapter 13). If the firm is production-orientated then it will develop and produce a product without market research, i.e. it is unaware of what the consumer wants. This is far more risky than market orientation.

3. **How should we produce it?** This question concerns the method of production and looks at production techniques, e.g. can the product be assembled by robots, can it be mass-produced or does it require skilled craftsmen?

4. **How much should we produce?** The amount of output that the firm decides to produce will be determined partly by its own objectives. If the firm wants to make as large a profit as possible – **profit maximisation** – it needs to know two things in order to decide how much to produce: (a) the revenue its gets from selling the product and (b) the costs of producing the product. The difference between the firm's revenue and costs is its profit. A firm's revenue will depend on the price of its product and the amount it sells at that price. Clearly, the price of the product will influence the quantity that is sold. The pricing policy of the firm is looked at in more detail in Chapter 12. The costs of production can be classified and calculated in a number of ways. This is examined in Chapter 11.

Production Location

One of the most important decisions a firm must make is where to site its factories. Since such decisions are not taken every day they are described as 'long term'. The decision to locate a factory in a particular place is influenced by many factors, including the following:

1. **Closeness of raw materials**: some firms have to locate near to their raw materials supply because such materials may be too bulky and expensive to transport. The 'extractive' or primary industries have very little choice of location. Mining, quarrying and oil exploration/drilling have to be based at the product's source. Similarly, the fishing and ship-building industries are located on the coast. Steel manufacture, which is centred in Sheffield, requires three basic raw materials: coked coal, iron ore and limestone, all of which are found close to this major city.

2. **The availability of power**: at the start of the Industrial Revolution a very important location factor was the availability of power. For example, one reason why the textile industry was established in the Pennine valleys of Lancashire and Yorkshire was that the rivers

running off the Pennines could be dammed to drive water mills to power the machines. The invention of the steam engine, which depended on coal, caused the location of the cotton mills to move to where coal was in plentiful supply, e.g. Manchester. Today, the growing use of electricity, oil and gas as sources of power has meant that many industries are far more flexible in terms of their location, they no longer need to be close to their direct source of power.

3. **Transport facilities**: a location close to good road, rail, sea or air links is important to many firms, especially as more and more products are being sold both nationally and internationally. During the Industrial Revolution many industries located along the banks of the canals. Today, location close to motorway links and airports is an important factor.

4. **Availability and cost of factors of production**: no matter where a firm locates it will always need an adequate supply of labour, i.e. not only a sufficient quantity of labour but also quality in terms of education, training and skills. If sufficient labour is available, the firm may have to do less training. The cost of labour is also important to the firm. One reason why firms in the 1980s have been locating away from the South East is that labour is not available in the right quantities and at the right price. Similar arguments apply to land, office space and rents in the South East.

5. **Closeness to the market**: firms which manufacture a product can choose to locate either near to their raw materials or close to their market, and the type of finished product is an important factor in this decision. If the product is fragile or very valuable, the firm may wish to be near its market so as to reduce the risk of pilferage or damage during transportation. Another important factor in the decision to locate near the market is the cost of transportation relative to the value of the product. If the finished item is bulky, low in value and expensive to transport, then it is better to site production near the market. On the other hand, if the finished product is lightweight, has a high value and is cheap to transport, then production does not have to be so close to the market. For example, if bulky and fragile valves had not been replaced by transistors and microprocessors, high transport costs would have made it more difficult for the Japanese to dominate the world electronics market.

One sector that has very little choice in its

Figure 10.1 A Modern Workplace

location is the service sector. The service industries, such as insurance, banking, restaurants, retail outlets and hairdressing salons, must be situated where the demand for those services exist. Typically, this will be in or around populated areas. However, the increase in car ownership has given greater mobility to families (and hence consumers), which means they can now do their shopping in 'out-of-town' locations where large hypermarkets and superstores are being sited.

6. **Government policy**: Britain is described as being a mixed economy (see p.12) in the sense that the government intervenes to try and improve the workings of the economy. Such influence extends to the location of industry. Government action on industrial location dates back to the 1930s and arose from concern over the regional imbalance of employment and unemployment. With the decline of many of the traditional industries in the North, e.g. mining, shipbuilding, steel and textiles, and the growth and prosperity of many new or 'sunshine' industries in the South, e.g. electronics, data processing, banking and finance, a 'gap' in economic prosperity has arisen – sometimes called the **North–South divide**. The government has attempted to persuade businesses to locate in certain parts of the country and has also tried to dissuade businesses from siting their firms in other areas. The various ways in which it can do this are examined in Chapter 21. It can offer subsidies, tax relief, rent-free premises and can prohibit development in areas designated as 'green belt' land. Government policy may also be important in encouraging multinational companies to locate in Britain. The Japanese firms, for example, seem increasingly attracted to Britain as a production site. This is explained in more detail in Chapter 20.

It is very unlikely that any one particular location will offer all the benefits of the factors described above and so a firm has to weigh up the advantages and disadvantages of a particular site. Today, largely as a result of the improvement in transport facilities and the ready availability of power, many businesses find themselves free to choose the location of their next factory. Such firms are said to be 'footloose' – they can literally locate anywhere.

The location of the car industry in general, and Ford UK in particular, offers some insight into the importance of the factors discussed above. The main production centres are at Dagenham on the outskirts of London (Ford UK), at Luton (Vauxhall's), at Cowley near Oxford (Rover Group), the West Midlands (Birmingham, Wolverhampton and Coventry) and Washington near Sunderland. Each of these sites is very near to a large centre of population. The plant at Sunderland was established partly as a result of government intervention and those in the West Midlands were the result of a strong engineering tradition. When siting his very first plant in Great Britain, Henry Ford was strongly influenced by the development of new housing areas at Dagenham in Essex. It represented a ready supply of educated labour of good quality. Cheap land was available and a large market was on hand in London. Further, the River Thames offered access for raw materials and made export of finished vehicles that much easier.

QUICK QUESTIONS 1

1. *What do you understand by the term 'location decision'?*
2. *How do firms decide on what goods and services to produce?*
3. *Why do a lot of firms locate in the South East, where factors of production are relatively more expensive?*
4. *What is a 'footloose' industry and why aren't firms in the service sector 'footloose'?*

Production Methods

The type of product or service produced by an organisation will not only influence its production location but also the type of production system or production method it adopts. There are three types of production method: job, batch and flow.

Job production typically occurs when a single product is to be made to a customer's own requirements. The production of certain cars (luxury sports cars, e.g. Morgans), the design and building of your own home, 'designer clothes' and double glazing are examples of job production. In the case of double glazing, the windows and doors of the house and what the customer wants, e.g. patio doors, different tinted and coloured glass and the shape of the windows, differs from person to person. For these reasons the double glazing manufacturer manufactures each door and window to meet each customer's individual requirements.

Batch production is where products are made in groups, sets or batches (hence the name) because a firm has similar orders for the same product from different customers. This production method is commonly found in the engineering industry. Many motor vehicle components are produced in batch. Other examples include aircraft, small housing estates, ships, printing of books and the manufacture of clothes.

Flow production is frequently found in manufacturing industry where the demand for a product is sufficiently large to justify production being arranged so that the product is assembled from a series of operations or repetitive tasks. Many durable goods such as washing machines, cars, televisions and radios are produced on a flow production or 'mass-produced' basis. In car production, for example, the production process is broken down into a series of very simple operations and the end product is highly standardised, with very few variations on the basic model. This method of production normally requires a large amount of capital machinery, and as each operation on the production line is simple and repetitive the people employed tend to be unskilled or semi-skilled.

Technological Change

Flow production methods have greatly increased the ability of firms to produce more and more goods and services for the consumer. **Technological change** has also altered the type of goods produced by firms and also the way in which they are produced. Technological change can be divided into 2 types. First, there is technological change in products (**product innovation**), which leads to the manufacture of new goods and services. Examples here include microwave ovens, cordless telephones, compact disc players and FAX machines. Secondly, there can be technological change in production methods (**process innovation**), which leads to new ways of producing goods and services. Examples here include the use of robots to manufacture and paint cars, to the use of computers to maintain our bank accounts, cash dispensers allowing us to with-

draw money even when the banks are shut, and bar codes, laser pens and computerised cash registers in retailing.

Such changes have a whole host of implications. Consumers benefit from technological change since it means there is a greater variety of goods available, and generally the price of new products falls as more units are produced. Good examples of this are video recorders, pocket calculators, television sets and compact disc players. For the firm, technological change in production methods should allow it to reduce production costs (which leads to lower consumer prices) but it may possibly lead to a fall in the number of people it employs. Against this some

Figure 10.2 New Products

people argue that technological change creates jobs because more labour is required to produce the new products that are bought by consumers as the price falls.

Quality Control

Having produced the product the firm has to ensure that it conforms to a given standard or quality. This is the aim of **quality control**. It involves setting a standard that the product is expected to conform to and then testing whether the product has reached that standard. A firm has 2 options for testing the quality of its products. First, it could examine and inspect each and every item made. This is time-consuming and expensive, although certain products do follow this demanding method of quality control. Ceramic tiles, for example, are individually checked and sorted into 'first' and 'second' quality and each box of tiles contains a ticket which verifies that they have been inspected. Each 'checker' is given a number so that if there has been a customer complaint about the product's quality the firm can trace back who was responsible for checking the product. The second system of quality control involves inspecting a group or sample of the products, and, providing the number of defective goods is below a certain level, the firm will allow the goods to be sold. Although this system is less time-consuming and less expensive, the firm runs the risk that some defective products will find their way onto the market. Customer complaints about these may damage a firm's reputation. The use of serial numbers on products has allowed firms to see whether there is a pattern of defects relating to goods produced. If this is the case the firm may call these goods back from the consumer for modification, repair or replacement.

QUICK QUESTIONS 2

1. *What are the 3 types of production method that a firm can adopt? Give examples of the sorts of products that are made by each method.*
2. *What are the 2 types of technological change?*
3. *How do consumers benefit from technological change?*
4. *What are the 2 types of quality control that a firm can adopt?*

The Scale of Production

A large amount of goods and services today are produced by large-scale firms. Here the word 'scale' means size. In examining the size of a business it is useful to distinguish between units of production and units of ownership. A **unit of production**, also known as an establishment or plant, may be an office, a factory or a shop. A **unit of ownership** or control is a firm or an enterprise. A firm may own a number of plants, e.g. Marks & Spencer PLC owns a number of stores throughout the country as well as having one in Paris. An **industry** consists of a collection of firms producing similar goods or services for a particular market.

Many of the large firms today began as small family businesses, e.g. Marks & Spencer started out as a small market stall in Leeds but it has grown to become a large PLC. Firms can also grow by taking over or merging with other firms. One of the main reasons why firms wish to grow is that in many industries 'bigger means better'. Larger firms can be more efficient in producing more output and can sell it at a lower price. In these circumstances small firms may find it difficult to compete with large firms. This is not true in all industries, and some small firms continue to survive and flourish. As an example, consider the brewing industry. In 1985 there were 75 brewery companies in the UK, although the output of the industry was dominated by 8 large companies, as shown in Table 10.1.

The output of the industry was 38 million barrels in 1985, and 78.3% of this was manufactured by the 8 largest firms. This is given by the **concentration ratio** figure (see p.228) which measures the importance of large firms in an industry. As the table shows, the largest firm, Bass, made 20.2% of the industry's output and the 2 largest firms, Bass and Allied, made 32.8% of the industry's output. Some small independent brewers do exist in the industry but there are advantages to being a large firm. These are discussed below.

Economies of Scale

Large firms dominate certain industries because their size or scale gives them advantages over smaller firms. By producing large amounts of output the

Table 10.1. *Beer Sales by 'National' Brewers and Concentration Ratios, 1985*

	Output	Share	Concentration Ratio
	(million barrels)	%	%
Bass	7.7	20.2	20.2
Allied	4.8	12.6	32.8
Whitbread	4.3	11.3	44.1
Scottish and Newcastle	3.5	9.2	53.3
Watney-Truman	3.4	8.9	62.2
Courage	3.3	8.7	70.9
Carlsberg	1.6	4.2	75.1
Guinness	1.2	3.2	78.3
Total production of the 'Big 8'	29.8		
UK Total	38.0		

Source: 'Industry Information' *The Economic Review*, January 1989.

large firm is able to reduce the average cost, cost per unit or unit cost of each item produced (see Chapter 11). Reductions in average costs due to increased output are known as **economies of scale**. These can be classified as either internal or external economies of scale.

Internal economies of scale occur inside the firm itself, regardless of what is happening in the industry or region where the firm produces. Car manufacturing, chemicals and brewing are examples of industries where individual firms can enjoy internal economies of scale. **External economies of scale** result from the expansion of the industry as a whole or when a number of firms locate together in a particular area. The Lancashire cotton industry is generally given as an example of external economies of scale.

Internal Economies of Scale

The major internal economies of scale can be classified under the headings below.

1. **Technical economies**: these arise from the technical nature of the production process itself and can be further divided into 4 categories: (a) specialisation, (b) indivisibilities, (c) increased dimensions, and (d) principle of multiples.

   (a) A large firm may be able to take advantage of the greater **specialisation** of labour and machinery. Even in the production of a product as simple as a pin there are 18 distinct operations, including drawing the wire, straightening it, cutting it, pointing it and grinding it to receive the head. Adam Smith, who wrote *The Wealth of Nations* in 1776, suggested that with labour specialising in these different tasks productivity (output per person) was 5,000 pins per day. If each employee was asked to make pins of their own they could only produce a few dozen per day. This is because people become better at performing one task and it is far easier to learn – practice makes perfect. It also means the person is stationed at one workplace and not having to move around to perform several operations, which costs time and money.

   (b) When production has been broken down into simple tasks, more machinery can be introduced to the production process. Automatic assembly, handling and packing machines can be used instead of manual labour. Some types of capital equipment though are only economic to use if they are producing a large amount of output. This is called **indivisibilities**, i.e. where large machinery can only be used effectively when it is producing large amounts of output. Two contrasting examples of scales of production are the modern oil refinery, which requires capital machinery of great size, and a fish and chip shop, whose capital equipment consists of small items like a fryer and oven.

(c) The greater size of capital equipment may also reduce the unit costs of production. This is sometimes called **increased dimensions**, and such arguments usually apply to the transport sector, e.g. buses, trains, planes and articulated lorries, all of which have been increasing in size (dimension) over time. Industries that make use of vats, storage tanks and furnaces, e.g. chemical production, iron ore production and petroleum refining, also benefit from increased dimensions. A simple example illustrates the benefits. Imagine a firm has the opportunity of buying one of two towing trailers. The dimensions of the larger trailer are twice those of the smaller trailer. The cost of the trailer is related to the amount of metal in it (the surface area), while the trailer's carrying capacity is related to its volume. Doubling the size of the trailer increases the surface area 4 times but increases its volume by 8 times. It can carry 8 times as much but will not cost 8 times as much to run.

(d) A lot of industries make use of a variety of machinery to produce components that go to make up the finished product. It is unlikely that the speed of these machines will produce the same number of components per hour, day or week. To illustrate this let us imagine that a firm uses 3 machines (X, Y and Z) that produce 3 separate components which go to make up a final product. If the speeds of the machines were such that X produces 10 units per hour, Y produces 2 units per hour and Z makes 5 units per hour then only 2 finished items would be produced per hour. The pace of production is dictated by the speed of the slowest machine. If the firm only possessed one machine of each type then machines X and Z would be idle for some part of each hour. In fact machine X would be idle for 48 minutes in the hour and

Table 10.2. *The Effect of Different Machine Speeds on Idle Time*

Machine	Production Speed Per Hour	Time Taken to Produce 2 Components (minutes)	Idle Time (minutes)
X	10	12	48
Y	2	60	0
Z	5	24	36

machine Z would be idle for 36 minutes every hour. This information is summarised in Table 10.2.

One way round this problem of having machines (and labour) standing idle is to use more machines in a combination that allows them to work all the time, i.e. at full capacity. In this case the firm has to find the 'lowest common multiple' (the minimum level of output where all machines are working all the time). In this case it is 10 units of the final product per hour. It could use one X machine producing 10 units per hour, 5 type Y machines ($5 \times 2 = 10$) and 2 type Z machines ($2 \times 5 = 10$). In this case no machine would be idle. This is sometimes called the **principle of multiples**, but the option of buying more machinery may only be open to the larger firm.

2. **Managerial economies**: in a small firm, e.g. a sole trader, the owner of the business may have to perform several roles, such as keeping the books, ordering stock, selling, selecting and recruiting employees, and wage and salary administration. A large company can employ specialists in charge of these functions, which brings with it the advantages of **labour specialisation**. Further, the large company can pay higher salaries to attract better staff and hence increase productivity.

3. **Marketing economies**: large firms often buy their raw materials in great quantities. Such bulk-buying allows them to get price discounts. Long-term contracts at fixed prices can also be negotiated with suppliers. The firm knows it can buy at a definite price and knows with certainty what its costs are going to be. The

larger firm is also more likely to employ specialist buyers who know the right time and the right price at which to buy. Again this allows the firm to get its raw materials at a cheaper price. Consumer products such as beer, cigarettes and detergents are sold in large quantities on a national scale and this allows the company to spread the costs of packaging, advertising and distribution over a large number of units sold, e.g. large firms can afford to advertise in the national press and on television. Although it is expensive to use such media, the cost per item sold is low because such a large quantity is sold.

4. **Financial economies**: a large firm has several financial advantages. Large organisations are regarded as more credit-worthy and can therefore obtain bank loans and overdrafts on more favourable terms than smaller firms. Large companies can also raise capital by selling shares on the Stock Exchange. A recent example has been the 'floating' of companies such as British Gas, which has spent large amounts of money advertising the share issue both on television and in the press. This cost of flotation does not rise in the same proportion as the amount of capital raised.

5. **Research economies**: as the number, size and sophistication of high technology industries increase, research and development (R & D) economies are becoming increasingly important. Large firms can usually afford research departments. These may discover new products and processes, which in turn lead to further economies of scale. Larger R & D activities are also likely to attract better researchers with greater productivity. If the firm produces a large amount of output these research costs can be spread over this large volume of output.

6. **Risk-bearing economies**: many large firms are able to reduce trading risks by a policy of **diversification**. They can manufacture a variety of products at different production plants. This means the company's eggs are not all in one basket, and so if the demand for one product falls then this may be offset by an increased demand for another product. A small, single-product firm is much more vulnerable to changes in market conditions.

QUICK QUESTIONS 3

1. *What do you understand by the terms 'plant', 'firm' and 'industry'?*
2. *What is meant by internal economies of scale?*
3. *Why has the size of aircraft, articulated lorries and boats been increasing in recent years?*
4. *What type of advantages may a large firm possess over a small firm?*

External Economies of Scale

External economies of scale are the advantages that a firm enjoys from the growth in the size of the industry in general, and they are especially important when an industry is heavily localised. In a case such as this, external economies are sometimes called **economies of concentration**. The following are some examples of external economies which may be available to firms:

1. **Labour**: the concentration of similar firms in one locality may lead to the creation of a local labour force that is skilled in the various techniques of the industry. Some areas are typically associated with particular products, e.g. the West Midlands and engineering, Staffordshire and the pottery industry, parts of Lancashire and Yorkshire for cotton and textiles, Leicestershire and Northamptonshire for footwear and leather, and Sheffield for steel. Schools and colleges may develop courses that are suited to the needs of local industry, thus providing firms with labour with the right qualifications and education.

2. **Ancillary services**: once a major manufacturer has established itself in a particular area, then a whole host of related services may grow around it. Banks and insurance companies may provide specialist financial information, component manufacturers provide raw materials, haulage companies offer particular types of transportation, and employment agencies could provide specific types of labour.

3. **Co-operation**: a collection of firms that specialise in the production of a particular product may well form a trade association or society which publishes its own trade journal, embarks on joint ventures and even establishes shared

research facilities. This co-operation is normally of mutual benefit.

4. **Disintegration**: this refers to the specialisation by individual firms in the manufacture of a single component or process. The classic example is the cotton industry in Lancashire, where the production of cotton cloth is broken down into four operations – spinning, weaving, dyeing and finishing. Each of these operations is carried out by a single firm before the product is passed on to another firm for the next process.

Diseconomies of scale

Increasing the size of a firm can bring advantages but it may also bring disadvantages. In other words, if a firm becomes too large for its own good, it starts to encounter disadvantages. These are referred to as **diseconomies of scale**. Diseconomies of scale occur when a firm grows too big and unwieldy to organise. In 1989 Sir James Goldsmith made a bid for BAT (British American Tobacco) Industries, the cigarette and financial services company. He argued that the company had become too large and would perform better if it was 'unbundled' or broken up into smaller companies. The diseconomies of scale that can arise in a large company are normally associated with the management functions of control, co-ordination, communication and motivation.

As seen in Chapter 3, a large company organises itself into specialist departments, e.g. accounts, personnel, production and marketing. If the firm is to operate successfully, the work of these departments needs to be co-ordinated. This becomes far more difficult as the company expands. Co-ordination may be hampered by long lines of communication, e.g. where 2-way communication from top to bottom and back again in a large business takes a long time. Communication breakdown and misrepresentation of information is more likely in large firms. Attitudes of employees and management are crucial to the success of a business. In large firms it may be that the company loses the 'personal touch' that a small firm can enjoy. Employees may feel unable to identify with the goals of the large company and may very rarely, if ever, see the Managing Director. The greater specialisation of labour and the increased use of machinery may make jobs less skilled, requiring far less craftsmanship. If an employee performs only one small part of the production process, they may have very little care or interest in their work. Motivation and control are made more difficult in these situations.

The Size and Survival of Small Firms

Although large firms do possess advantages, as described earlier in this chapter, small firms continue to exist in many industries. But what is the definition of a small firm? The Bolton Committee Report on small firms suggested in 1971 that a small firm was one that employed less than 200 people and had 3 other main characteristics:

1. It had a relatively small market share.
2. It was managed in a personalised way by its owners, who took the major decisions and carried out the main management functions.
3. It did not form part of a larger organisation.

Whilst evidence suggests that the number of large firms is increasing, small firms continue to survive and flourish. There are a number of explanations, including the following:

1. **The limited size of the market**: the ability of a firm to benefit from mass production is limited by the demand for the product. The demand for the product may be too small to justify large-scale production. In isolated, rural communities there is often a general store that sells everything – groceries, drapery, stationery and ironmongery. The market for each of these products is too small to support specialist retail outlets in such a community.
2. **Exclusive products**: the market for a product could be limited by its price where the emphasis is on quality and hand-manufactured goods. In the fashion trade and interior decoration, for example, exclusive and high-quality products are particularly attractive to buyers. The same is true of expensive cars, e.g. from Rolls-Royce and Porsche.
3. **Capital requirements**: in some industries the amount of capital that a business requires is small, e.g. window cleaners need only ladders, leathers, buckets and a van or bicycle. Business

couriers need a motorbike and a phone. These are relatively cheap items of capital compared with, say, the capital required to begin oil refining or chemical manufacture.

4. **Differences in tastes**: firms in some industries have to deal with customers who have different preferences or tastes, e.g. wedding dresses and wedding cakes are typically chosen with a certain design, colour and style in mind. This means the firm cannot mass-produce the item as no other consumer will want exactly the same thing. For this reason dressmakers, tailors and bakers tend to be small businesses.

5. **The personal touch**: in the service sector, as opposed to manufacturing, the emphasis is on personal attention, e.g. hairdressing, dentistry, motor car repairs and equipment hire. The need for individual attention restricts the size of business to sole traders and partnerships.

The Growth of Firms

A business can grow by 2 principal means. First, by **internal growth**, where the firm uses ploughed-back profits and finance raised from banks and other institutions. Growth by this method tends to be slow because profits for reinvestment in the business may not be large and external finance may be difficult and costly to obtain. The second means by which a firm can grow is by combining with other firms. This is called **integration** and involves either a **merger**, where 2 companies agree to join together, or a **takeover**, where one company buys out another. Integration is normally classified into three types: horizontal, vertical and conglomerate.

Horizontal integration occurs when firms producing similar products join together, e.g. 2 car manufacturers, 2 banks or 2 building societies. The objectives of horizontal integration may be to achieve economies of scale, eliminate competition and increase the market share of the company.

Vertical integration occurs when firms at different stages of the production process combine together. It takes 2 forms: **forward vertical integration** is when a firm combines with another at the next stage of the production process. For example, a brewery could expand vertically forwards towards the market by securing more retail outlets, such as public houses or off-licences. **Backward vertical integration** occurs when a firm expands backwards towards its source of supply. A

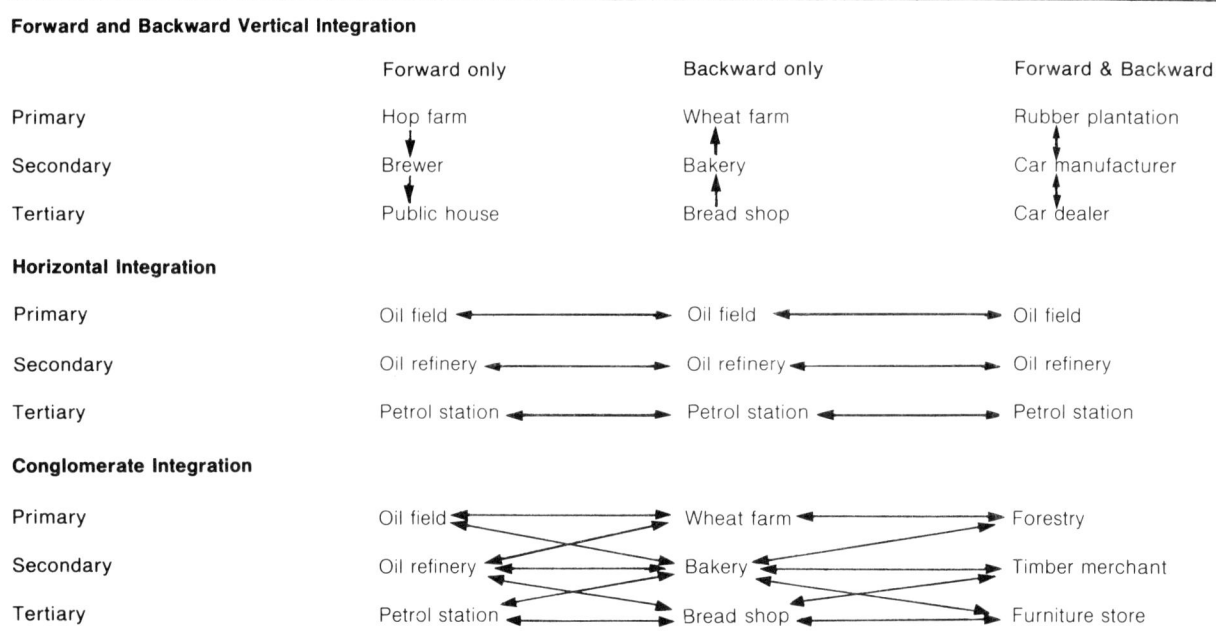

Figure 10.3 Types of Integration

brewery, for example, might try to secure its raw materials by purchasing its own hop farm and bottle manufacturing plant. Alternatively, a clothing retailer may combine with a textile manufacturer.

Conglomerate integration is when there is very little or no link between the products or processes of the 2 combining firms. An example would be a frozen food manufacturer combining with a hotel chain. The idea behind conglomeration is to diversify the product range of the company and spread business risks over a wider range of markets and products.

The various forms of integration are illustrated in Figure 10.3.

QUICK QUESTIONS 4

1. *What type of disadvantages could a large firm suffer?*
2. *What is meant by a small firm and why do small firms continue to survive?*
3. *Classify the following examples of business integration:*
   (a) Alliance Building Society joining with the Leicester Building Society.
   (b) Virgin Records Ltd buying jets to fly people across the Atlantic.
   (c) Shell UK acquiring more petrol stations.
4. *What are the motives for backward and forward integrations?*

STUDENT EXERCISE
Industrial Location and Structure

Study Tables A and B below and answer the questions that follow.

Table A. *The Industrial Structure of Milton Keynes, 1986*

Sector	Jobs	% of Total	Number of Plants	Average size of Plant
1	2	3	4	5(2 ÷ 4)
Agriculture, forestry & fishing	138	0.2	37	3.7
Mineral oil & natural gas	17	*	2	8.5
Electricity, gas & water supply	691	1.1	9	76.7
Extraction of ores & mineral products	0	0	0	0
Metal manufacture	57	0.1	4	14.3
Non-metal products	530	0.9	17	–
Chemicals & man-made fibres	1173	1.9	20	58.7
Mechanical engineering	1552	2.5	75	–
Electrical & electronic engineering	4026	6.5	77	52.3
Motor vehicles & parts	381	0.6	16	–
Other transport equipment	2166	3.5	6	361
Metal goods & instruments	1359	2.2	56	–
Food, drink & tobacco	594	1.0	13	–
Textiles	97	0.2	5	–
Leather, footwear & clothing	600	1.0	16	–
Timber & wooden furniture	581	0.9	44	–
Paper products, printing & publishing	1890	3.1	53	35.7
Rubber, plastics & other manufacturing	1138	1.8	40	–
MANUFACTURING SECTOR	16006	25.9	405	39.5
CONSTRUCTION	3795	6.1	271	14.0
Distribution & repairs	12583	20.4	785	16.0
Hotels & catering	2184	3.5	176	12.4
Transport & communication	3778	6.1	112	–
Banking, finance & insurance	8068	13.1	437	–
Public administration	3694	6.0	89	41.5
Education & health	7845	12.7	199	39
Other services	2830	4.6	255	
SERVICE SECTOR	40982	66.4	2053	20
TOTAL	61767	100.0	2814	21.9

Source: Milton Keynes Development Corporation.   *Percentage too small to be given.

Table B. *Regional Differences in Factor Prices and Labour Supply*

Area	Average Weekly Pay (1987)	Town/City	Unemployment Rate (May 1985)	Office Rent	Commercial Rates
	£		%	£ per square foot	
South East	206.30	Milton Keynes	13.3	9.00	2.60
East Anglia	186.90	Peterborough	13.2	6.50	2.40
South West	189.30	Bristol	11.2	7.00	2.70
Yorkshire & Humberside	188.90	Bradford	15.7	2.50	2.00
North West	190.00	Warrington	13.1	6.50	2.30
Wales	187.20	Swansea	16.5	4.00	1.20

Source: The Observer, 18 May 1986; New Earnings Survey, Department of Employment, 1987; and *Department of Employment Gazette*, June 1985.

In March 1988 there were 137,700 people living in Milton Keynes. The population is generally younger than the average in England and Wales, with a higher proportion of schoolchildren and younger families. The population has grown by 25,700 people since 1983. Between 1984 and 1988 38% of people moving into the area came from the South East and 35% moved from London. The town has excellent communication links with the rest of the country. There were 61,767 employees in employment in 2,814 firms. The distribution of these is shown in the Table A.

1. In which area is labour the most expensive?
2. In which area is labour cheapest?
3. Which city has the highest unemployment rate?
4. Why do firms still locate in Milton Keynes where labour, land and office space is expensive?
5. Which is the most important sector to Milton Keynes? Is this a 'footloose' sector?
6. Which is the most important manufacturing sector? Why do you think the firms in this sector decided to locate in Milton Keynes?
7. Which is the least important industry in Milton Keynes? What does this tell you about the location decision in this industry?
8. In column 5 the average size of establishment is given by the average number of employees per plant. Calculate the missing figures and from this find the sectors that contain (a) the largest firms and (b) the smallest firms on average. Why do you think there is a difference between the size of firms in these sectors?
9. In the construction sector the typical firm has 14 employees. Nationwide, however, there are a few giant firms such as John Laing, Wimpey and Tarmac. Why do the small firms manage to

survive in this sector? What does it tell you about economies of scale in this sector?
10. In the Hotels and catering sector the typical firm has around 12 employees. However, some hotels are very large, e.g. the Savoy, the London Hilton, and others are in large chains, e.g. Grand Metropolitan. In August 1989 the Bass Brewery took over the Holiday Inn chain of hotels. What type of 'integration' is this?

PROJECT AND ASSIGNMENT SUGGESTIONS

1. Find a business which has recently located or relocated in your area. Contact the business and try and find out what factors were important in its location decision. To help you in your investigation you could design a questionnaire based upon the information in the chapter concerning locational considerations. You could extend your investigation to a comparison between two or more businesses to see if the same locational factors are important in each case.
2. Arrange a visit to a local manufacturing business and investigate the organisation of its production process. In particular you should aim to answer the following questions:
   (a) What product or products does the business produce and in what quantities?
   (b) What type of production methods does the firm employ? Does it use different methods for different products?
   (c) What type of technology does the business employ? Is the production process largely capital or labour intensive?

(d) What system is used to check the quality of the goods the business produces?

(e) Are economies of scale important to the business? If so, which types of economies are most important?

Write up your findings in the form of a report. Where appropriate, include statistics referring to the production process to illustrate your answer.

CHAPTER 11

Costs, Revenues and Break-Even Analysis

The Costs of Production

Production costs are usually measured in money terms, and they include items such as payments for wages, rent, machinery, fuel, power and raw materials. The costs that an organisation incurs are normally divided into 2 components: **fixed** and **variable**. A simple cost classification is illustrated in Figure 11.1.

Fixed Costs

As their name implies, fixed costs remain the same as the output of the firm changes. They are sometimes called **indirect costs** or **overheads** and are associated with the fixed factors of production such as land and capital. Fixed cost items include interest on loans, depreciation of machinery and the rent and rates paid on land and buildings. These items do not change as output varies. So, for example, a firm pays the same rent and rates whether it produces 5,000 or 10,000 washing machines.

Variable Costs

These are the cost items that are directly related to output, and for this reason they are sometimes called **direct costs**. The most obvious items are the wages paid to production labour, the cost of raw materials and power. If, for example, a furniture manufacturer wanted to double his production of wicker chairs, he would need to use more wood. The firm may also have to pay overtime rates of pay to production labour if they work beyond their normal hours of work.

Problems in Cost Classification

There are some costs that do not fit neatly into this cost classification. For example, certain administrative expenses such as postage and telephone bills may vary with the firm's output, although in the case of a telephone bill there is a fixed element not related to the use of the phone (the quarterly standing charge) and a variable element which is related to the number, distance and time of day of the calls. Other administrative costs, such as salaries, tend to be fixed (so much per month) and will not vary with output.

Another problem is that some fixed costs do alter with the output of the firm, e.g. depreciation or wear and tear on capital equipment is classified as a fixed cost although this is related to how frequently the machine is used. These examples serve to illustrate how difficult it sometimes is to distinguish between fixed and variable costs.

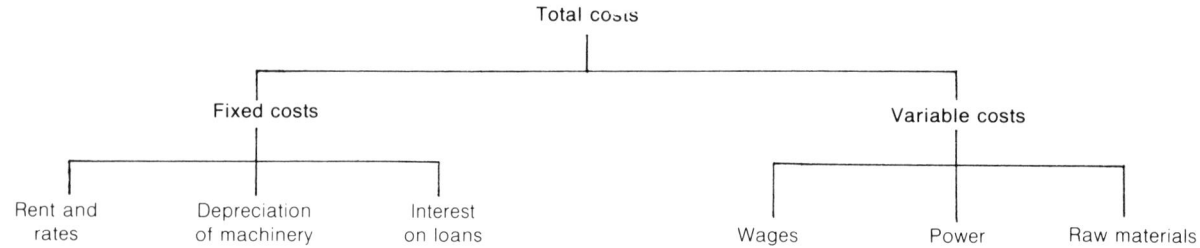

Figure 11.1 The Classification of Costs

Total Costs

Total costs represent the sum of fixed and variable costs. They are calculated by the following formula:

Total costs (TC) = total fixed costs (TFC) + total variable costs (TVC)

The relationship between the firm's output and the cost items given in the formula are illustrated in Table 11.1 and Figure 11.2.

Table 11.1. *The Costs of Production*

Output	Total Fixed Costs £	Total Variable Costs £	Total Costs £
0	100	0	100
1	100	5	105
2	100	8	108
3	100	29	129
4	100	60	160
5	100	105	205
6	100	152	252
7	100	201	301
8	100	252	352
9	100	305	405
10	100	360	460

In Figure 11.2 output is plotted along the horizontal axis and costs are plotted along the vertical axis. When the firm produces nothing it has no variable costs – it doesn't use raw materials, labour or power. Its only costs at zero output are fixed costs, which are equal to £100. These remain the same whatever output the firm decides to produce, and they are given by the horizontal line which starts on the vertical axis. As output increases, total costs rise. The sole reason for this is the increase in variable costs, e.g. when the firm increases its output from 5 to 6 units total costs rise from £205 to £252 – an increase of £47. Similarly, this is also the increase in total variable costs (£152 − £105 = £47). The total cost and total variable cost curves in Figure 11.2 are always the same distance apart since the difference between total cost and total variable cost is total fixed cost. This can be seen by rearranging the formula for total cost as follows:

Total cost = total fixed cost + total variable cost

Taking total variable cost onto the left-hand side of this expression gives:

Total cost − Total variable cost = Total fixed cost

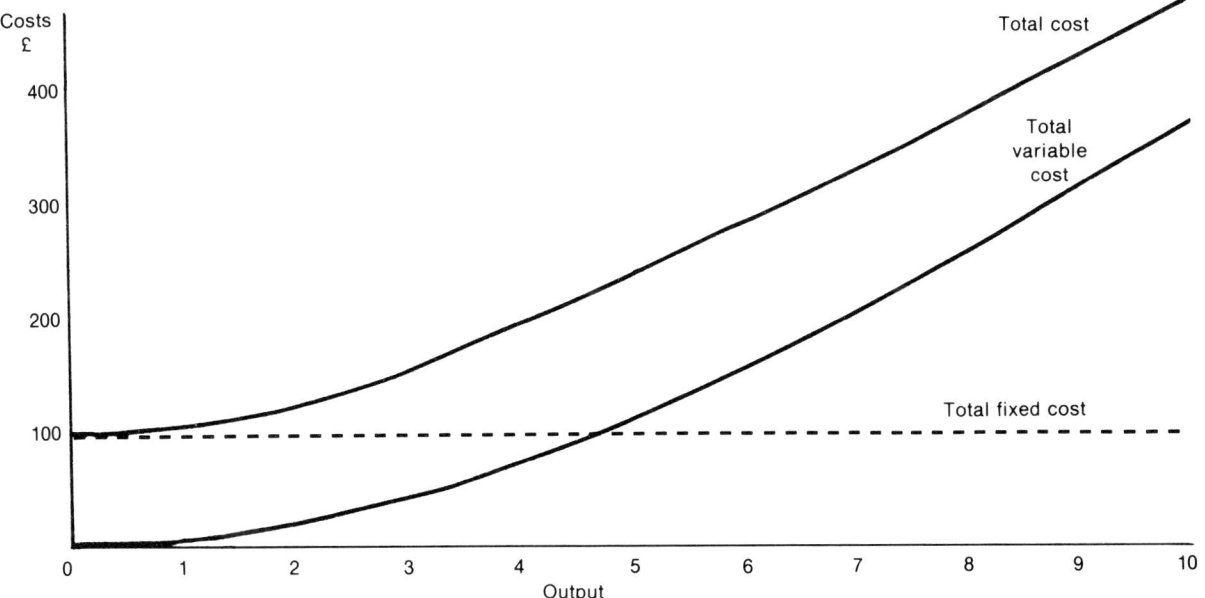

Figure 11.2 The Relationship between Total Costs and Output

131

Average Cost Relationships

There are 3 types of average cost relationship: average total cost (ATC), average fixed cost (AFC) and average variable cost (AVC).

Average total cost is found by dividing total cost by output. Our expression for total cost given previously was:

Total cost = total fixed cost + total variable cost

Dividing both sides of this expression by output gives:

$$\frac{\text{Total cost}}{\text{Output}} = \frac{\text{total fixed cost}}{\text{output}} + \frac{\text{total variable cost}}{\text{output}}$$

where

$$\frac{\text{Total cost}}{\text{Output}} = \text{average total cost (ATC)}$$

$$\frac{\text{Total fixed cost}}{\text{Output}} = \text{average fixed cost (AFC)}$$

$$\frac{\text{Total variable cost}}{\text{Output}} = \text{average variable cost (AVC)}$$

Average total cost is therefore made up of 2 elements – average fixed cost and average variable cost, i.e.:

Average total cost (ATC) = average fixed cost (AFC) + average variable cost (AVC)

These cost relationships can be illustrated diagrammatically. Using the figures from Table 11.1 it is possible to calculate average fixed, average variable and average total costs. The relevant calculations and diagram are set out in Table 11.2 and Figure 11.3.

Average fixed costs are high at low levels of output, since the total fixed cost is only being spread over a few units of output. As output expands, average costs progressively decline, which is shown in Figure 11.3 by the falling ATC curve. The fall in average fixed costs as output expands is sometimes referred to as 'spreading the overheads'.

Table 11.2. *Total and Average Cost Relationships*

Output	Total Fixed Cost £	Total Variable Cost £	Total Cost £	Average Fixed Cost £	Average Variable Cost £	Average Total Cost £
0	100	0	100	Infinity	–	Infinity
1	100	5	105	100.0	5.0	105
2	100	8	108	50.0	4.0	54
3	100	29	129	33.3	9.7	43
4	100	60	160	25.0	15.0	40
5	100	105	205	20.0	21.0	41
6	100	152	252	16.7	25.3	42
7	100	201	301	14.3	28.7	43
8	100	252	352	12.5	31.5	44
9	100	305	405	11.1	33.9	45
10	100	360	460	10.0	36.0	46

Average variable costs fall from £5 to £4 between 1 and 2 units of output respectively. Thereafter average variable costs rise as output expands. This is explained by the law of diminishing returns, which is examined in more detail in the section below on short and long run.

Average total costs fall at first until they reach a minimum of £40 per unit when the firm produces 4 units of output. When average costs fall in this way, **increasing returns** are said to be operating. The point at which average total costs are at a minimum is known as **optimum** (best) **output**. It is called this because the firm cannot produce at a lower average

total cost. Beyond 4 units of output, average total costs rise. When this happens we have something called **diminishing returns**. If the firm wishes to expand output beyond 4 units, its average total costs will increase and this may mean higher prices for the product. One way round this problem is to increase the amount of capital the firm uses. This is where the distinction between the 'short' and 'long' run becomes important.

The Short and Long Run

Economists distinguish between the short and long run in production to illustrate how a firm can change its output using different amounts of factors of production. The short run is defined as the period of time when at least one factor of production (land or capital) is fixed. The long run is the period of time when all factors of production are variable. It is important to bear in mind that there is no definite period of time that describes the short and long run. In some industries it may be relatively easy to change capital, e.g. the installation of a new weaving machine in a textile firm may take a few days, whereas in the electricity industry it may take 5–10 years before a new power station can be built.

In the short run, when capital is fixed, the firm can only increase its output by changing the labour input. It can do this in one of two ways. First, it could ask its existing labour force to work longer hours, e.g. overtime or shiftwork. Here the firm will have to pay higher hourly rates of pay and it may be that workers become tired as their working hours increase, i.e. their productivity decreases. This combination of higher hourly pay and falling productivity increases the average total cost of production. Secondly, the firm could recruit more labour but it may find that as it adds more labour to a given sized factory with a fixed number of machines employees may get in one another's way. This again will increase average total costs. This is referred to as the principle of diminishing returns, and in Table 11.2 and Figure 11.3 it occurs beyond the fourth unit of output.

One option available to the firm to try and overcome diminishing returns is to increase the size of its factory or install more capital equipment. This will change the cost structure of the firm and the firm may benefit from economies of scale, as discussed in

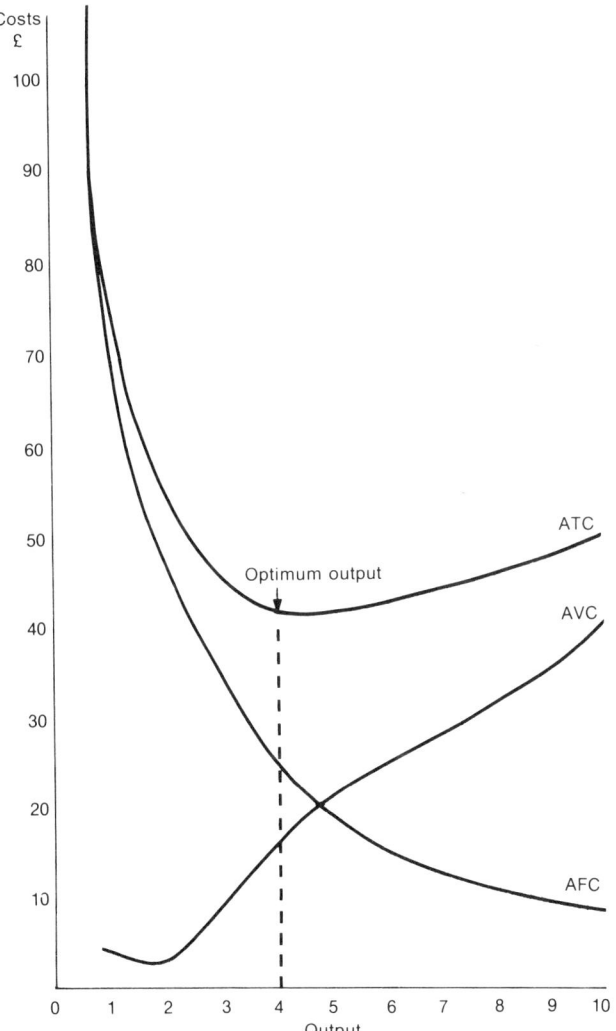

Figure 11.3 The Relationship between Average Costs and Output

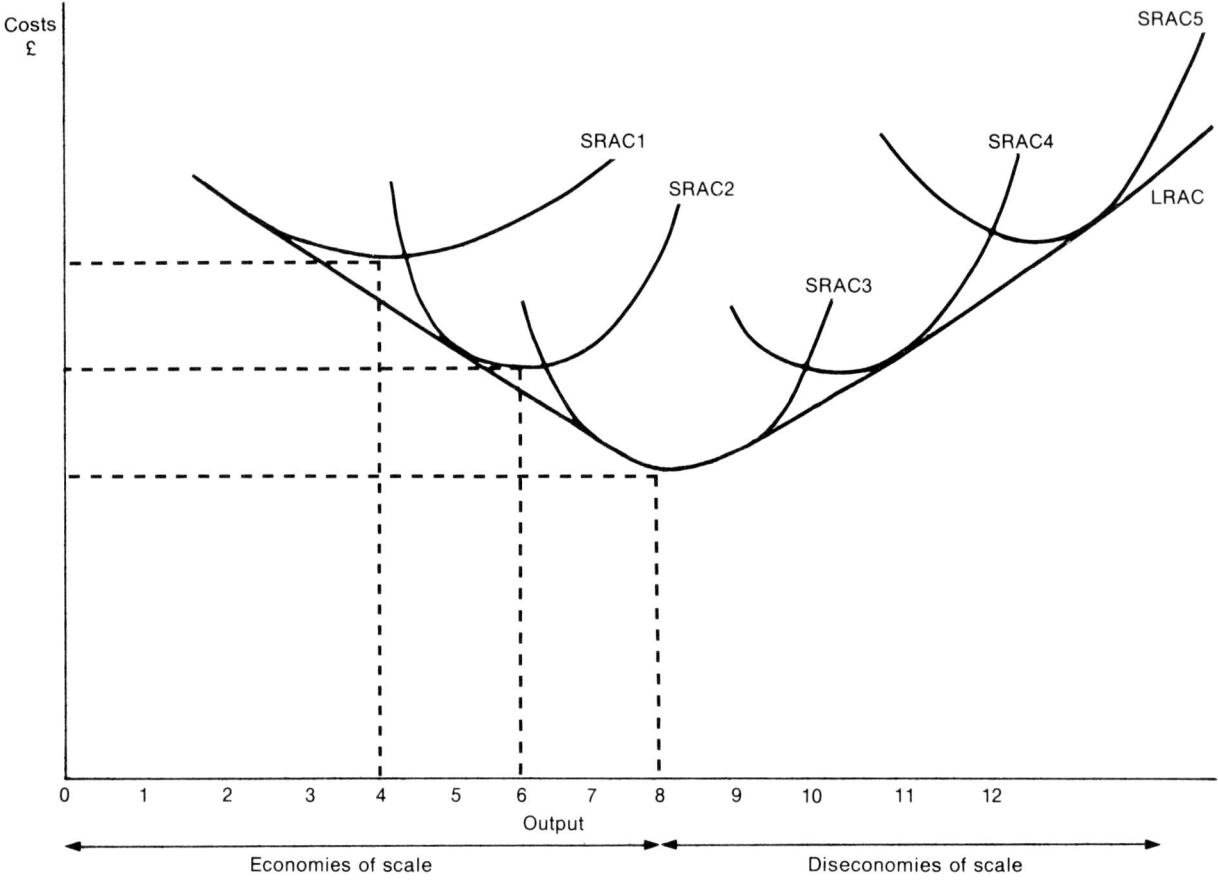

Figure 11.4 Economies and Diseconomies of Scale

Chapter 10. The effect that increasing the amount of capital has on the structure of the firm's costs is shown in Figure 11.4.

Assume that the firm is originally producing on the short-run average cost curve SRAC1. The optimum output of the firm is 4 units. Increasing output beyond this level increases average total costs. The firm encounters diminishing returns. The firm may increase the amount of capital it uses in production and the corresponding cost curve becomes SRAC2. The average cost of production is now at its minimum point when the firm produces 6 units of output. The firm has benefited from economies of scale. It could continue to increase the amount of capital it uses in production, as shown by the cost curves SRAC3, SRAC4 and SRAC5. But there will come a point where diseconomies of scale trouble the firm. This is at the output level of 8 units. The envelope curve LRAC is the long run average cost curve and it traces out the series of short run average cost curves.

Marginal Cost

The final important cost relation to consider is marginal cost. This can be defined as what the next unit of output adds to total cost of the firm. Table 11.3 shows how marginal cost is calculated.

The marginal cost of the first unit of output is £5. This is because as a result of output rising from 0 to 1, total costs rise from £100 (when nothing is produced) to £105 (when 1 unit is produced). Hence, the first unit of output adds £5 to total costs and this is known as the marginal cost. To calculate the marginal cost of the seventh unit of output we need to have a look at how total costs change when output rises from 6 units to 7 units. When 6 units are produced total costs are £252 and when 7 units are produced total costs are £301. Therefore, the marginal cost of the seventh unit of output is £49. In general the marginal

Table 11.3. *The Calculation of Marginal Cost*

Output	Total Fixed Cost £	Total Variable Cost £	Total Cost £	Marginal Cost £	Average Total Cost £
0	100	0	100	–	Infinity
1	100	5	105	5	105
2	100	8	108	3	54
3	100	29	129	21	43
4	100	60	160	31	40
5	100	105	205	45	41
6	100	152	252	47	42
7	100	201	301	49	43
8	100	252	352	51	44
9	100	305	405	53	45
10	100	360	460	55	46

cost of a unit of output can be calculated by the following formula:

$$\text{Marginal cost } (n_{th} \text{ unit}) = \text{total cost } (n_{th} \text{ unit}) - \text{total cost } (n - 1_{th} \text{ unit})$$

As mentioned earlier, the only reason why total costs increase when output increases is because of changes in variable costs. Fixed costs, by definition, cannot change. It is therefore possible to calculate marginal cost by another method – by looking at changes in variable costs. Consider what happens when the firm increases output from 6 to 7 units. Total costs rise from £252 to £301. The increase in total variable costs is from £152 to £201 – an increase of £49, which is the marginal cost of the seventh unit of output. Both methods of calculating marginal costs give the same result.

QUICK QUESTIONS 2

1. You are given the following cost information about a ball-bearing manufacturer. Output can only be produced in batches of 100 units.

Output	TFC £	TVC £	TC £	AFC £	AVC £	ATC £	MC £
0	80	0					
100	80	30					
200	80	75					
300	80	125					
400	80	170					
500	80	300					
600	80	500					

(a) Calculate TC, AFC, AVC, ATC and MC.
(b) Plot the information on a graph.
(c) Describe what happens to AFC as the output of ball-bearings increases. What is this called?
(d) What happens to ATC as output increases? What is the reason for this?
(e) What is the firm's optimum output? What are average costs at this level of output?

2. What do you understand by the terms 'short run' and 'long run'?

3. What do you understand by the term 'marginal cost'?

The Revenue of the Firm

As with the cost side of the production process, the revenue relationships divide into total, average and marginal revenues. The total revenue of the firm is simply the number of units of output sold multiplied by the price at which they sell. Total revenue is sometimes called **turnover** or **sales revenue**. It is given by the following formula:

Total revenue (TR) = Price of the Product (P) × Quantity Sold (Q)

Average revenue (AR) can be found by dividing total revenue by quantity sold, and average revenue is equal to the price of the product, as shown in the following formula:

$$\text{Average revenue} = \frac{\text{total revenue}}{\text{quantity sold}}$$

$$= \frac{\text{price} \times \text{quantity sold}}{\text{quantity sold}} = \text{price}$$

Marginal revenue is simply the change in total revenue as a result of the sale of one more unit of output, and is given by the following formula:

$$\text{Marginal revenue } (n_{th} \text{ unit}) = \text{total revenue } (n_{th} \text{ unit}) - \text{total revenue } (n - 1_{th} \text{ unit})$$

The Profit of the Firm

Although there are various profit terms, profit can be defined as the difference between total revenue and total cost. It is given by the following formula:

Total profit = total revenue − total cost

To calculate profit per unit we simply divide the above formula by quantity sold:

$$\frac{\text{Total profit}}{\text{Quantity sold}} = \frac{\text{total revenue}}{\text{quantity sold}} - \frac{\text{total cost}}{\text{quantity sold}}$$

Profit per unit = average revenue − average cost

Break-Even Analysis

A firm breaks even when the total revenue it gets from selling its product just covers its total costs of production. In a situation where the firm breaks even, the profit of the firm, given by the above expression, will be zero. The simplest way to illustrate the principles of break-even analysis is to use a diagram. Using the cost figures in Table 11.3 and assuming the firm can sell each unit of output for £54 gives Table 11.4.

From the table it can be seen that the firm breaks even when it produces 2 units of output. If it produces less than this it will make a loss. Above 2 units of output the firm is making a profit. The profit figure is presented in 2 ways. First, as an absolute amount of profit, which is shown to rise beyond 2 units of output, although it falls from £81 to £80 if the tenth unit is produced. Second, as an amount of profit per unit. In this example, profit per unit is highest when 4 units of output are produced. Beyond this level of output profits per unit fall.

This same information can be shown graphically in the form of the break-even chart in Figure 11.5. The volume of production/sales is plotted along the horizontal axis and the revenue and costs are on the vertical axis. The chart shows the amount of profit or loss at various levels of sales/production. Total fixed costs are shown as a horizontal straight line. Total costs are shown as starting on the vertical axis, and they increase as output increases. To find the break-even point a third line must be added – total revenue. The total revenue line starts at the origin since when output is zero total revenue must be zero. It is a straight line because the firm gets the same price for each unit produced.

It is possible to read off the diagram the total revenue and total costs associated with any particular level of output. To find the break-even point you simply look where the total cost and total revenue curves intersect. At this point neither profits nor losses are made. The break-even point is important to the firm since it shows the minimum level of sales that is necessary to ensure the survival of the firm. Beyond the break-even point the firm makes a profit.

Table 11.4. *Profitability at Different Levels of Output*

Output	Price Per Unit £	Total Revenue £	Average Revenue £	Total Cost £	Average Cost £	Profit £	Profit Per Unit £
0	54	0	54	100	Infinity	− 100	–
1	54	54	54	105	105	− 51	− 51
2	54	108	54	108	54	0	0
3	54	162	54	129	43	33	11
4	54	216	54	160	40	56	14
5	54	270	54	205	41	65	13
6	54	324	54	252	42	72	12
7	54	378	54	301	43	77	11
8	54	432	54	352	44	80	10
9	54	486	54	405	45	81	9
10	54	540	54	460	46	80	8

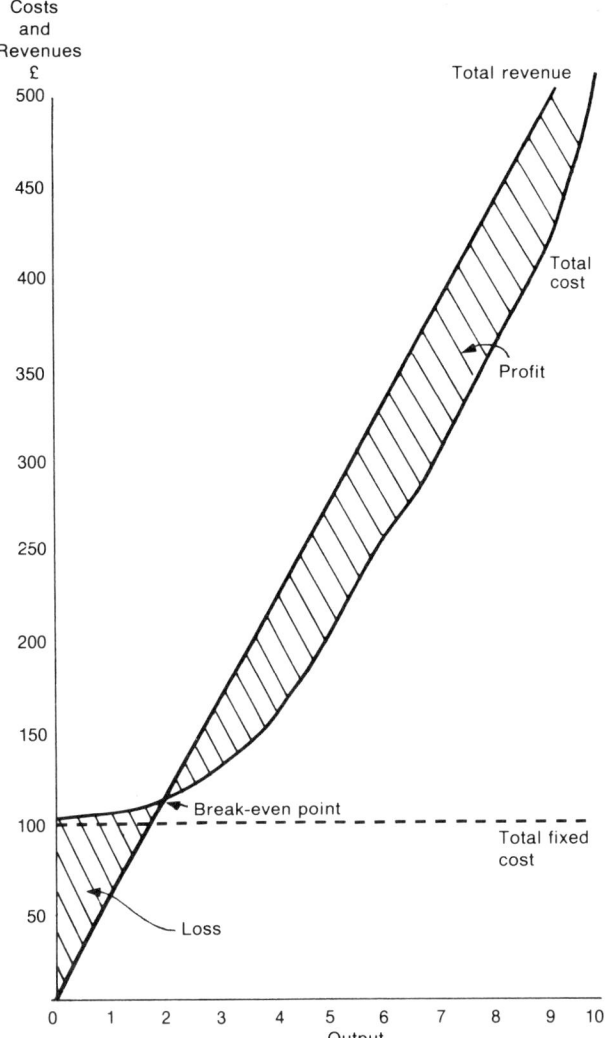

Figure 11.5 Break-Even Analysis

Deciding on the Level of Output

One problem confronting the firm is to decide at what level of output to produce. This depends on the firm's objective. Clearly, it must produce more than 2 units of output otherwise it will either break even or make a loss. It could aim to maximise the profit per unit sold, in which case it would produce 4 units of output. However, the overall level of profit would not be being maximised since it only makes £56 profit at this level of output. Higher levels of output do offer the firm a greater level of absolute profit although the profit per unit is not as great. If it decides to maximise the level of absolute profit it will produce 9 units of output where the level of profit is £81. No other level of output offers a higher profit level. If the firm wished to maximise its sales (or increase its market share) it could produce 10 units of output although it would not be maximising its profit level or profit per unit. Finally, the firm may try to minimise its average costs, in which case it would be producing at the so-called 'optimum output' level. Average costs are minimised at 4 units of output and this is where the firm makes the largest profit per unit.

Break-Even, Shut-Down Point and Contribution Costing

If the firm produced 2 units or fewer it would either break even or make a loss. If it was faced with this situation persistently the firm would close down and leave the industry. However, should the firm close down soon after it starts to make losses or could it continue to produce output even though it was making a loss? Imagine the demand for the firm's product suddenly dropped and it found itself in the situation where it could only sell 1 unit of output. Should it continue to produce? Looking at Table 11.4, the firm would be making a loss of £51. If it produced zero units of output it would make a bigger loss of £100. This is because the fixed costs of the firm – £100 in this case – still have to be covered, even though the firm is producing nothing. The revenue received for the first unit of output – £54 – is sufficient to cover all the variable costs of producing it (which is £5), and further, it is making some contribution to fixed costs. The firm should therefore make the first unit of output. This is sometimes called

---

QUICK QUESTIONS 3

1. *How does a firm calculate its total revenue?*
2. *How can a firm calculate its average revenue?*
3. *What is meant by the profit of a firm?*
4. *What is meant by break-even analysis and why is it important?*

---

contribution costing since it looks at whether the revenue from the sale of the product covers its variable costs and makes some contribution to the fixed costs of the firm.

The following example is another illustration of contribution costing. Imagine a company has been making and selling 1,000 watches at £6, each with an average cost of £5. A discount store offers to buy an extra 500 watches if the price is reduced to £4. Should the company accept this offer? It would appear that the company would make a loss of £1 per watch on the new order but the firm needs to consider its production costs more carefully. In particular, how its total costs are divided between variable and fixed costs. The relevant cost information is set out in Table 11.5.

Originally the firm is making a profit of £1,000 by selling 1,000 watches. The new order for an extra 500 watches at a price of £4 boosts the profit of the company to £1,250, and so the company should accept the order. The reason why the profits of the firm go up, even though the selling price of 500 of the watches has gone down, is to do with contribution costing. The variable cost per watch (labour, materials and power) is £3.50 and so if the firm receives £4 for some of the watches this price covers the variable cost of producing them and makes some contribution to fixed costs.

Table 11.5. *Profitability at Different Output Levels*

		1000		1500
Units of Output		£		£
Variable Costs				
Labour	£2 per unit	2000		3000
Materials	£1 per unit	1000		1500
Power	£0.50 per unit	500		750
Total Variable Costs		3500		5250
Fixed Costs				
Rent and rates		400		400
Administration		800		800
Interest on loans		300		300
Total Fixed Costs		1500		1500
Total Costs		5000		6750
Cost per Unit		5		4.50
Total Revenue	£6 per unit	6000	£6 for 1000 £4 for 500	8000
Profit		1000		1250
Profit per Unit		1		0.83

QUICK QUESTIONS 4

1. *How does a firm decide on what level of output to produce?*
2. *Why do some organisations, e.g. certain football clubs, stay in business even though they make losses?*
3. *Explain what you understand by the term 'contribution costing'.*
4. *How does contribution costing explain why some schools are prepared to hire out their facilities, e.g. sports halls, to the local community?*

STUDENT EXERCISE

Costs, Revenues and Profitability

Everlast Ltd is a medium-sized pocket battery manufacturer. Currently it produces 15,000 pocket-sized batteries each year. A battery has a selling price of 80 pence (or £0.80). Variable costs of manufacture include 30p labour per battery, 5p power per battery and 15p per battery in raw materials. Fixed costs include rates of £1,000, rent £1,500 and machinery depreciation of £500.

1. From the information given, calculate
   (a) Total variable cost
   (b) Average variable cost
   (c) Total fixed cost
   (d) Average fixed cost
   (e) Average total cost
   (f) Total revenue
   (g) Profit
   (h) Profit per unit.
2. Illustrate your answers to Question 1 in the form of a break-even chart which should contain total fixed costs, total costs and total revenue.
3. Using the break-even chart, or by another method of your choice, calculate the break-even level of output of batteries for Everlast.
4. The company receives a 'special order' for 5,000 batteries from a large toy store. They will only purchase the batteries if the price is 60p, which is 20p below the current price. Should you accept the order? Explain your answer by completing the right-hand side of the table. Would you accept the same order if the price were 45p? Explain your decision.

Costs, Revenues and Profit of Producing Batteries

Output	15,000	20,000 (5,000 special order)
Variable Costs (Per Unit)		
Labour		
Power		
Raw materials		
Total Variable Cost	——	——
	——	——
Average Variable Cost	——	——
Fixed Costs		
Rates		
Rent		
Depreciation		
Total Fixed Cost	——	——
	——	——
Average Fixed Cost	——	——
	——	——
Total Cost	——	——
	——	——
Average Total Cost	——	——
	——	——
Total Revenue 15,000 × £0.80	——	——
	——	——
Profit	——	——
	——	——
Profit Per Unit	——	——

PROJECT AND ASSIGNMENT SUGGESTIONS

1. Make a list of all the costs involved in running your school or college. Divide these costs into fixed costs and variable costs, according to whether they are affected by the number of students on the roll.
   (a) Present this information in the form of a chart or table and draw attention to any problem you encounter in trying to classify costs in this way.
   (b) Explain how the cost per student (which is average total cost in this case) is affected by changes in student numbers.
   (c) In the light of the above analysis, write a brief report explaining why in recent years Education Authorities in many areas have adopted a policy of closing or merging schools in response to a decline in the size of the school-

age population. If possible include examples from your local area.

2. You wish to set up a shop at your school or college to sell crisps and cans of soft drinks during the lunch-break. A suitable room is available but you will have to pay a weekly sum to use it. You can buy the stock you need at cost price from the local cash and carry, and you intend to sell the items at normal retail prices.

    (a) What information would you require to be able to calculate (i) the fixed cost of running the shop each week, and (ii) the variable cost each week?

    (b) What information would you need to be able to calculate the total revenue of the shop per week?

    (c) Explain how you would go about finding out the minimum amount you have to sell to make the business a viable concern.

    (d) Undertake an investigation to find out all the information you need to write a feasibility study on the project. Illustrate your study with diagrams showing the cost and revenue information you have calculated.

CHAPTER 12

Prices and Pricing Policy

Price is a very important weapon that can be used to persuade consumers to buy. For example, the purpose of winter and summer sales is to clear out old stock in preparation for the new season. One means of doing this is to reduce the price of goods and services in the hope that consumers will buy more. When garages have cheap petrol days, they are normally confronted with queues, and now that the price of unleaded fuel is cheaper than leaded fuel it has started to take a larger market share. Price is one of many factors that determine the demand for a product. In this chapter the following subjects will be examined: how price is determined using supply and demand analysis; what other factors determine consumer demand; and the pricing policies that firms can adopt.

Supply and Demand Analysis: The Determination of Market Price

A market can be defined as any form of contact between buyer and seller. The prices of most products are determined in markets. Markets always have two sides: the demand side, composed of buyers, and the supply side, made up of sellers. Price in a market is determined by supply and demand forces.

Demand

The demand for a product is the amount of a good that people are willing to buy over a given time period at a particular price. For most goods and services the amount that consumers wish to buy (the quantity demanded) will increase as price falls. For example, if the price of cassettes becomes cheaper, there would be a tendency to buy more cassettes and

perhaps fewer records, a substitute product.

The relationship between price and quantity demanded can be shown in 2 forms: a **demand schedule** and a **demand curve** or **line**. Table 12.1 and Figure 12.1 are examples of these two methods.

Table 12.1. *A Demand Schedule*

Price (£)	Quantity Demanded (units per week)
10	20
9	30
8	40
7	50
6	60
5	70

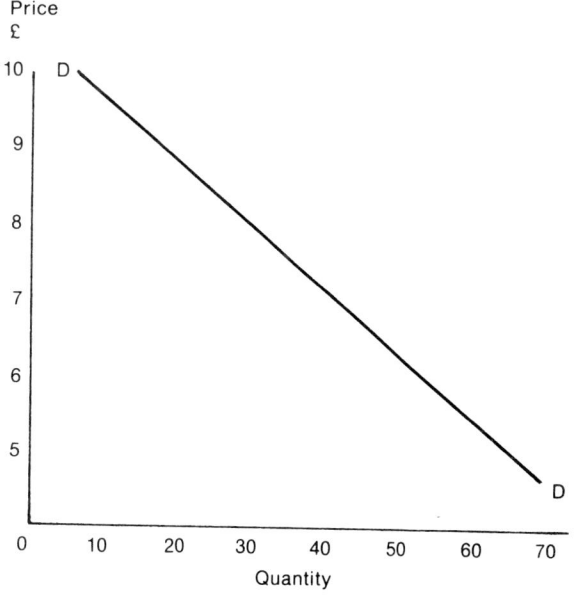

Figure 12.1 A Demand Curve

The information given by the demand schedule shows the amount of the product that consumers are willing to buy at different prices – not what they actually do buy. In this sense it is said to be a **desired demand**. For example, some consumers would like to buy a Rolls-Royce but they lack the purchasing power (income) to do so. When consumers have the ability to purchase what they would like, this is called **effective demand** – demand backed by the ability to pay. In the table, when the price of the product is £10, consumers would like to buy 20 units per week. At a lower price, say £9, consumers would like to buy 30 units per week. This is sometimes called **the first law of demand** – as the price of a good falls (rises) quantity demanded increases (decreases).

The demand curve in Figure 12.1 shows the demand schedule information in the form of a graph. The price of the good is measured along the vertical axis and the quantity demanded is measured along the horizontal axis.

The demand for a product is not only influenced by price. An individual may be influenced by factors such as personal tastes, the size of income, advertising and the cost and availability of credit. The total market demand will be affected by the size and age distribution of the population and government policy. These factors are discussed below.

Personal Tastes

The demand for goods and services is likely to change according to tastes, habits and fashions. Tastes and fashions can change quite quickly, while habits may be harder to break. They can also be influenced by advertising and the development of new products. The clothing and footwear industries are particularly affected by fashions, with particular colours and shapes being fashionable one season or year and not the next. Habits are much slower in changing, e.g. there has been a decline in the percentage of the population who smoke, and this has affected the demand and sales of the cigarette companies. There has also been a trend towards taking more exercise, e.g. squash and jogging, and eating healthier foods. The so-called 'green lobby' has made consumers more aware of the damaging effect that some consumer products, e.g. aerosols, can have on the environment, and this has changed shopping habits. Health scares, e.g. the possibility of

eggs and yoghurt containing harmful bacteria, can also affect the demand for a product.

QUICK QUESTIONS 1

1. *What is a market?*
2. *What is the difference between effective demand and desired demand?*
3. *What is the first law of demand?*
4. *Think of some products that have recently (a) come into fashion and (b) gone out of fashion. What have been the reasons for this?*

Incomes

For most goods and services an important influence on what and how much is bought is the level of a person's or household's income. Throughout most of this century the real incomes of the majority of the population have been rising. This has led to more people owning colour TVs, videos, cars, compact disc players, washing machines, dishwashers and telephones. This rise in incomes has also affected the demand for holidays abroad. Goods whose demand rises with income are called **normal goods**. Not all goods experience a rise in demand when income rises. In fact the demand for some goods falls as income rises. Examples include matches, salt, cheaper foodstuffs such as mince and sausage, and cheaper clothes such as plastic shoes. These are known as **inferior goods**.

It is important to realise that it is disposable income and not gross income that is significant in determining the demand for a good, i.e. income after deductions such as income tax, national insurance and pension contributions. If the government were to cut income tax, as it did between 1979 and 1988, then the demand for normal goods and services would rise. The distribution of income is also significant, e.g. if the government were to increase pensions then there might be an increase in the demand for food and heating.

Prices of Other Goods

The demand for a good may also depend on the price of other goods. It may be that 2 goods are **substitutes** for one another, e.g. lamb and beef or pork and veal. Alternatively, 2 goods may be **complementary** to one another, e.g. cars and petrol, bread and butter and gin and tonic.

If 2 goods are close substitutes for one another, then an increase in the price of one, e.g. butter, will lead to an increase in demand for the other, e.g. margarine. This is called **competitive demand**. The products are literally competing against one another.

If 2 goods are complementary to one another, the price of one may affect the demand for the other. For example, a rise in the price of cars may lead to a fall in the demand for petrol. This is sometimes called **joint demand** because the products are consumed or demanded together.

Advertising

This can be both informative – telling consumers that a product exists, the price at which it can be bought and where – and persuasive – persuading consumers that a particular product is desirable and should be bought. The idea behind advertising is to increase the demand for a product, and there have been some very successful advertising campaigns, e.g. the lager adverts. Some firms, e.g. those which produce washing powders and pet foods, respond to the advertising of their competitors.

Cost and Availability of Credit

The demand for a lot of consumer durables, e.g. cars, houses, TVs and compact disc players, depends on the cost and availability of hire purchase or credit. This may involve making a deposit for the item (say 10% of the purchase price) and then paying for the good over a period of time. A lot of people use credit or charge cards when buying goods. Any change in the terms on which credit is available will affect the demand for durable goods, e.g. an increase in the rate of interest may reduce the demand for housing because mortgages become more expensive. This in turn will affect retail sales. Some companies try to get consumers to purchase their product by the offer of 'interest free credit' or 'buy now pay later'.

Size, Age and Sex Distribution of the Population

An increase in the population tends to increase the demand for most goods and services. The age structure of the population is also important. For example, a baby boom like the one in the 1960s will tend to increase the demand for nappies, prams and pushchairs. When this group reach the teenage years there may be an increased demand for records and

clothes. As the population ages there may be a greater demand for health care and social services.

Government Policy

In the UK the government purchases a large amount of goods and services and it can also affect other people's demand for goods and services by changes in pensions, unemployment benefit and income tax. Cuts in the rate of income tax may increase the demand for normal goods.

QUICK QUESTIONS 2

1. What are (a) normal goods and (b) inferior goods? Give 3 examples of each.
2. What do you understand by (a) substitute and (b) complementary goods? Give 3 examples of both.
3. How would you expect (i) a cut in income tax and (ii) a fall in interest rates to affect the demand for (a) housing (b) steak (c) compact disc players (d) holidays abroad?
4. How would a successful advertising campaign for coffee affect the demand for tea?

Supply

Demand is concerned with the buying side of the market. Supply is concerned with the firm's or producer's side of the market. Unlike demand, the quantity supplied of a good will increase as price rises. The relationship between quantity supplied and price can be shown by a supply schedule and a supply curve, as in Table 12.2 and Figure 12.2.

Table 12.2. *A Supply Schedule*

Price £	Quantity Supplied (units per week)
10	60
9	50
8	40
7	30
6	20
5	10

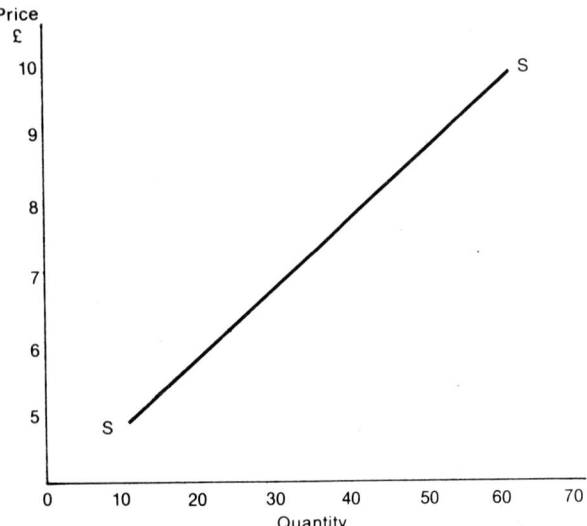

Figure 12.2 A Supply Curve

The supply schedule shows the amount of the product that firms are willing to sell at different prices. The supply curve in Figure 12.2 shows the supply schedule information in the form of a diagram. The price of the good is measured along the vertical axis and the quantity supplied along the horizontal axis.

The supply of a product is not only influenced by price. Supply will be affected by anything that helps or hinders production or alters the costs of production. Some factors that influence supply are discussed below.

Technological Change

This refers to improvements in the quality of the factors of production, e.g. capital and labour which leads to increased productivity. New production methods can increase supply of goods and services such as the use of robots on car assembly lines and chemical fertilisers to increase crop yields.

The Price of the Factors of Production

The cost of labour, materials and machinery determines the firm's costs of production. If costs rise then the firm may no longer find it profitable to produce the same amount of output or offer the same service as before, e.g. the rise in interest rates in 1988/89 led to a number of estate agents closing certain branches, and the washing machine manufacturer Hoover blamed high interest rates on their decision to make redundancies at their plant in South Wales in 1989.

Government Policy

Taxation on goods and services such as VAT and subsidies can influence supply. For example, one reason why the Common Agricultural Policy of the European Community has managed to give us 'wine lakes' and 'butter mountains' is that production is subsidised. Farmers are willing to grow and supply more of a product if it carries a subsidy.

Weather

Certain goods, e.g. agricultural products, depend on the weather. A wet summer may lead to a poor grain harvest, while a hot summer may lead to lower production of milk and cheese because the grass necessary for dairy farming isn't as plentiful.

Market Equilibrium

To see how price is determined in a market it is necessary to bring supply and demand together. This is done in Table 12.3 and Figure 12.3.

Table 12.3. *Supply and Demand Schedules*

Price £	Quantity Demanded (units per week)	Quantity Supplied (units per week)	Description
10	20	60	Excess supply
9	30	50	Excess supply
8	40	40	Market equilibrium
7	50	30	Excess demand
6	60	20	Excess demand
5	70	10	Excess demand

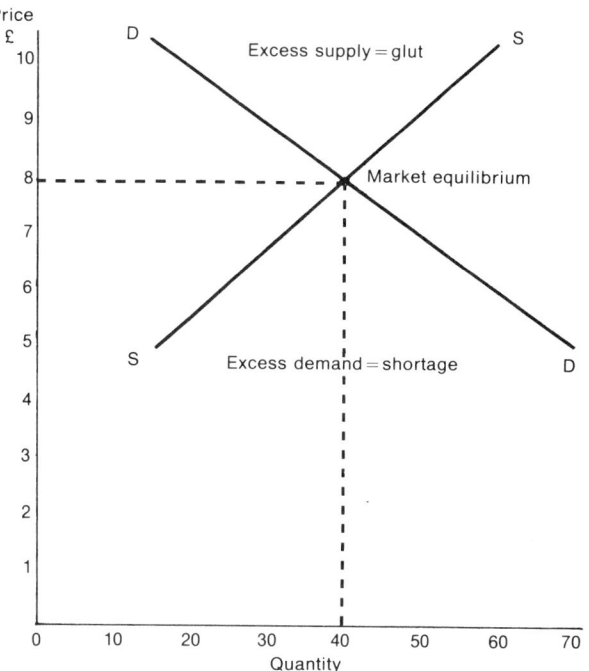

Figure 12.3 Supply, Demand and Market Equilibrium

If the price differed from the equilibrium level, market forces would move it back towards the equilibrium. For example, if the price of the good was £10 – above the market equilibrium – there would be an excess supply or glut. Consumers are only willing to buy 20 units per week at that price, although firms are willing to sell 60 units per week. There is an excess supply of 40 units. Firms may start to accumulate unsold stocks and in order to sell them will reduce prices. As the price falls the quantity demanded rises and the quantity supplied falls. The reverse analysis applies when the price is below the market equilibrium. In this case there will be an excess demand and the tendency of price will be to rise back towards the market equilibrium.

Changes in the market equilibrium

The prices of goods and services are continually changing and so too is the amount that is bought and sold. In winter the price of tomatoes tends to be a lot higher than in the summer and fewer tomatoes are bought in the winter. These changes can be explained by a movement in the supply curve of tomatoes. Similarly, the price of turkey tends to increase at Christmas and so too does the number of turkeys bought. These changes can be explained by an increase in demand. To show the effect of an increase in demand on the market equilibrium consider what happens if there is a successful advertising campaign which increases demand by 20 units per week at each and every price. The effect is shown in Table 12.4 and Figure 12.4.

It can be seen from Table 12.3 that at a price of £8 the quantity demanded is equal to the quantity supplied. This is known as **market equilibrium**. An equilibrium simply means a state of balance between 2 forces, in this case supply and demand. In Figure 12.3 the equilibrium is shown as the point where the supply and demand curves cross one another. The market equilibrium price and quantity are £8 and 40 units per week respectively.

Table 12.4. *The Effect of an Increase in Demand*

Price	Old Quantity Demanded	New Quantity Demanded	Quantity Supplied	Description
£	(units per week)		(units per week)	
10	20	40	60	Excess supply
9	30	50	50	Market equilibrium
8	40	60	40	Excess demand
7	50	70	30	Excess demand
6	60	80	20	Excess demand
5	70	90	10	Excess demand

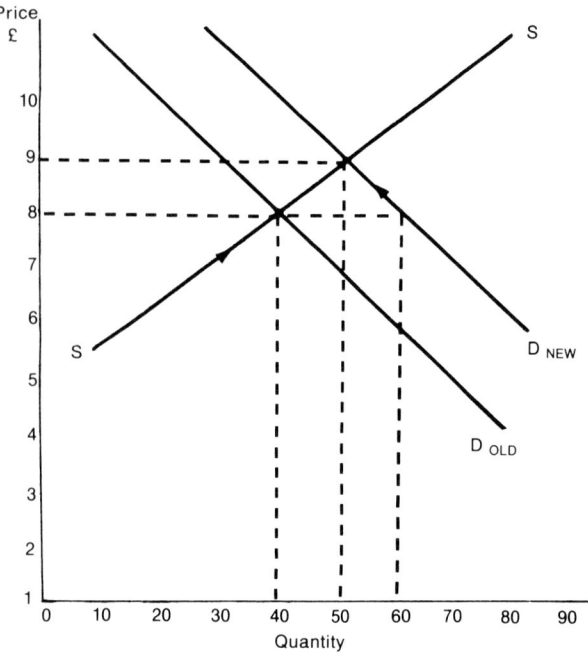

Figure 12.4 The Effect of an Increase in Demand

price and quantity are £9 and 50 units per week respectively.

In Figure 12.4 the original equilibrium is shown by where the first demand curve (labelled D_{OLD}) cuts the supply curve at a price of £8 with 40 units per week being bought. The successful advertising of the product shifts the demand curve to the right, giving a new demand curve D_{NEW}. The new equilibrium price and quantity bought is £9 and 50 units respectively. This movement to a new equilibrium does not happen straightaway. At the old price of £8 consumers are now willing to buy 60 units of the product, firms are only willing to supply 40 units. This creates an excess demand of 20 units per week. The effect of this excess demand is to pull the price of the product upwards. The upward movement in price causes 2 things to happen: (a) consumers are willing to buy less of the product (causing a movement up the new demand curve as shown by the arrow), and (b) as the price rises firms increase quantity supplied (causing a movement up the supply curve as shown by the arrow). Eventually a new equilibrium at a price of £9 with 50 units bought is established.

Changes in the market equilibrium can also come about as a result of a decrease in demand, an increase in supply or a decrease in supply. Table 12.5 provides a summary of these influences, together with their impact on market price and the quantity bought and sold.

Before the increase in demand the market equilibrium price and quantity were £8 and 40 units per week respectively. Demand, as a result of the advertising campaign, has risen by 20 units at each price, which gives us the new demand schedule. The new equilibrium is where demand and supply are equal, and in Table 12.4 the new market equilibrium

Table 12.5. *The Effect of Changes in Supply and Demand on Price and Quantity*

Change	Illustrated as	Effect of Change	Caused by
Increase in demand	Shift of demand curve to right	Increase in price and quantity	Changes in: tastes, incomes, prices of other goods,
Decrease in demand	Shift of demand curve to left	Decrease in price and quantity	advertising, credit, population, government policy
Increase in supply	Shift of supply curve to right	Decrease in price and increase in quantity	Changes in: subsidies, taxes on expenditure, technological,
Decrease in supply	Shift of supply curve to left	Decrease in quantity and increase in price	progress, weather, costs of factors

QUICK QUESTIONS 3

1. *How has technological change altered the price and ownership of (a) compact disc players, (b) walkmans and (c) calculators? Illustrate this effect using a supply and demand diagram.*
2. *What is meant by the term 'market equilibrium'?*
3. *The following information relates to the market for crisps:*

Price p	Quantity Demanded (units per month)	Quantity Supplied (units per month)
30	100	600
25	150	400
20	200	350
15	300	300
10	380	250
5	400	200

(i) *What is the market equilibrium price and quantity?*

(ii) *What would happen if the price of crisps were 25p per bag?*

(iii) *A new type of fast-growing potato has recently been developed which increases supply by 130 units at each and every price. What is the new supply curve? What is the new market equilibrium price and quantity?*

The Price Elasticity of Demand

The **price elasticity of demand** (PED) measures the responsiveness of quantity demanded of a good or service to a change in price. It is important for a firm to have some understanding of how changes in its pricing policy will affect the quantity bought of the good and hence its total revenue (total revenue = price × quantity sold).

Where quantity demanded is **very responsive** to a change in price, demand is said to be **elastic**. Where quantity demanded is **unresponsive** to a change in price, demand is said to be **inelastic**. The PED can be given a numerical value and is calculated using the following formula:

Price elasticity of demand (PED)
$$= \frac{\% \text{ change in quantity demanded}}{\% \text{ change in price}}$$

The PED can be measured in connection with either a price rise or a price fall. Consider the demand schedule in Table 12.6.

Table 12.6. *A Demand Schedule and Total Revenue*

Price £	Quantity Demanded (units per week)	Total Revenue (Price × Quantity) £
10	20	200
9	30	270
8	40	320
7	50	350
6	55	330
5	60	300

Let us calculate the PED when price falls from £10 to £9. The percentage fall in price is given as:

% fall when price drops from £10 to £9
$$= \frac{10 - 9}{10} \times 100 = -10\%$$

The drop in price is -10%.

The percentage increase in quantity demanded is given as:

% increase in quantity demanded
$$= \frac{30 - 20}{20} \times 100 = +50\%$$

From the formula for PED given above it is now possible to calculate the price elasticity of demand when price falls from £10 to £9.

$$\text{PED} = \frac{\% \text{ change in quantity demanded}}{\% \text{ change in price}}$$
$$= \frac{+50\%}{-10\%} = -5$$

The value of the PED is a number, and in this case it is -5. It is quite straightforward to interpret this number. It means that for every 1% reduction in price between £10 and £9 ($-$) there will be a 5% increase ($+$) in quantity demanded of the product. This means that the quantity demanded is responsive to price reductions and so it is said to be elastic. The firm has increased its total revenue as a result of dropping price. So if demand is elastic and price falls then total revenue will increase.

It is important to emphasise that the PED value will be different if we consider a price rise (rather than a fall) from £9 to £10. In this case the working is set out below.

Price elasticity of demand when price rises from £9 to £10:

$$\% \text{ increase in price} = \frac{10 - 9}{9} \times 100 = +11.1\%$$

% fall in quantity demanded

$$= \frac{20 - 30}{30} \times 100 = -33.3\%$$

$$\text{PED} = \frac{\% \text{ change in quantity demanded}}{\% \text{ change in price}}$$

$$= \frac{-33.3\%}{+11.1\%} = -3$$

For a price increase between £9 and £10 the PED value is −3. This means that for each 1% increase in price between £9 and £10 the quantity demanded falls by 3%. Note that the firm's total revenue has fallen from £270 to £200 when price has increased and PED is elastic.

Table 12.7 provides a summary of all the PED values from the demand schedule information given in Table 12.6 for both price increases and price decreases. It also shows the effect of these price changes on the firm's total revenue.

It can be seen from Table 12.7 that when PED is elastic and the firm drops its price then total revenue increases. When PED is elastic and the firm increases price then total revenue falls. When the PED is inelastic and the firm drops price then total revenue falls. If the PED is inelastic and the firm increases price then total revenue rises.

When the PED takes on a value of 1 it is said to be **unit elastic** and in this case a 1% change in price brings about a 1% change in quantity demanded and the total revenue of the firm will remain unchanged in response to a price change. In the example shown, the firm will receive most revenue if it charges a price of £7. If it increases price above this level, demand is elastic and total revenue will fall. If it reduces price below this level demand is inelastic and revenue will fall. Exactly what determines whether a product has an elastic or inelastic price elasticity of demand is discussed below.

Factors Determining the Price Elasticity of Demand

Different products have different values for their PEDs. There are a number of factors which influence the PED for a product. They include:

1. **The availability of close substitutes for the product**: if a product has very few close substitutes then the PED will tend to be more

Table 12.7. *PED Values and their Effect on Total Revenue*

	% Change in Price	% Change in Quantity	PED Value	Description of PED	Effect on Total Revenue
Price Falls					
10–9	− 10.0	+ 50.0	− 5	Elastic	Increase
9–8	− 11.1	+ 33.3	− 3	Elastic	Increase
8–7	− 12.5	+ 25.0	− 2	Elastic	Increase
7–6	− 14.3	+ 10.0	− 0.69	Inelastic	Decrease
6–5	− 16.7	+ 9.10	− 0.54	Inelastic	Decrease
Price Rises					
5–6	+ 20.0	− 8.30	− 0.42	Inelastic	Increase
6–7	+ 16.7	− 9.10	− 0.54	Inelastic	Increase
7–8	+ 14.3	− 20.0	− 1.40	Elastic	Decrease
8–9	+ 12.5	− 25.0	− 2	Elastic	Decrease
9–10	+ 11.1	− 33.3	− 3	Elastic	Decrease

inelastic. This is because when the price of a good rises consumers may have very few alternative substitute products from which to choose. If a product has a large number of substitutes then the PED for it will tend to be more elastic. The PED for a particular type of breakfast cereal is likely to be elastic since there is a vast array of cereals on the market. The PED for petrol is likely to be inelastic because there are so few alternative fuels available.

2. **The proportion of income spent on the commodity**: certain items make up a large percentage of a household's budget, e.g. mortgage payments, food and holidays. Other commodities account for a small percentage of a consumer's spending, e.g. matches and newspapers. These cheaper products tend to have inelastic PEDs because a large percentage increase in their price does not have a drastic effect on a consumer's income.

3. **Habit-forming/addictive goods**: these products tend to have inelastic demands because the consumer is 'hooked' on the product, so even when the price of the good rises they still carry on purchasing the product.

4. **Necessities**: it is argued that products which are necessities, e.g. food, must have inelastic demands. By contrast, luxury items tend to have elastic demands. However, although food may have an inelastic demand in general it all depends on how we define a particular good, e.g. meat is likely to have an inelastic PED although the PED for particular types of meat such as beef, pork, lamb, bacon and veal are likely to be more elastic. This is because they could be regarded as substitutes for one another. Whether necessities have an inelastic demand thus depends on how widely or narrowly the product is defined.

Pricing Policy

How firms set the price of their goods and services is a complicated issue. A number of factors will affect the price a firm sets for its product, including such things as the cost of producing the product, the rival firms' prices, the type of product, and the desired market share of the company.

The 3 most common pricing methods adopted by firms are:

1. **Cost-plus pricing** is a very simple pricing method and is perhaps the most common. A firm may calculate its average costs of producing a product and then simply add a profit 'mark-up', say 10%, on to average costs. This mark-up could be changed to allow for the effects of competition and economic conditions, e.g. where there is a lot of competition this mark-up may be lowered or when business is good the mark-up could be raised.

2. **Marginal-cost pricing** differs from the above in that the firm looks not at its average costs but at marginal costs, i.e. the firm calculates the additional cost of producing the next unit or set of units of output and then charges a price (plus a 'mark-up') according to marginal cost. A typical example is found in the shoe repair business. There appears to be no standard price for repairing shoes. What tends to happen is the cobbler examines the shoes and makes a quick estimate of how much material and time it will take to repair them. Larger shoes, those made of leather and those in greater disrepair have a higher marginal cost and therefore a higher price is charged for their repair.

3. **Price discrimination**: several firms are able to charge different prices for a similar product. This is known as price discrimination. British Rail, for example, charges different consumers such as businessmen and women, children, senior citizens and students different prices and also charges different prices according to the time of the journey, e.g. peak, off-peak, weekday and weekend. BT also price discriminates according to the time of day/week and distance of the call. The price charged to the consumer is made up of 2 elements: a fixed charge or quarterly rental, which is designed to cover BT's fixed costs, and a variable charge related to the use of the phone. The ability of a firm to price discriminate depends on whether it can split or segment its market. In the case of BT and BR this is quite straightforward. Other industries and firms price discriminate, e.g. the breweries charge different prices in the different regions of the country, cinemas offer cheap

tickets for afternoon and late shows, and the Electricity Boards operate an Economy 7 system where consumers pay less for night-time electricity.

In addition to adopting a particular pricing method, a firm can also follow a number of pricing strategies or tactics. The more common of these include:

1. **Penetration pricing** is a tactic adopted by a company when it is first entering (or penetrating) a market and is trying to establish a market share. It tends to be used where there is very little or no consumer 'brand loyalty' and where the demand for the good is price elastic.

2. **Skimming price** is where a firm charges a high price for a product in order to 'skim' the 'top end' of the market. It is most likely where the product is new and consumers have not had a chance to establish a 'price plateau'. This refers to the price that consumers expect to pay for a product, e.g. would anybody expect to pay 40p for a standard size Mars bar? Clearly this would be above the price plateau. When products are new a price plateau has not had the chance to be established and some consumers are willing to pay a high price to buy the new product because of its novelty value.

3. **Loss-leader pricing** is when firms offer prices below the cost of producing the item (hence making a loss) in order to encourage the sale of other products. Supermarkets frequently adopt this tactic to encourage people into the stores so that once inside they may buy additional items on impulse.

4. **Limit-pricing** occurs when a firm which normally has a large market share drops the price of its product to limit or deter the entry of other new competitors. The success of this strategy depends on the size of the price drop, the potential profits to be gained by new firms, and the determination of other firms to enter the industry.

5. **Predatory pricing** typically occurs when a firm holds the price of its product below those of its rivals for long periods of time in the hope of driving them out of the industry and establishing a monopoly position.

6. **Dumping pricing** happens when a firm 'dumps' its goods onto a market at below the cost of producing them in the hope that it can establish a foothold in the market. Once a market has been established the price of the product may rise to those of competitor firms.

7. **Competitive pricing** is when the firm prices its product in line with those of its competitors. There is little price variation between the types of goods being sold. In this situation there may be a substantial amount of 'non-price' competition, e.g. on packaging and design of the product.

QUICK QUESTIONS 4

1. What do you understand by the term 'price elasticity of demand'?
2. A firm is advised that if it drops the price of its chocolate bar from 30p to 25p its sales will increase from 20,000 bars per week to 25,000 bars per week. Calculate the PED of the chocolate bar. Should the firm adopt this strategy?
3. Would you expect the following goods to have elastic or inelastic PEDs:
   (a) bread
   (b) holidays abroad
   (c) cigarettes
   (d) safety pins
   (e) a Sony walkman?
   Give reasons for your choice.
4. What are the names given to the following types of pricing policy illustrated in the following situations:
   (a) a taxi charging a higher fare on journeys after midnight
   (b) Marks & Spencer charging higher prices for its peanuts and toilet rolls
   (c) a baker who charges an engaged couple for a specially designed wedding cake?

STUDENT EXERCISE

BPP Ltd manufactures and sells ballpoint pens. The table below shows the market information for ballpoints.

Price £	Demand Per Year (millions)	Supply Per Year (millions)
4.00	38	60
3.50	40	52
3.00	43	49
2.50	45	45
2.00	50	42
1.50	58	40
1.00	60	38

1. Illustrate this information on a diagram.
2. What is the market equilibrium price and quantity for ballpoint pens?
3. What would happen if the market price were (a) £4 and (b) £1.50?

Firms in the fibre-tip pen industry decide they are going to drop the price of their pens substantially. The predicted effect of this will be to reduce demand for ballpoints by 8 million pens at each and every price shown in the table.

4. Calculate and draw the new market demand curve.
5. What has happened to the market equilibrium price and quantity of ballpoint pens?
6. How would you describe the relationship between the 2 products?

The market share of BPP Ltd is 10%. A consultancy firm has estimated BPP's demand curve as follows:

Price £	Demand (millions per year)
4.00	3.8
3.50	4.0
3.00	4.3
2.50	4.5
2.00	5.0
1.50	5.8
1.00	6.0

7. From this demand curve calculate the price elasticity of demand for BPP Ltd pens when the price falls from £2.50 to £2.
8. Is the price elasticity of demand elastic or inelastic?

The Sales and Production Departments of BPP Ltd produce the following information:

Price £	Sales (millions per year)	Costs Fixed £m	Costs Variable £
2.50	4.5	3	£1 per pen
2.00	5.0	3	£0.60 per pen

The Sales Director argues that BPP should not drop price because the firm will lose sales revenue. The Production Director suggests that output should be increased to 5 million because average costs of production would be lower.

9. What would be the argument of the Finance Director, who is concerned about the company's profit?

PROJECT AND ASSIGNMENT SUGGESTIONS

1. Choose a common household commodity and a more expensive luxury item and investigate the factors which are important in determining the demand for each. You can use the information from the chapter to construct a table listing the major influences on demand, and then indicate the importance of each influence on the 2 commodities you have selected.
2. Choose 3 goods or services that you and your friends regularly buy, e.g. records, articles of casual clothing, visits to the cinema and so on.
   (a) Check the prices of each item in a number of shops or outlets.
   (b) Using this information as a guide, construct a realistic range of prices for each item you have chosen.
   (c) Ask your friends whether they would buy the good or service at each price and if so how much they would buy over a given period.
   (d) Use the information from your survey to calculate the elasticity of demand of each item over the range of prices. State whether the good or service seems to be price elastic or price inelastic.
   (e) If the price elasticity differs considerably among the different commodities, try to explain the reasons for this.

CHAPTER 13

Market Research and Product Development

The Market for Goods and Services

A market has previously been defined as any form of contact between buyers and sellers for the purpose of buying and selling goods and services. These markets can be local, e.g. window cleaning services, national or even international. A market typically has 4 elements:

1. Buyers – people wishing to acquire goods and services.
2. Sellers – people wishing to sell goods and services.
3. The goods and services which are going to be exchanged.
4. A means of payment – that includes cash, cheque, credit, direct debit, standing order and hire purchase.

Chapters 13–15 are about the market for consumer goods, i.e. the provision of goods and services to the general public. However, the principles and ideas apply equally to industrial markets – just as there is a market for toothpaste so there is a market for multi-million-pound oil rigs and aircraft.

Market Orientation and Product Orientation

Consumers have a wide variety of choice in how they spend their income, and there is a large quantity and many different types of goods and services that the consumer can buy. One difficulty that confronts a firm is to decide what to produce. Satisfying the wants and needs of consumers and anticipating these wants can make the difference between success and failure in business. Some things, such as food, are essential. Food is an example of a **single-use consumer good**. Most people, having satisfied their needs, can attempt to satisfy their wants by the purchase of items such as cars, TVs, microwave ovens and compact disc players. These are sometimes called **consumer durable products**. Alternatively, they may purchase services such as dry-cleaning, haircuts, trips to the cinema and meals out.

Today, a successful company is one which tries to discover what the consumer wants or could be persuaded to buy and then makes that product and sells it at a profit. Such firms are said to be **market-orientated**. In a market-orientated firm one of the functions of the marketing department is to find out consumer requirements. This is in complete contrast to a **product-orientated** firm, which first produces a product and then tries to sell it in the hope that the consumer will buy it.

Marketing and the Marketing Department

The Institute of Marketing has defined marketing as 'the process responsible for identifying, anticipating and satisfying customer requirements profitably'. The Marketing Department of any company must first establish what the customer wants before that product can be designed and manufactured. Once it has been made, it is the Marketing Department's responsibility to see that the product is sold to the consumer. The typical functions of a Marketing Department in a large company are shown in Figure 13.1. Each of these functions will be examined in the next 3 chapters.

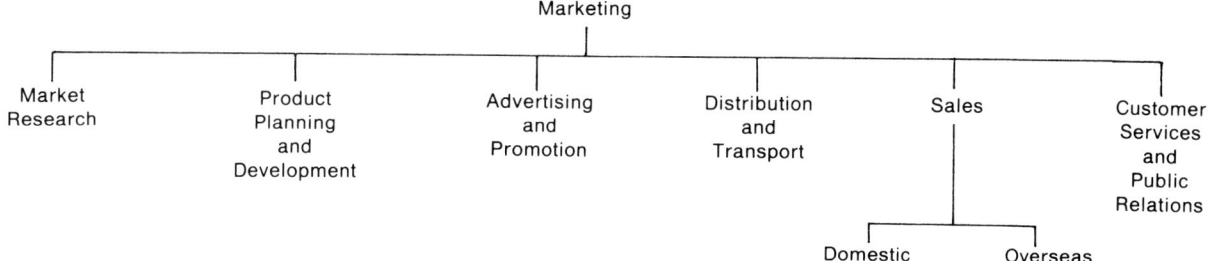

Figure 13.1 The Organisation of the Marketing Department

Market Research

This involves studying the market to discover exactly what the customer really wants. Companies collect information in order to build up a picture of consumer requirements. It can come from 2 main sources.

1. **Primary information** is information that is not already available. One of the techniques used to collect this information here is **field research** – questioning consumers directly about their tastes and preferences.
2. **Secondary information** is information that is already available to the firm. It can come from a variety of sources, such as government statistics and business and trade publications. Gathering information this way is called **desk research**.

A firm usually possesses its own internal information about the popularity of its products and about its own sales. This information, although useful, may be of limited value since it tells the firm nothing about the total size of the market, competitors' products and prices, or consumer preferences. Here the firm will have to acquire external information from sources such as the Department of Trade and Industry (DTI), trade associations, banks, chambers of commerce, national and local press and trade journals. The DTI has its own Statistics and Market Intelligence Library, which is freely available for public use and contains information on market size and trends, which products consumers are buying and the market position of different firms.

QUICK QUESTIONS 1

1. *What are the 4 elements of a market?*
2. *Give examples of (a) single-use consumer goods, (b) consumer durable goods.*

3. *What is marketing and what are the functions of a Marketing Department?*
4. *From what 2 sources can a company obtain its market research information?*

Identifying Consumer Wants: Questionnaires and Interviews

Consumer research can be carried out by the Market Research Department of a company or by a business which specialises in providing this service for others, e.g. Mintel and MORI. Market research companies have enjoyed a boom in the last decade, and in 1986 the industry was estimated to have a turnover of £204 million. When the Market Research Society celebrated its fortieth anniversary in 1986 it had a membership of 5,500 as against 23 when it first started in 1946.

Identifying the tastes and preferences of consumers is not simple because there are many different types of consumers with different tastes. Before market research can get under way, the firm needs to ask itself 2 questions:

1. **Who is our consumer?** Firms normally try to build up a consumer profile, i.e. the age, sex, occupation and location of its consumers. The most widely used method of identifying consumers is according to their socio-economic group. It has been established that social position and occupation often determine consumers' spending habits. Table 13.1 shows the various socio-economic groups in the UK.

   Newspapers, for example, often provide information on readership by socio-economic groups. This enables advertisers to decide on the most appropriate newspaper for their advertising campaigns.

Table 13.1. *Socio-economic Groups in the UK*

Social Grade	Social Status	Occupation	% of UK Population
A	Upper middle class	Professional	3.1
B	Middle class	Managerial	13.4
C1	Lower middle class	Supervisory	22.3
C2	Skilled working class	Skilled manual	31.2
D	Working class	Semi-skilled/Unskilled	19.1
E	The poor	Pensioners/Unemployed	10.9

2. **What information does the company wish to find out and by what means?** This is concerned with the type of questions that consumers are going to be asked and how they are going to be asked. A firm has 2 principal methods of seeking information from consumers: the questionnaire and the interview. The major difference between the 2 methods is that with a questionnaire the answers are completed on a form whereas during an interview consumers are asked questions by an interviewer who then records the answers given.

Questionnaires

It is difficult to design a sensible and usable questionnaire. To be of any use the replies need to come from well-worded and well-presented questions. The following points need to be kept in mind during the design process:

1. The purpose of the questionnaire must be clearly stated – people tend to be suspicious about answering questions and giving confidential information.
2. Try not to rely too much on the person's memory.
3. All questions need to be as clear as possible – avoid asking questions that are ambiguous.
4. The questions need to follow a logical pattern.
5. Use everyday language and try to avoid jargon.
6. Offer a range of answers if possible rather than 'yes' or 'no' – the responses must not be too restricted otherwise the person may not feel able to answer the question.

7. Keep the questionnaire as short as possible – people will not feel like answering a lot of questions, particularly if they have to write long answers. It saves time and encourages people to complete the questionnaire if all they have to do is tick a box.

Table 13.2, which contains examples of questions and their weaknesses, illustrates how difficult it is to design good questions.

Once the firm has decided on the questions it is going to ask, it then needs to distribute the questionnaires. This can be done in a number of ways: by post in the form of a postal survey; to consumers who have already bought a product by including the questionnaire in the product's packaging; by using a market researcher to distribute the questionnaires and collect the completed form or by supplying a pre-paid stamped addressed envelope. Some companies include questions, e.g. about the place of purchase or the age/sex of the consumer, on their guarantee. This is a relatively cheap method of gathering research information.

Interviews

In comparison with the questionnaire, the interview does have a number of advantages over the questionnaire in that the interviewer can ask more difficult questions and can also explain the questions. The **response rate** also tends to be higher because people are more likely to agree to being questioned when approached by somebody in the street than they are to complete a questionnaire that comes through the door. Finally, the interviewer can also select certain types of consumers that the company is

Table 13.2. *Typical Faults in the Way Questions are Phrased*

Question	Faults
1. Do you buy sweets regularly?	What type of sweets and what does regularly mean? To some people the word regularly may mean every day. To others it could be once a week or twice a month.
2. Are your curtains lined?	The word 'lined' could mean with curtain linings or with a lined pattern.
3. Would you buy T-shirts if they were available in more colours and had different designs?	This question involves two issues. First, the colour, and second, the design. The answers would not give the particular reason why they bought T-shirts.
4. How many times have you bought a 'Big Mac' in the last year?	This is relying too heavily on the person's memory and the answers are likely to be very approximate.
5. Do you think Mars bars are reasonably priced?	What is meant by a 'reasonable' price? To some people it could be 10p to others it may mean 30p.

particularly interested in, e.g. somebody local, aged between 18 and 25, and female. This cannot be done so easily by postal questionnaire. However, these advantages are bought at a price – the interviewer has to be paid and interviewing is a time-consuming process.

QUICK QUESTIONS 2

1. *What is market research?*
2. *Which is (a) the largest and (b) the smallest socio-economic group in the UK? Why is it useful for organisations to know this information? Give examples to support your answer.*
3. *Look at the questions in Table 13.2. Redesign them so that they make more sense.*
4. *What are the advantages of gaining market research information by interview rather than by question-naire?*

Other Methods of Gathering Market Information

A company can also gather market research information from other sources. The most important include:

1. **Group interviews**: in a group interview a number of consumers with similar interests are brought together and they are asked to discuss a particular topic under the guidance of someone experienced in consumer research. This allows argument and discussion to take place, which is not possible with a straightforward question-naire.
2. **Hall tests**: consumers are invited to a 'hall' to look at or taste a particular product and give their reaction to it. It is a method that is frequently used in supermarkets when they are testing new types of coffee, cheese, pizza, margarine, etc.
3. **Telephone surveys**: these are an important part of UK market research and they now account for about one third of all interviews carried out by market research companies. Telephone interviews tend to be shorter and less costly than both personal and postal surveys. But the cost of using the telephone means that detailed questions cannot be asked. There are 2 reasons for the growth in telephone surveys. Firstly, a larger proportion of households now own a telephone (about 80%). Second, telephone research produces more im-

mediate results. The information can be collected and analysed very quickly. A number of TV programmes now conduct telephone research into people's opinions on particular topics. It is also used by life assurance, double glazing and fitted kitchen companies.

4. **Consumer panels**: in a situation where a continuous flow of information is required over a period of time it may be too costly and too time-consuming to carry out market research on a regular basis. To get round these problems a consumer panel can be established. This is a group of consumers who agree to use and report on a particular product. Consumer panels are often used for testing reactions to a new product or changes to an existing product. The consumer gets free use of the product, e.g. a new steam iron, and is then asked to fill in a questionnaire about it.

In 1985 it was estimated that members of the Association of Market Survey Organisations (AMSO) conducted 7.1. million interviews. The importance of the various methods discussed above is illustrated in Table 13.3.

Table 13.3. *Principal Interviewing Methods of AMSO 1985*

Method	%
Personal interview	55.2
Telephone	32.0
Hall test	5.8
Postal interview	6.1
Group discussion	0.9
TOTAL	100

Source: Financial Times Survey, 11 November 1986, p. 19.

Sampling

With a population of 58 million people in the UK no method of consumer research could possibly find out all their tastes and preferences. In order to try and find out what consumers want or prefer it is necessary to question a **sample** of the population. Meaningful results and conclusions can then be drawn. A sample is simply a group that reflects the population at large. There are 2 methods of choosing a sample: (a) random or probability sampling and (b) quota sampling.

With **random sampling**, names and/or addresses can be pre-selected, e.g. every 20th person in the telephone directory. This is of course a completely arbitrary method of choosing a sample. With **quota sampling**, the sample has to be designed so as to reflect the characteristics of the total population. The information about a large school given in Table 13.4 can be used to illustrate the principle of quota sampling.

Table 13.4. *School Population Divided According to Year Group and Sex*

Whole School Population			% of Total		
Year	Boys	Girls	Boys	Girls	Year Group
One	90	95	9.0	9.5	18.5
Two	70	80	7.0	8.0	15.0
Three	80	60	8.0	6.0	14.0
Four	90	90	9.0	9.0	18.0
Five	100	100	10.0	10.0	20.0
Six	70	75	7.0	7.5	14.5
TOTAL	500	500	50.0	50.0	100

There are 1000 children in the school, split equally between boys and girls. To construct a representative sample, 100 pupils would be picked for questioning. This 100 would be known as a 10% sample, and it would have to reflect 2 things: (a) the sex difference and (b) the year group difference. For example, the third form is smaller than the fifth form and so the sample should contain more people from the fifth form than from the third form, e.g. 8 boys and 6 girls from the third year and 10 boys and girls from the fifth year. These principles apply to the construction of samples for opinion polls taken before a General Election, e.g. by Marplan or MORI.

The information gained from market research can be used in a variety of ways. It is particularly important in the development of new products or in the refinement of existing ones. Product development is examined below.

Product Development

This section of the Marketing Department's work may follow up the findings of the market research section. Design of a new product and refinements to existing products entail co-operation between a number of departments, including Design, Production, Finance and Marketing. A company often sets up a product planning committee to make decisions about product changes. There are a number of reasons for developing new products: sales of the existing product may be falling; another firm may have introduced a new product; or a technological change may have happened that enables the firm to build something that they weren't able to build before. The idea of product development is to keep the company ahead or up with its rivals, e.g. motor car manufacturers change the specification and styling of their cars at regular intervals after the introduction of the original model.

Having established whether there is sufficient potential demand for a product and the type of product that the consumer wants, the design team then has to work out what the product is going to look like and the materials that will be used to make it. The Production Department has to be consulted to see if it is possible to build the new product, and the Finance Department's job is to make sure that the product can be sold at a profit – they will have to look at the cost of the product and its potential sales. If it cannot be supplied profitably there is no point in making it. Technological change has speeded up the process of product development. **Computer-aided design** (CAD) has enabled car designers to use computer simulations to decide on the design of a new vehicle. Previously the only way to find out about a vehicle's performance was to build and then test it. When Sir Alec Issigonis first designed the Mini, for example, he started with a freehand sketch on the back of a postcard. Now such designs are done on computer.

Once the product has been designed, a **prototype** or test product is manufactured and tested by the firm. In the light of these test results, the company may modify the product before allowing it to be tried by a sample of consumers or launching it onto the market. The advertising, promotion and distribution involved in the launch of the product are examined in Chapter 14.

QUICK QUESTIONS 3

1. *Why have telephone surveys become a more popular method of getting market research information?*
2. *What is a consumer panel?*
3. *What is quota sampling and why is it necessary?*
4. *Why may a firm decide to introduce a new product?*
5. *Which departments will be involved in the development of a new product? Outline briefly the work of each in this process.*

STUDENT EXERCISE

Market Research and Product Development

You work for a company called Houseware Ltd that manufactures 2 electric household goods: microwave ovens and electric cooking pots. These products have a reputation for reliability and long life. However, sales of these products have been falling and the Market Research Department is asked to find out why. Here is its response:

Factors Affecting the Sale of Microwave Ovens

Price	Size of family
Credit facilities	Convenience
Cooking capacity	Ownership of freezer
Colour	Age of person
Free utensils	Marital status
Income/Socio-economic group	

1. Design a questionnaire that could be used to find out the importance of these factors when people are deciding to buy a microwave oven.
2. Explain how you would expect any 5 of the factors listed above to influence the purchase of microwaves.

The Market Research Department decides that it is going to use your questionnaire on a random sample in 7 major cities of Britain: London, Manchester, Birmingham, Leeds, Liverpool, Newcastle and Bristol. The response rate was very good – 85% of people approached gave answers.

3. Explain what you understand by the terms: 'random sample' and 'response rate'.

In addition to conducting this primary research, the Market Research Department also uses desk research and discovers the following statistics on the sale of household products.

Analysis of the Purchase of Household Goods

Product	First-Time Buyers	Replacement of Old Item	Total Sales
Microwave ovens	100,000	20,000	120,000
Electric cookers	400,000	80,000	480,000
Irons	200,000	100,000	300,000
Deep freezes	80,000	10,000	90,000
Cooking pots	10,000	1,000	11,000
Toasters	70,000	35,000	105,000
Food blenders	20,000	2,000	22,000

A lot of market research information is often presented in ways that are easily understood, e.g. bar charts, pie charts and percentage tables.

4. From the above information calculate for each product: (i) The % of sales accounted for by first-time buyers and replacement buyers (ii) Show this information diagrammatically.

From the above list of products the company has decided to manufacture another 2 products apart from microwave ovens and cooking pots. You suggest that they should produce the products with the largest number of first-time buyers because this shows (a) that there is a healthy demand for the product and (b) that not all people possess the product.

5. Which 2 products would you choose?
6. Design one of these products and point out any of its features that you think will be attractive to potential customers. How does this product compare with the product of one of your competitors?

PROJECT AND ASSIGNMENT SUGGESTIONS

1. Assume you wish to establish a business which specialises in printing colourful designs on T-shirts. Your idea is that customers can either select one of your range of designs or ask for a design of their own choosing. You believe there is a market for this type of service but you wish to test out the idea before going ahead.
   (a) Design a questionnaire which can be used to carry out a market research exercise to help you decide if your idea is worth pursuing.
   (b) Explain how you would organise your market research exercise and who you would include in your samples.
   (c) Organise a sample survey in your school or college in order to test the suitability of your questionnaire for obtaining the information you require.
   (d) After your survey, briefly explain any changes you would make to your questionnaire and why you would make them.
   (e) Describe what other methods you could use to research the market for your idea.
2. Find out what you can about the work of market survey organisations. If there is a specialist market research company in your area write for information about the type of work it undertakes. Using this information write a report on how this type of business helps other firms to improve their products and increase their sales.

CHAPTER 14

Advertising, Distribution and Customer Relations

Advertising and Promotion

If consumers are going to buy a good or service they must be made aware of its existence. The advertising function of the Marketing Department communicates with the customer through media such as newspapers, television, the cinema and posters. It will also be concerned with the design and distribution of catalogues, special offers (price reductions and free gifts), sponsorship, displays, competitions and product launch campaigns. Some companies prefer to leave the advertising of a product to a specialist advertising agency. The agency is said to have the company's account.

Advertising

In Chapter 4 on communication it was established that the purpose of communication – which is what advertising is – is to inform and influence people's behaviour. The 4 elements of communication, the sender, the message, the media and the receiver, are all found in advertising.

Advertising can be classified into 2 broad categories: **informative** and **persuasive**. Typically an advert contains elements of both. When a product is first launched, sales are low because very few customers are aware that it exists. The role of advertising here may be to inform the public of the product's existence and its particular uses. The same applies when a product has been modified or improved. In other cases, e.g. new cars or scientific calculators, the nature of the product may be such that a large amount of technical information has to be supplied, and advertising again may have to be informative. Advertising that informs and educates consumers gives them greater choice in their selection of goods and services. It can be seen as a form of competition between firms and may encourage manufacturers to improve their products to the benefit of the consumer.

Persuasive advertising, as its name implies, is used to try and persuade a consumer to buy a particular product. Such advertising is subjective and contains many statements of opinion rather than fact, e.g. 'Carlsberg – the best lager in the world ... probably'. Persuasive advertising is normally associated with consumer products and is used heavily where differences between products are minor, e.g. toothpaste, baked beans, soap powder, washing liquids and lager. Persuasive advertising has been criticised because it emphasises the advantages of a product and attempts to make those who do not use the product feel as if they are missing out. It plays on jealousy, envy and 'keeping up with the Joneses'. However, there are a number of regulations that control the content of advertisements, and firms are required to follow the British Code of Advertising Practice. Some important extracts from this code are:

1. All advertisements should be legal, decent, honest and truthful.
2. All advertisements should be prepared with a sense of responsibility to the consumer.
3. All advertisements should conform to the principles of fair competition as generally accepted in business.
4. No advertisement should bring advertising into disrepute or reduce confidence in advertising as a service to industry and to the public.

When the code is breached advertisers are quick to amend or withdraw the advertisement concerned. If they do not do this the media may agree not to sell them advertising space or airtime and they may risk unwelcome publicity from the Advertising Standards Authority. In the case of TV commercials, every film must be approved for transmission before it can be screened, to ensure that it complies with the

Independent Broadcasting Authority's Code of Practice.

It is normally very difficult to distinguish between the persuasive and informative elements in any advertisement. There is generally a blend of both. Examples of newspaper and magazine advertising are shown in Figure 14.1.

Perhaps the best example of informative advertising is the advert for Begee's, which simply states what the company sells, its address and telephone number. The advert for Charles King has elements of both. It informs the consumer of opening times for parts and accessories, and of the location of the company, but also tries to persuade the consumer by the offer of a free gift for Sunday shoppers. The advert for Vitapointe is obviously the one that contains the largest persuasive element.

Once the firm has decided that advertising is going to play some role in the marketing of its product(s), it must then decide on the message, the media and the receiver. All these factors will be linked. It could be that the receiver – the so-called **target audience** – will determine the message and the media. If, for example, the product is a children's toy, the advert should be placed on television at particular times of the day.

In designing the message the advertiser will need to consider the following:

1. **The content of the message**: this will depend on the type of product and the market in which it is to be sold.
2. **Who is the receiver?** The message may be directed at a particular group of the population, in which case it may have to be delivered in a particular way using a certain media.
3. **The person used to send the message**: very often large firms use celebrities that they think are appropriate for the product, e.g. Steve Cram and Start breakfast cereal, Jerry Hall and Bovril and Daley Thomson and Lucozade.
4. **The timing and number of messages**: an advertiser has a choice between 2 approaches to an advertising campaign. It can be extensive, where the object is to reach as wide an audience as possible using different media. On the other hand, it can be intensive, where the object is to reach a particular group repeatedly (e.g. products such as lager, coffee, washing powder and

toilet rolls are advertised intensively on television).

QUICK QUESTIONS 1

1. *What is advertising and how can it be classified?*
2. *Write down examples of persuasive and informative advertising on the TV at the moment.*
3. *Study some adverts from the TV and the press (a newspaper or magazine). Say whether they are good or poor adverts and why.*
4. *How are firms limited in what they can say in an advert?*

Having decided on the message, the advertiser then has to choose the most cost-effective medium (or media). This means choosing the medium that delivers the message to the right (and largest) audience at the lowest possible cost. Examples of the media available are: commercial television, independent local radio, newspapers, magazines, billboards, buses, trains and bus shelters. For a firm advertising an industrial product the choice may be limited to exhibitions, specialist magazines and direct mail (see pp.164–5).

Table 14.1 shows how much was spent on advertising in the UK in 1985 and how it was allocated among the different media. Table 14.2 shows the companies that spent the most on advertising in 1988.

Table 14.1. *Advertising Expenditure in the UK, 1985*

Medium	£m
Cinema	18
Radio	82
Posters and transport	164
Television	1,376
Total press	2,801
Press made up of:	
Regional newspapers	1,003
National newspapers	747
Business/Professional	344
Magazines and periodicals	253
Press production costs	245
Directories	209
TOTAL EXPENDITURE	4,441

Source: Financial Times Survey, 22 October 1986, p. 1.

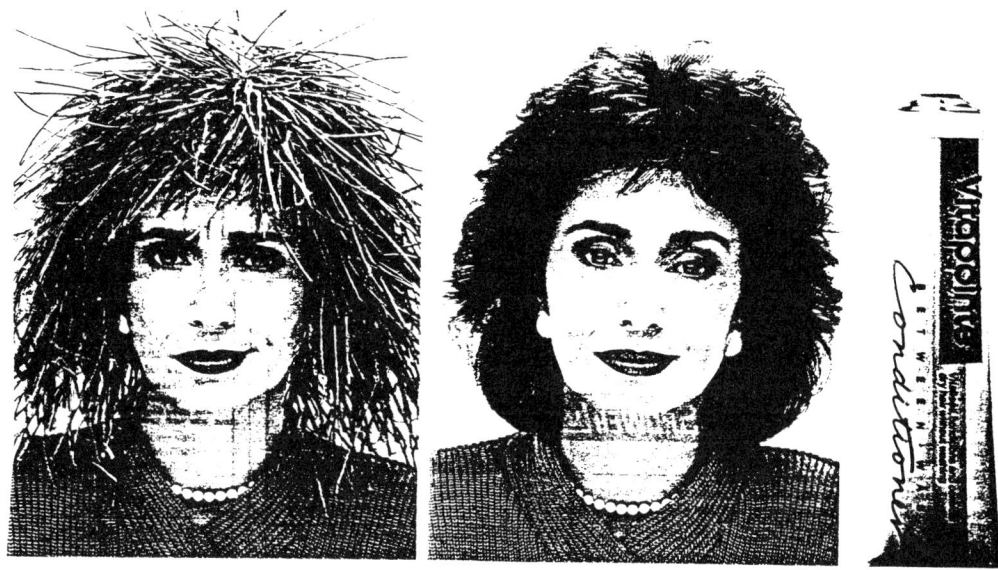

ALL DRY HAIR NEEDS IS A DROP OF VITAPOINTE.

You don't have to get wet to control dry hair. Because Vitapointe is specially formulated to work between washes.
Take one drop of Vitapointe and you can replace all the natural oils and lanolin that dry hair lacks. At the stroke of a brush.

Figure 14.1 Examples of Newspaper and Magazine Advertising

Table 14.2. *The Top Ten Advertisers in 1988*

By Holding Company	£m	By Company	£m
Unilever	118.1	Proctor and Gamble	58.0
Proctor and Gamble	77.4	British Telecom	45.6
HM Government	76.1	Kellogs	41.2
Mars (UK)	73.3	Nestlé	36.1
Nestlé Holdings (UK)	71.5	Pedigree Petfoods	34.5
Kingfisher	46.5	Mars Confectionery	33.9
British Telecom	45.6	Electricity Council	32.9
Electricity Council	42.6	Vauxhall Motors	32.8
Kellogg (UK)	41.2	Austin Rover Group	30.9
General Motors (US)	33.3	Brooke Bond/Batchelors	30.1

Source: Media Expenditure Analysis Survey (MEAL), 1988.

In total almost £4.5 billion was spent on advertising in 1985. The majority of this was in the press (£2.8bn) – mainly regional newspapers – followed by television.

The largest advertisers were Unilever and Proctor and Gamble, which manufacture detergents, followed by companies that advertise consumer food products and motor cars. The government spent a lot on advertising in 1988 on things such as health and privatisation campaigns.

Although each advertising medium is in competition with the other media, this may not be direct competition. Each medium has its own characteristics and covers different areas of a potential market. A summary of these is provided in Table 14.3.

The advantages and disadvantages of each medium must be weighed up when a firm comes to select the means used to deliver the message. The choice of medium is also governed by the **impact** the firm wishes to make, the number of times the firm wants the advert displayed (**frequency**), the **coverage** of the advert and the **cost** of advertising.

Impact

This has a number of aspects, including the use of colour, movement, size of advert, the content of the advert, e.g. humorous or serious, and the placing of the advert.

Frequency

This is the number of times or length of time the advert is shown, e.g. if the campaign is intensive the advert may be shown on TV many times on 2 or 3

nights a week for several weeks or even longer. The campaign may involve taking out a single advert in a newspaper on one particular day. The type of product may dictate the timing of the advert and when it is advertised, e.g. toilet rolls are advertised all the year round whereas summer holidays are more likely to be advertised in the winter, and children's toys are more likely to be advertised between children's programmes.

Coverage

This looks at the breadth of the medium that is being used to conduct an advertising campaign and also at the number or percentage of the target audience that is being reached. One factor that is important in determining coverage of an advertising campaign is its cost.

Cost

The cost of using the different media varies. For example, the average cost of producing a 30-second TV commercial is said to be around £80,000. To put this commercial 'on the air' using Thames Television would have cost £10,000 in 1984. In the same year a full-page advertisement in the national press would have cost between £10,000 and £20,000, according to the circulation of the paper.

A firm has to ask itself a number of important questions in relation to advertising:

1. What effect does advertising have on the company's sales? Lord Leverhulme, founder of

Table 14.3. *The Advantages and Disadvantages of Different Media*

Medium	Advantages	Disadvantages
Television	• Exposure on a national scale. • The advert reaches all socio-economic groups. • Sound, vision, movement and colour can all be used.	• Expensive. • There may not be a nationwide interest in the product, so TV advertising would be inappropriate.
Daily newspapers	• Exposure on a national scale. • People tend to believe what is in the papers. • They have a high attention value.	• Only read by particular groups. • Can be expensive.
Sunday newspapers	• They have a greater attention value as more people have time to read them. • They have a large circulation. • Colour and good quality paper in magazines makes the advertising in them more attractive.	• Expensive. • Difficult to pin down the composition of the readership. • A single advert in one issue may not inform the majority of readers.
Local newspapers	• Readers tend to scrutinise their local paper more closely than they do the nationals. • Evening editions which come into the home are read at leisure. • Greater density of readership on a local basis.	• Local papers do not have the authority of the nationals. • Newsprint is sometimes of poor quality.
Trade magazines	• Circulation is rising. • Read by people who take an interest in trade adverts. • Less expensive than newspapers.	• Only reach small percentage of the population. • Tend to be published less frequently. • Advertising normally agreed on annual basis.

Lever Bros., is credited with making the famous statement: 'We know that one half of our advertising budget is wasted but we do not know which half.' This suggests that advertising does have some impact on a product's sales but that the exact effect is uncertain.

2. When should the company advertise?
3. Which medium or combination of media will work best?
4. How much should the company spend on advertising? Companies tend to use simple rules of thumb to decide this question. One method is to have a fixed amount to spend on advertising, although there is a weakness in this policy because the amount may not match what the company's competitors are spending, and they may be taking a bigger share of the market. A second rule is to follow your competitors and match their spending. This could lead to an advertising war and could be counter-productive because sales may not increase at the same rate as the advertising expenditure. A third rule is to set your advertising spending as a percentage of the actual (or forecast) sales of the product. But one problem here is that a sales lull would lead to a cut-back in advertising. Whereas it may be that the company needs to increase its expenditure on advertising the product in order to boost sales.

QUICK QUESTIONS 2

1. *What is meant by cost-effective advertising?*
2. *Imagine you were given the following products and services to advertise: toothpaste, window cleaning, a FAX machine, a local restaurant. Which types of advertising media would you choose and why?*
3. *Select 3 of the companies shown in Table 14.2 and try to discover what they produce. See if you can find adverts for their products in the different media. What does this tell you about the company's advertising campaign?*
4. *What factors are involved when a company decides how much to spend on advertising?*

Promotion

Sales promotion is often thought of as being the same as advertising. However, although the objectives of promotion and advertising are the same – to persuade the consumer to buy – there are differences in the way they are practised. Sales promotion often takes the form of an incentive, e.g. a free sample or a special offer, or 'Buy two and get one free'. The following examples should make the difference between advertising and promotion clear.

Firms use a number of sales promotion methods, including the following most typical ones:

Packaging and Design

The packaging and design of a product is very important if it is to catch the customer's eye. It may have to compete with other products for shelf-space, e.g. a supermarket may stock several types of a product but the one that catches the consumer's eye is likely to be the one put in the shopping basket. The key elements of packaging and design include colour, size, display and a brand or trademark. A company uses packaging and labels or trademarks to separate its product from those of close rivals. This is sometimes called **branding** and brand names are a common form of promotion. Some products are so closely associated with a particular manufacturer that consumers may refer to them by their brand name, e.g. Hoover in the case of vacuum cleaners and Parker in the case of pens. Companies hope to create a so-called 'brand image' e.g. 'Beanz Meanz Heinz', and Marks & Spencer using the St Michael label. The use of a brand name is designed to capture 'brand loyalty' – consumers will continue to buy products that are familiar and have a good reputation. They may also buy an unfamiliar product if they like others from the same brand. Other retailers, particularly in food retailing, have tried to hit back with the use of 'own label' products, e.g. Tesco baked beans and Sainsbury's washing powder.

The packaging of products has undergone a revolution in recent years. Soft drinks, for example are now sold in cans or plastic bottles rather than in large and heavy glass bottles. Sometimes the consumer may dictate the packaging of the product, e.g. with the current concern over the environment consumers are demanding biodegradable packaging. One area where packaging and design is important is the toothpaste market. Mentadent developed a pump dispenser to get over the problems of toothpaste tubes which crack, make a mess and do not dispense toothpaste even when there is still some left in the tube. Toothpaste is also a product where use is made of colour, e.g. different coloured stripes.

Personal Appearances

Celebrities often appear on 'chat shows', e.g. *Wogan*, to promote a new product. A group may perform a new record, a writer may promote a new book or an actor may be 'plugging' the new play in which he or she is performing. Authors and sportsmen sometimes make personal appearances at bookshops to sign copies of their novels or biographies to promote sales.

Exhibitions and Demonstrations

Many products are displayed at exhibitions open to the general public, e.g. The Ideal Home Exhibition and the annual Motor Show. A product may sometimes be tasted by the public in a supermarket, e.g. coffee, pizza and cheese. In large department stores aftershave and perfumes are available for testing and make-up demonstrations are arranged by cosmetics manufacturers. Sometimes a firm provides a demonstration in the home, and a party may be held to promote the sales of a product. In such settings, products are generally offered to the customer on a 'free demonstration no obligation to buy basis'.

Sampling

One means of launching a new product is to

provide free samples of it to households. These samples can be delivered door to door or through a particular magazine. Hair products, washing powders/liquids and fabric softeners are often launched in this way. The company hopes that once consumers have tried a small sachet sample of the product, they will go and buy the larger size bottle or packet at the shop.

Competitions

These are becoming commonplace in promoting sales of a product or service. Supermarkets, garages and travel agents often run competitions to increase sales. Newspapers have tried bingo games to increase their circulation. The prizes to be won are very attractive, e.g. £1 million, a 2-week holiday, or a car. Some consumers have even started to become competition addicts and have developed the art of devising catchy slogans and catchphrases.

Coupons

These can be used to further the sales of a product in 3 ways: they can be delivered through the door; they can be cut from newspapers to take to a store; or they may be attached to the product itself. To get the consumer to buy the product over and over again the offer may require the consumer to collect 10 packet tops in order to get £2 back or a free book. Petrol companies are heavily engaged in promotional activity, e.g. collect 10 tokens and receive a free tankard or tumbler. Some have now started to print gift brochures which show the gifts that can be gained with different numbers of tokens or stamps.

Pricing Promotions

Pricing has already been considered in Chapter 12. The idea behind a pricing promotion is to try and persuade consumers that they are getting value for money, e.g. 25% extra free, special bonus pack, 2 for the price of 1, and 10p off. A seasonal sale to clear out stock from the previous season to make room for the new season's collection is a further example of pricing promotion.

Direct Mail

The use of computers to maintain consumer records has enabled more and more companies to use 'junk mailing' methods to promote their products.

Companies use computer-stored information to make up mailing lists, and can send households personalised letters to urge them to change insurance policies or to convince them of the benefits of belonging to the Readers' Digest. A local company may employ somebody to drop handbills through the door, e.g. 'Top Prices Paid for Old Furniture or Scrap Metal'.

Sponsorship

This is frequently done to promote the name of the company rather than a particular product. It can be done by both large and small companies. Large companies may favour sponsoring a sports league or event, e.g. the Dunlop Matchplay Golf Championship or the Barclays League. Local firms may sponsor local teams and provide the players with shirts that display the company logo.

Merchandising

This involves the layout of the shop, the placing of the item in the store, the use of colour and point-of-sale material. It is often called the 'silent salesman' or 'selling through technique'. The best or 'prime' selling spots in a supermarket are the check-out areas, the shop perimeter and eye-level shelves. A child's attention is easily caught by the sweets at the check-out. Less popular products may be placed near the front of the store, with the popular items at the back. Customers may then pick up some of the less popular items on their way through the shop. In the fashion trade displays are very important. Shop windows are regularly changed by professional designers to prevent familiarity and to entice the customer into the shop. Once in the store, the careful placing of items may encourage a 'multiple sell', e.g. accessories such as shoes, belts and hats may sell better if placed near complementary trousers and skirts.

QUICK QUESTIONS 3

1. *Choose 2 well-known products. Look at how they are packaged and designed. Is it effective? Is it eye-catching? Design your own method of packaging for these 2 products and give reasons why you think your design is better.*

2. *Find some companies that are running competitions on particular products. Write down the conditions of*

taking part, what has to be collected and the gifts that are on offer. Make up your own competition to promote one of these products.

3. *Why do shops put a great deal of effort into the layout of the store and the placing of the items in the store?*

4. *Make a list of companies that sponsor national and local events. What products do they produce? Try and find out how much the sponsorship costs the company.*

Distribution and Sales

The term 'distribution' is not confined to the physical distribution of goods from the producer to the consumer, e.g. road and rail transport. In the business context it refers to the channels of distribution, i.e. the sort of retail outlets that the goods and services are sold in. These channels of distribution are examined in this section.

Many industrial products and services are sold directly to the consumer or user, e.g. aircraft and lathes. Most consumer products are usually distributed through retail organisations. By tradition many manufacturers sell their products to a wholesaler who warehouses the goods until they are required by the retailer. This so-called **full chain of distribution** offers advantages to both the manu-

facturer and retailer. The manufacturer can mass-produce the goods, get the money for the goods straight away, and does not have to worry about storage and distribution costs. The retailer can order goods from the wholesaler and does not have to worry about holding large stocks. The full chain of distribution has disadvantages for the manufacturer and the retailer. The wholesaler does not have any particular incentive to promote the sale of the manufacturer's goods, and the retailer will have to pay a higher price for the goods from the wholesaler than if they were bought directly from the manufacturer. Some industries have cut out the 'middleman' (wholesaler), and the manufacturer sells directly to the retailer. In other industries the wholesaler may sell the goods directly to the customer and no retailer is involved. Finally, the manufacturer may sell directly to the customer without a wholesaler or retailer being involved. Figure 14.2 provides a summary of these different chains of distribution.

Full Chain of Distribution

This tends to be used when the producer makes a limited range of products, storage costs are high and the product is perishable.

No Wholesaler

The wholesaler is eliminated in industries where the producer makes a number of standard products that it sells to similar kinds of retail outlets.

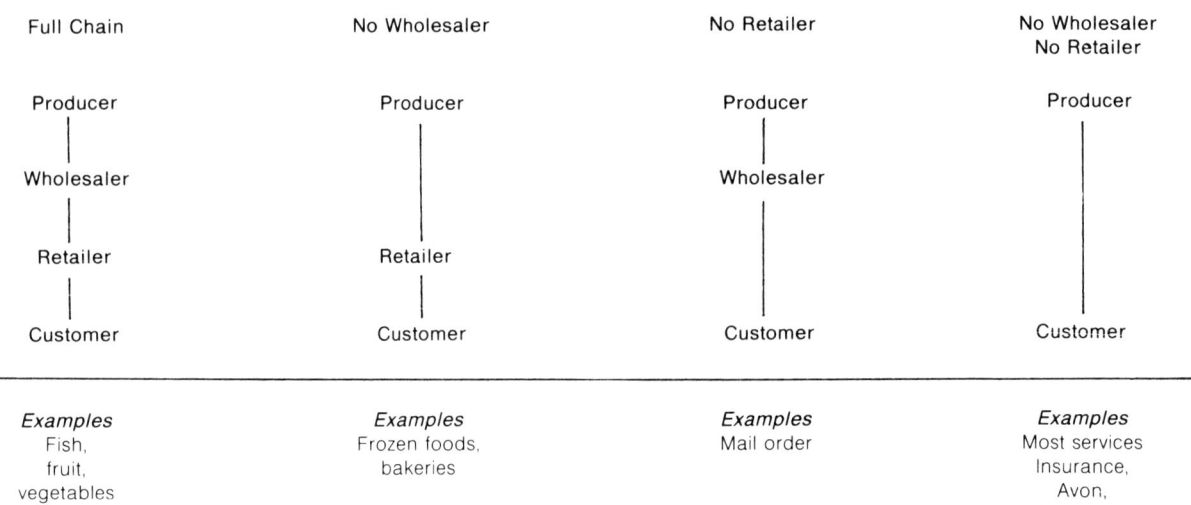

Figure 14.2 Different Chains of Distribution

Frozen-food firms and large bakeries tend to have their own distribution network and their own fleet of delivery lorries.

No Retailer

There has been a growth in the use of wholesalers which sell direct to the general public. These large discount stores sell furniture and other household products in warehouse-style buildings with relatively poor customer facilities. Mail order companies such as Great Universal Stores, where local selling agents run a catalogue and canvas for orders, are a good example of distribution without a retailer. These local agents work on a commission basis and deal with the ordering of goods and the means of payment.

Direct Selling

Direct selling to the customer is typically found in the sale of services, e.g. insurance and double glazing. In the case of industrial products such as chemicals and manufacturing machines, firms generally employ a full-time sales force to try and sell products to other firms. Such sales teams may be organised on a regional basis, with specific areas of the country to cover, e.g. North West, East Midlands and South Wales. The sales team is a very important part of the marketing function. Although its major role is to sell the company's product, it may also be a source of important market research information, e.g. salesmen can find out customers' reactions to products and can ascertain their future requirements. They can also find out what competitors are doing and supply this information back to the company. The sales team may also be the first link that a customer has with the company, and so the presentation of a good image may be important.

Retail Outlets

There are various retail outlets through which a manufacturer can decide to sell a product. In 1984 it was estimated that there were 343,153 retail outlets controlled by 230,789 organisations – which indicates that the vast majority are 'one-shop' operations. A summary of the different types of retail outlets is provided in Table 14.4.

Public Relations and Customer Service

Public relations (PR) is sometimes a separate department outside the marketing function. PR can be defined as the attempt to present an acceptable or

Table 14.4. *Different Types of Retailer*

Type of Retailer	Comments and Examples
Small-scale retailers	Market traders, door-to-door, mobile vans, newsagents, tobacconists, hairdressers, florists, jewellers
Department stores	Harrods, Browns of Chester and Ricemans of Canterbury
Multiple stores	A number (minimum 10) of retail shops owned by one firm, e.g. Halfords, Richard Shops, W. H. Smith, Curry's and Dolcis
Variety chains	Marks & Spencer, Woolworth, BHS and C & A
Co-ops	
Discount stores	Superdrug
Supermarkets	Tesco, Asda, Sainsbury's, Gateway, Keymarkets
Hypermarkets	Much larger than supermarkets and based on out-of-town sites. They tend to be owned by the large supermarket chains
Leased shops, franchises, concessions*	Miss Selfridge pays for 'concessions' in large department stores. This allows the company to sell its own products on somebody else's premises. Cosmetic manufacturers also tend to lease stands in Boots, John Lewis, etc.
Automatic vending	Not strictly a retail outlet. Generally found in pubs, railway stations and hotels. Cigarettes, sandwiches, chocolate and drinks are sold

* A leased shop involves renting floor space within a store in return for a commission based on sales. Franchising is where a smaller firm is allowed to trade under another firm's brand name in return for a fee and royalty payments, e.g. Benetton or Burger King.

favourable image of the company to the general public. This can be done in a number of possible ways: advertising, sponsorship, involvement in charity work, exhibitions and trade fairs, press releases and conferences.

Customer service is slightly different from PR in the sense that the company here is concerned with keeping the customer happy and satisfied. Areas that are important in good customer relations include: servicing and repair, after-sales service (installation, maintenance and spare parts), guarantees, enquiries and complaints. Having sold a product to the customer, the Service Department must see that the consumer is content with the product. A dissatisfied customer may be a future sale lost and bad publicity.

QUICK QUESTIONS 4

1. *What do you understand by the term 'full chain of distribution'?*
2. *What are the advantages to a manufacturer of using the services of a wholesaler? What are the disadvantages to the retailer?*
3. *What is direct selling? Give examples of where this method of selling is used.*
4. *What are the main functions of a sales team?*
5. *What is customer service and why do firms consider it to be important?*

STUDENT EXERCISE

Read the following extract and answer the questions that follow.

After years of decline from 450 million cinema visits in the UK in the late 1940s to just 54 million in 1984, attendances are on the increase. After British Film Year in 1985 the cinema is looking towards 80 million admissions in 1986. This gives the cinema something to sell the advertisers. The 2 great sales points of cinema are the dramatic impact of big screen advertising and the nature of the audience – the elusive young who watch little television. Seventy-eight per cent of the cinema audience is under 35 and 60 per cent under 25. This determines the nature of the advertising. Grocery brands and financial services are recent additions to cinema advertising. Brooke Bond with Red Mountain coffee, Nescafé, Weetabix and Kellogg's Start are just

some of the major brands on the screens, while Natwest, Barclays and TSB jostle with the building societies.

Cinema remains a cheap medium, with only a few advertisers, like Levi, Holstein and Pernod, spending over £500,000 a year. At the other extreme the local Chinese restaurant can book a spot for between £10 and £15 a week but it must commit itself to a 65-week contract. *Time Out* has booked a three-month campaign through Rank cinemas in the London area for £50,000, the cost of a couple of peak time spots on Thames TV. And it knows it will be screened at its target audience.

Source: The Financial Times, 22 October 1986.

1. Why has the cinema now got 'something to sell the advertisers'?
2. What are the advantages of cinema advertising?
3. Why have food retailers and the financial services companies started making more use of the cinema as an advertising medium?
4. What is the disadvantage to a small local firm of booking a cinema advertising slot?
5. What would be the contract cost to the local Chinese restaurant of using the cinema?
6. What are the advantages to *Time Out* of using the cinema rather than Thames TV?

PROJECT AND ASSIGNMENT SUGGESTIONS

1. Choose a good or service which is available from a number of competing producers. Undertake a study comparing the way the individual firms advertise their respective products, e.g. a comparison by the advertising undertaken by the main High Street banks or by the motor manufacturers. Your study should try and answer the following questions:
   (a) How does the advertising of each firm differ with respect to the degree of information provided to the customer?
   (b) Are the advertisements similar in style? Do they employ the same or different techniques of persuasion?
   (c) Is the advertising aimed at the same type of customer or do different firms try to appeal to different sectors of the market? How does your answer to this question compare with your

findings in (b) above?

(d) What are the similarities or differences in the media the firms use to advertise their product(s)?

(e) If possible try to discover how much the firms spend on advertising and compare the size of their advertising budgets.

Write up your findings in the form of a report, including examples of advertisements from the different firms you have studied.

2. Draw up a list of all the different promotional methods businesses can employ to increase the sales of their products. In each case find an example of a product where this type of promotion is particularly important, and a product where the method seems relatively unimportant. Choose different products for each type of promotional activity. In each case explain why you think the producer either places emphasis on this aspect of promotion or appears to reject it. Summarise your findings in the form of a table.

3. Visit a local corner or village shop and a large supermarket or hypermarket. Make a study of the different features of these types of retail outlets. In particular you should consider:

(a) How does the chain of distribution from producer to consumer differ for the kind of goods sold by each type of retailer?

(b) Are these different types of retailer used by different types of consumer?

(c) What are the advantages and disadvantages to the consumer of each type of retail outlet?

(d) How has the growth of the out-of-town hypermarket affected the role of the small retailer?

Summarise your findings in the form of a report.

CHAPTER 15

The Marketing Mix and Product Life Cycle

The Marketing Mix

The functions of the Marketing Department were examined in Chapters 13 and 14. This chapter looks at a firm's marketing strategy or **marketing mix**. The marketing mix is made up of 4 components, sometimes called the 4 Ps. These are:

1. **Product**: the firm has to identify what products the consumer wants and the way existing products can be adapted to meet consumer preferences more successfully. Consideration of new product development is essential here as tastes change and technology progresses.
2. **Price**: a firm has to decide on its pricing policy for list prices, discounts for bulk-buying and interest-free credit. What competitors are charging and what consumers are willing to pay are also important. A low price may make consumers suspicious ('cheap and nasty') or the low price may be thought of as a bargain ('cheap and cheerful'). If the price of the product is too high then the company may be pricing itself out of the market. If the price of the product is higher than what competitors are charging then it must be justified in some way, e.g. because the quality of the product is higher.
3. **Promotion**: this amounts to choosing methods that can generate sales of the product. Possibilities here include personal selling, advertising and other promotional work (see Chapter 14).
4. **Place**: the product has to be in the correct place – retail outlet – in order to capture sales. Exactly where a firm decides to sell its product will depend on the nature of the product.

A summary of the marketing mix and its components is given in Figure 15.1.

Figure 15.1 The components of the Marketing Mix

Product	Place
Quality	Distributors
Design	Retailers
Performance	Location
Features	Mail order
Size	Department stores
Name	Wholesalers
Services	Machine vending
Guarantees	
Colour	
Price	**Promotion**
Discounts	Advertising
List prices	Personal selling
Credit	Competitions
Hire purchase	Coupons
Payment period	Publicity
	Packaging

The components of the marketing mix are illustrated below using the example of cigarettes and tobacco companies.

The **product** itself comes into different size categories, e.g. standard, king size and now 'super-kings'. Cigarettes may come tipped or untipped, and there is also variety in terms of the tar content (low, middle and high). The tobacco, and hence the flavour of the cigarettes, also differs, e.g. some brands taste very strong while others are mild or menthol. The size, design and flavour are therefore variable, as are the number of cigarettes in a box – generally 10 or 20. Some brands, e.g. Park Drive, used to be sold in boxes of 5.

As far as **place** is concerned, cigarettes are sold through a wide range of retail outlets – tobacconists, newsagents, corner shops, garages, supermarkets, pubs, off-licences, hotels, duty-free shops and vending machines.

The **price** of cigarettes can vary enormously, particularly between the different types of retail outlets, e.g. supermarkets and newsagents. A favourite ploy of the tobacco companies is to have special offers at particular times to try and increase sales. Price also differs according to the size of the cigarette.

The **promotion** aspect of the marketing mix for cigarettes is a vast area. The tobacco companies are not allowed to advertise on television and each packet must carry a government health warning. Due to these restrictions, promotional activity takes a number of forms: sponsorship of sporting events, e.g. the Silk Cut Cricket Challenge and the Embassy World Darts Championship; competitions where the prices include holidays and cars; an offer of money in exchange for a certain number of packet tops. Embassy has had a long-running coupon collection promotion whereby coupons can be exchanged for gifts. The forerunner to all these competitions of course was the picture cards contained in cigarette packets. Some of these card collections are now worth a lot of money.

Even though the tobacco companies are not allowed to advertise their product on TV, they do spend considerable amounts of money on advertising in other media. Now that smoking is generally considered to be an antisocial habit (it is prohibited in some public places, e.g. certain train carriages and the London Underground, and some firms do not allow smoking in certain parts of their buildings), and because of the greater emphasis placed on health and fitness, smokers are now in a minority. Tobacco companies have therefore had to adopt a very attacking selling strategy. Advertising in magazines – particularly the colour supplements to the weekend papers – on billboards and on bus shelters is commonplace. The advertising is often very subtle, thought-provoking and eye-catching, e.g. Silk Cut and Benson and Hedges. Other companies adopt an entirely different approach, e.g. to conjure up the idea that people who smoke Marlboro are rugged, the smoker is portrayed as a cowboy on a horse.

It is quite noticeable that the marketing mix differs according to the type of product that is being sold. The fact that the term 'mix' is used implies that the four Ps – product, price, promotion and place – can be combined in different ways. One important factor that affects the marketing mix is the position of the product in its life cycle.

QUICK QUESTIONS 1

1. *What do you understand by the term 'marketing mix'?*
2. *Why may consumers be put off buying a product if it has too low a price?*
3. *How can a company justify charging a price for a product that is way above those of the competition? Give examples to support your answer.*
4. *Think of a product known to you and find out (a) the features (colour, design) of it, (b) the price of the product, (c) how it is promoted, (d) the places where it is sold.*

The Product Life Cycle

The period of time over which a product appeals to customers is called the product life cycle. At a given point in time a product will be at a particular stage of its life cycle. The length of this product life cycle differs from product to product, e.g. the life cycle of certain items such as clothing (flared or drainpipe trousers) and pop records may be very short indeed, perhaps a matter of months, or a few years at the outside. Other products, particularly consumer durable products such as telephones and colour TVs, may have a much longer product life cycle. Figure 15.2 shows a typical life cycle in diagram form.

In Figure 15.2 the **sales volume** (quantity of sales) or **sales revenue** is plotted along the vertical axis. Time (measured in weeks, months or years) is plotted along the horizontal axis. The figure shows the 5 stages of the product life cycle: introduction, growth, maturity, saturation and decline. Examples of products at the various stages of their life cycle are shown in Table 15.1.

Before a product is introduced, it generally has to be tested on a sample of consumers. During the development period, the product is often given a code name, e.g. Cadbury's Wispa had the secret

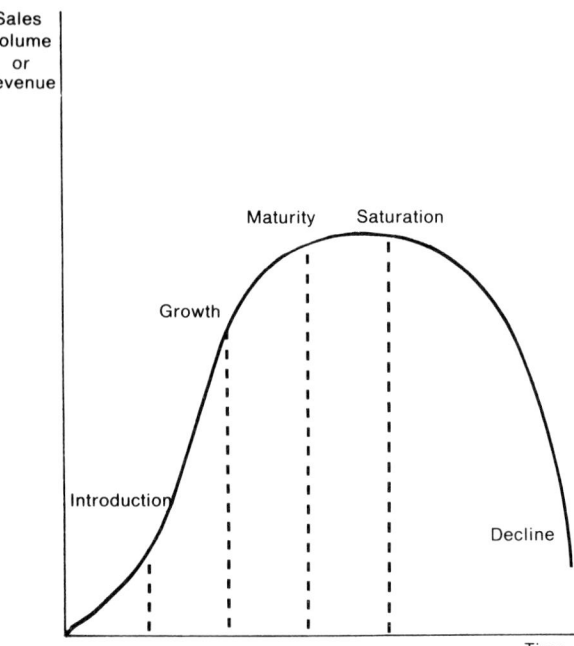

Figure 15.2 The Product Life-Cycle

Table 15.1. *Products at Different Stages of the Life Cycle*

Stage	Products
1. Introduction	On-board computers in cars, satellite TV stations and dishes
2. Growth	Washing liquids, microwaves, home computers, unleaded petrol
3. Maturity	Colour TVs, freezers, automatic washing machines
4. Saturation	Telephones, ironing boards, vacuum cleaners, pocket calculators
5. Decline	Black and white TVs, hair curlers, push garden mowers, tupperware plastic products

project code name p46. The product's **introduction** may be accompanied by a blaze of publicity, heavy advertising and promotional work, e.g. the launch of a new car typically involves large amounts of advertising expenditure to inform the consumer of its existence and features. A lot of new cars are first

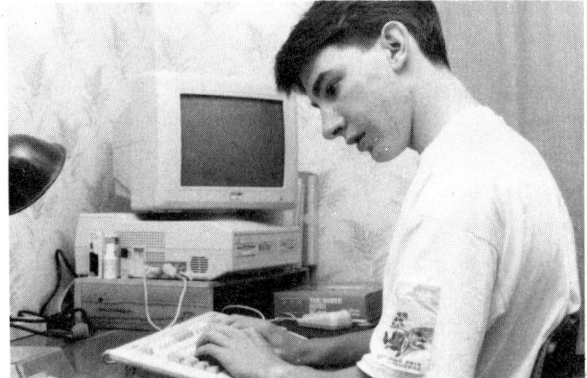

Figure 15.3 Products at Different Stages of the Life-Cycle

172

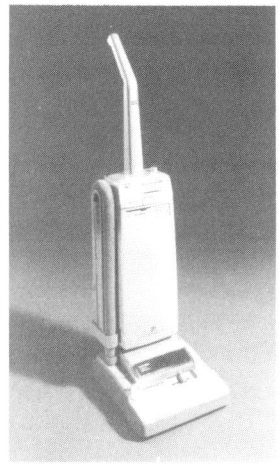

introduced at a prestigious motor show. In the introductory phase the sales of the product tend to be low and sluggish, and the price of the product may be higher than it will be at later stages in the product life cycle due to the lack of competition and because the firm is trying to get back some of the costs of developing and launching the product. Very few retail outlets may stock the product because they are unsure about the likely consumer reaction to it.

During the **growth** stage of the product life cycle, sales start to increase rapidly as more consumers become aware of the product as a result of the heavy informative advertising. The few people who owned the product in the introduction stage may have told friends about it (and shown it to them), and word of mouth encourages further sales. There may well be a slight reduction in the price of the product because of greater competition with the entry of rival firms. More retail outlets start to stock the product.

When the product is in its **maturity** phase, sales reach a peak. The product may become standardised with very little variation on a standard model. With standardisation comes a drop in the price of the product and an increase in the amount of competition between firms.

In the **saturation** phase most people own or use the product and sales remain static. Most sales are due to consumers replacing an old product – rather than new consumers buying the product. Advertising tends to become persuasive rather than informative, with firms trying to lure the customer towards their product and away from that of their competitors. The Marketing Department will try to develop variations on the standard product – especially if there have been technological changes, by the addition of extra features. It is trying to stop sales from declining and it may look (if it hasn't already) for another market to sell the product, e.g. overseas. Colour TVs now have considerably more features – teletext, remote control, stereo sound and different shaped and size screens – than when they were first introduced. When people replace their old TV they may purchase one that incorporates these different features.

The **decline** phase of the product life cycle is characterised by falling sales. Advertising ceases, prices drop considerably and few retail outlets stock the product.

QUICK QUESTIONS 2

1. *What do you understand by the phrase 'product life cycle'?*
2. *What are the 5 stages of the product life cycle?*
3. *Write down further examples of products that are at different stages of the product life cycle.*
4. *What type of marketing activity tends to be associated with (a) the growth stage and (b) the saturation stage of the product life cycle?*

The Marketing Mix in Action

In developing a marketing strategy there are 2 important areas that the Marketing Department must concentrate on: firstly, the identification of the market segment(s) which the company intends to target, and second, the elements in the marketing mix which will successfully sell the product at a profit.

The Marketing Department must be aware that

consumers will not only differ in the price they expect to pay for a product but also in the benefits they expect to receive from it. Consider the market for electronic calculators. This market is made up of a number of segments, e.g. scientists, office workers, and the general public. Clearly, each group or segment is likely to be willing to pay a different price. In addition, each segment is likely to expect a different product. The scientific segment will require the calculator to perform more sophisticated functions and the office segment may be looking for a more robust product. The channels of distribution will also differ: scientific calculators will be best sold through specialist journals and personal selling, office calculators through specific distributors, and the general public through the major retail chains such as W. H. Smith and Argos. Likewise, the advertising and promotional strategies will differ in both media and message.

The purpose of the marketing mix is to establish a product which makes consumers 'brand loyal' to it so that they will not switch to an alternative product. This loyalty to the product could be the result of any of the marketing mix elements – creating a superior product (Porsche, for example, is positioned in the prestige segment of the car market with an advantage based on quality/technical performance), more attractive product designs (aerodynamically shaped cars are an example here), better service during and after the sale (Volvo has a lifetime care commitment to its customers) and good quality advertising. In order to illustrate the way the marketing mix can vary, for different products, here are 2 case studies: Beecham's rejuvenation of 2 'old' products, Brylcreem and Lucozade, and the battle for the washing liquids market.

Marketing Mix Case Study 1: 'Beecham's Born Again Brands'

Bob Bauman, Chairman of the Beecham Group, faced the task of getting this slumbering giant moving again. In trying to move the Group forward to what it was once famous for – marketing with flair – he needed to look no further than the consumer division with those two born again brands, Brylcreem and Lucozade.

In 1982 both products were heading at various speeds for oblivion, stuck in time with dated images, shrinking markets and shrinking sales. Today, they are rejuvenated and repositioned at the forefront of their fields. Together they have helped, along with other Beecham products like Bovril, Ribena and Horlicks, to restore some gloss to the company's marketing reputation, established in the 1950s and 1960s.

Brylcreem and Lucozade are two 'golden oldies', both more than 50 years old. Here, first, is the Brylcreem story.

Brylcreem was launched with instant success in the hair-slicking roaring twenties. During the war patriots sent it to the troops to boost morale. The Royal Airforce took particularly to the hair-gluing cream to complete their neat disciplined profiles, earning the reputation of the 'Brylcreem Boys'. In 1947 England test cricketer Denis Compton endorsed the product (the first British sportsman to mix sport and business in this way) and made it famous. Then came the 1960s when the flower power and flowing locks screwed the lid on Brylcreem for the next 20 years and sales slumped.

Graham Neale, Marketing Manager of hair care products, believes there was much to thank the 'punk movement' for. 'It showed that you didn't need a mass consumer following to be in vogue.'

Research showed that Brylcreem had an ageing consumer profile and scarcely any new users. 'Users were dying and taking Brylcreem with them,' said Neale. Yet for all its heritage there was considerable public affection for the brand name and it's distribution was second to none, with 100% of chemists and most supermarket chains stocking the white gel in the red pot.

Roger Edwards, Chairman of the advertising agency Grey, which was given the task of bringing the product back explained 'It seemed almost impossible. We had to capture two entirely different groups, the ageing lapsed user and the new market of trendy young males.'

The reason for bringing the product back in 1985 and not earlier was Beecham believed the time was right. Style was back in fashion and the market for men's toiletries was fast emerging. As the best-known brand in the men's hair styling field – it claims 60% of the market – Beecham saw a huge opportunity. The 'noticeably combed' hair styles adopted by today's young men offered a way back.

The aim of the advertising was to shift attitudes towards Brylcreem specifically to remind lapsed users of what they were missing and excite young users by the fashion look. Only then would Beecham expand its product range. Such a task dictated a television advertising campaign. Brylcreem took to the small screen for the first time in 12 years in October 1985.

The campaign of three commercials soon gained cult status. The acclaimed Girl in a Tube ad showed a girl diving out of a Brylcreem tube followed by a close-up of a well-groomed Clark Kent lookalike being caressed by the girl. Slowly she turns him towards her and removes his spectacles before planting a kiss on his lips.

The agency creative team chose nostalgia as a means of appealing to both young and old target groups. Soundtrack from the rockband Art of Noise put the ad firmly in the 1980s while original footage revived memories for older consumers. Response was immediate. Media coverage was unprecedented, from TV programmes like the *Six O'Clock Show* to women's press and cult style magazines, *The Face* and *ID*. Research soon showed that awareness of Brylcreem in the London area, where the campaign broke first, reached 84%.

Having established this, Beecham then launched two new Brylcreem products, the mousse in November 1985 and the gel in April 1986. New product development continued with a 'hair style and hold spray' and gel being launched in November 1986. For Christmas Brylcreem was gift-packed.

Like Brylcreem, Lucozade, too, needed to position itself differently in consumers' minds. First launched in 1929 by a Newcastle pharmacist onto a flu-stricken world, Lucozade stood for convalescent drink. 'Lucozade aids recovery' ran the punch line. Early ads showed the patients recovering in hospital and sickly children finding a new lease of life with Lucozade at the ready.

Improved health care and self-medication undermined the drink's selling platform. The decision was made to reposition it as a healthy everyday energy replacement drink. Ads in the early 1980s showed a moving wavy orange graph line, on which walked an animated family group, depicting the ups and downs of the day. When the

Figure 15.4 Changes in Advertising: Brylcreem

downs got to them a gulp of Lucozade pepped them up for the ups ahead. From then on the drink came in a variety of packages – plastic bottles, one drink bottles, bulk packs and cans. Two new barley drinks were launched in April 1986.

The shift in image to an everyday health drink was boosted by an apt endorsement from Daley Thompson, the then world champion decathlete. These commercials featured the athlete during one of his punishing workouts, getting parched and then downing the amber liquid. There was also a witty 'traffic lights' ad in TV and poster form, showing the colours red, amber (signalled by a bottle of Lucozade) and green in sequence. Results showed that sales of Lucozade in 1985 rose by 21% over the previous year. Between 1979 and 1985 sales tripled to £46 million, 75% of that coming from products not around in 1979.

QUICK QUESTIONS 3

1. *Why were both Lucozade and Brylcreem 'heading for oblivion'?*
2. *When was Brylcreem first launched and why do you think it was so successful at first?*
3. *Why and when did Brylcreem begin to enter the decline phase of the product life cycle?*
4. *What is meant by the term 'ageing consumer profile'? Give other examples of products that have this profile.*
5. *Why do companies use particular people to endorse their products? Why do you think it works? Give examples of products that are endorsed by celebrities.*
6. *Why did Beecham bring back Brylcreem in 1985?*
7. *Outline the main features of the Brylcreem advertising campaign? Are there any other products known to you that use a similar campaign?*
8. *What is meant by the term 'gift-packed' and why are a lot of products gift-packed at Christmas time?*
9. *What product image was Lucozade stuck with before the 1980s?*
10. *How did Lucozade change this image and what new product and packaging changes took place? How does Beecham measure the success of this change in its marketing mix?*

Marketing Mix Case Study 2: 'Battle for the Washday Lead'

Britain's longest running soap opera – the blood, sweat and understains saga – began in the 1920s when Proctor and Gamble (P & G) launched green Fairy to challenge Lever Brothers' yellow Sunlight bar soap.

The battle for market leadership is now in heavy-duty liquid detergent – a new grade of liquid detergent used for washing clothes. It is the most revolutionary launch in the industry since 1950 when P & G launched Tide, the first synthetic washing powder, to take on Lever's Persil.

Lever launched Persil liquid at the end of July 1988 and spent £1.8 million advertising it in its first month on the shelves. The average monthly spending on all 12 branded washing products on sale in Britain in 1987 was a mere £4 million. Such extravagant advertising is a clear indication of the battle for supremacy.

P & G and Lever share 86% of the £500 million low-suds, heavy-duty detergent market in the UK and have used a whole range of marketing tricks. Stunts include free watches with Liquid Ariel, £2 cash back for two Wisk labels and the liberal application of 'BOGOF' – the 'buy one get one free' principle. Jean-Paul le Courant, Lever's Marketing Director, has promised more goodies. 'We certainly need six months of very heavy promotion to reach the level we want', he says, promising lots of free samples until Persil liquid is market leader.

The tally from stores fitted with electronic checkout scanners for the week ending 5 September 1988 showed that Ariel liquid had 12.9% of all heavy-duty detergent sales, including powders; Daz liquid with 5.4%; Persil liquid with 7.2% and Wisk with 3.9%. At its peak Wisk had almost 9%.

The market is growing very quickly. Before the arrival of liquids the detergent market had been growing at about 3–5% per year. Between July 1987 and July 1988 the detergent market had expanded by 14% and washing liquids were taking a 26% slice. In just two years Britain has become the second largest market in the world for these new products, topped only by the USA, where they have around 35% of sales. P & G and Lever both agree on the reasons for this growth: increased affluence, almost daily use of the washing machine at lower temperatures (90% of all washes are done at 60 deg C or less), and demand for products which are gentle and kinder on coloured clothes and natural fabrics.

The way products are launched in the detergent business is through a long testing period in regional markets with lesser brands. Wisk was on trial in the Midlands for a full year before it went national. Lever started with Wisk, established in the USA for 30 years but unknown in Britain, rather than an established name like Persil, so that if it failed there would be no adverse effect on the main brand. Supplies of Wisk were rationed for most of its first year and it proved a runaway success until P & G launched its main brand Ariel liquid four months after the Wisk launch. P & G claimed it had 60% of the UK liquids trade and launched Daz liquid in the Spring of 1987. Lever scrambled to get Persil liquid on the shelves and had not time for scientific market testing. The company's guinea pigs living around Port Sunlight, who normally try out new products, had been asking when they would be able to test a liquid version of Persil. That was the extent of the test. Consumers had already shown they liked liquids, they found them less messy to use, they gave good results at low temperatures and they felt that powders were harsh.

Recent research by the Economist Intelligence Unit has shown that consumers have heard the cry 'new' and 'improved' once too often. They feel advertisements insult their intelligence and are doubtful about the lavish promotions of the industry. They say they would rather see the 12% of sales spent on detergent advertising passed back to the consumer in the form of lower prices. Despite the heavy advertising and promotional activity given to washing liquids there has only been one casualty. Breeze, a new Lever powder detergent was withdrawn from UK sales after a year's test. With liquids going so well this was hardly the time to be coming out with new powders.

QUICK QUESTIONS 4

1. How much did Lever spend on advertising Persil liquid in its first month of sales?
2. Why was this described as being 'extravagant'? Use figures to support your answer.
3. Give examples of the marketing tricks that the detergent companies have used to sell their products.
4. Think of some products known to you. What promotional offers have been tried to boost their sales?
5. Why have electronic check-out scanners proved useful to these companies?
6. What reasons are given for the growth of the liquid detergent market? Can you think of any other factors?
7. How are products normally launched in the detergent business? Why do they adopt this method? Give an example to support your answer.
8. What evidence is there to suggest that the advertising of detergents may not work?
9. What percentage of sales is spent on detergent advertising? Are there any other products that have such a large amount of advertising? Give examples.
10. Why is now not the time to be introducing new washing powders?

STUDENT EXERCISE MARKETING MIX

You are the Marketing Director of LMS Foods Ltd, a company that manufactures food and drink for the consumer market. Your department has recently given you the following table:

The Performance of LMS Ltd and the National Food Market

Year	Annual Sales of LMS Ltd £m	Total Market Sales £m
1984	20	100
1985	25	140
1986	30	200
1987	35	250
1988	40	325
1989	45	400

1. You have been asked to present a report to the board of directors to show the market position of your company between 1984 and 1989, drawing particular attention to the growth of your sales compared with the market, and to your company's

market share. The information needs to be illustrated.

2. The company is thinking of moving into the health food market with the launch of several new brands of honey, bread and cereal. You have been asked to devise a marketing mix for these products, paying particular attention to:

   (a) the market segments to aim at
   (b) the channel of distribution
   (c) the pricing of your product compared with your competitors
   (d) the style of the advertising campaign and other promotional activity.

   The report that you have to prepare on the marketing mix must contain information on what other competitors are doing in this area.

PROJECT AND ASSIGNMENT SUGGESTIONS

1. Select a product and undertake a detailed analysis of its marketing mix. Your study should pay particular attention to the following:

   (a) The design and quality of the product. Does it possess any special features? How does it differ from similar products? Is it designed to appeal to a particular segment of the market?

   (b) The price of the product. Towards which end of the price range for this type of product is it situated? How are price and quality related? Is it marketed as a high quality product which is worth paying more for, or is price competitiveness an important element in the marketing mix?

   (c) The promotional strategy. How important is the packaging of the product? What forms of advertising are used and in which types of media? What other promotional techniques are employed?

   (d) The availability of the product. What is the chain of distribution from the producer to the customer? Is the product widely available or can it only be bought from certain outlets?

   Write up the results of your research in the form of a report and explain what elements of the marketing mix of the product you think are most important and why.

2. Select one example of a product from each phase of the product life cycle. Investigate how the products differ in the way they are marketed to the consumer.

SECTION D

Financing Business Activity

CHAPTER 16

Financial Accounting and Financial Control

Finance is central to the operation of any business. More or less every activity a business undertakes will require some form of funding. Finance is needed to rent or buy premises, to purchase capital equipment, to hire labour and to obtain raw materials. Therefore, without finance a new business could not be set up and an existing business could not continue to function.

Financial Objectives

Although finance is required for so many different aspects of business activity, it is usual to group a business's financial needs under the following broad headings.

Survival

This is the most fundamental objective of all businesses. In order to ensure survival there must be enough money flowing into the business to finance the necessary day-to-day expenditure, e.g. purchasing raw materials, paying employees' wages and so on. This type of expenditure is **current expenditure** and will normally be financed from current income, that is the money generated from the sale of the business's goods or services.

Growth and Development

Whilst survival is the fundamental short-run objective of the business, in the long run businesses are concerned with growth and development. Old machinery must be replaced with more modern technology to maintain and increase efficiency in order for the company to remain competitive. Growth allows the firm to diversify its product range and open up new markets. With growth come the benefits of **economies of scale** and a more secure

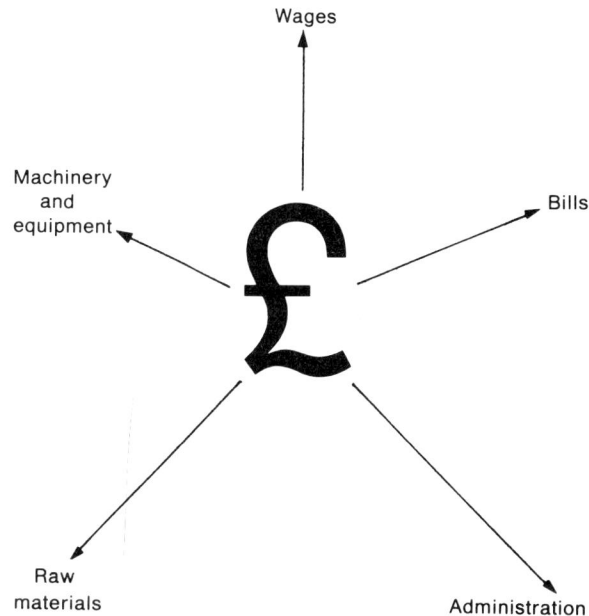

Figure 16.1 Why the Money is Needed

position in the market. To pursue these objectives the business requires **capital finance**. The difference between current and capital finance is dealt with in detail in Chapters 17 and 18.

Survival and growth and development are obviously closely related. A business which does not develop and grow will encounter problems in the long run in maintaining its market share and its survival may be threatened. These objectives determine how a business uses financial resources, often referred to as a business's **application of funds**.

181

Sources of Funds

Closely related to how money is used by a business is how it is obtained, i.e. the various **sources of funds**. Sources and application of funds are closely related because generally the most important factor in deciding the method of obtaining the finance is the reason the finance is required. Sources of funds can also be summarised under 2 broad headings.

Internal Finance

This refers to the money a business generates from its own assets. Internal finance can be obtained from the following sources:

1. Careful management of the business's income and expenditure. This is known as the **cash flow** of the business. It needs to be carefully monitored to ensure there is enough money flowing into the business to meet current commitments.
2. The profits from the previous trading activities of the business. Some of the profits will be distributed to the owners of the business as a return on their investment. However, it is usual to **reinvest** part of the profits in order to allow the business to expand. This is a very important source of finance for capital expenditure.
3. The sale of the business's assets. Often the finance required for new assets can be partly obtained by selling older equipment. The business may also sell assets to a third party under an agreement which allows the assets to be retained in return for an agreed rental. This **sale and lease back** generates finance for the purchase of new assets at the cost of increasing the business's current expenditure.

External Finance

External finance refers to the injection of funds from outside the business. Essentially this type of finance can be obtained from 2 sources.

(a) Borrowing money. All businesses borrow in order to finance a whole range of business activity. Materials can be bought on credit to help finance current expenditure and loans are obtained from many sources to help purchase new assets. However, borrowed money usually has to be repaid and will normally have to be serviced, i.e. interest will be charged on the amount borrowed. This increases the current expenditure of the business.

(b) Extending ownership. This means attracting finance from people outside the business who are prepared to invest in its future. This occurs when a sole proprietor takes a partner or when a private limited company 'goes public' or when a public limited company issues more shares. Unlike borrowing, this form of finance does not have to be repaid and as it does not generate a debt there are no interest charges. However, in the long run the business will have to make enough profit to give a return on this investment or the investors are likely to wish to withdraw their money and invest it elsewhere.

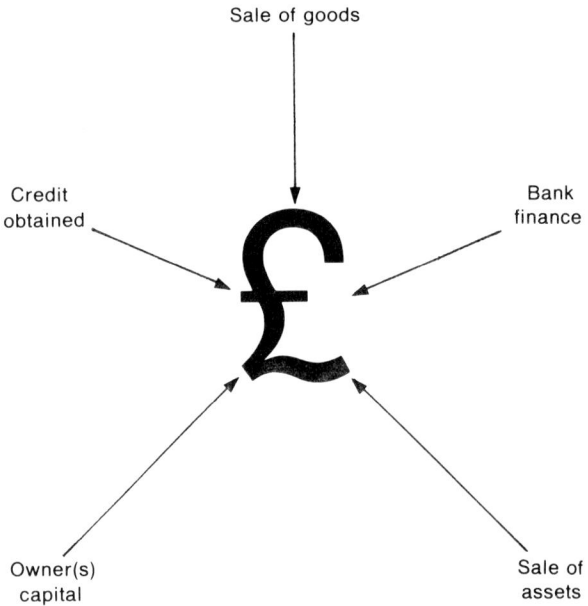

Figure 16.2 Where the Money Comes from

QUICK QUESTIONS 1

1. *Divide the following list of business expenditures into 2 groups according to whether they are current or capital items: redecorating the offices, payment to the window cleaner, settling the telephone bill, the purchase of a new delivery van, the servicing of a company vehicle, buying a plot of vacant land next to the factory, a business lunch for an important customer.*

2. *In one sentence distinguish clearly between internal and external finance.*
3. *If profits are retained in the business to finance expansion, who is actually providing the finance for this investment?*
4. *Name one advantage and one disadvantage to the business of borrowing to finance capital expansion rather than extending ownership.*

Therefore financial decisions are concerned with both the sources of funds and the application of those funds. In larger businesses this financial planning and decision-making is the responsibility of the Finance Department.

The Role of the Finance Department

The staff employed in the Finance Department are concerned with 3 principal tasks:

1. Monitoring **when** the money is coming in and going out.
2. Monitoring **where** it is coming from and going to.
3. Monitoring **how much** is flowing backwards and forwards.

The structure of a typical Finance Department in a large or medium-sized company is shown in Figure 16.3.

Figure 16.3 The Structure of a Finance Department

These various subdivisions of the department are responsible for preparing the financial accounts of the business, budgeting, and giving advice on the advisability of new investment proposals.

In order to undertake these functions effectively, accurate and up-to-date financial information is needed. Therefore the collection, presentation and evaluation of financial data are central to the work of the department. This can be seen as a 4-stage process:

Recording – interpretation – advice – control

The first stage is the preparation of the various financial statements required by the business. The principal statements are the **balance sheet** and the **profit and loss account**.

The Balance Sheet

The balance sheet is like a 'snapshot' of the business showing its financial position at a particular point in time – usually at the end of the financial year. It shows what the business owns, what it is owed and what it owes. There are 2 ways of presenting this information, shown in Figures 16.4 and 16.5. In these figures the 2 methods of presenting the balance sheet are shown for a medium-sized company called Style Fashions Ltd. This company is a textile business specialising in casual clothes for the teenage market. Figure 16.4 shows the traditional or **horizontal format** for presenting the balance sheet, which is still used for the accounts of small business, e.g. sole traders. Companies such as Style Fashions are much more likely to present the balance sheet in the **vertical format** shown in Figure 16.5. This second method of presentation highlights certain important elements in the accounts, e.g. the size of the business's working capital, and makes comparisons with previous years easier.

Style Fashions Ltd
Balance Sheet at End of Financial Year 1989–90

Assets (£)			Liabilities (£)		
Fixed Assets			Capital Liabilities		
Land and buildings	80,000		Share capital		100,000
Plant and machinery	25,000		Plus net profit	20,500	
Vehicles	15,600		Less drawings	10,500	
		120,600			110,000
			Long-Term Liabilities		
			Bank loan		25,000
Current Assets (£)			Current Liabilities (£)		
Stock	11,500		Trade creditors	9,000	
Debtors	8,500		Other creditors	4,000	
Cash	7,400				13,000
		27,400			
		148,000			148,000

Figure 16.4 The Horizontal Presentation of the Balance Sheet

Style Fashions Ltd
Balance Sheet at the End of Financial Year 1989–90

Fixed Assets		£
Land and buildings	80,000	
Plant and machinery	25,000	
Vehicles	15,600	120,600
Current Assets		
Stock	11,500	
Debtors	8,500	
Cash	7,400	27,400
Less Current Liabilities		
Trade creditors	9,000	
Other creditors	4,000	13,000
Net Current Assets		14,400[1]
		————
		135,000
		————
Financed by		
Loans outstanding		25,000
Share capital	100,000	
Net profit retained	10,000	110,000[2]
		————
		135,000
		————

Notes
[1] Working capital
[2] Net worth = owners' equity

Figure 16.5 The Vertical Presentation of the Balance Sheet

The main items in the balance sheet are explained below.

Assets

Assets consist of everything the business owns plus any money owed to the business by its debtors. It is usual to list assets in order of increasing liquidity, i.e. the ease with which they can be turned into cash. Assets are of 2 main types:

1. **Fixed assets** are the assets purchased for use in the business on a permanent basis and consist of such items as land, buildings, plant, machinery, furniture and fittings, and vehicles. They are known as fixed assets because they do not change during the normal trading activities of the business.
2. **Current assets** are the assets of the business which change during the normal trading activities of the business. They consist of stock, debtors and cash.

Liabilities

Liabilities are items and money in the business which belong to or are owed to those outside it. They can be divided into 3 types:

1. **Capital liabilities**: the money which has been used to purchase the fixed assets of the business and therefore represents the investment of the owner(s) in the business. In the case of a limited company, this figure is the value of the issued share capital of the company. In the horizontal format of the balance sheet shown in Figure 16.4, retained profit is also included as a capital liability because it represents a further investment in the business by its owner(s). This format is not generally used to present the accounts of a company because the method of recording how the business uses its profit is a little more complex.
2. **Long-term liabilities**: the debts of the business which will be paid off over a long period of time, e.g. a bank loan. If the business is organised as a limited company and has issued debentures (see Chapters 2 and 18), these appear on the balance sheet as a long-term liability.
3. **Current liabilities**: the short-term debts that the business has incurred during the course of its trading activities, including such items as trade credit or a bank overdraft.

Notice that if the balance sheet is presented in the horizontal format both sides must **balance** because they show different measures of the value of the business. This is expressed separately as:

1. **Assets**: what the business owns and is owed.
2. **Liabilities**: the claim on those assets by the business's owners and its creditors.

Therefore the sum total of the assets of the business does not represent the value of the business to its owner(s) because part of this total will be owed to creditors, e.g. the bank or suppliers. So if the owner(s) were to **liquidate** the business, i.e. sell its assets for cash, they could only expect to receive a sum equal to the value of the assets **minus external liabilities**. In the example in Figure 16.4 this is equal to:

£148,000 − £38,000 = £110,000

This figure of £110,000 is known as the **net worth**

of the business. In the case of a limited company net worth is generally referred to as **owners' equity** or **shareholders' funds** as it represents the investment of the owners (shareholders) in the company. In the vertical format of the balance sheet in Figure 16.5, owners' equity appears as an identifiable item.

QUICK QUESTIONS 2

1. *Why is the balance sheet of the business likely to be out of date as soon as it has been prepared?*
2. *In one sentence explain the principal difference between a fixed asset and a current asset.*
3. *What is the difference between a long-term liability and a current liability?*
4. *Why is it unlikely that the value of a business to its owner(s) will be as great as the value of its assets?*

STUDENT TASK

1. What is the main purpose of drawing up a balance sheet of a business?
2. The following information is known about the present financial situation of Justin Time Ltd:

Share capital	£140,000
Trade creditors	£2,200
Cash at bank	£800
Value of machinery	£25,000
Expense creditors	£600
Debtors	£3,700
Value of premises	£120,000
Value of stock	£6,300
Bank loan	£13,000

Set out the above information in the form of a balance sheet. As the business is organised as a limited company you should use the vertical format for the presentation of the account.

The Interpretation of the Balance Sheet

A degree of care is required when trying to assess the exact financial position of a business from its balance sheet. The apparent precision of the figures can be misleading. In reality it is very difficult to place exact values on many items in the balance sheet and some of the figures are little more than estimates or rough guesses by the accountants who have drawn up the balance sheet. Some of the main problems involved in the interpretation of the balance sheet are outlined below.

1. Fixed assets are difficult to value because what they are worth changes over time. Some assets **appreciate**, i.e. become worth more, because of inflation. This applies especially to land and buildings. Other assets **depreciate**, i.e. become worth less, because they wear out with use. This affects the value of such assets as machinery and vehicles. Therefore, if care is not taken to estimate the value of these assets accurately, the balance sheet can give a false picture of the worth of the business. Particular problems can result from an undervaluation of the business's assets:

   (a) The profit the business has made will appear to represent a greater return on the assets employed than is actually the case. It is very common to express the business's profits as a percentage of the assets employed to generate that profit. In the example given in the balance sheet of Style Fashions Ltd, net profit is £20,500 and the value of the business's assets is given as £148,000. Thus the return on these assets can be calculated as

   $$\frac{£20,500}{£148,000} \times 100 = 13.85\%$$

   However, if the assets of Style Fashions Ltd have been undervalued and are actually worth more than £148,000, then the percentage return gives a false impression of how profitable the business really is.

   (b) Undervaluation makes the business vulnerable to a take-over. If the actual value of the assets is more than has been recorded (the book value), then the shares of the business are worth buying because the assets can be obtained for less than their real worth. Sometimes this is done with a view to selling off the assets at a profit rather than running the enterprise as a business. This process is known as **asset stripping**.

2. The balance sheet only records the value of the business's physical assets: land, buildings and so on. It does not indicate the value of the

business's intangible assets, such as:

(a) Goodwill: the reputation the business has built up over its years of trading obviously adds to its value. It is not usual to include a value for this asset in the balance sheet but if a business is valued for the purpose of being sold, goodwill will have to be taken into account.

(b) Patents and licences: the business may possess legal or contractual rights to produce certain products. This may greatly increase the possibilities for profit if other businesses are prevented from also producing these products. Although these rights are a definite asset to the business, they will not normally be included in the balance sheet.

3. Finally there is a problem in recording the value of the business's debtors. This represents the total amount of money owed to the business by individuals or other businesses which have bought goods from the business on credit but have not yet settled their accounts. This item is valued as an asset because the business will be paid that money in due course. However, it is not uncommon for debtors to fail to pay what they owe. When this occurs it is known as a **bad debt**. Often this money cannot be recovered, e.g. if the money was owed by a company which has ceased trading with debts much greater than the value of its assets. Sometimes the costs involved in trying to recover the debt are greater than the value of the money owed. In these circumstances the debts will have to be **written off** by the business, i.e. the value of these debts must be removed from the balance sheet as they are not recoverable. The problem is trying to estimate what proportion of the money currently owed to the business will turn out to be bad debts. It is the job of the accountants to estimate a realistic figure for bad debts based upon the previous trading experience of the business. This means that the debtors' figure recorded in the balance sheet is not an exact one.

QUICK QUESTIONS 3

1. Why do certain assets of the business appreciate over time?
2. What is the cause of the depreciation of assets?
3. If the true value of Style Fashions Ltd assets is £170,000 rather than £148,000, what would be the rate of return on assets employed?
4. Explain what is meant by the term 'asset stripping'.
5. Why do bad debts occur?

STUDENT TASK

Mr Choudhry owns a corner grocery shop which he bought 4 years ago with a mortgage from a building society. He is about to draw up a balance sheet showing the current position of his business.

1. Make a list of all the different items which are likely to appear as assets on the balance sheet of Mr Choudhry's business.
2. Mr Choudhry will divide these assets into groups. Distinguish between the 2 types of assets which appear on a balance sheet and give examples of each.
3. Explain why Mr Choudhry may find it difficult to place an exact value on the assets of his business.
4. The outstanding value of the mortgage on Mr Choudhry's shop must be recorded as a liability on the balance sheet. What other liabilities may the business have?
5. What important information can Mr Choudhry find out by subtracting the external liabilities of the business from the value of its assets?

The Profit and Loss Account

The balance sheet has been described as a 'snapshot' of the business. The profit and loss account is the history of the business. It shows what has happened in the business between the publication of one balance sheet and the next. Whereas the balance sheet only shows the amount of profit the business has made, the profit and loss account shows how this profit has been made. The profit and loss account of Style Fashions Ltd set out in Figure 16.6 shows how the net profit retained of the business is arrived at. It is important to note that there are 2 profit figures

Style Fashions Ltd
Profit and Loss Account at End of Financial Year 1989–90

Income from sales		200,000
Less material costs		108,700
Gross Profit for Year		91,300
Less financial overheads		
Bank charges	800	
Loan interest	2,400	3,200
Less selling and distribution overheads		
Salaries and commissions	21,000	
Advertising	10,000	
Depreciation of vehicles	2,000	
Transport expenses	3,100	36,100
Less administration overheads		
Salaries	19,200	
Depreciation of office equipment	1,500	
Telephone, telex, postage	2,800	
Rates	4,600	
Lighting and heating	3,400	31,500
		70,800
Net Profit for Year		20,500
Less tax paid		5,500
Net Profit after Tax		15,000
Less dividends paid		5,000
Net Profit Retained		10,000

Figure 16.6 The Profit and Loss Account

which will interest the managers of the business: the **gross profit** and the **net profit**.

Gross Profit

Gross profit represents the difference between the cost price and the selling price of the goods the business has sold. The total income to the business from the sale of its goods or services is known as its **turnover**. Therefore gross profit can be expressed as:

$$\text{Gross profit} = \text{turnover} - \text{cost of goods or materials}$$

The profit and loss account in Figure 16.6 shows that Style Fashions Ltd purchased materials to the value of £108,700 and used these to produce goods which have been sold for £200,000, giving a gross profit of £91,300.

However, it is not only the size of gross profit which is important but the relationship between gross profit and the turnover of the business. This is

known as **gross profit percentage** and is calculated using the formula:

$$\text{Gross profit percentage} = \frac{\text{gross profit}}{\text{turnover}} \times 100$$

Applying this formula to the profit and loss account of Style Fashions Ltd gives a gross profit percentage of:

$$\frac{£91,300}{£200,000} \times 100 = 45.65\%$$

Although this looks a very high figure it does not represent the final profit percentage of the business because it relates to gross profit. However, it is an important figure because it can be used to compare the gross profit on sales from one year to the next. If gross profit falls this should be investigated by the management of the business. There are a number of reasons which could account for a fall in gross profit percentage:

1. The staff are stealing the takings or the stock.
2. There could be increased stock breakages or in some businesses too much stock is being allowed to perish.
3. The rising cost of the materials purchased by the business is not being passed on to customers.

By identifying the cause of the fall in gross profit percentage the management can take the appropriate action, e.g. better security, improved training of staff, a change in pricing policy and so on.

Net Profit

In the calculation of gross profit only the direct costs of production are included. Therefore the expenses incurred by the business are ignored. These expenses are known as **overhead costs** and are the costs of actually running the business. These have to be taken into account before the final profit figure can be declared. The subtraction of overheads from gross profit gives the business's net profit.

$$\text{Net profit} = \text{gross profit} - \text{expenses}$$

The result is the actual profit of the business before tax. In the example of Style Fashions Ltd given in Figure 16.6, overheads are divided into 3 groups: financial overheads, selling and distribution overheads and administration overheads, although for smaller businesses it is unlikely that overheads would be itemised in such detail. Notice that depreciation is recorded as an expense of the business. This is simply an allowance made to cover the cost of replacing worn-out assets. If the business did not make this allowance its profit would be artificially high and it would pay a larger amount of tax on its profit.

As with gross profit it is the size of net profit in relation to the business's turnover which is of particular importance. This is known as **net profit percentage** and is calculated using the formula:

$$\text{Net profit percentage} = \frac{\text{net profit}}{\text{turnover}} \times 100$$

Therefore, the net profit percentage of Style Fashions Ltd is:

$$\frac{£20,500}{£200,000} \times 100 = 10.25\%$$

Once again net profit percentage should remain roughly the same from year to year, and any significant fall should be investigated. A fall in net profit percentage could be the result of a fall in gross profit percentage. However, if gross profit percentage has remained stable over the period then a fall in net profit percentage could be the result of a rise in any one of the expenses of the business. The management should therefore examine each item carefully to see if there has been any change in the ratio of the expense to the turnover of the business.

Any rise in overheads, e.g. administration costs or salaries, in relation to the sales income the business is generating can be identified using the formula:

$$\frac{\text{Expense}}{\text{Turnover}} \times 100$$

Appropriate action can then be taken.

The final part of the profit and loss account shows what happens to the net profit made by the business. This is known as the **appropriation account** and is shown in simplified form in Figure 16.6. Once declared, a business's net profit can be appropriated in the following ways:

1. **Taxation**: the business may be liable for tax on its profits. This is **corporation tax** and is an unavoidable payment, although it may not have to be paid immediately. However, there is a threshold below which profits are not liable for taxation, and a lower rate which applies to small businesses.

2. **Distribution to owners**: once any tax liability has been met the remaining profit belongs to the owner(s) of the business and represents the return on their investment. In the case of a business organised as a limited company, this is paid as a dividend to the shareholders.

3. **Retained profit**: it is very unlikely that all the net profit of the business will be distributed to the owner(s). Retained profit represents a very important source of finance for the business, and so some of the profit will generally be **ploughed back** into the business to finance further expansion. Note that when this occurs it means that the existing owner(s) are increasing their investment in the business.

QUICK QUESTIONS 4

1. *Explain why the profit and loss account constitutes the recent history of the business.*
2. *How is the gross profit of the business calculated?*
3. *Explain the difference between gross profit and net profit.*
4. *In what ways can net profit be distributed by the business?*

The balance sheet and the profit and loss account represent the principal accounts drawn up by the Finance Department, and they form a very important part of the business's annual report. However, the efficient management of the business requires a great deal of financial information and therefore the Finance Department's work is much wider than simply the preparation of the statements referred to above. Another key function of the department is budgeting and financial control.

STUDENT TASK

A summary of the profit and loss account of Howe and Wye Ltd for 1989 is given below.

	£
Sales	200,000
Cost of goods	150,000
Gross profit	50,000
Operating expenses	12,000
Net profit	38,000

1. What is the gross profit percentage of the business?
2. What is the net profit percentage of the business?
3. The management of the business is rather concerned by the fact that the gross profit percentage is significantly lower than in 1988. Suggest possible reasons for this and recommend any action the business should take to help restore the gross profit percentage.
4. Name 4 items which might be included in the operating expenses of the business.
5. The net profit of the business (after any liability for tax has been met) can be retained by the business or distributed to the business's owners. Why is it unlikely that all the net profit will be distributed to the owners?

The Financial Control of the Business

Financial control means the directing and monitoring of the financial resources within the business. It is exercised internally by managers and accountants and co-ordinated by the Finance Department. In addition, a further degree of control may be exercised externally by the business's auditors, who are independent financial advisers who verify the business's annual accounts.

In order to make financial control possible it is first necessary to set objectives and targets within which each department is expected to work. This process is known as **budgeting** and it is central to financial management.

Essentially a budget is a financial expression of intentions or expectations. Budgeting occurs at several levels within the business and over different time scales. However, common to all budgets is that they relate to the future and are therefore based upon forecasts rather than facts. This is in contrast to the balance sheet and the profit and loss account, which relate to the business's past performance.

The preparation of a budget consists of a number of stages which can be expressed as the following sequence:

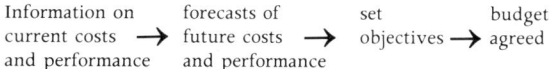

Information on current costs and performance → forecasts of future costs and performance → set objectives → budget agreed

Information

A department will start its budgetary process by looking at the information relating to its present situation. For example, in the case of the Sales Department this means analysing the current sales figures, identifying trends and taking care to interpret any figures which may be the result of unusual circumstances.

Forecasts

The next stage is to look forward to the period under consideration and try to estimate as accurately as possible the situation which will prevail in the future, e.g. estimate the amount the business is likely to sell over the coming year. Experience will be of great help here but other techniques may also be employed, e.g. market research and statistical analysis. Where accurate predictions are difficult to make it is common to prepare more than one set of forecasts, e.g. an optimistic forecast and a more pessimistic one.

Objectives

Once the business has framed its various forecasts, e.g. production, sales, marketing and so on, then it is possible to set realistic performance objectives. These will normally take the form of a series of targets that each department is expected to meet, e.g. how much is to be produced, the increase in sales the business is aiming for, etc.

The Budget

The final stage of the process is to budget to meet the business's performance targets. This means setting out the level of expenditure within which each department or sub-department (usually known as **cost centres**) will have to work. The materials budget will be agreed on the basis of the production targets, the marketing budget on the basis of the sales target and so on. It is very important that all the various parts of the budget are carefully co-ordinated. It obviously makes no sense to budget to sell 100,000 units if a production target of only 80,000 has been set. Therefore, at each stage of the budgetary process close interdepartmental consultation will be necessary.

The accountants working in the Finance Department will be closely involved in the preparation and co-ordination of the budget, which will be the blueprint for the operation of the business over the period concerned.

How the Budget Helps the Management of the Business

Once the budget has been agreed it is used to monitor the performance of all departments in the business. The management will be interested in any difference between the planned targets and the actual performance of the business. This is known as **variance** and is central to the financial control of the business. It is important to investigate the cause of any variance before action is taken. This means it is necessary to distinguish between the controllable and uncontrollable elements of any variance, e.g. if material costs begin to run over budget, an investigation may reveal the cause to be a combination of:

(a) increased wastage of materials by machine operators
(b) a greater than anticipated rise in suppliers' prices.

The first factor is controllable in the sense that it is within the control of the business and is open to improvement, e.g. a better training programme for machine operators. However, the second factor is uncontrollable because its cause lies outside the business (unless a cheaper supplier can be found). In this case the budget will have to be amended to take account of the inaccurate forecast. It would make no sense to stop buying materials purely because the original forecast of their expected cost was too low. This shows that budgets must be flexible and open to amendment as circumstances change. A summary of the complete budgetary process is shown in Figure 16.7.

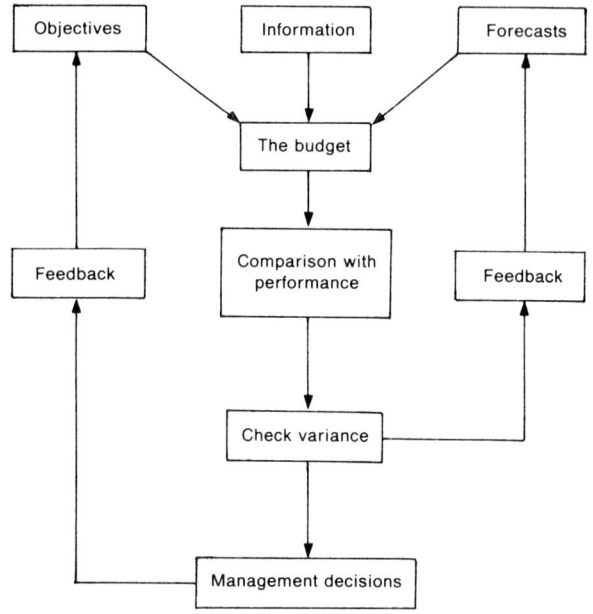

Figure 16.7 The Process of Budgetary Control

QUICK QUESTIONS 5

1. *Why do you think financial control is important to the business?*
2. *Why is it important to base the budget on as much accurate information as possible?*
3. *Why is it often necessary to prepare more than one set of forecasts concerning the business's expected performance?*
4. *Explain why it is important that the business's budget is flexible.*

The Importance of Budgeting to the Business

The process of budgeting is central to financial management and the efficient operation of the business. The main advantages to the business can be summarised as follows:

1. Budgeting requires the business to consider its objectives and it therefore clarifies its aims and policies.
2. Each department or sub-department is required to plan its expenditure. This identifies the

different areas of management responsibility within the business.

3. It gives the people who work in the business targets to aim for, which improves incentives and motivates employees.

4. Budgeting requires co-operation and communication between the various departments within the business. This helps to develop a corporate identity and reduces departmentalisation.

5. Budgeting improves the central control of the business by senior management.

6. Finally, budgeting identifies strengths and weaknesses within the business and therefore helps to improve efficiency.

PROJECT AND ASSIGNMENT SUGGESTIONS

1. Find out as much as you can about the work of the Finance Department of a medium-sized or large business. Draw up an organisation chart to show the structure of the department and write a short description of the type of work undertaken by each person in the department.

2. Assume an uncle has left you the lease on his bicycle repair shop in his will. The business is rather run down and desperately requires the injection of some capital if it is to survive. Nevertheless, you believe you could make a success of the business. The bank has indicated that it would consider lending you the money you require if you can show that the business represents a worthwhile investment. The bank has asked you to prepare financial statements showing:

(a) the present value of the business
(b) its recent trading history
(c) how you intend to spend the money you wish to borrow.

Explain how you would go about collecting the information the bank requires and present the information in the form of separate financial statements. What are the main problems you are likely to encounter in preparing accurate statements?

3. Obtain copies of the annual reports of 2 similar companies and compare their accounts. Compare the businesses with respect to:

(a) the value of their share capital
(b) the size of their assets
(c) the size of their net profit in relation to these assets
(d) their gross and net profit percentages
(e) the proportion of net profit which is distributed to the shareholders as a dividend.

Assume you have to decide which of the 2 businesses you are going to invest in. Which business would you choose? Write a brief report explaining your choice.

CHAPTER 17

The Finance of
Trading Activities

As has already been mentioned in Chapters 3 and 16, the most immediate objective of any business is to survive. In order to ensure survival there must be sufficient funds flowing into the business to meet the necessary expenditures incurred during its day-to-day trading activities. This process can be represented as a continual flow of money through the business.

Figure 17.1 shows that money is flowing in and out of the business all the time. The sale of the business's goods (or services) generates finance which is used to purchase more materials, pay wages and so on in order to generate more production, more sales and hence more income. Provided income from sales is sufficient to meet these necessary immediate expenditures then the business can continue to trade.

The business is said to be **solvent**. If the business is successful then the amount received from sales will be greater than the costs of production and therefore a profit will be made. This profit can then be used to reward the owner(s) and possibly improve or expand the business in order to generate higher profits in the future.

However, the flow of money through the business as illustrated in Figure 17.1 is an over-simplification. First, it assumes that when the business sells its products it will receive the income from these sales immediately. This may not be the case. In business it is very common to sell goods on credit and so there will be a period of time between the sales and the receipt of the money from those sales. Therefore, at any point in time, the business will be owed money by customers who have received goods but not yet settled their accounts, i.e. the business will have incurred **debtors**. Secondly, it is unlikely that the business will always have to pay for materials and various services immediately. It is usual to purchase these items on credit and pay for them at a later date when the business has had time to generate sales income from the use of these materials and services. Therefore, at any point in time the business will owe money to suppliers for goods and services received but not yet paid for, i.e. the business will have incurred **creditors**. The existence of both debtors and creditors has an important effect upon the finance of the trading activities of the business.

The Working Capital of the Business

The items which change continually during the normal trading activities of the business are known

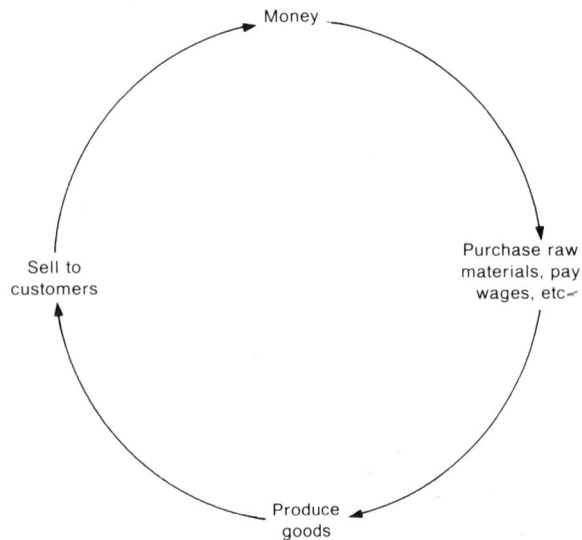

Figure 17.1 The Money 'Merry Go Round'

collectively as the business's **working capital**. Working capital can be defined as:

> The current assets available to the business minus any current claims on these assets.

This is generally expressed in the form:

> Current assets — current liabilities
> = net working capital

The individual items which make up the business's working capital were referred to in Chapter 16 when the components of the balance sheet were examined. Whichever format is used to present the balance sheet, current assets and current liabilities are listed separately from the other assets and liabilities of the business in order to identify the resources available to finance the business's trading activities. By referring back to the accounts of Style Fashions Ltd (see pp. 183–4), it can be seen that the items included in working capital form the bottom half of the horizontal-format balance sheet.

Current Assets		Current Liabilities	
Stock	11,500	Trade creditors	9,000
Debtors	8,500	Other creditors	4,000
Cash	7,400		
	27,400		13,000

It can be seen that current assets are those items owned by or owed to the business which change during day-to-day trading, i.e.:

> Stock + debtors + cash

Current liabilities are the short-term debts of the business which will have to be paid in the near future from current assets. The items making up current liabilities are the various sums owed to the business's creditors. It is normal to distinguish between the following different types of creditor:

1. **Expense creditors** have supplied a necessary service to the business but have not yet been paid, e.g. British Telecom for the telephone, the Electricity Board, even the window cleaner. Bills for these services fall due regularly and the business must have the resources to make payment.
2. **Trade creditors** have supplied goods to the business on credit and the accounts have not yet

been paid e.g. raw material and component suppliers.
3. **Financial creditors** are the institutions which have lent money to the business which has to be repaid in the short run e.g. the bank providing overdraft facilities.

Therefore the business's working capital is made up of the following items:

$$\left.\begin{array}{c} \text{Stock} \\ + \\ \text{Debtors} \\ + \\ \text{Cash} \end{array}\right\} - \left\{\begin{array}{c} \text{expense creditors} \\ + \\ \text{trade creditors} \\ + \\ \text{financial creditors} \end{array}\right\} = \begin{array}{c} \text{net working} \\ \text{capital} \end{array}$$

To ensure the efficient operation of the business, working capital needs to be carefully managed. This involves a system of stock control, a debtor policy and cash flow forecasting.

QUICK QUESTIONS 1

1. *Explain the meaning of the term 'solvency'.*
2. *Distinguish between a creditor and a debtor.*
3. *What is the formula for calculating the size of a business's working capital?*
4. *To which part of a business's accounts would you refer in order to find the value of its working capital?*

Stock Control

Figure 17.1 shows that the trading activities of the business involve purchasing raw materials and then manufacturing these into finished goods for sale. This means that at any one time the business holds stocks of items which are part-way through this cycle. There are 3 types of stock which the business can hold:

1. raw materials and components
2. semi-finished goods (work in progress)
3. finished goods awaiting sale.

However, a business will not necessarily hold all 3 types of stock, e.g. a retail business would only be likely to have stocks of finished goods awaiting sale. Only manufacturing businesses are likely to have all 3 types of stock.

These various types of stock are the **least liquid**

items of the business's current assets, i.e. they cannot generally be turned into cash immediately if the business suddenly requires the money. Stock generates cash gradually as goods are produced and the finished items sold. It is therefore important not to tie up unnecessarily large amounts of cash in stock because this money may be needed to meet current expenditures.

The process of ensuring that the business has a sufficient level of stock while at the same time minimising the cost to the business of holding stock is known as **stock control**.

The efficient stock control of raw materials is particularly important to a manufacturing business. If stocks of any one item run out it could mean that the whole production line comes to a standstill until new stocks can be obtained. This could prove very costly to the business. Therefore a **minimum safe level of stocks** must be established. Provided stocks are kept above this level the business should not encounter any problems regarding stock shortages. To maintain stocks above the minimum safe level requires a stock control system involving the following:

1. An efficient stock monitoring system to ensure that the level of stock at any time is known as accurately as possible.
2. Accurate information regarding the rate at which stock is used. This depends on the speed of production and can be estimated from the production targets set during the budgetary process.
3. Knowledge of the time it will take to replace stock from the time of placing the order with the supplier to delivery to the factory.

These 3 elements form the bare essentials of an efficient stock control system. However, it should be noted that often the information required is difficult to obtain or to predict. If the business can manage stock levels efficiently, it can benefit from major savings in 3 areas:

1. As mentioned above, holding large amounts of stock ties up money which may be needed for other purposes. If this causes the business to run short of cash, it might have to borrow to meet short-term liabilities, and this is expensive.

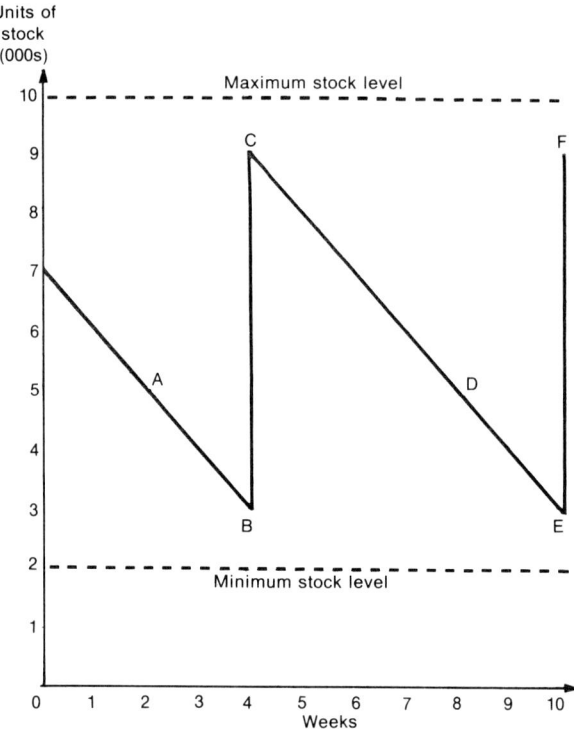

Figure 17.2 Stock-Holding Pattern

2. Storage costs can be reduced. Holding large amounts of stock takes up space and incurs warehousing costs. In addition, in certain industries the insurance of stock may be expensive.
3. Some stock items may have a limited shelf-life, which means they will become useless if held for too long. Efficient stock control is particularly important in minimising the wastage of such items as food.

There is an added complication in the management of stock levels: even if it is possible to keep stocks very close to the minimum safe level, it may not always be desirable to do so. This is because it would then be necessary to order fairly small amounts of stock frequently, and this may not be very efficient. The business also has to consider:

1. The costs involved in ordering stock – principally administration costs. Continually placing orders for small amounts of stock is expensive in terms of staff time and this may outweigh the

costs of carrying larger stocks and ordering less frequently.

2. The discount which is often available on larger stock orders.

Since there are a number of factors which must be taken into account when determining the stock control policy of the business, the result is likely to be a compromise between keeping stocks above the minimum safe level and not allowing stock ordering and stock-holding costs to rise to an unacceptable level. A possible stock-holding pattern is given in Figure 17.2. In this example the business has set a minimum stock level of 2,000 items to ensure it will not encounter stock shortage problems, and a maximum stock level of 10,000 items based upon storage capacity and holding costs. Stock is used at the rate of 1,000 units per week and the stock delivery time is 2 weeks from placing the order to the receipt of the goods.

Stock is ordered at points A and D, and BC and EF represent the size of the orders. Notice that the stock does not fall to the minimum safe level. This is to allow a margin in case, for example, the order is delivered late. The same is true for the maximum stock level. The business retains the capacity to carry slightly higher stocks if the opposite occurs and the order is delivered sooner than expected.

The above analysis of stock-holding policy refers to stocks of raw materials and components. However, the same principles apply to other types of stock the business may carry.

QUICK QUESTIONS 2

1. *In a tailoring business, what items would constitute work in progress?*
2. *How would you define a business's minimum safe level of stocks?*
3. *Why is the Manager of a supermarket likely to be more concerned about efficient stock control than the Manager of an electrical store?*
4. *What are the disadvantages to the business of holding too much stock?*

STUDENT TASK

Stan Ellis is the Production Manager of Fun and Games Ltd, a medium-sized toy manufacturer. The business is in the process of organising production to meet the pre-Christmas demand from its customers. One of Stan Ellis's jobs is to estimate the size of the orders the business needs to place with its suppliers over this period.

Reg Turner, his Production Foreman, is concerned that they do not have a repeat of last year's problems, when they ran out of an important stock item and production was seriously affected. He advises Stan to double their existing orders and send them out immediately to be sure they have everything they need before production is stepped up. Stan explains that ensuring they never run short of an item of stock is not the only consideration, and asks Reg to prepare more accurate estimates of their requirements.

1. What other considerations is Stan Ellis referring to in his discussion of stock levels with Reg Turner?
2. What particular problems may prevent the business from ordering all its stock requirements before it begins to increase production?
3. What information will Reg Turner need to find out before he can make accurate estimates of the business's stock requirements?

Debtor Policy

If a business sells its goods or services for cash then it will not incur any debtors. However, it is very common in business to offer credit facilities to customers as a way of increasing sales. Attractive credit terms often form an important component in the **marketing mix** of the business. However, offering credit terms to customers can result in 2 major problems for the business:

1. **The risk of default**: when the business sells goods on credit there is always the possibility that the customer will fail to pay what is owed. It was noted in the previous chapter that when this occurs the result is a bad debt which must be written off by the business. To avoid this problem the business will endeavour only to deal with creditworthy customers. However, it is not easy to establish the creditworthiness of all customers and bad debts are always a possibility. Creditworthiness is frequently based upon previous trading experience – businesses are generally more willing to offer credit facilities to long-standing customers

whom they know and trust. It is also possible to use the services of Credit Reference Agencies to investigate the creditworthiness of customers.

2. **The effect on cash flow**: as stated above, the trading activities of the business must generate enough money to meet current outgoings. If the business has a large amount tied up in debtors, it may not be able to meet these commitments.

In order to avoid these problems the business has to ensure that (a) it is not offering an unrealistic amount of credit to its customers, and (b) that the debts are not outstanding beyond the period that was agreed.

The cash position of the business is clearly affected by how long it takes to convert debtors into cash. This is known as the **average credit period**, and it should be regularly monitored to ensure it remains at a realistic level. It is common for businesses to send out accounts to customers at the end of the month and allow one month for settlement. This means that the credit period can vary from around 8 weeks for customers who receive goods at the beginning of one month and settle at the end of the next, to just a few days for customers who receive goods at the end of the month and settle almost immediately. Therefore, the average credit period under these circumstances is likely to be around six weeks. (This takes into account the fact that customers do not generally settle their accounts before they are required to do so.)

A business can check its average credit period by comparing its total sales income with the size of its debtors. This can be done on an annual basis using the following formula:

$$\frac{\text{Debtors}}{\text{Annual sales}} \times 100$$

For example, if the business's annual turnover was £130,000 and its outstanding debtors at the end of the year are £11,500 then the percentage of sales income outstanding can be calculated as:

$$\frac{11,500}{130,000} \times 100 = 8.8\%$$

If it is assumed that the business trades for 50 weeks of the year, then 8.8% represents approximately 4.5 weeks (4.5 weeks is 9% of 50 weeks). This is the average credit period. Given the business's debtor policy, this figure is quite acceptable. How-ever, if the figure should rise above the 6 weeks the business expects, it indicates that the debt control policy needs to be tightened up. This may mean sending out accounts or reminders more quickly or possibly giving discounts for prompt payment. In the last event it may be necessary to refuse to supply more goods to customers who have not yet settled their account for previous deliveries.

The problem of debtors reducing the cash available to the business can be a serious one, especially for small businesses with limited resources. It is therefore common for smaller businesses to make use of outside agencies to help improve cash flow. Debt control policy can be helped by employing the services of the following types of business:

1. **Finance companies** provide facilities for customers to purchase goods on credit, generally in the form of **hire purchase agreements**. These companies form a very important part of the consumer credit market. By having an arrangement with a finance company, a small retail business can still offer goods for sale on credit but does not have to tie up assets in the form of debtors. The business receives the cash from the finance company once the sale is agreed and the customer then owes the finance company and not the retailer. The finance company makes its profit from the interest charged on the hire purchase agreement.

2. **Debt factoring agencies**: debt factoring means selling debts to an outside agency and thus increasing the flow of cash into the business. Generally the agency purchases the debts as they occur. They pay a given percentage – usually up to 80% – when the invoice is first issued, less a given sum which is the charge they make for the service. The balance of the debt is paid by the agency when the account has been settled by the customer. This is a very useful service to the small business because it greatly reduces the amount of money tied up in debtors and eases the cash flow position.

1. *What is the major reason why businesses offer credit to their customers?*
2. *What are the main risks involved in offering credit on sales?*
3. *What does the term 'average credit period' mean?*
4. *How can a debt factoring agency help a business to improve its cash flow position?*

STUDENT TASK

Ray Dempster runs a small electrical company which supplies components to a number of large electrical engineering firms. Although his business is doing quite well, he operates in a very competitive market and has to work hard to keep his bigger contracts.

When an order for components is received, the goods are despatched from stock and an invoice is prepared for sending to the customer. This means that there is always a certain amount of money owing to the business from its customers. Some invoices are settled quickly but certain firms take a considerable time to pay for the goods they have received. This is causing problems because the business is quite small and doesn't have the resources to have large sums tied up in debtors. Ray Dempster realises he must take action to deal with this problem or there may not be enough cash in the business to meet his monthly commitments. He sees there is the need to devise a sensible debtor policy for the business.

1. Why would it be unwise for Ray to insist on payment before any goods are despatched as a way of dealing with his debtor problem?
2. Explain what Ray means by a 'sensible debtor policy'?
3. In order to tackle the problem Ray must first work out the present average credit period on the goods he is selling. How can he go about calculating this?
4. What action could Ray consider to try and reduce the average credit period?
5. If he fails to find a solution to this problem, what could be some of the consequences for the business?

Cash Flow and Cash Forecasting

Cash refers to the liquid assets which the business can use to meet payments and settle debts. This money is generally held in the business's bank account. It is very importnat that the business manages its finances efficiently to ensure it has an adequate cash flow. If the business experiences cash flow problems it will have to take action to either increase the money flowing into the business or reduce outgoings. However, the business does not want to hold too much cash as this means it has money lying idle in the bank account which could be used profitably in the business, e.g. to purchase further assets.

As cash flow is so vital to the business it is very important that cash requirements can be foreseen and planned for. This is the reason why cash flow forecasting is such an important part of the budgetary procedure described in Chapter 16. Cash flow is affected by a number of factors, including the current level of sales, the percentage of sales for cash, previous sales on credit and the average credit period, the level of outgoings and the credit available from suppliers and so on. The following information must therefore be available before a cash forecast can be produced.

1. The estimated income from cash sales.
2. The estimated income from debtors who purchased goods previously on credit.
3. The level of expected outgoings on running costs and overheads during the period, taking into account any credit which may be available.
4. The amount which must be paid to creditors over the period for goods and services previously received.
5. Any planned expenditure on capital items which will affect cash flow, e.g. a new office word processor.
6. Any special expenses which are foreseen during the period.

From this information it is possible to estimate the cash requirements over the period and take any action which may be necessary to avoid cash flow problems.

The process of cash flow forecasting can be clearly illustrated by the following example of quite a simple business venture.

Fineprint: The First Year of a New Business

A print worker who is made redundant has difficulty in finding another job in printing. He therefore considers using his £10,000 redundancy money to start his own printing business. He makes enquiries and finds he can rent suitable premises at a cost of £2,400 a year payable quarterly in advance. A second-hand printing press will cost him £7,500. He is advised that he qualifies for assistance from the Government Enterprise Allowance Scheme, which will pay him a weekly sum in his first year. This means that he will not have to draw an income from the business during the first 12 months of trading. He makes careful estimates about his likely income and expenditure during the first year.

1. He expects sales during the first 3 months to be at the level of £1,000 a month. As he becomes more established, this should rise to £2,000 a month for the next 6 months and £3,000 a month for the final 3 months of the year.
2. He will have to give one month's credit to his customers.
3. The cost of the necessary materials is estimated to be half the value of sales and must be bought for cash at the time of purchase.
4. The expenditure on such overheads as heating, lighting, advertising and so on is expected to be £350 a month.
5. His administration costs are expected to be £150 a month.

A simple profit forecast based upon these estimates shows that the business would have a successful first year of trading. This can be seen by looking at the estimated profit and loss account in Figure 17.3.

	£
Estimated sales revenue	
(3 × 1,000) + (6 × 2,000) + (3 × 3,000)	24,000
Cost of goods sold	12,000
Gross profit on sales	12,000
Rent 2,400	
Production and sales overheads 4,200	
Administration costs 1,800	
8,400	
Estimated net profit	3,600

Figure 17.3 Estimated Profit and Loss Account for Fineprint

However, a cash flow forecast for the year indicates that he could encounter problems in financing his trading activities. Figure 17.4 shows the cash flow forecast for Fineprint based upon the estimates of income and expenditure set out in Figure 17.3. Notice that after he has bought the printing press he starts the business with £2,500 in cash. This is reduced to £900 after the first month's trading.

As with the profit and loss account, the cash flow forecast indicates that if the business achieves its expected level of sales it will be in quite a sound position at the end of the year. Income from trading comfortably exceeds outgoings and the cash balance is quite healthy. However, during the year it makes a

	Jan	Feb	Mar	Apr	May	June	July	Aug	Sept	Oct	Nov	Dec
Sales	1000	1000	1000	2000	2000	2000	2000	2000	2000	3000	3000	3000
Revenue	–	1000	1000	1000	2000	2000	2000	2000	2000	2000	3000	3000
Materials	500	500	500	1000	1000	1000	1000	1000	1000	1500	1500	1500
Rent	600	–	–	600	–	–	600	–	–	600	–	–
Production and sales overheads	350	350	350	350	350	350	350	350	350	350	350	350
Administration costs	150	150	150	150	150	150	150	150	150	150	150	150
Total expenditure	1600	1000	1000	2100	1500	1500	2100	1500	1500	2600	2000	2000
Revenue – expenditure	– 1600	–	–	– 1100	500	500	– 100	500	500	– 600	1000	1000
Cash balance	900	900	900	– 200	300	800	700	1200	1700	1100	2100	3100

Figure 17.4 Cash Flow Forecast for Fineprint (£)

trading loss in 4 months of the year and only just breaks even in 2 of the months. Most importantly, it encounters a cash flow problem in April, when there are not sufficient cash resources to meet the business's commitments. Therefore, at one point during the year extra cash resources will be needed to overcome a cash flow problem and allow trading to continue.

There are a number of options the business can consider to deal with this type of situation.

Solutions to Cash Flow Problems

If the business has a problem with its cash flow then either a temporary source of external finance must be sought or the situation must be addressed by better management of working capital. The major ways this can be done are outlined below.

1. **Bank finance**

   Banks are an extremely important source of financial assistance to business, especially to small businesses. The 2 main methods of obtaining bank finance are via a **bank loan** and a **bank overdraft**.

   (a) A bank loan is negotiated between the business and the bank. It is a way of borrowing a fixed sum over a given period at a given rate of interest. The amount the bank charges for a business loan depends upon a number of factors, e.g. the size of the loan, the period of the loan, the bank's estimate of the risk involved and so on. This type of borrowing is **formal** in the sense that it generally takes the form of a signed agreement between the 2 parties. Loans are often used to purchase further fixed assets and the business may be required to provide **collateral**. This means securing the loan against the assets of the business so that if the loan repayments are not met then the bank has a claim on the assets as a way of recovering its money.

   (b) A bank overdraft is an **informal** method of borrowing from the bank. The bank allows the business to make payments from its account totalling a greater amount than it has in the account – usually up to some pre-arranged limit. No agreement is signed and the bank expects the overdraft to be cleared

as quickly as possible. In most circumstances when the business only needs temporary finance an overdraft is preferable to a loan because interest is only charged on the amount that the account is overdrawn. This is normally calculated on a daily basis. Whereas with a loan the business pays interest on the full amount borrowed regardless of whether the whole amount is required or not.

A bank overdraft is the obvious solution to the cash flow problems outlined above. The business is likely to be able to negotiate overdraft facilities on its account and its temporary shortage of cash will be covered by the bank. This will then be paid off from the sales income the following month. The business will only pay interest on the amount overdrawn for the number of days the account is in deficit. A bank loan would not be a suitable method of finance in this situation. (The use of loan facilities as a method of business finance will be dealt with in the next chapter.)

2. **Obtaining credit**

   If the business can delay payments to its suppliers of materials until it has generated sales income from those materials, it will improve its cash flow. In the above example, Fineprint is selling its service on one month's credit but paying cash for its materials. If it could obtain one month's credit on purchases then it would not encounter a cash flow problem during the year, in fact its cash balance would not fall below £800. As Fineprint becomes more established it may be able to negotiate credit facilities with its suppliers and so improve its cash flow.

3. **Reducing debtors**

   As explained earlier, debtors tie up cash which may be required by the business. In the example of Fineprint, the delay in receiving payment for sales does not help its cash flow, and customers who are late in settling their accounts would make the problem worse. A reduction in its average credit period would help overcome the cash flow problem but this is probably not a sensible solution in this particular situation.

The business may well lose sales by not offering this facility, especially if other printing businesses offer credit to their customers. Nevertheless a business with cash flow difficulties may well have to investigate its debtor policy and consider making adjustments if other solutions are not available. One policy it may consider is debt factoring so as to increase its sales income by the sale of its debts.

4. Reducing expenditure

This means examining carefully all the outgoings of the business to see if costs can be cut and cash flow improved. In our example the printing business is very small and therefore the ability to make savings is very limited. In this case even reducing expenses to an absolute minimum would not help the situation very much. However, with larger businesses substantial savings may be possible by careful monitoring of all expenditures.

5. Reducing the scale of operations

Often businesses encounter cash flow problems because they grow too quickly and do not have the resources to finance their increased level of trading. In the above example, Fineprint encounters its cash flow problem in the first month of increased sales. This is an example of how lack of finance may frustrate the development of a small business. However, in this case the business has to increase its sales above the level of the first 3 months in order to be able to meet expenditures later in the year and be in profit at the end of the year. In this instance a delay in increasing turnover would therefore only lead to a cash flow problem later in the year. Businesses with different financial commitments may nevertheless find that such a solution is the answer to cash flow problems.

6. The sale of assets

This is really a last-resort solution to address a cash crisis. If the assets have to be sold to keep the business solvent then generally the business is facing very severe problems. However, a business which is intending to sell off certain assets may well adjust the timing of such sales in order to assist cash flow. In the above example

the business only has one fixed asset, its printing press, and hence this solution could not be contemplated since the business would be forced to close down. In addition, the business does not have to contemplate such a drastic solution since other methods of finance are available and much more suitable.

The above alternatives show some of the internal and external methods of generating cash resources which may be available to a business. If the cash flow problem is temporary, as in the example of the Fineprint printing business, then it can be fairly easily solved. However, more fundamental financial problems may require a more long-term solution, e.g. borrowing over a longer term or the injection of more capital into the business. The sources of such medium-term and long-term finance are dealt with in the next chapter.

STUDENT TASK

Tyler and Slater Ltd is in the process of drawing up its budget for the next 6 months. It estimates that monthly sales over this period will be as follows:

July	August	September
£10,000	£15,000	£15,000
October	**November**	**December**
£10,000	£8,000	£8,000

The goods purchased to produce each month's sales cost half the sales value and are purchased in the month before sales. Both purchases of raw materials and the business's sales of its product are on 2 months' credit. Other expenses of the business are as follows:

Rent of factory: £10,000 each quarter (the June rent has just been paid)

Wages: £5,000 per month

Administration: £1,000 per month

1. Assuming the business will have £3,000 in its account at the beginning of October, draw up a cash flow forecast for each of the last 3 months of the year.
2. What problem does the forecast suggest the business will face?
3. Outline the possible solutions the business could adopt to deal with this situation.

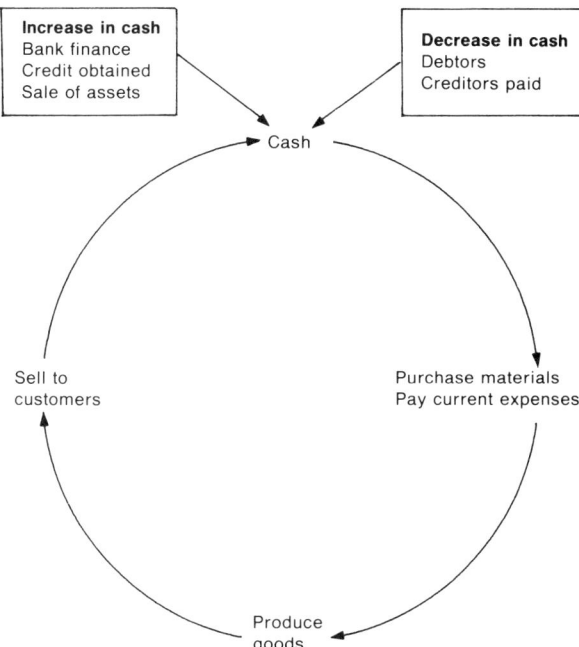

Figure 17.5 Influences on the Cash Position of the Business

The various influences affecting a business's cash position can be summarised by a more detailed illustration of the flow of working capital than was originally shown in Figure 17.1.

QUICK QUESTIONS 4

1. *Why is careful management of cash flow so important to the business?*
2. *Is there any disadvantage to the business of holding too much cash?*
3. *Give 2 major differences between a bank loan and a bank overdraft.*
4. *Name one other external source of finance to help the business overcome a cash flow problem.*

The Size of the Business's Working Capital

The survival of any business depends on it remaining **solvent**. Solvency refers to the ability of the business to meet its immediate liabilities and continue to undertake trading activities. Therefore, solvency depends upon maintaining a sufficient level of working capital.

Working capital has already been defined as **current assets minus current liabilities**. This calculation gives a specific monetary figure for the business's working capital. However, the important question is whether this sum is sufficient to ensure the business can continue to trade successfully. A safe level of working capital will ensure that the current assets of the business are large enough to meet its immediate liabilities. Therefore, solvency is dependent upon the size of current assets **in relation to** current liabilities. This relationship is known as the business's **working capital ratio** or its **current ratio** and can be expressed as:

$$\frac{\text{Current assets}}{\text{Current liabilities}} : 1$$

This ratio should not fall below 1:1 as this would indicate that assets are not sufficient to meet immediate liabilities, which means that the business faces insolvency. However, a working capital ratio of 1:1 could still mean the business may run into liquidity problems and find it difficult to meet current commitments. Therefore, the ratio should be in the region of 2:1 (current assets equal to twice current liabilities) to avoid any problems. A figure significantly higher than this would indicate that the business is probably holding assets in liquid form which could be put to profitable use in the business.

The accounts of Style Fashions Ltd discussed above (see pp.183–4) show that the current financial position of the business is as follows:

Current Assets		Current Liabilities	
	£		£
Stock	11,500	Trade creditors	9,000
Debtors	8,500	Other creditors	4,000
Cash	7,400		
	27,400		13,000

The business's working capital can be calculated as:

$$£27,400 - £13,000 = £14,400$$

Applying the formula to test whether this is a sufficient level of working capital the result is as follows:

$$\frac{27,400}{13,000} = 2.1$$

This gives a ratio of current assets to current liabilities of just over 2:1, which is perfectly satisfactory and indicates that the business should not encounter any problems in meeting its immediate commitments.

However, care must be taken in interpreting this ratio. In particular a large sum tied up in stocks may give a satisfactory working capital ratio but the business may still encounter liquidity problems because stocks cannot generally be converted into cash at very short notice. For this reason it is useful to look at the size of current assets **excluding stock** in relation to current liabilities. This is known as the business's **liquid capital ratio**, or the **acid test ratio**. This can be expressed as:

$$\frac{\text{Current assets} - \text{stock}}{\text{Current liabilities}} : 1$$

As a general rule the business should aim to keep this ratio around 1:1, i.e. cash and debtors at least equal to current liabilities, to ensure it can meet its immediate commitments. The acid test ratio of Style Fashions Ltd can be calculated as follows:

$$\frac{27,400 - 11,500}{13,000} = 1.2$$

This shows that liquid assets are just greater than current liabilities, which again is satisfactory and indicates that the business should have no problems in meeting its immediate commitments.

QUICK QUESTIONS 5

1. *How does a business calculate its working capital ratio?*
2. *Why may the business be concerned if its working capital ratio falls below 2:1?*
3. *Why may a business exclude the value of its stocks when evaluating its current financial position?*

Successful Trading

To conclude it can be seen that the success of the day-to-day trading activities of the business is dependent upon the efficient management of working capital. This requires adequate stock control, a realistic debtor policy and, most importantly, careful management of cash flow. To remain solvent the business must ensure there are sufficient current assets to meet the immediate liabilities generated in the course of trading.

STUDENT TASK

The balance sheet of a business contains the following items:

Assets	£	Liabilities	£
Premises	120,000	Capital	200,000
Machinery	70,000	Loan	28,000
Vehicles	30,000	Creditors	5,800
Stock	14,400	Overdraft	2,100
Debtors	1,500		
	235,900		235,900

The management of the business is rather worried about its current financial position. It therefore looks closely at the balance sheet to see if the business is likely to face any immediate problems.

1. What is the present working capital of the business?
2. How would the management judge whether this is a sufficient level of working capital?
3. Shortly after the balance sheet was drawn up, the following amendments had to be made:
   (a) Stock costing £4,000 was sold for £7,000 cash.
   (b) A careful check of the records revealed that one creditor had in fact been paid £500 but the accounts had not been amended to show this.
   (c) More stock was purchased at a cost of £4,500, one-third of which was paid in cash and two-thirds on credit.

What is the effect of the above changes on the working capital of the business? Has the current financial position of the business improved as a result of these changes?

PROJECT AND ASSIGNMENT SUGGESTIONS

1. Assume you have won £20,000 in a competition. You decide to use the money to open a travel agency business. You have found suitable premises to rent near the centre of the town and are

keen to get the project under way as soon as possible.

(a) Write an account of how you will set up the business, the equipment you will need, the number of people you will employ and so on.

(b) Make an estimate of all the expenses you are likely to incur in the first 6 months of trading and the likely monthly income over this period. Present this information in the form of a cash flow forecast.

(c) Assume your estimates of the monthly income of the business are rather over-optimistic and you enter a cash flow problem in the first few months of trading. Explain the nature of your cash flow problem, suggest ways of dealing with this problem and indicate the best course of action.

2. Contact one or two of the main high street banks and ask for information about the services they offer to small businesses. See if you can find out:

(a) The main differences between a personal bank account and a business account.

(b) How the banks try to attract business accounts.

(c) The various ways the business can use its bank account to make payments and settle debts.

(d) The different methods of borrowing from the bank.

(e) What specialist services the bank provides for its business customers.

If the bank has a specialist small business advisor, see what you can find out about the sort of work he or she does.

3. Look at a copy of the annual report and accounts of a large company, which can be obtained by writing to the company's head office. You can use the information from the balance sheet to analyse the current financial position of the business. Look at the size of current assets and liabilities and the amount of working capital. Calculate the company's working capital ratio and its liquid capital ratio. Do these ratios fall within acceptable limits? You could repeat this exercise for a number of similar companies and write a brief report comparing their current financial position.

CHAPTER 18

The Capital Financing
of Business

Capital financing refers to the raising of funds to purchase fixed assets for use within a business organisation. In Chapter 16 it was explained that fixed assets are those items which are employed in the business on a permanent basis, i.e. they do not change during the normal trading activities of the business. Fixed assets (or fixed capital) therefore include land and buildings, plant and machinery, fixtures and fittings, and vehicles.

However, it is important to understand that the term 'capital' is not only used to describe the business's actual fixed assets. Capital can also refer to the finance used to purchase these items. Therefore, a distinction must be made between:

1. **Physical capital**: the fixed assets themselves, e.g. premises, machine tools and so on. The process of purchasing these items is known as **investment**.
2. **Financial capital**: the money raised for the purpose of purchasing physical capital.

It is the sources of financial capital available to the business which are examined in this chapter. In simple terms, there are 2 reasons why the business needs to purchase fixed assets.

1. To replace those assets which wear out. The process of wearing out and replacement is known as **depreciation**, as explained in Chapter 16. If a business does not replace assets as they depreciate its productive capacity and its efficiency will decline and it will find it difficult to compete. This threatens its long-term survival.
2. To expand the business. This can mean purchasing new fixed assets for use within the business or buying the assets of another busi-

ness, as is the case in a **take-over**. This may enable the business to become more efficient by securing **economies of scale** (explained in detail in Chapter 10), to improve its market share, to diversify its product range and so on.

The total level of investment undertaken by the business is called **gross investment**. Investment above that necessary to cover depreciation of assets is known as **net investment**.

All investment within the business requires a source of financial capital. As with the finance of trading activities, which was dealt with in the previous chapter, there are 2 types of funds available to the business as sources of financial capital. These are **internal sources** and **external sources**.

Internal Sources of Financial Capital

Internal capital financing refers to the money generated from the business's own assets which is available to purchase further assets. There are 3 main ways the business can finance investment from internal sources.

1. Profits

As was explained in Chapter 16, once the business has declared its profit for the year and met any tax liability it can either distribute the remainder to the busuiness's owners (shareholders in the case of a limited company) as a return on their previous investment or retain the profit for use within the business. Retained profit is held in the business's reserves and constitutes a very important source of capital for investment. This process is known as

ploughing back profits. Small businesses in particular rely greatly on past profits as a source of capital, partly because of the difficulties of raising capital from other sources. However, large businesses also reinvest significant sums from their previous profits. In 1989, for example, British Gas made a net profit of £620 million after tax. It retained £237 million of the sum in its reserves.

It should be remembered that retaining profits for use within the business represents a further investment in the business by its owner(s) because this money has been generated by the use of the business's existing assets.

2. The Sale of Assets

It was noted in Chapter 17 that one possible method of generating liquid funds to meet trading commitments is to sell some of the assets of the business. However, selling assets for this purpose usually indicates the business is in very severe financial trouble and such a course of action is generally a last resort to try and keep the business afloat. The same is not true when a business is considering the sale of assets to finance capital expenditure. Selling assets to generate the financial capital for further investment is common practice and can be sound financial management. If a business is trying to maintain its efficiency and keep ahead of its rivals it may well need to replace existing physical capital with more up-to-date technology before this equipment has reached the end of its useful life. In such circumstances it is sensible to finance the purchase of the new machinery partly by the sale of the existing equipment. In a similar way many businesses have agreements with local garages concerning the provision of company cars. These are changed at regular intervals and the new cars are financed partly by the trade-in of the old vehicles. Therefore, the timing of the sale of older assets to generate funds to purchase new assets is an important part of financial management.

3. Sale and Lease Back

A leasing agreement allows the business to secure the use of capital assets without having to raise the necessary finance to purchase those assets. In effect the business is hiring the assets, e.g. a building or a piece of capital equipment, for a specific period of time in return for an agreed payment. As an operating lease separates the use of the asset from its ownership, this process does not constitute investment in the business. The payment for the use of the asset is met out of trading income and thus the business does not need to raise extra financial capital. This type of agreement is becoming more popular, particularly in heavy industries such as oil exploration, where capital equipment is extremely expensive and may only be required for a specific period.

One particular type of leasing agreement is **sale and lease back**. This is when a business enters into an agreement to sell the assets it currently owns to a specialist institution and then lease them back for continued use within the business. The main reason for such an agreement is that the business may have large sums tied up in fixed assets which it wishes to release in order to finance further expansion. This is particularly true in the case of land and buildings. Such fixed assets appreciate over time and become worth a great deal but as they are **illiquid assets** (not readily converted into cash), the benefit of their increasing value can not be utilised by the business. Certain institutions with liquid capital to spare, e.g. insurance companies and pension funds, are prepared to purchase these assets in return for a regular income from the business. The institution has a fairly secure and predictable return on its investment and the business releases usable funds from its fixed assets. These funds can then be used to purchase further assets and expand the business. This type of agreement is therefore another way of generating financial capital internally from the business's assets.

QUICK QUESTIONS 1

1. *What characteristic distinguishes a fixed asset from a current asset of the business?*
2. *Explain in one sentence the difference between physical capital and financial capital.*
3. *What do we mean when we say that a business's assets depreciate?*
4. *Explain why retaining past profits represents a further investment by the owner(s) of the business.*
5. *What are the advantages to a financial institution of entering into a sale and lease back agreement with a business?*

External Sources of Financial Capital

External capital financing refers to obtaining the money required for investment from outside the business. This can be done in 2 ways – via **borrowing** or via the **extension of ownership** of the business. Decisions concerning the type of external finance will determine the business's **capital structure**. Raising money by borrowing creates a debt which has to be serviced (i.e. interest has to be paid on the debt), and is therefore often referred to as **debt finance**.

Sources of Debt Finance

1. Bank Finance

Certain aspects of bank finance were referred to in Chapter 17 in relation to the business's working capital. A distinction was made between borrowing in the form of a bank loan and a bank overdraft. Whereas an overdraft is generally the most suitable form of borrowing to finance a temporary cash flow problem related to the business's trading activities, this method is not appropriate for financing capital expenditure. For capital finance the business requires a given sum over a given period of time at an agreed rate of charge. Therefore, when a business is considering capital expenditure it is its ability to obtain a bank loan which is important. This allows a fixed sum to be borrowed and to be paid back either on an agreed future date or in instalments over the period of the loan, generally the latter. All busi-

nesses, large and small, borrow from banks in this way but bank financing of this type is particularly important to small businesses because their ability to raise capital from other sources is limited.

Traditionally banks in Britain have tended to lend over a rather short term, e.g. over periods not exceeding 3 or 4 years. However, in recent years they have moved away from their insistence on short-term lending, and loans over a period of 7 or even 10 years have become more common.

It is important to realise that there is no standard charge (i.e. rate of interest) on business loans. Banks determine the rate to charge according to a number of factors, including the following:

(a) The degree of risk that the business will not be able to repay the loan. Where the bank considers the risk is significant it is unlikely to grant the loan at all unless it is secured against the assets of the business.

(b) The bank's knowledge of the business, i.e. its previous record in meeting its commitments, the size of its account with the bank and so on.

(c) The current economic climate and the availability of funds. Borrowing from banks (and other financial institutions) is more expensive in times of economic restraint when liquid funds are less freely available.

(d) The specific conditions of the loan, particularly the length of time before repayment.

The above points show that borrowing in the form of a bank loan is likely to be less expensive for larger businesses than for smaller concerns. This is an example of a financial **economy of scale**.

2. Building Society Finance

Building societies are institutions which provide long-term capital finance for the purchase of land and buildings. Finance is provided in the form of a **mortgage**, which is the method most people use to buy their own houses. Typically a mortgage is spread over a very long period of time, generally 25 years, although shorter-term mortgages can also be obtained. A mortgage is a very important source of capital for smaller businesses because it allows the business to buy rather than rent its premises. Mortgages are secured against the property on which they are lent, which means they are widely available to small businesses which have limited assets and

Figure 18.1 The Stock Exchange

therefore limited opportunities to borrow from other sources. However, having mortgaged property reduces the value of the owned assets of the business, i.e. the value of the land and premises given in the balance sheet is their current market value minus the outstanding mortgage. Mortgaged property cannot be used as security (collateral) for other forms of borrowing in the way that property owned outright can. Nevertheless, as property appreciates in value over time, the mortgage becomes a decreasing percentage of the market value of these assets, and so it becomes possible to raise further capital on the unmortgaged value of the property.

3. Finance Houses

Finance houses are institutions which offer facilities for buying goods on credit, usually in the form of a **hire purchase agreement**. As was explained in Chapter 17, smaller businesses may use the services of a finance house in the process of selling their goods. However, a business can also use a finance house to supply the finance for the purchase of assets. Again this is only likely to occur in the case of a small business, particularly one which is just starting up and needs to purchase assets. Items such as office furniture, typewriters and so forth can be purchased with finance obtained in this way. The business pays a deposit and the balance is then paid off over a given period, e.g. 2 or 3 years. The business has the use of the assets from the beginning of the agreement but does not own them until the last payment is made. Finance obtained in this way is quite expensive and so this method is not used by businesses which can raise the necessary capital in other (cheaper) ways. For this reason it is not used as a source of financial capital by larger businesses.

4. Finance for Industry Ltd

This is a holding company, i.e. a company which holds a majority shareholding in a number of other businesses. It was established in 1973 to manage 2 specialist finance institutions: the Industrial and Commercial Finance Corporation (ICFC) and the Finance Corporation for Industry (FCI). These 2 institutions were founded in 1946 jointly by the Bank of England, the London clearing banks and the Scottish banks to make loans available to businesses which are experiencing difficulties in raising capital.

5. Debentures

Debentures were mentioned in Chapter 2 as a method used by companies to borrow from the public over long periods of time. A debenture certificate is essentially an IOU which guarantees repayment of the sum borrowed at a given date in the future, the **maturity date**. The person holding the debenture certificate is entitled to a fixed annual sum as an interest payment on the money borrowed. Although it is not possible to secure the repayment of the loan from the business before the maturity date, it is possible to sell the certificate to someone else at any time. In this way debenture certificates change hands in a similar way to share certificates. However, as was explained in Chapter 2, debenture holders are not owners of the business in the same way that shareholders are; they are **creditors** of the business. If the business becomes insolvent and has to be wound up (liquidated) then the debenture holders have the same rights as other creditors. In fact if the business gets into financial difficulties and is unable to pay the interest due on its debentures then the debenture holders can force the business into liquidation in order to secure the return of the money they have lent.

However, it is quite common to issue **mortgage debentures**. These are secured against particular assets of the business and therefore carry less risk. If the business is forced into liquidation these assets are sold to raise the money to pay back the mortgage debenture holders. As mortgage debentures carry less risk they normally earn a lower interest payment, e.g. 6% instead of 8%.

The main advantage of issuing debentures is that they are a method of long-term borrowing, whereas bank loans are essentially short or medium term. As some investment projects take many years to implement, long-term finance is more suitable.

The above 5 sources of financial capital constitute the main ways in which a business can borrow. The alternative method of attracting external finance is through an extension of the ownership of the business.

QUICK QUESTIONS 2

1. *What are the 2 broad types of external finance available to the business?*
2. *Why does the rate of interest a bank charges on a business loan vary?*
3. *Why is building society finance particularly important to small businesses?*
4. *Give 2 major differences between a share and a debenture.*

STUDENT TASK

Margret Pearson is the Finance Director of Write Stuff PLC, a company manufacturing various stationery items. The company is currently considering a large investment programme in order to update its capital equipment and expand its productive capacity. Margret has advised the board that the modernisation programme can be partly financed from the business's own resources but it will need to borrow some of the capital required. She told a recent board meeting:

> ... given the current economic climate and the recent performance of the business we should not have any problem in raising the finance we need at a reasonable rate of interest.

1. What type of investment increases the productive capacity of a business?
2. What do you think Margret Pearson meant when she said the expansion could be partly financed from the business's own resources?
3. What sources of borrowed capital could the business consider to raise the external finance it requires? Which do you think is the most suitable source?
4. What factors will determine the rate of interest the business will have to pay on the money it borrows?

Extending the Ownership of the Business

Extending ownership means attracting finance from individuals or institutions who are prepared to take a stake in the business in return for a share of the profits. Finance provided in this way does not create a debt because investors become part-owners of the business not creditors. They are not guaranteed a fixed return on their investment; what they receive will be dependent upon the profitability of the business. The attraction of raising external finance in this way is that it does not increase the size of the business's creditors and hence there is no liability to pay interest on the capital. However, extending the ownership of the business will obviously mean that existing owners lose some control over the management of the business.

The process involved in extending ownership of a business depends upon the type of business concerned. In the case of a sole proprietor, capital can be raised to expand the business by taking a partner. If it is to be an equal partnership, then a sum equal to half the value of the business will be invested by the partner and he or she will be entitled to a half share of the profits. In addition, all decisions concerning the running of the business will now be made jointly by the 2 partners. The principle is the same if more partners join the business. External finance can also be raised by attracting investment from **sleeping partners** (see Chapter 2).

In the case of a private limited company (see Chapter 2), the existing shareholders can decide collectively to extend the ownership of the business by allowing new shareholders to take a stake in the company. This process spreads the ownership of the company among a larger number of people and increases the claim on the business's profits. The new shareholders also have rights with regard to electing the board of directors and determining the policy of the company. It should be remembered that a private limited company can also raise extra capital by issuing more shares to the existing shareholders. This does not spread the ownership any wider but represents an increased investment in the business by its present owners.

However, the raising of financial capital by offering a part of the business for sale to those who might wish to invest in it is particularly important to public limited companies. This is because the shares are available to anyone through the **capital market**. The capital market is composed of all those financial institutions concerned with the provision of capital finance for industry and commerce.

The Workings of the Capital Market

Central to the operation of the capital market is the London **Stock Exchange**. Here shares in public limited companies are bought and sold. However, the Stock Exchange is essentially a **market for second-hand securities**. This means it deals principally in shares which have already been bought and sold before. It is the market through which individuals and institutions which have money to invest can purchase shares in public limited companies and where those who wish to liquidate (turn into cash) their investments can find buyers for their shares. These transactions do not affect the finances of the companies themselves, it is simply the ownership of the shares that changes. Therefore, when considering raising new capital we must investigate the process of issuing more shares. This involves another part of the capital market known as the **new issues market**. There are a number of ways of raising capital via a new issue of shares, as outlined below.

1. **An offer for sale**. If a company wishes to undertake an offer for sale, it employs the services of an **issuing house**. These are specialist merchant banks who act on behalf of companies in the issuing of new shares. A prospectus will be drawn up to present all the relevant information about the company required by a would-be investor before making a decision on whether or not to invest. The prospectus gives a history of the company, its present financial structure, its past profitability and so on. The issue is then advertised and individuals and institutions are invited to **subscribe** (apply) for shares. The issue can either be at a fixed price, i.e. applicants are invited to subscribe for so many shares at a price per share stated in the prospectus, or it can be an issue by **tender**. A tender is a way of selling shares to the highest bidder. Applications are invited in the same way but potential investors have to state the price they are prepared to pay per share. This method reduces the opportunity for investors to make a quick profit by buying shares in an over-subscribed issue and then selling them immediately they are traded on the Stock Exchange for a higher price. In an issue by tender it is the company rather than the speculating investor that benefits from a well-subscribed issue.

With an offer for sale there is always the risk that not all the shares the company wishes to issue will be taken up by the public. In order to cover themselves against this risk the company will have the share issue **underwritten**. This means the company pays a fee to the issuing house in return for a guarantee that they will buy any shares not taken up by the market.

An offer for sale is the most expensive method of issuing shares and must be used if more than £3 million is to be raised.

2. **A Stock Exchange placing**. In the case of a placing, all the shares to be issued are 'placed' in large blocks with the big institutional investors. The institutions interested in buying shares in this way are pension funds, insurance companies and union funds, which have large amounts of liquid capital held in reserve ready to take advantage of investment opportunities in reliable businesses. Issuing shares in this way is cheaper than through an offer for sale.

3. **A rights issue**. In a rights issue new shares are offered to existing shareholders at a more favourable price than they will be offered to the general public. Existing shareholders are generally given the right to subscribe for these shares in proportion to their existing shareholding.

These 3 methods of issuing shares relate to larger public companies which have a **Stock Exchange listing**, i.e. their shares, once issued, can be traded on the Stock Exchange. However, for smaller public companies which do not have a Stock Exchange listing their share can still be issued to the public via the **Unlisted Securities Market (USM)**. This was created in 1980 to help smaller businesses which had previously been discouraged by the requirements of a full listing on to the Stock Market. It is essentially a natural half-way stage between a small business and a mature listed company. It is considerably cheaper to join the USM than to gain a full listing and it enables the company to attract capital from a wider area.

It is clear that a business has a large number of options when considering external sources of capital finance. In particular, it has to make the choice between debt finance and extending ownership. This decision is very important because it will determine the **capital gearing** of the business.

QUICK QUESTIONS 3

1. *Explain what is meant by the description of the Stock Exchange as 'a market for secondhand securities'?*
2. *Explain the difference between a fixed price issue of new shares and an offer by tender.*
3. *Why do companies have a new issue of shares underwritten?*
4. *To whom are shares offered when a company undertakes a rights issue?*
5. *What is the main function of the Unlisted Securities Market?*

Capital Gearing

A gear determines how a movement in one variable will affect the movement in another, e.g. it is the gearbox in a car which determines how the speed of the engine affects the speed of the vehicle. Gears are ratios between different variables, and one of the most important ratios to a business is its capital gearing ratio. Gearing in this context refers to the ratio between a company's **equity** and its **permanent loan capital**.

1. **Equity** is the money invested in the business by the ordinary shareholders. There is no guaranteed return on this investment, it will depend upon the profitability of the business. However, when the size of the dividend to be paid to ordinary shareholders has been decided, all such shares will receive an equal amount – that is why they are called equities.
2. **Permanent loan capital** refers to the debt finance which must be serviced (i.e. interest must be paid on the amount borrowed) regardless of the profitability of the business.

Therefore, gearing is essentially the ratio of share capital to borrowed capital. However, this is not always the case because of the nature of preference shares. (The different types of preference shares are explained in Chapter 2.) They are shares which have first call on the company's profits after all expenses have been met – including interest on loan capital and any liability for taxation. Since preference shares earn a **fixed rate of return**, the amount which must be paid will not rise with profitability (unless the company has issued participating preference shares).

In this respect the payment to preference shareholders is similar to the payment to long-term creditors. For this reason fixed rate preference shares are commonly treated in the same way as loan capital when gearing is being calculated because they are both **fixed rate securities**.

Thus the size of a company's gearing can be expressed by the following formula:

$$\frac{\text{Fixed rate securities}}{\text{Ordinary share capital}} \times 100$$

A **highly geared** company will have a large amount of fixed rate securities in relation to the value of its ordinary shares. A **low geared** company will have a small amount of fixed rate securities in relation to the value of its ordinary shares.

Gearing is important because it determines how fluctuations in profitability affect the size of the dividend paid to the ordinary shareholders. This is because fixed rate securities have to be paid a given sum regardless of the size of the company's profits. However, as profits rise the amount paid to these fixed rate security holders does not increase, so the amount paid declines **as a proportion** of the profit made. This means that the more highly geared the company the more any change in profitability will affect the dividend to ordinary shareholders. The effect of capital gearing on the ordinary share dividend is illustrated in the following comparison of the dividends paid to the shareholders of 2 different companies.

Both companies have a capital structure composed of just ordinary shares and fixed rate preference shares. Company A has a very low gearing ratio of fixed interest securities to equity of 1 : 5. Company B is very highly geared, with a ratio of 5 : 1. The capital structures are compared below.

	Company A	Company B
£1 ordinary shares	500,000	100,000
10% preference shares (£)	100,000	500,000

Note that if both companies are profitable then each must pay 10% of the value of their preference share capital in the form of a dividend to preference shareholders. This amounts to only £10,000 for company A (low gearing) but £50,000 for company B (highly geared). If all the remaining profit is distributed to ordinary shareholders, we can analyse the effect of various different levels of profitability on the dividends paid to the ordinary shareholders in each company.

If each company makes a post-tax profit of £50,000, then the distribution of this profit will be as follows:

	Company A	Company B
Payment to preference shareholders (£)	10,000	50,000
Amount available for ordinary shareholders (£)	40,000	–
Rate of dividend per ordinary share	8%	–

In this case the preference shareholders take all the profit in company B but only 20% of the profit of company A. This allows a dividend of 8% to be paid to each ordinary share in company A. No ordinary share dividend can be declared in company B.

Compare the way the companies' profits are distributed when the profit levels are higher – at £75,000 and £100,000.

Profit Level of £75,000

	Company A	Company B
Payment to preference shareholders (£)	10,000	50,000
Amount available for ordinary shareholders (£)	65,000	25,000
Rate of dividend per ordinary share	13%	25%

Profit Level of £100,000

	Company A	Company B
Payment to preference shareholders (£)	10,000	50,000
Amount available for ordinary shareholders (£)	90,000	50,000
Rate of dividend per ordinary share	18%	50%

It can be seen that the variation in the ordinary share dividend is much greater if the company is highly geared than if the gearing is low. The following summary makes this clear.

Profit variation from £50,000 to £100,000:

Company A (low gearing): dividend varies from 8% to 18%

Company B (high gearing): dividend varies from 0% to 50%

Therefore the higher the capital gearing of the company the more the dividend paid to ordinary shareholders will fluctuate for any given variation in profitability.

QUICK QUESTIONS 4

1. *Explain briefly what is meant by the term 'capital gearing'.*
2. *Why are ordinary shares often referred to as equities?*
3. *Explain why a company which has a high gearing ratio may encounter difficulties if its financial performance falls below expectations.*

STUDENT TASK

Platt Products PLC has the following capital structure:

100,000 £1 ordinary shares
£200,000 10% preference shares
£100,000 8% debentures

In 1989 the profit of the company net of all expenses except debenture interest was £50,000. It must first pay interest to the debenture holders and the remaining sum is then liable for tax at a rate of 25%. The business pays the dividend to preference shareholders and decides to retain 50% of the remaining profit for reinvestment. The balance of the profit is then distributed as a dividend to ordinary shareholders.

1. What is the capital gearing of the company?
2. How much is paid as interest to the debenture holders?
3. What is the company's pre-tax profit?
4. What is the net profit after tax?
5. What sum will be paid in dividends to preference shareholders?
6. How much profit will the business retain?
7. What is the percentage dividend paid to each ordinary share?
8. What would be the percentage ordinary share dividend if the profits of the company doubled to £100,000? Comment on the size of this change in dividend.

The Financial Decision

Businesses require finance for a wide variety of reasons, and most businesses can obtain finance from a number of different sources. Therefore, decisions have to be made regarding the most appropriate source of finance. The provision of advice concerning the best method of financing different aspects of business activity is one of the key responsibilities of the Finance Department. When considering which method of finance is most suitable for any type of business activity, a number of factors must be taken into account:

1. **The purpose for which the finance is required**. It was explained in Chapter 16 that the reason a business requires finance – the application of funds – is often the most important factor in determining how the finance will be obtained – the source of funds. This means that funds required to bridge a temporary cash flow problem are likely to be sought from a different source than funds for capital expansion.

2. **The cost of the finance**. Certain types of finance are expensive to raise, e.g. an issue of new shares. Other forms of finance can be expensive to service, e.g. interest charges on borrowed funds. The various costs must be carefully considered to ensure the business is obtaining its finance as cheaply as possible.

3. **The availability of finance**. Some sources of finance are not available to all businesses and this restricts the choice of funding.

4. **The present financial structure of the business**. It is important to take account of the existing liabilities of the business when considering further finance. The capital gearing of the business is particularly important in this respect.

5. **How quickly the finance is required**. If the funds are needed immediately, e.g. to supplement cash flow, then the choice is likely to be restricted to a small number of sources, e.g. a bank overdraft. The more time the business has to plan for its financial needs the wider the choice will be.

Finally, it should be noted that the larger the business the greater the number of possible sources of funds available. Small firms face particular difficulties in raising the finance they need. This is one of the major reasons preventing the growth and development of such businesses. Some of the problems small businesses face in obtaining finance are:

1. Small businesses generate small profits, which means that there are limited funds for reinvestment.

2. Small profits also mean that the amount the business can borrow is constrained. Banks and other financial institutions base the amount they are prepared to lend on the ability of the business to service and repay the loan. Therefore, low past and projected future profits also affect the amount which can be raised through borrowing.

3. Lending to small businesses is seen as more of a risk than lending to large companies. This is because small businesses are often dependent upon a narrow product range, have only limited assets, and so on. This also makes borrowing difficult.

4. Borrowing for small businesses can be more expensive than for larger companies. Financial institutions may charge a higher rate of interest to compensate for the greater risks involved.

5. Finally, some sources of finance may involve a loss of control over the running of the business. A sole trader wishing to expand may find the only sensible course of action is to seek a partner or turn the business into a limited company. The owner may not wish to do this because of the loss of control over how the business is run. Many sole traders are in business precisely because they wish to be their own boss.

QUICK QUESTIONS 5

1. *Distinguish between source of funds and application of funds.*
2. *List 3 factors a business will take into account when considering the most suitable source of finance.*
3. *Why is lending to a small business likely to be more of a risk than lending to a larger business?*

STUDENT TASK

Snape Mouldings PLC is a medium-sized company producing plastic kitchenware, e.g. bowls, brushes etc. The Managing Director wishes to expand the business into the production of moulded plastic garden furniture in order to diversify the product range and benefit from the economies of large-scale production. The expansion will require the extension of the present plant, installing new moulding equipment and improving the transport fleet. There is land behind the factory which is owned by the company and could be built upon. The main problem is raising the necessary capital to finance the expansion project. Given the fact that the Finance Director has recently pointed out that the company is already quite highly geared, suggest the most appropriate sources of capital to finance

1. the new factory extension
2. the new capital equipment
3. improvements to the transport fleet.

PROJECT AND ASSIGNMENT SUGGESTIONS

1. Find out as much as you can about the City institutions concerned with the capital finance of industry. The Stock Exchange provides a great deal of information about the operation of the stock market and how shares are bought and sold. You should also investigate the functions of merchant banks in raising capital within the market.

2. Send for details about a new issue of shares or a company floatation and write an account of the different stages involved in raising capital by this method. Your report should try and answer the following questions:
   (a) What type of shares is the company issuing?
   (b) Is the issue being undertaken as an offer for sale or an offer by tender?
   (c) How much capital does the company intend to raise?
   (d) Which City institutions are involved in the issue?
   (e) What information is provided about the company and the issue to potential investors?
   (f) How do individual investors go about subscribing for some of the shares?

3. Obtain a copy of the annual report and accounts of a public limited company and analyse its capital structure. The report will contain a sources and application of funds statement giving the annual capital expenditure of the company and explaining how this has been financed. You can work out what proportion of its capital expenditure has been financed from internal sources and how much has been raised externally. The report will tell you what type of shares the company has issued and the extent of its borrowing. Try to calculate the gearing ratio of the business. You may find the accounts appear very complex, although there will be explanatory notes to help you.

SECTION E

External Influences on Business Behaviour

CHAPTER 19

The Business Environment and the Interests of the Community

In previous chapters the various objectives of businesses and how the management of business tries to achieve these objectives have been examined. Businesses are concerned with the immediate aims of survival and profitability and the more long-term objectives of expansion, growth and improving their market share. However, in the preceding investigation of the conduct of business in relation to these objectives, the business has generally been viewed in isolation from the community in which it operates. In reality of course any organisation is closely linked to the local community in which it is located. Think for a moment of the many ways your school or college is linked to the local area in which it is situated. The same is true of business, which has close links with not only the local community but possibly the national and international community as well. This is known as the **environment** in which the business operates, and its decisions will both affect and be affected by this environment.

The environment of a business is composed of various groups of people and organisations which will both place demands on the business and directly or indirectly be interested in the conduct of the business. The major groups which form the environment of the business are summarised below.

1. The **shareholders** of the business (if it is organised as a limited company), who provide the risk capital and require a return on their investment. The management must ensure the shareholders are satisfied with the performance of the business or they are likely to withdraw their capital and invest it elsewhere.
2. The **customers** of the business. No business can survive for long if its customers are not satisfied with its products or services. An effective customer-care policy has become increasingly important to ensure the business can both retain its present customers and attract new buyers.
3. The **employees** of the business. The business must be able to recruit and retain employees with the relevant skills and ensure its workforce is efficient and well motivated.
4. The **local community** in which the business is located. The business draws its employees from the local community and its actions will have an impact on people who live nearby. It is also important that the business maintains a good image within the local area.
5. The **country**. All businesses are bound by the laws of the country in which they operate, and these laws affect many aspects of the management of the business. In addition, the success or failure of the business affects to a greater or lesser degree the performance of the economy as a whole.

The business has to take account of the demands of a wide variety of different groups if it is to be successful in achieving the objectives outlined above. It is only by being aware of the interests of others that its own interests will be served. This is often referred to as a policy of **enlightened self-interest**.

Such a policy is not generally as simple as it sounds. The aims and aspirations of the various interest groups are rarely the same, which inevitably leads to a conflict of interests. For example, a business wishes to introduce a new product to the market. This will require the building of a new plant. However, the manufacturing process of the new product will cause a certain amount of atmospheric pollution in the form of smoke and exhaust gases from the factory chimneys.

A decision to build the plant would be welcomed by certain groups: the shareholders would view the development as a way of improving the profitability of the company and thereby increasing the return on their investment; the workers are likely to view the expansion as improving their job security, and the success of the development may lead to higher wages; the potential customers of the new product would also wish the company to proceed with the project as more suppliers generally means lower prices as a result of increased competition. However, the local community is likely to have certain reservations about the building of the factory in its area. Although it may welcome the new jobs resulting from the development, it may take the view that the pollution created is unacceptable. This may lead to local opposition in the form of protests and demonstrations against the siting of the factory. The government, which has the responsibility to take account of the national interest, will welcome any new industrial development which creates jobs (particularly in areas of high unemployment) and helps exports, but is also becoming increasingly concerned about **environmental** or **'green'** issues.

This conflict of interest between different groups means that management is often faced with the need to compromise. It will try to find a solution which takes account of the views of all those concerned and minimises opposition. In the situation outlined above, the management may consider how it could reduce the level of pollution by changes to the production process or by installing special filters to the factory chimneys. This may have the effect of increasing the costs of production and result in higher prices to customers and a lower return to shareholders. However, it is likely to reduce local or national opposition to the development.

Therefore, the management of a business must take account of the views and wishes of a range of different interested parties. In particular it must be aware of the effects of its actions not only on the business itself but also on the wider community. The negative and positive effects of business activity on the community as a whole are known as **social costs** and **social benefits**.

QUICK QUESTIONS 1

1. *Explain what is meant by the environment of the business.*
2. *What are the main groups which constitute this environment?*
3. *Why is it often difficult for a business to satisfy the interests of all these groups?*

Social Costs and Benefits

The managers of a business are concerned with achieving objectives such as survival, profitability and growth, although these objectives may differ according to the type of business or the stage of development of the business. Therefore, management decisions are taken in the light of how these objectives can best be fulfilled. For example, if the managers of a business are considering the development of a new product, they will be interested in such questions as:

1. What are the development costs?
2. How expensive is the product to produce?
3. How will the finance be raised?
4. How will the new product affect the sales of the business's existing products?
5. Will the new product give a satisfactory return on the assets employed to produce it?
6. How will the dividends to shareholders be affected, both in the short run and in the longer term?

The answers to these questions will determine the costs and benefits **to the business** of introducing the product. These are the **private costs** and **private benefits** of the decision. They are known as private costs and benefits because they are internal or private to the business itself. Naturally the management is interested in finding out if the private benefits exceed the private costs before making a decision to proceed with the development.

However, the decision will also affect groups outside the business, i.e. those that make up the business environment. These effects are the social costs and benefits. A **social cost** is a harmful or unwanted effect which is borne not by the business itself but by the community, as in the case of the pollution referred to previously. A **social benefit** is a desirable effect on the community, e.g. the creation of employment.

In some cases the social costs and benefits of business activity can be very significant indeed. This can be illustrated using the example of one of the largest business ventures currently being undertaken: the building of the Channel Tunnel.

Digging into the Future – The Channel Tunnel

There has been a proposal for a tunnel (or fixed transport link, as it is often referred to) between Britain and France since 1751. In more recent times there have been a number of failed attempts by governments to put the idea into practice. However, in 1986 the 2 countries agreed to a scheme put forward by Eurotunnel to build a privately financed link which is due for completion in the mid-1990s.

Eurotunnel is an Anglo-French consortium, i.e. a group of independent companies which have combined together, which will finance the building of the tunnel in return for the expected revenues from its operation. Their decision to undertake this project is based upon their estimation of the private costs and benefits involved. However, with such an important project as this there are a great many social costs and benefits which must also be considered. Figure 19.3 considers both the private costs and benefits and the social costs and benefits involved in this project.

Eurotunnel and consumers face nightmare of tunnel safety

GATEWAY TO EUROPE

CHUNNEL CHUNNEL TOIL AND TROUBLE

TUNNEL GROUP SET FOR FAST GETAWAY

This is the tunnel that buried itself

BR plans 80 passenger trains a day for tunnel

Is there relief at Chunnel's end ?

CHUNNEL STARTS RACE TO MAKE ENDS MEET

Figure 19.1 The Channel Tunnel in the Headlines

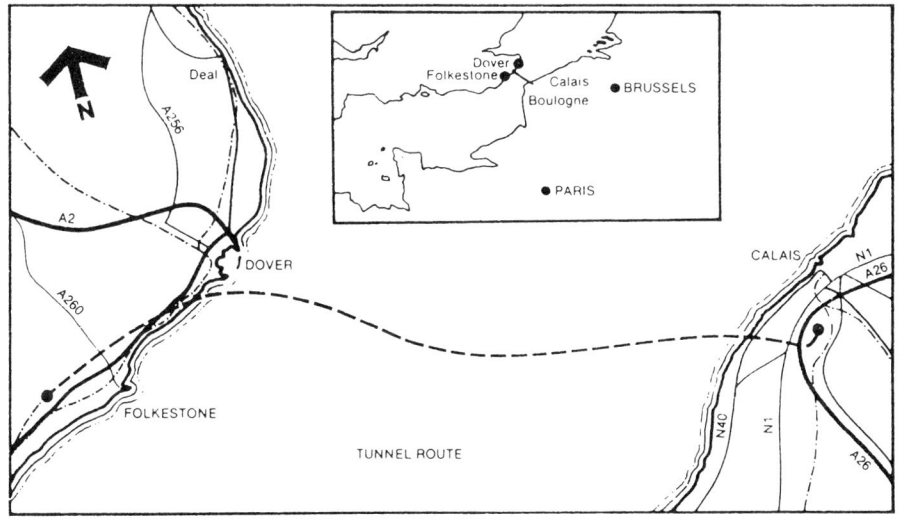

Figure 19.2 Diagram of the Proposed Channel Tunnel

Private Costs	Private Benefits
• The costs of setting up the consortium and raising the necessary finance for the project	• Receipts from passengers using the tunnel
• The cost of purchasing land for the terminal buildings	• Income from the carriage of freight through the tunnel
• Construction costs	• Income from catering and other passenger services
• Purchase of rolling stock and other equipment	• Rents from business operating concessions in terminal buildings
• Running costs when the project becomes operational	• Revenue from the sale of advertising space in trains and terminal buildings
• Depreciation and maintenance costs	

Social Costs	Social Benefits
• The environmental effects on local residents while the tunnel is being constructed, e.g. noise, disruption, falling house prices	• Increased orders for British firms supplying materials for the construction of the tunnel
• Increased congestion on transport links to the tunnel	• Employment created during construction and operation
• Unemployment in the cross channel ferry industry	• Quicker journey times between Britain and France
• Loss of business to nearby ports, e.g. Folkestone and Ramsgate	• Lower costs of travelling as a result of competition between cross channel ferries and the tunnel operators
	• Possible reduction in exporting costs to British industry

Figure 19.3 The Costs and Benefits of the Channel Tunnel

Figure 19.3 lists some of the effects of building the tunnel on both the local community living in the South East of England and the country as a whole. You may be able to think of other social costs and benefits which may result. This exercise is called a **cost–benefit analysis**.

A cost–benefit analysis is an attempt to evaluate the overall impact of important economic decisions on the community. Such an analysis is very often undertaken when the government is considering a major item of public expenditure, e.g. the various proposals for a third London airport. There are a number of problems in undertaking a cost–benefit analysis for projects of this size and importance. While the private costs and benefits can usually be identified and valued with a fair degree of accuracy, social costs and benefits present more of a difficulty. In particular there are the following problems:

1. Identifying what constitutes a social cost or a social benefit.
2. Placing a monetary value on these costs and benefits, e.g. a reduction in travelling time, or an increase in noise levels.

However, increasingly sophisticated techniques are being employed in the construction of cost–benefit studies and they are the best method available for evaluating the effects of business and government activity on the community.

What is clear from this type of analysis is that it would not always be in the best interests of the community to allow businesses to make decisions based only on whether or not it benefits the business itself. If this was the case then only the private costs and benefits would be considered and the external effects on the local area or on the country would not be taken into account. For this reason the government is involved in influencing and regulating business activity to try and ensure that the interests of all groups in society are safeguarded.

QUICK QUESTIONS 2

1. *Explain what is meant by private costs and private benefits.*
2. *How do social costs and benefits differ from private costs and benefits?*
3. *Why might social costs and benefits not be taken into account by the management of a business?*
4. *Give one social cost and one social benefit which are likely to result from a decision by a business to introduce new labour-saving machinery in its factory.*

STUDENT TASK

The old cattle market in the centre of the market town of Westbury closed several years ago and the site has been left vacant ever since. A large property company has recently acquired the land and has applied to the local council for planning permission to build a leisure complex consisting of a cinema, casino and nightclub. The council has decided to undertake a cost–benefit analysis before making a decision regarding the proposed development.

1. What is the purpose of the cost–benefit analysis the council is about to undertake?
2. Make a list of all the costs and benefits you think the council is likely to consider and present them in the form of a table similar to the one shown in Figure 19.3.
3. Assume you are a resident of Westbury and write a letter to the council either supporting or opposing the proposed development.

Government Policy and Business Behaviour

The government has the responsibility to see that the activities of the business sector are compatible with the interests of the wider community. Although the Channel Tunnel project is being undertaken by private businesses, it was the governments of Britain and France who decided the tunnel would benefit both their countries and invited offers from private companies to build it. In some cases business activity is directly or indirectly undertaken by the government because of the social benefits which result from this activity, e.g. road building, the National Health Service and the state control of certain important industries.

However, the link between government and business goes far beyond the direct provision of goods and services. Both central and local government can also exert considerable influence over the activities of privately owned businesses. Although the government has no automatic power directly to control the activities of the private sector of the economy, it can influence business behaviour in a variety of ways:

1. Business is subject to the laws of the country in the same way as individuals are. Central government can pass legislation aimed at regulating the activities of the business sector, e.g. laws related to health and safety at work.
2. Legislation is administered by government departments and government controlled agencies which can use their powers to influence the behaviour of the business sector, e.g. regular checks on restaurants and food retailers by health officials.
3. The government can also influence business behaviour via public expenditure. Provision of financial assistance of various types can be used to induce businesses to undertake activities which the government believes will benefit the economy as a whole, e.g. grants to influence location or aid research.
4. The government can also adopt the reverse policy through its powers of taxation. Taxation can be used selectively to affect specific aspects of business behaviour, e.g. differing rates of taxation on leaded and unleaded fuels.
5. The operation of general economic policy. The government can use a number of economic measures to affect the economic environment in which business operates. In particular it can influence the level of demand in the economy for goods and services, e.g. by using high interest rates to discourage consumer spending.

It can be seen from this list that the government has the power both to induce businesses to act in accordance with what it considers to be the interests of the community, and to prohibit or discourage behaviour which imposes social costs on the community. This is very often referred to as the use of **the carrot and the stick**.

The extent to which the government of the day chooses to use these powers of influence depends upon its political colour. Conservative governments take the view that it is best to leave businesses as free as possible to pursue their own objectives and believe in only limited interference by government. Labour governments place more emphasis on social factors and therefore believe there is a strong case for government control of the private sector.

However, governments of all political persuasions recognise the need for a certain amount of government influence over business behaviour in order to achieve certain national objectives. These objectives are generally divided into 2 broad groups – **social objectives** and **economic objectives**.

Social Objectives

1. **Maintaining a democratic decision-making process.** In Britain this is centred around regular elections for local councils and the national parliament on the basis of one person one vote.

2. **The protection of the rights of the individual.** Certain freedoms are generally regarded as being essential in a democratic society. These include freedom of speech, freedom to demonstrate, the freedom to join a trade union and so on. In addition there are various economic freedoms which are necessary for the operation of a market economy, e.g. the right to set up in business, attract investment, hire labour and so on.

3. **Equality of opportunity.** This means that everyone should have the opportunity to achieve success and a reasonable standard of living if they are prepared to work hard and contribute to society. Individuals should not be condemned to a particular position in society just because of where they were born or who their parents were.

4. **A clean and healthy environment.** This objective has received more attention in recent years, with the government giving a higher priority to so-called 'green issues'. These include the control of pollution, measures to protect the ozone layer, concern over the disposal of waste products and so on.

Economic Objectives

1. **Full employment of the labour force.** In a market economy based upon freedom of economic choice it is not possible to avoid some degree of unemployment because there will always be some people who are unable to work and others who are in the process of changing jobs. However, the government is concerned that the percentage of people unemployed should not rise to an unacceptable level.

2. **The control of inflation.** Inflation describes the rate at which the general level of prices are rising and hence the rate at which the value of money is falling. The stability of business depends upon money retaining its value over time. High inflation does not affect everyone to the same degree and so it has an important impact on the distribution of wealth. It can also adversely affect business confidence.

3. **Stability in the balance of payments.** The balance of payments is a record of all the transactions between residents of the UK and residents of the rest of the world. The UK is a trading nation and requires food and raw materials as well as manufactured goods from abroad. The government is concerned to ensure that the earnings from selling UK goods and services overseas are at least sufficient to cover the payments for those items we buy from abroad.

4. **Promoting economic growth.** Economic growth refers to the rate at which the output of the economy increases from year to year. Growth allows the standard of living to rise through the increased availability of goods and services and improvements in health, education and other welfare services. Economic growth requires investment by the business community, e.g. new factories and equipment, and public sector investment by the government. Therefore it is important that the government aims to create the economic conditions necessary to induce businesses to invest.

5. **Improvements in the welfare of the population.** Government is concerned to reduce deprivation and poverty within society. This requires not only a general increase in prosperity but also a redistribution of income from the better-off to those in more need, e.g. the old, the sick, the homeless.

Although governments of all political persuasions are in broad agreement on these economic and social objectives, it is difficult to pursue all the objectives simultaneously. This applies particularly to economic objectives where policies aimed at achieving one goal often tend to frustrate others. A policy to control inflation is likely to reduce economic activity and so lead to a rise in unemployment and a slowdown in economic growth. Similarly, attempts to stimulate the economy in order to reduce unemployment can increase the level of imports and hence cause problems with the balance of payments.

Therefore, governments have to seek a balance in their economic policies in order to take into account the consequences of an attempt to achieve any one objective.

QUICK QUESTIONS 3

1. *What is the basic principle which guides government policy aimed at influencing business behaviour?*
2. *What are the principal ways the government can exert influence over the business sector?*
3. *What are the main social and economic objectives the government is trying to achieve through its regulation of business?*

In this chapter it has been shown that business activity has important consequences for the wider community. The decisions taken by business affect many different groups in society and help determine the success or failure in achieving a number of social and economic objectives. For these reasons the government is concerned to influence and regulate the activities of businesses in order both to protect the interests of various groups and to help achieve a number of wider objectives. In the following chapters the nature of this government influence, regulation and control is explored. It is helpful to investigate the many aspects of government policy aimed at influencing the conduct of businesses in terms of 3 key areas: aiding and controlling the producer (Chapter 20), safeguarding the interests of the workforce (Chapter 21) and protecting the consumer (Chapter 22).

STUDENT TASK

Kevin Allen is a Trainee Manager with a large retail chain. He is about to get married and is in the process of buying his own house. He hopes to go abroad on his honeymoon. His grandfather, who still lives in the council house where he was born, thinks life is a lot easier for Kevin than it was when he was young.

'I was on the dole for six years,' he tells Kevin, 'I've never owned a car or been abroad.'

'In that case why do you always talk about the "good old days" when beer cost 4d a pint and the river was full of fish instead of chemicals?' Kevin replies.

1. What economic and social objectives of the government are referred to in this conversation between Kevin and his grandfather?
2. What indication does the conversation give as to whether the government has been successful in achieving these objectives?
3. Why do you think the government has not been successful in achieving all its social and economic objectives? Illustrate your answer with examples.

PROJECT AND ASSIGNMENT SUGGESTIONS

1. Assume a proposal has been made to close a secondary school in your area because of a decline in the school-age population. The proposal will increase the intake of other schools in the area which also have fewer pupils than they were designed to accommodate. This will enable them to make more efficient use of their resources. The money saved by closing the school will be redistributed to the other schools to reflect their increased numbers.

   (a) Make a list of all the groups which would be affected by a decision to accept the proposal and close the school.
   (b) Select one of the groups which is in favour of the proposal and explain the arguments they are likely to put forward to support their case.
   (c) Undertake the same exercise for a group which is opposed to the proposal.
   (d) What factors will the Local Education Authority take into account before it decides whether to accept the proposal?

   This case study could be treated as a role-play exercise, with different members of the class representing the various interest groups in a meeting with the education authority.

2. Use your local paper to find an example of an important development currently being undertaken by a local business or the local council. Construct your own cost–benefit analysis of the development, taking into consideration all the effects on the local community. On the basis of your analysis, write a report indicating your reasons for either supporting or opposing the development.

CHAPTER 20

Aiding and Controlling Business Activity

The previous chapter considered the wider implications of business activity. It was explained that different groups are affected by various aspects of business behaviour and that many social costs and benefits result from business activity. Therefore a certain degree of regulation and control of business is necessary in order to protect the interests of these groups and achieve wider social and economic objectives.

This chapter investigates the main areas of government industrial policy. This is concerned with the methods of influence, regulation and control the government exercises over producers within the economy.

Influencing Location and Development

Since the end of the second world war the country has experienced growing prosperity as a result of economic expansion. However, not all parts of the country have benefited to the same extent from the effects of economic growth. Certain areas were dependent on industries which have suffered a large decline in the demand for their products in recent years. The decline of these industries, e.g. cotton in Lancashire, shipbuilding in the North East and on the Clyde and mining in South Wales, has caused serious economic and social problems in the regions in which they were concentrated. These include high unemployment, lower incomes, poor housing and a general deterioration in the social environment. At the same time the new and expanding industries, e.g. light engineering, and electronics (where closeness to markets rather than raw materials is the most important factor in the location decision), have

tended to locate in other areas, e.g. the South East, the M4 corridor and around the M25. Consequently these areas have experienced shortages in skilled workers, increased congestion, rapidly rising house prices, and so on. The result of these changes has been referred to as 'the regional problem' or the **North–South divide**. This regional difference can be illustrated by the fact that in 1985–6 the average household income for a family in the South East was £269.06 per week whereas in the North of England it was only £187.72.

In order to address these problems, particularly regional unemployment, the government has adopted policies to try and influence business to locate where there are workers available. The government offers a variety of incentives to business in the form of grants, loans and tax allowances if they are prepared to locate in certain areas. Government policy in this matter is expressed largely through inducements ('carrots') to attract business to locate in certain parts of the country. In the past the government has also used the opposite approach ('the stick') by restricting development in the more prosperous areas of the country. However, this policy may mean that a business decides not to put its expansion plans into practice at all if it is prevented from doing so on its chosen or present site. In addition to these direct measures, the government has attempted to make certain areas more attractive to business by improving road and rail links, housing, recreational facilities, and so on.

The 3 major initiatives undertaken by government in the second half of the 1980s are outlined below.

1. Assisted Areas

Certain regions of the country have been given the status of Assisted Areas. This means that businesses locating in these areas qualify for various types of government assistance. The regions with the worst problems of unemployment, e.g. parts of the North East, Merseyside, Strathclyde and certain parts of Wales, have been denoted as **Development Areas**. Areas where the problems are less acute but still give cause for concern, e.g. parts of the Midlands, the area around Plymouth, and the Highlands and Islands of Scotland have been made **Intermediate Areas**. The assistance available to businesses locating in Intermediate Areas is correspondingly lower. However, this distinction was reduced in the late 1980s as there was a change in emphasis of government regional policy. In addition, Northern Ireland, which has a very serious unemployment problem, is eligible for incentives at a higher rate than that available in other parts of the country.

During the 1980s the government reviewed the role of Assisted Areas within its overall policy for tackling regional unemployment. In particular it took the view that the previous policy of giving automatic assistance mainly benefited companies which would have undertaken the investment even if no government help had been available. Therefore, the government moved away from the automatic assistance provided in the form of the old Regional Development Grants to more selective aid to business. The emphasis now on **Regional Selective Assistance**, which is only available if companies can demonstrate that their planned investment would not go ahead without government money. In addition, since April 1988 businesses in Assisted Areas employing fewer than 25 people have been able to apply for 2 new types of grant:

(a) An investment grant to finance 15% of the cost of new fixed assets up to a maximum of £15,000.
(b) An innovation grant of 50% to support product and process development up to a maximum of £25,000.

This shows that the thrust of regional policy in the late 1980s was to encourage the expansion of small- and medium-sized companies in areas of high unemployment while maintaining the means to attract larger-scale investment. This move towards more selective assistance was also pursued through other government initiatives, particularly the creation of Enterprise Zones and Urban Development Corporations.

2. Enterprise Zones

These were established between 1981 and 1984 as a method of targeting help to a number of specific locations which had experienced particular problems of high unemployment and had become quite run down. A total of 25 such zones were established.

3. Urban Development Corporations (UDCs)

The changing pattern of Britain's economic development since the war has brought with it a general movement of people and jobs out of the older inner cities. New industries have tended to locate on the outskirts of towns and cities or in the new towns which have been built over the last 40 years. The result has been the increasing dereliction and urban decay of some of the inner cities, characterised by areas of industrial wasteland, abandoned factories, poor housing and the associated problems of poverty, crime and drug abuse. Urban Development Corporations have been established to try and deal with these problems and restore a degree of economic prosperity to the inner city. The first 2 UDCs were set up in London's Dockland and in Liverpool, and the scheme has since been extended to cover other areas, e.g. Teesside, the Black Country and Cardiff Bay. Assistance for these areas is available from both local and central government in a number of ways: Urban Development Grants, Derelict Land Grants and Urban Regeneration Grants. In addition, the UDCs constitute the planning authority in these areas and can therefore give speedy consent for new developments. They also have the power to acquire land for development. To date the scheme has been most successful in Docklands because of its prime location on the doorstep of the City of London.

As well as these 3 main initiatives of central government, local authorities are also involved in schemes to attract new businesses and increased investment, and some areas of the country qualify for assistance from the European Community's Regional and Social Funds. The result is a rather complex patchwork of assistance which can be very confusing to businesses which are in the process of deciding where to locate.

1. *Name one economic objective the government is trying to achieve through a policy aimed at influencing the location of industry.*
2. *Distinguish between 'carrot' and 'stick' measures.*
3. *What benefits are available to a business if it locates in an Assisted Area?*
4. *Why has the government moved away from automatic grants to businesses in Assisted Areas towards a more selective approach?*
5. *What is the main reason for the establishing of Urban Development Corporations in certain areas of the country?*

STUDENT TASK

The following table shows employment trends in different regions of the country between 1979 and 1986.

	Employees in Employment: Manufacturing Jobs % Change	Employed Labour Force (includes Self-Employed) % Change
South East	− 24	+ 2
East Anglia	− 3	+ 13
South West	− 15	+ 5
West Midlands	− 29	− 7
East Midlands	− 18	−
Yorkshire and Humberside	− 35	− 6
North West	− 35	− 12
North	− 34	− 10
Wales	− 36	− 13
Scotland	− 38	− 8
Northern Ireland	− 33	n/a

Source: Department of Employment

1. What information does the table provide about regional trends in employment?
2. Briefly suggest reasons for the trend shown in the table.
3. Outline the initiatives the government has introduced to address regional differences in unemployment rates.

Encouraging New Businesses

In any market economy there is an ever-changing demand for goods and services. This means that there will always be industries which are experiencing decline in the demand for their products, resulting in falling output, businesses closing down and workers being made redundant. Therefore, if the country's economy is to be successful, new businesses must be continually established to both meet the demand for new products and create employment opportunities for the workforce. Thus the government is concerned to encourage people with new ideas, inventions or innovative production techniques to set up in business and put these ideas into practice. Particular emphasis has been placed upon encouraging new business ventures following the recession in economic activity which occurred in the early 1980s. During this time many businesses were forced to close and others had to cut back on production and shed labour to survive. One of the government's responses to the rising level of unemployment was to try and create an **enterprise economy** within which new businesses could flourish and, it was hoped, grow to replace the older declining industries.

Nevertheless, people setting up in business face a number of difficulties. The risks involved mean that over half the new businesses established in a given year are likely to fail before they are 4 years old. Therefore, the government's aim is to try and reduce the initial difficulties of starting a new venture in the hope that more people with ideas and energy will come forth and set up in business. It has already been mentioned that the government is targeting particular assistance at new businesses in areas of high unemployment. More general government initiatives are outlined below.

1. The government provides a **Small Firms Service** free of charge. This gives information on a wide variety of problems which a business may encounter whether it is just starting out or is already established. It also advises in detail on a number of schemes which encourage growth and expansion of small businesses. In addition, a business counselling service staffed by experienced business people is available to give sound practical, impartial and confidential ad-

vice in such areas as finance, premises, production, marketing and business law.

2. The **Enterprise Allowance Scheme** is intended to help unemployed people who have a business venture in mind but who may be discouraged from working for themselves because they would lose their entitlement to unemployment and other state benefits. It was referred to in Chapter 17 as a financial incentive which encouraged a redundant print worker to set up his own business. Those over 18 and under 65 who are receiving Unemployment Benefit or Family Credit, and who have been out of work for more than 8 weeks, are eligible. The first step is to attend a self-employment awareness day to find out about the scheme and get advice about setting up a new business. Those who wish to apply must have at least £1,000 to invest in their business or be able to raise it by loan or overdraft. In return the government will pay the successful applicant a weekly sum of £40 for the first year to supplement the receipts of the business while it is being established. It is hoped that this financial assistance will enable the business to survive the difficult first year of trading and so enhance its chances of long-term success.

3. The **Loan Guarantee Scheme**. Many small businesses cannot attract the financial backing they need because the owner is unable to offer the security needed. This scheme is designed to encourage banks to lend money to support business ventures by guaranteeing 70% of the loan. Up to £75,000 can be covered by the scheme, although many guarantees are for much smaller amounts.

4. The **Business Expansion Scheme** gives top-rate tax relief to independent investors who provide equity investments in unquoted companies. It is therefore designed to encourage investors to take the risk of making finance available to smaller businesses and thereby extend the sources of capital available for expansion.

5. Many people may be discouraged from undertaking a new business venture because of the bureaucracy and 'red tape' involved. The government has tried to sweep away as many of these rules and regulations as possible to ease the burden on small businesses.

6. Finally the government has acted to reduce the tax burden on small businesses. A business with a turnover of less than £35,000 per annum is not eligible for value added tax, and profits below £250,000 are liable for a lower rate corporation tax (25% rather than 34%).

Many of the above initiatives are administered through the Department of Trade and Industry (DTI), which the government now refers to as the **Department for Enterprise** to show its intention of creating a dynamic and thriving enterprise economy.

QUICK QUESTIONS 2

1. *Why does the government believe the encouragement of new business is so important to the economy?*
2. *Give the 2 problems which are likely to face someone starting their own business?*
3. *List 3 ways the government can help in overcoming these problems.*
4. *Which government department is most actively involved in the policy of encouraging new business ventures?*

STUDENT TASK

The table below shows the failure rate of businesses according to the size of their turnover.

Turnover Size 1980 £000	Number of Businesses	Failures	Failure Rates %
1–13	172,976	43,321	25.0
14	18,870	3,209	16.1
15–49	424,106	50,955	12.0
50–99	237,230	17,185	7.2
100–499	277,239	12,299	4.4
500–1999	64,769	2,306	3.6
2000+	22,389	871	3.9

Source: P. Ganguly, 'UK Small Business Statistics and International Comparisons' (1985), from *The Economic Review*, September 1987.

1. What information does the table give about the relationship between the size of a business and the likelihood that it will fail?
2. Suggest some reasons for this relationship.
3. Outline the ways in which the government aims to improve the chances of survival of small businesses.

Influencing the Market Place

A market economy is generally considered to operate in the best interests of the consumer by ensuring the production of the goods and services people want using the most up-to-date technology available. Competition between producers should ensure that prices are kept as low as possible because firms are continually aiming to cut costs and improve efficiency in order to survive.

However, although some markets are characterised by this highly competitive behaviour this is not always the case. In some markets the degree of competition is affected by the existence of a monopoly supplier or by various restrictive practices undertaken by producers, as described below. The government is concerned about these market imperfections because they often act against the interests of the consuming public.

Monopolies and Mergers

A monopoly is a situation where one producer is the only supplier of a given product to a particular market, i.e. the business and the industry are the same thing. Monopolies are generally accused of 2 activities which are contrary to consumers' welfare. They take advantage of this position to:

1. restrict output so that consumers cannot buy as much of a product as they might wish to, in order to
2. charge high prices, since people have no alternative but to buy the product from the monopolist.

In this situation the government would be expected to intervene to protect the consumers' interests. Indeed the traditional argument for state ownership of natural monopolies (i.e. those industries where a single supplier is the only practical type of market structure), such as the Post Office, gas, electricity and telephones, has been that only by incorporating these industries into the public sector could the interests of the consumer be adequately protected. Since the Conservative government was elected in 1979 many of these industries have been returned to the private sector. This has created large private monopoly producers, e.g. British Telecom and British Gas. However, when this has occurred the government has also established specific regulatory bodies, such as the Office of Fair Telecommunications (OFTEL), to try and ensure that the industries do not operate against the interests of the consumer.

It is important to realise that monopoly-type behaviour is not the exclusive province of single-firm industries. There is general agreement among economists that once a firm controls more than 20% of a particular market it is able to exert considerable influence on that market – perhaps in the form of raising prices. Therefore, the government is also concerned with merger activity because this increases the size of firms and their market power. This process of firms joining together is normally called **integration** (see the section on the growth of firms in Chapter 10). There are 3 types of integration: horizontal, vertical and conglomerate. It is horizontal integration which directly affects the percentage of the market a firm can command because it involves the joining together of firms producing the same or similar products, e.g. the merger of 2 building societies, as in the case of Nationwide Anglia or the Alliance and Leicester. Merger activity of this type increases the degree of **concentration** in the market. Concentration refers to the importance of large firms in a particular industry. It is most commonly measured by the **concentration ratio**, which shows the market share of a specified number of the industry's largest firms. A 4-firm concentration ratio, for example, can be calculated as:

$$\frac{\text{Output of 4 largest firms}}{\text{Output of whole industry}} \times 100$$

The higher the concentration ratios in any market the less competitive the market is likely to be. Therefore, the government is interested in mergers which will increase market concentration and in the behaviour of firms which have a large share of a particular market.

The Monopolies and Mergers Act 1965 set up the Monopolies and Mergers Commission (MMC) to investigate mergers and monopoly behaviour which were likely to act against the public interest. Any proposed amalgamation is referred to the MMC if 25% or more of the market would, as a result of the merger, be controlled by one supplier, or where the value of the assets involved in the merger exceeds £5 million. The role of the MMC is to investigate the merger or the monopoly concerned and recommend the appropriate course of action to the Secretary of

State for Trade and Industry. In this way the government can design its competition policy on the basis of the national interest as a whole rather than the interests of the businesses concerned. Although mergers are undertaken for sound business reasons, it is possible that other groups may suffer as a result. If the price offered for shares is unreasonably low and if the new company is not as successful as the old one, the shareholders are likely to suffer. It often takes time to marry management teams together and some managers may be surplus to requirements, so managers may suffer. Streamlining may mean a loss of jobs or the possibility of having to move to another area to work – so workers may suffer. Also, with a reduction in competition there may be less choice of products and higher prices. This is a clear example of a cost–benefit situation. It is the government's responsibility, through the MMC, to examine each case on its merits, taking into account the effects on all these various groups, and come to a judgement. However, the MMC has no power to implement its recommendations. Its role is advisory and it is the government, in the form of the Department of Trade and Industry, which decides what action should be taken.

Restrictive Practices

Another way in which competition may be reduced within a market is through agreements between firms to undertake collective policies, e.g. keeping prices at a given level or jointly restricting output or agreeing to divide up the market and trade on the same terms. The government is concerned to eliminate such anti-competitive behaviour and has passed a numer of Acts of Parliament to control such agreements. Under the Restrictive Trade Practices Acts of 1956, 1968 and 1976 these types of restrictive practices are unlawful unless it can be clearly shown that they are in the public interest. In order to prove this a firm must send details to the Office of Fair Trading, which maintains a register of all such agreements. The Director General of Fair Trading then has the power to refer the case to the **Restrictive Practices Court**. The court will find all such agreements unlawful unless the benefits to the consumer can be shown to be greater than the costs. Approval may be granted if a proposed agreement complies with one of the following 'gateways':

1. The restrictions protect the public against injury.
2. Removal of the restrictions would deny customers and clients substantial benefits.
3. Removal would adversely affect exports.
4. Removal would increase unemployment.
5. The restriction does not directly or indirectly discourage competition.

In practice very few agreements have been given approval; the sale of books and drugs are 2 examples. Generally the view of the court is that such agreements are not in the interest of the public. Under the 1987 Act the Director General of Fair Trading has the power to instigate proceedings to prevent the continuance or repetition of any unlawful restrictive practices. Any organisation found guilty of breaking previous undertakings to the court can be fined for contempt. Also, any consumer affected by such practices can bring an action for damages against the companies involved.

QUICK QUESTIONS 3

1. *Why are monopoly producers generally considered to act against the public interest?*
2. *Why are industries such as gas and the Post Office often referred to as 'natural monopolies'?*
3. *Why did the government set up the Office of Fair Telecommunications when it privatised British Telecom?*
4. *What role does the Monopolies and Mergers Commission play in influencing the government's policy towards the operation of markets?*
5. *Why would a secret agreement between the major oil companies to keep petrol prices at a given level be unlawful? What action could be taken against the companies in this situation?*

STUDENT TASK

The following table contains information about the structure of the UK brewing industry.

Beer Sales by 'National' Brewers and Concentration Ratios, 1985

	Output (million barrels)	Share of UK Output %	Concentration Ratio %
Bass	7.7	20.2	20.2 (1 firm)
Allied	4.8	12.6	32.8 (2 firms)
Whitbread	4.3	11.3	44.1 (3 firms)
Scottish and Newcastle	3.5	9.2	53.3 (4 firms)
Watney-Truman	3.4	8.9	62.2 (5 firms)
Courage	3.3	8.7	70.9 (6 firms)
Carlsberg	1.6	4.2	75.1 (7 firms)
Guinness	1.2	3.2	78.3 (8 firms)

Source: 'Industry Information', *The Economic Review*, January 1989.

1. What indication is there in the names of some of the brewers of previous merger activity?
2. What information do the concentration ratios give about the structure of the industry?
3. In 1989 the Monopolies and Mergers Commission published a detailed investigation into the brewing industry. Looking at the information in the table, why do you think the government called for the investigation?
4. One of the recommendations of the MMC was that no brewer should be allowed to own more than a specified number of public houses. Why do you think this recommendation was made?
5. Which government department will consider the MMC report and decide whether to implement its recommendations?

Helping Exports

As explained in Chapter 20, one of the economic objectives of the government is to try to ensure that overseas earnings are sufficient to pay for the goods and services that the country imports. Another function of the Department of Trade and Industry is the formulation of general overseas trade policy, including specific duties in connection with the encouragement of export trade through the British Overseas Trade Board (BOTB) and the Export Credits Guarantee Department (ECGD).

The British Overseas Trade Board

The BOTB operates in a variety of ways to inform, help and encourage exporters. Through the board there is access to the commercial posts of the Diplomatic Service overseas. These 200 or so posts supply information of every kind affecting trade within their territories, e.g. the local economic and commercial conditions. In particular they help exporters overcome the difficulties which may arise out of government regulations in the country to which the goods are bound. The BOTB also advises on the financial standing of potential overseas customers. In addition, international exhibitions and trade fairs are organised in order to promote British goods overseas.

The Export Credits Guarantee Department

The ECGD protects exporters, merchants, investors and bankers against credit risks overseas. All exporters face considerable risks in that they are dealing with customers in other countries. This risk is increased when the exporter is selling goods on credit. The business may find it difficult to establish the creditworthiness of potential customers, rates of exchange may change between despatch and payment, there may be doubts about the stability of the government or the possibility of changes in the country's regulations. The ECGD enables the exporter to insure against the non-payment of overseas debts and also provides loans at low rates of interest to help exporters with the initial costs of selling abroad. The ECGD is self-financing and charges exporters a premium for its services. However, it is non-profit making and so its premiums are low. It covers about a third of British Exports and it is generally believed that without the security it provides exporting would be a much less attractive proposition to many firms. In this way the government is indirectly helping the country's overseas earnings.

Encouraging Research and Development

As mentioned above, an economy that competes effectively in international markets requires an efficient business sector able to adapt to changing demands, develop new products and discover new techniques of production. This means that research and development (R & D) is extremely important to the long-term future of business and for the international competitiveness of the economy.

However, one of the major characteristics of R & D is that it requires a financial outlay which does not bring immediate benefits to the business. The development of new products in some industries can take many years; particularly with technical, highly engineered products, e.g. motor cars, computer hardware, telecommuncations. The problem is one of balancing short-term costs with long-term benefits. This means that many smaller firms do not have the resources to place large sums in R & D because there is no prospect of a return in the short run. Larger companies which encounter difficulties and have to cut costs can reduce or suspend R & D expenditure with no immediate damage to the business. This was noticeable during the recession of the early 1980s.

In order to encourage R & D the government funds research itself and aids private industrial research. The government has its own research establishments and finances a great deal of the work undertaken in university research departments. Much of this expenditure is concentrated in a number of specific areas, particularly defence-related research. However, there are spin-off effects from this research which can be beneficial to business, e.g. the development of light metal alloys or satellite navigation. In addition, the government supports industry with advice and research grants and through the British Technology Group.

QUICK QUESTIONS 4

1. *Name 2 ways the British Overseas Trade Board can assist a firm in selling abroad.*
2. *How does the Export Credits Guarantee Department reduce the risk of exporting?*
3. *Why is it that money spent on research and development does not usually bring immediate benefits to a business?*
4. *In what ways does the government try to encourage research and development?*

Overall Economic Policy

Influencing location, encouraging new businesses, influencing the market place, helping exports and encouraging R & D represent the main ways in which the government directly tries to aid and control business behaviour. In addition to these examples of specific industrial policy, the government must also consider the effects on the business community of its overall economic policy. The government aims to achieve the economic objectives outlined in Chapter 19 by employing a range of policy instruments. These economic policy measures can be divided into 3 types.

1. Fiscal Policy

Fiscal (or budgetary) policy refers to the alteration of government expenditure and tax rates in order to affect the overall level of demand in the economy. Lowering taxes or increasing public expenditure stimulates demand while raising taxes or lowering expenditure has the opposite effect.

2. Monetary Policy

Monetary policy involves the use of interest rates, credit controls and the regulation of financial markets in order to affect the growth of the money supply. The policy is primarily aimed at influencing the level of bank lending, which in turn affects the purchasing power in the economy.

3. Direct Economic Policies

The government can directly intervene in the operation of the economy in order to secure particular economic objectives. Direct economic policies include the examples of industrial policy outlined above aimed at influencing business behaviour, e.g. regional policy and monopoly policy. The government can also adopt policies to control prices and incomes, affect the foreign exchange value of the pound, and so on.

These types of policies can be co-ordinated in order to expand economic activity to promote growth and reduce the level of unemployment or alternatively to hold back demand to control inflation or to reduce imports and help the balance of payments. These policies have an important effect on business activity. An expansionary economic policy works to the benefit of domestic businesses if the increase in demand is directed towards home-produced goods and services. However, if the policy increases the rate of inflation, production costs are likely to rise and business confidence may suffer. A policy to control inflation could adversely affect sales and turnover and squeeze profitability. High interest rates make borrowing more expensive and tend to exert upward pressure on the exchange rate making exporting more difficult, and so on. Therefore, the government must take account of the views of the business sector in framing its overall economic policy, and it must endeavour, within the constraints of its other objectives, to create an environment which is likely to promote the success of industry and commerce.

PROJECT AND ASSIGNMENT SUGGESTIONS

1. Undertake an investigation into either an Assisted Area or an Urban Development Corporation. See if you can answer the following questions.
   (a) Are there particular types of businesses which have traditionally located in the area?
   (b) What changes occurred in the area at the end of the 1980s?
   (c) What is the present rate of unemployment? Has this risen or fallen in recent years?
   (d) In what ways is the government trying to address the economic and social problems facing the area?
   (e) How effective are the various forms of assistance in attracting new businesses to the area?
   Write up your findings in the form of a report. Include a map of the area and a table of important statistics relating to the area.

2. Find out more about the help available to firms involved in exporting. You could contact a local firm which sells abroad and ask them to help you or you could write to the Department of Trade and Industry. Try to produce a 'Guide to Exporting' which explains the problems a business is likely to encounter and the ways the government can help the business to overcome these problems.

CHAPTER 21

Government Intervention and the Workforce

Chapters 19 and 20 examined the government's concern to protect the interests of various groups in society which are affected by the activities of businesses, and the principal types of government influence over certain aspects of business behaviour. This chapter continues the analysis of government regulation, control and influence with regard to one specific group of people who are central to the operation of any organisation – the workforce.

Although businesses employ a variety of factors of production, their most important resource is their labour force. The human skills they employ are vital to the success of the business itself and to the economy as a whole. The government is therefore concerned that the workforce is productive and efficient and has the relevant skills to meet the needs of industry. In addition, over the years the government has framed regulations and controls aimed at protecting the interests of the workforce in such areas as health, safety and welfare (general physical well-being) and in their dealings with employers.

Influencing Training and Education

A successful economy requires a workforce with the relevant skills to meet the needs of industry. Enterprise is stifled and the country's competitiveness is undermined if business cannot recruit employees with the necessary skills and abilities. This has become particularly important in recent years as the pace of industrial change has increased and many older occupations have disappeared to be replaced by new jobs requiring different types of skills. Some jobs have changed out of all recognition in terms of the work done (e.g. that of a print-worker). In the 1980s there was a growing recognition that people must be able and willing to change jobs during their working life – perhaps 3 or 4 times. The government is aware that this will require a workforce that is more flexible and able to adapt to the demands of a changing world. To achieve this the government aims to influence both the general educational standards of the population and the opportunities available for more specifically vocational training.

The dividing line between education and training is a thin one. Many students choose their GCSE or A-level subjects with a particular career in mind but this could not really be described as specific training for a clearly defined job. This has meant that in Britain education and training have traditionally been treated as separate issues. Although the Department of Education and Science (DES) exercises overall control over education policy, in practice Local Education Authorities (LEAs) and individual schools have been given a fair degree of autonomy to determine what children are taught and how they are taught. Training has been regarded as something which occurs after people have left school and entered the labour market. Therefore, overall training policy has been the responsibility of the Department of Employment.

Vocational Initiatives in Schools

However, over the last few years this view has been changing and education and training are being increasingly treated as closely related areas of government policy. One very visible sign of this change was the introduction of the **National Curriculum** into all state-maintained schools in 1989. This aims to ensure that all pupils study certain core subjects until the age of 16. The curriculum puts emphasis on such areas as English, mathematics, science and foreign languages, which shows the government's concern both to develop the skills of literacy and numeracy and to improve pupils' scientific and linguistic abilities – skills which are very relevant to an increasingly technical and international world. In addition to the overall objectives of the National Curriculum, the government has also directed a number of other more specifically vocational initiatives at schools.

1. The Technical and Vocational Education Initiative

TVEI is a scheme which was introduced in 1983 to improve school pupils' awareness of how industry works and to encourage job-related education in schools. There is no single TVEI curriculum or approach to teaching. The stated aim of the scheme is to

explore and test a variety of methods of organising, delivering and managing programmes of technical and vocational education.

Local authorities are expected to relate the technical and vocational elements of any TVEI course to potential local employment opportunities and to link courses with subject training or educational opportunities. Each project has a co-ordinator who is expected to bring together the different interest groups involved in TVEI, such as the local authority, local industry and commerce, teachers, lecturers, parents and interested local bodies. It is worth noting that TVEI is financed by the Department of Employment rather than the Department of Education and Science. This again shows how the government's attitude to the division between education and training is changing. The money provided through the scheme has allowed many schools to improve their facilities, particularly in the areas of computing and technology.

2. The Certificate of Pre-Vocational Education

Schools and colleges of further education have introduced CPVE as an alternative to studying for more traditional qualifications. This is a 12-month course, usually taken at 16 +, which involves specific training for a job, sometimes incorporating day release to a local college and perhaps one or two GCSE

(Mature) subjects. This is another attempt to make education more relevant to the world of work and prepare students more directly for employment.

Training Initiatives for the Workforce

As well as giving serious thought to what students are taught in schools and colleges and the skills they should acquire before they enter the job market the government is also concerned with the training and retraining of people already in the workforce. Until the 1980s the training and retraining of industrial workers was largely the responsibility of the **Industrial Training Boards** (ITBs). These were established by the Industrial Training Act of 1964 and covered a wide range of industries, e.g. the Construction Industry Training Board, the Engineering Industry Training Board and so on. The government became dissatisfied with the performance of many of these training boards. It considered that they were failing to provide the quality of training which was required at a time of increasing unemployment. Therefore from 1982 the Manpower Services Commission (which before it was replaced in 1988 by the Training Agency had overall control of industrial training) significantly reduced the number of Training Boards and began to introduce new employment and training initiatives. Training and Enterprise Councils (TECs) are being established over the period from 1989 to 1993 and part of their function is to take over the planning and overseeing of vocational education and training on a local basis.

1. The Youth Training Scheme

Detailed information on the organisation of YTS was given in Chapter 7. The scheme was launched in 1983 as a more comprehensive attempt to deal with unemployment among young people than the Youth Opportunities Programme, which had been introduced 5 years earlier. The government had become increasingly concerned over the number of teenagers who were leaving school and going straight onto the unemployment register. There was a belief that unemployment should not be an option for the school-leaver and that those young people who did not enter further or higher education or were unable to find a job should be able to undertake a period of training and work experience to improve their chances of employment.

The government introduced YTS with the following stated objectives:

(a) To provide all participants with a better start in working and adult life through an integrated programme of learning, education and work experience, and a 'record of achievement' which could serve as a foundation for subsequent employment, for continued training, or for relevant further education.

(b) To provide participating employers with a better equipped young workforce which has acquired some competence and practical experience in a range of job-related skills.

(c) To develop a more versatile, readily available, highly motivated and productive workforce to assist Britain's competitive economic performance.

YTS represents one of the government's main initiatives in the area of vocational education and training and it is hoped that the scheme will lead to an increasing number of young people acquiring the skills and qualifications relevant to the needs of industry.

2. Employment Training

Employment Training, or **ET** as it has become known, is aimed at helping unemployed workers to gain the skills and experience they need to improve their chances of finding a job. It is hoped that ET will reduce the 'skills gap', i.e. help to resolve the problem that the unemployed do not possess the necessary skills and qualifications to fill the vacancies available in industry. The government has referred to ET as 'training the workers without jobs to do the jobs without workers'.

The scheme is open to anyone aged 18 or over who has been unemployed and signing on at an Unemployment Benefit Office for the previous 26 weeks. The first stage is a period of assessment, usually lasting about a week, to discover the hobbies, interests and aptitudes of the unemployed person in order to find suitable training and possible attainable qualifications, and to look for a specific career direction. The scheme itself consists of a free training programme and practical workplace experience which give the unemployed the opportunity to learn

Figure 21.1 Advertisement for Employment Training

new skills, update existing skills, become familiar with new technology, learn about self-employment, learn job search skills and possibly acquire a recognised vocational qualification. The training lasts from 3 to 12 months, depending on the individual's needs. During that time participants in the scheme receive at least £24 per week plus any other state benefit entitlement and travelling expenses.

3. Training Grants for Employers

These grants are available to help businesses identify and meet their training needs. They include local grants towards the cost of retraining existing employees or training new recruits for hard-to-fill vacancies, local consultancy grants to help firms analyse their retraining needs, and a national priority skills scheme where special grants are given to help finance the training of workers in areas where there is a recognised national skill shortage.

4. Open Learning

This is designed to make it easier for people to gain access to training by using specially prepared self-instructional material, with a little help, if necessary, from a local college or training centre. It eliminates the need for attendance on a full-time course and means that study can be at a time and pace which suits the individual's needs. Through this scheme the unemployed can update abilities and knowledge without affecting their eligibility for Unemployment Benefit, and the learning can continue even if unemployment changes to employment. One important open learning scheme is the **Open Tech Programme**. This has made available some 30,000 hours of open learning material in such subjects as agriculture, engineering, construction, information technology, health services, hotels and catering, management, robots and computer-aided design. In addition to the open learning material the scheme also provides support services at technical, supervisory and management level. Courses are not free and can cost the individual or the employer (or both) anything from under £10 to over £250. However, help may be available from the Local Education Authority or through the Training Agency.

5. The Community Programme

This scheme is designed to give people who have been unemployed for 12 months or more the opportunity to undertake some paid employment on projects contributing something to the community at large. The idea is to help the long-term unemployed get back into a work routine, acquire up-to-date work experience and an up-to-date reference, perhaps trying new jobs, updating skills or learning new ones. The wide variety of jobs available include the following types of work:

(a) making homes burglar proof
(b) running an advice centre
(c) gardening and decorating
(d) helping the disabled, the aged and infirm
(e) renovating footpaths, cycleways and canals.

Training is provided where appropriate and pay is the local rate for the job for the hours worked. Unemployment Benefit is not paid in addition to the Community Programme wage but families may still be entitled to other benefits such as Income Support or Family Credit.

QUICK QUESTIONS 1

1. *Which government department is most closely associated with industrial training?*
2. *What do the initials TVEI and CPVE stand for?*
3. *What does the government mean when it refers to the 'skills gap'?*
4. *Explain what is meant by Open Learning.*
5. *Briefly outline the purpose of the Community Programme.*

Regulating Working Conditions

Another very important area of government regulation of business concerns the working environment. The government has passed successive Acts of Parliament aimed at ensuring that the conditions in which people work are both safe, in the sense that life and limb are not placed in jeopardy, and healthy, in the sense that workers are not going to come into contact with germs, diseases or materials which are likely to make them unwell. The major legislation which places the responsibility on the employer to provide a safe and healthy working environment is outlined below.

1. The Factories Act 1961

This Act covers not only factories but also brick and cement works, construction sites, laundries and dry cleaners, potteries, printing shops, abattoirs and many other businesses which use machinery. The principal provisions of the Act are as follows:

(a) The workplace must be well ventilated and well lit.
(b) Washing and toilet facilities must be provided and must be adequate for the size of the workforce.
(c) There must be a guard around moving machinery.
(d) Lifts and hoists must be constructed and maintained in a proper manner.
(e) Stairs, passages and floors must be kept unobstructed and must not be slippery.
(f) Well-maintained fire escapes must be provided.

2. Office, Shops and Railway Premises Act 1963

This Act applies to these places of work in the following ways:

(a) Rooms must not be overcrowded and a minimum of 12 square metres of floor space should be provided on average per person.

(b) The temperature of rooms must be at or above 16°C.

(c) Supplies of fresh or artificially purified air must be sufficient.

(d) There must be suitable lighting whether it be natural or artificial.

(e) Sanitary provision should be suitable, sufficient, accessible, clean and properly maintained.

(f) Washing facilities must be adequate and accessible with hot and cold running water, soap and clean towels.

3. Health and Safety at Work Act 1974

This Act (normally referred to as HASAWA) is the most far-reaching of recent legislation. It completely overhauled and modernised previous legislation dealing with safety, health and welfare in the workplace. The Act also covers members of the general public who come into contact with the work situation. It places responsibility on both the employer and the employee with regard to matters of health and safety. It is the employer's responsibility to provide a safe workplace, including adequate provision of fire-fighting equipment, fire doors and notices of the procedures in case of emergency, and the maintenance and safety of equipment. It is the employees' responsibility to take reasonable care of their own safety and that of their colleagues and to co-operate with their employer at all times on matters relating to safety. The act created the Health and Safety Commission to oversee the legislation, and reorganised the various government inspectorates into one body called the **Health and Safety Executive**.

Under the Act all employers with more than 4 staff must provide a statement, in writing, of their health and safety policy. In unionised workplaces employees may elect safety representatives who are encouraged by the Act to

(a) inspect the work areas at least every 12 weeks

(b) inspect all accidents and dangerous events

(c) inspect any relevant health or safety documents

(d) record inspections in a register.

Where there are elected safety representatives, employers are required to set up safety committees at the request of a minimum of 2 of these elected representatives. The committee's purpose is constantly to review all aspects of health and safety within the workplace.

STUDENT TASK

George Palmer is a foreman in the machine shop of an engineering company. The business is currently undergoing a reorganisation which involves the machine shop moving to a new location in a different part of the factory. A number of new machines are also being installed as part of the reorganisation. As an elected health and safety representative, George is concerned that the new location conforms to the statutory requirements on health and safety. He therefore decides to make a thorough inspection of the new location before the next meeting of the Health and Safety Committee.

1. List some of the safety aspects George will be concerned to investigate in his inspection.
2. Give examples of facilities which the company will have to ensure are available in the new location.
3. What assurances will George want from the company about the new machines which are being installed in the factory?
4. If George is satisfied that the new location and the new machines comply with the requirements of government legislation on health and safety, what duties will he be expected to perform in the future to ensure health and safety standards are maintained?

Regulating Terms and Conditions of Employment

The basic law regarding employment is the Contract of Employment Act 1972, which became incorporated into the Employment Protection (Consolidation) Act of 1978. It is important at this point to examine what constitutes a valid contract. A contract can be defined as 'any agreement between 2 or more parties which is intended to be enforceable at law'. The following are essential features of a valid contract:

1. **Offer and acceptance**: one party must make an offer to perform a role or pay a price and the other party to the agreement must unconditionally accept the offer.
2. **Consideration**: there must be something given or performed in return for the benefits received, so payment must be made for goods received or work undertaken for wages received: you can't get something for nothing.
3. **Intention**: parties to a contract must intend to make a legally binding relationship, unlike the case in social or domestic arrangements (e.g. an agreement to meet a friend or do the washing up).
4. **Capacity to contract**: parties entering into contractual arrangements must be fit to do so. The law defines certain people whose capacity is either limited or removed, such as those under 18 years of age, the mentally sick or the blind drunk.
5. **Validity**: sometimes a contract may have the above 4 features but will be considered invalid because:
   (a) One of the parties has made a genuine error, e.g. mistaken identity by one party either of the nature or the person of the other party.
   (b) One of the parties indulges in deliberate misrepresentation.
   (c) Facts which are material to the contract have not been declared, e.g. previous illness not declared on life assurance policies. This is a breach of what is known as *uberrima fides* (utmost good faith).
   (d) A contract is drawn up to perform certain activities which are unlawful, e.g. contracts drawn up to restrict competition contravening the Restrictive Trade Practices Act (1976). This is referred to as unlawful intent.

A contract does not have to be written. It can be a verbal agreement between 2 parties. Therefore a person starting a job does not have to be given a written contract. However, the contractual agreement between employer and employee will involve an offer of employment by the employer indicating the terms of employment which the employee accepts; the payment of a wage or salary on the part of the employer and the work to be done on the part of the employee constitutes the consideration. It may be assumed that there is an intention here to make a legally binding contract between employer and employee, that both parties have the capacity to contract, e.g. the employee is fit and competent to do the work which is required and that the contract is valid in that none of the invalidity clauses apply (the person is not being employed to rob a bank, for example).

1 March 1990

Job Title	Car mechanic
Company	Wilson's Motors Ltd
Employee	Mr Stephen Sharpe
Commencement of employment	25 February 1990
Pay	£5 per hour for standard working week. Time and a half for any overtime up to 10 hours; time and three-quarters thereafter.
Hours	8 a.m. to 5 p.m. four and a half days per week, 8 a.m. to 12.30 p.m. on Saturdays. Flexible break of 1 hour each full day and one half hour each half day. Standard working week of 40 hours.
Duties	To carry out all standard mechanical car repairs and servicing as directed by garage foreman.
Holidays	24 working days with full pay plus all bank holidays. Holidays cannot be carried over and must be arranged not less than 1 month in advance and in consultation with the garage foreman.
Sickness	Half pay for time lost up to a maximum of 3 months in any 12-month period. Notice of sickness should be given on first day of absence by telephoning 246 1001. Normal self-certification rules apply.
Notice	One month, in writing.
Pension	Normal National Insurance arrangements, plus company superannuation scheme.
Rules	All employees are advised to read carefully the notices entitled 'Rules & Regulations' which are placed on all employees' noticeboards around the garage.
Discipline	All mechanics are encouraged to join the local TGWU branch. In any case, in the event of any grievance contact Mr Walter Jackson (body shop), who acts as shop steward.

Figure 21.2 Example of the Terms and Conditions of Employment

Under the 1972 Act employees have the right to be given written terms and conditions of employment within the first 13 weeks. This statement is not the contract but the terms and conditions agreed. By law this statement must contain certain information, e.g. the title of the job, the rate of pay, working hours, holidays and so on. A hypothetical example of what is likely to be found in such a written statement is shown in Figure 21.2.

QUICK QUESTIONS 2

1. *Give 4 examples of government regulations designed to improve health and safety at work.*
2. *What responsibilities are placed upon employees under the Health and Safety at Work Act?*
3. *What are the basic features of a contract of employment?*
4. *Give an example of a factor which would make a contract of employment invalid.*

Employment Protection

The government helps employees in a whole variety of ways, not the least of which are the steps which the government has taken to try to ensure that employees are treated fairly in their job. The government considers it unfair for employees to be discriminated against because of their race or place of birth, their sex or marital status. There are 3 major Acts which address these potential sources of unfairness in employment:

1. The Equal Pay Act 1970

The aim of this Act was to stop the practice of employers paying females less than males in broadly similar types of employment for the same hours worked. Prior to the legislation this was not uncommon. If a male or female worker considers that another worker is receiving more money for doing ostensibly the same thing, he or she can appeal to an **Industrial Tribunal** (see below).

This legislation was amended in 1984 to allow a claim for equal pay to be based upon the criterion of **work of equal value**. There are obvious difficulties in determining what constitutes equal value, and it is the function of Industrial Tribunals to make rea-soned judgements on whether the criterion is applicable. Since the amendment was incorporated into the Act there have been a number of test cases which have given some guidelines to employers concerning the circumstances under which the legislation can be enforced.

2. The Sex Discrimination Act 1975

The Act makes discrimination between the sexes in employment, training and education illegal — unless there is a '**genuine occupational qualification**'. There are 8 of these:

(a) **Physiology**: e.g. male actors are needed to play male roles in the theatre; females are needed to model women's fashion.
(b) **Decency**: e.g. male changing rooms at sports centres have male attendants.
(c) **Single-sex establishment**: e.g. female prisons have female warders.
(d) **Nature of the establishment**: where employees are required to live in and share accommodation, e.g. girls' school boarding houses have female staff (although it seems to be accepted that boys' boarding houses may have female staff).
(e) **Education or welfare**: e.g. female marriage guidance counsellors to counsel females.
(f) **Legislation**: e.g. females are not allowed to work in factories on the night shift because of the Factories Act (an example of discrimination promoted in legislation).
(g) **Other countries' legislation**: e.g. women lorry drivers are not permitted in some countries.
(h) **Married couples**: e.g. according to historical precedence the tenants of public houses are, ideally, married couples.

The legislation permits anyone to take an employer to an Industrial Tribunal if they consider they have been discriminated against because of gender (this includes anyone who thinks they weren't offered a particular job simply because of gender). Discrimination in the context of the Act is said to occur when one person treats another person less favourably because of his or her sex than that person would have treated an individual of the opposite sex, when one person applies conditions to another person that are not applied to the opposite sex. It can be seen that this law applies to both males and females. It is therefore illegal to advertise a job specifying sex unless there is a 'genuine occupational qualification'. The Act also established the **Equal Opportunities Commission** to be both promoter and watchdog of equal opportunities.

3. The Race Relations Act 1976

This Act makes discrimination on grounds of colour, race, nationality and ethnic or national origins illegal, again unless there is a 'genuine occupational qualification'. There is only one of these and it is called **authenticity**, e.g. an employer can state that he or she wishes to employ an Indian waiter in a curry house for reasons of 'authenticity'. Discrimination is said to occur when one person treats another person less favourably on racial grounds that he or she would have treated someone else. The Act established the **Commission for Racial Equality** to be both promoter and watchdog of racial equality.

QUICK QUESTIONS 3

1. *Give 3 examples of a 'genuine occupational qualification' which would justify sex discrimination in employment.*
2. *What institution has been established by the government to promote equal treatment of men and women at work?*
3. *Give an example of an employment situation where discrimination based upon race or colour would be legal.*

Redundancy and Unfair Dismissal

Another area where the government attempts to promote fairness is in matters of redundancy and dismissal.

Redundancy

Under the Redundancy Payments Act 1965 a worker is considered redundant when the job no longer exists. This can come about when the business is wound up, when the business is contracting, or when the particular type of work is no longer required, e.g. when machines replace workers. The government has a **Redundancy Fund** financed from National Insurance contributions in order to assist businesses in making redundancy payments. Any employee who has 2 years' service and has worked for at least 21 hours per week is entitled to the minimum rate of tax-free redundancy pay. The amount an individual worker is entitled to receive depends on such factors as age, weekly wage and the number of years worked for the business. Industrial Tribunals look into disputed cases of redundancy. Below are some hypothetical examples of redundancy payments.

1. Freda Williams, aged 40, has worked as a salesperson for Smellit & See Cosmetics (Sunderland) Ltd for 15 years. She earns £150 per week but is being made redundant because of a decline in sales. She is entitled to a redundancy payment of £2,250, which is equal to 1 weeks' pay for each of the 15 years of employment.
2. Joe Camay earns £70 per week working as a forecourt attendant at a local garage. He is 17 years old and has worked at the garage since leaving school the year before. The job ceases to exist because the garage is changing to self-service. As Joe has worked for the company for less than a year and is under 18 no redundancy payment is made.
3. Mr Solly Bergman, aged 56, has worked as a conveyancing clerk for a legal firm for 20 years and is currently on an annual salary of £9,500. He is made redundant because the firm is being wound up on the retirement of the 3 senior partners. Solly is entitled to a minimum of £5,025 on the basis of 1 week's pay for each of 5 years, and one and a half week's pay for each of 15 years. In the event the company award him a half a month's salary for each 2 of the first 4 years and one month's salary for each 2 of the remaining 16 years, making a grand total of £7,125.

Many companies act according to redundancy agreements negotiated between employers' organisations and employees' organisations, others have an internal company agreement made by mutual agreement or specified as part of a written contract. These may involve larger sums than the minimum stipulated, as in example 3 above.

Unfair Dismissal

Although the Industrial Relations Act of 1971 was repealed and replaced by the Trade Unions and

Labour Relations Act of 1974, some of its provisions were retained, in particular those relating to unfair dismissal. Under the Act an employer cannot sack an employee without proper reason or correct procedure. An employee who thinks that he or she has been unfairly dismissed can take the employer to an Industrial Tribunal, provided that the employee has been employed for 2 years and works at least 16 hours per week, **or** works for 15 hours per week or less but has been employed for at least 5 years.

An employer cannot dismiss an employee because he or she refuses to join a staff association or is a member of a trade union. It can also be considered unfair dismissal if the employee has no alternative other than to resign from a job because of the employer's actions, e.g. when an employer insists on an employee working with materials to which the employee is severely allergic when alternative products could be used, e.g. if a cleaner is allergic to a specific scouring powder. The Act recognises the need to ensure that not all dismissals are assumed to be unfair. It therefore specifies reasons for fair dismissal. These are as follows:

1. The employee can't do the job: e.g. a salesman who has been taken on because he said he had a driving licence is fairly dismissed if, in fact, he failed his driving test.
2. Redundancy.
3. The employee's conduct is unsatisfactory: e.g. a nurse looking after the mentally handicapped resorts to violence when the patients are unable to respond to the nurse's exhortations.
4. The employee is not properly qualified: e.g. a teacher is fairly dismissed when, on investigation, it is discovered that his or her stated qualifications are totally bogus.
5. When to employ the person would break the law: e.g. a bus driver is fairly dismissed if he or she has been banned from driving as a result of offences committed whilst driving a private vehicle.
6. Other substantial reason: e.g. the Marketing Director's secretary is fairly dismissed on marrying the Marketing Director of a rival company.

Businesses must be seen to go about dismissal fairly. For instance, a business must state codes of discipline clearly and not simply make them up as they go along in order to cause difficulties for employees, e.g. the employer cannot change working hours at random and then dismiss employees who have transport difficulties. The worker must be given the opportunity to explain his or her conduct and to make an appeal, e.g. employers cannot simply dismiss someone for absence without first finding out the circumstances – there may, for example, have been a death in the family. If an employee's conduct is considered unsatisfactory over a period of time it should be pointed out to that employee before the situation deteriorates to the point of no return. Employees cannot be blamed for a lack of proper instruction and training where the provision of such training is the responsibility of the employer. Therefore, according to the law, employees can no longer be fired on the basis of whim or fancy. However, that does not mean that it never occurs. In some occupations, e.g. the armed forces and the police force, there is no protection against unfair dismissal because the Trade Unions and Labour Relations Act is not applicable here. Similarly, in cases where employees are denied their legal rights as a result of the terms of their contract, the law is not enforceable.

Industrial Tribunals

If an employee meets the necessary requirements for appeal against dismissal and feels that his

LAW LORDS BACK EQUAL PAY CLAIM
Notable victory for women workers
Equal pay ruling may deepen disagreement

Figure 21.3 Industrial Tribunals in the Headlines

or her dismissal is unfair, the employer may be taken to an Industrial Tribunal. These tribunals, established in 1964, also deal with claims of sex and race discrimination and matters arising from the Equal Pay Act and the Redundancy Payments Act. These tribunals are to be found nationwide, and there are approximately 60 sitting at any time. There is an informal atmosphere about them, and the claimant or applicant can choose to put his or her own case to the tribunal. There is no need for legal representation, but trade unions can, and often do, represent their members. Each tribunal has 3 independent members – a legally qualified chairperson, an employer representative (elected by the CBI) and an employee representative (elected by the TUC). If an employee wins a case at a tribunal, compensation may be paid; reinstatement can be recommended but not enforced. If an employer does not wish to reinstate then an additional compensatory award may have to be made. The amount of compensation varies, but substantial sums, in excess of £10,000, are awarded where loss of earnings and earning power in the future are severe.

QUICK QUESTIONS 4

1. *Give 2 circumstances in which a worker could be made redundant.*
2. *What is the difference between redundancy and unfair dismissal?*
3. *Give 2 examples of a situation where a worker could be fairly dismissed.*
4. *Besides unfair dismissal, what other types of cases are dealt with by Industrial Tribunals?*
5. *If an Industrial Tribunal finds a worker has been unfairly dismissed, will he or she automatically be reinstated?*

STUDENT TASK

The following article refers to the case of Mrs Sandra Winton, who took her claim for equal pay to an Industrial Tribunal.

Woman wins fight for pay parity with manual staff

By John Gapper, Labour Correspondent

A WOMAN records assistant employed by Northern Ireland Electricity has been awarded equal pay with a male manual worker in the first case in which parity has been established between white-collar and blue-collar jobs.

The industrial tribunal judgment in the case of Mrs Sandra Winton could have a marked effect on the pay scales of UK white-collar electricity workers, which lag behind the pay of mainly male manual employees.

Unless the company appeals against the ruling, it may have to pay white-collar workers in Mrs Winton's grade a scale from £9,422 reaching £10,139 in four years, compared with the present £7,625 to £9,995 over eight years.

The judgment, which compared the value of Mrs Winton's work in terms of physical demands, skill and decision-making with that of a mains recorder, means she will also receive the recent 9.2 per cent manual pay settlement.

The case was taken on Mrs Winton's behalf by the white-collar section of the GMB general union. Mr John Edmonds, GMB general secretary, said the award by a Belfast tribunal was a breakthrough in public sector pay.

The ruling follows other judgments in favour of equal pay for women under equal value amendments of the 1970 Equal Pay Act which came into force in 1984. One of the most prominent was that of Ms Julie Hayward, a shipyard cook.

Ms Hayward, also a member of the GMB, was awarded equal pay with three male craftsmen at the Birkenhead shipyard of Cammell Laird by the House of Lords, which said benefits in kind should be treated as part of pay.

The GMB said that unless the Belfast decision was applied to 25,000 other women white-collar workers in the electricity industry, it would take many other individual cases to industrial tribunals.

Mrs Winton, who first took the case five years ago, was awarded several thousand pounds backpay to November 1982, despite Northern Ireland Electricity's argument that backpay should only be counted from 1984.

Source: The Financial Times, 15 June 1989.

1. On what basis was Mrs Winton awarded equal pay with certain male manual workers?
2. Under what Act of Parliament did Mrs Winton make her claim for equal pay?
3. What would have been the composition of the Industrial Tribunal which heard the case?
4. Who supported Mrs Winton in her claim to the tribunal?
5. Write a short account explaining why you think this case received such interest and attention and list some of the possible results of the judgement.

PROJECT AND ASSIGNMENT SUGGESTIONS

1. Visit your local job centre and find out as much as you can about government initiatives concerned with the training and retraining of workers. There are leaflets available explaining how the various schemes are organised and who can take advantage of them. With the help of these leaflets write a report describing the different types of help available for workers who wish to learn a new skill.
2. See if you can obtain a copy of the Health and Safety Policy of your school or college. Investigate how the institution implements this policy. Your investigation should try to answer the following questions:
   (a) What are the responsibilities of the institution with regard to health and safety?
   (b) In what ways are the employees of the institution involved in health and safety matters?
   (c) Who are the health and safety representatives?
   (d) What duties do the representatives perform?
   (e) Is there a Health and Safety Committee?
   (f) If so, have there been any recent recommendations from the committee concerning ways of improving health and safety?
   (g) Are there any aspects of health and safety which you think could be improved? Explain what action you think should be taken.
3. See what you can find out about recent judgements of Industrial Tribunals. Make a collection of any press cuttings you can find. You can organise these cuttings according to the type of case involved. Write a short summary of each judgement, including the basic facts of the case and the details of the tribunal's ruling.

CHAPTER 22

Consumer Protection

This final chapter on government influence, control and regulation of business activity concerns the important area of consumer protection. The purchase of goods and services is not always a straightforward exchange between buyer and seller which results in satisfaction for both parties. The consumer in particular is vulnerable in a number of ways when buying goods and services.

1. Consumers may be persuaded to purchase on the basis of incorrect or bogus information.
2. They may be pressurised by the seller into buying something they do not want or cannot afford.
3. They may be misled about the quantity they are buying.
4. The service they receive may be substandard.
5. The terms of the sale may be unfair.

Early Legislation

A hundred years ago the general attitude towards the problems and pitfalls listed above could be summed up in the doctrine of *caveat emptor*, which means 'let the buyer beware'. It was taken to be the responsibility of buyers to ensure that the goods they bought were suitable for the purpose for which they were bought. If a consumer bought a load of rubbish or struck a bad bargain it was just hard luck. The first attempt to give any legal protection to the consumer came with the passing of the **Sale of Goods Act 1893**. This Act laid down that all goods must be of **merchantable quality**, i.e. fit to be sold for their intended and expected purpose, and should match the description given. This means that a consumer who asks a butcher for a pound of fresh prime fillet steak should not be given a pound of fatty scrag-end which is unfit to eat.

This Act served as the basis for consumer protection for a great many years. However, in the latter half of the twentieth century it became apparent that changes in products, channels of distribution and methods of payment rendered the simple provisions of the 1893 Act insufficient adequately to protect the interests of consumers. Products have increased in sophistication and complexity, with a greater chance of the sort of breakdown which no consumer could be expected to rectify. This has put a greater responsibility on manufacturers and retailers regarding the quality of the goods they sell. A large number of products are now pre-packed and weighed; this is especially true of food products, which are sold in a variety of tins, jars, polystyrene containers, plastic bags, hermetically sealed polypropelene wrappers, and so on. This makes it difficult or impossible to inspect the goods before purchase. It was also felt that the consumer was increasingly at a disadvantage when dealing with business organisations, especially where the supply of the product is concentrated among a few manufacturers or retailers, because they cannot take their custom elsewhere if they are not satisfied with what they are offered. Another change concerns the methods of payment for goods and services. Consumers are increasingly using methods other than a straight cash payment, and retailers now offer credit facilities which can place consumers in a vulnerable position. In addition, over the years advertising has become increasingly persuasive rather than informative and so safeguards are needed to protect consumers from deliberately misleading methods of promotion.

When purchasing a good or service the consumer is entering into a contract with the seller. However, it is clear from the above that it is extremely difficult for the consumer to be aware of all the factors involved in the contract. Therefore, today consumers are protected in a number of ways when making a purchase. The government provides protection in the form of a variety of consumer laws which have been passed by parliament over the last 30 years. Various organisations, both government funded and independent, exist to provide additional help and protection for the consumer.

QUICK QUESTIONS 1

1. *What does the term 'caveat emptor' mean?*
2. *Give 3 reasons why this principle is not thought to be an adequate basis for consumer protection today?*
3. *The Sale of Goods Act 1893 introduced the concept of 'merchantable quality'. What does this mean?*

The Advertising of Goods and Services

In many cases the first contact the seller makes with the consumer is through the advertising of goods and services. To ensure the consumer is not subjected to misleading or dishonest advertising practices there are a number of statutory regulations governing advertisements, and the advertising industry itself has its own code of practice. The main aspects of consumer protection in the area of advertising are as follows:

The Trades Descriptions Acts 1968 and 1972

These two Acts made producers, sellers and advertisers responsible for telling the truth both orally and in writing when describing goods and services for sale. It is a criminal offence falsely to describe goods and services in advertisements or on product labels, e.g. with respect to size, materials used, method of manufacture or place of manufacture. It is also an offence to make false comparisons between present and previous prices. If a pair of shoes is described as 'real leather, hand-made in the United Kingdom, original price £40, sale price £25', then each piece of information must be the absolute truth. The shoes must have been on sale at £40 for at least 28 consecutive days in the previous 6 months (unless the seller clearly states to the contrary). The responsibility for the enforcement of the Act lies with local government. Local authorities employ **Trading Standards Officers**, who have the power to initiate prosecutions against sellers who fail to comply with the provisions of these Acts.

The Advertising Standards Authority

This is an organisation which has been established by the advertising industry to supervise the industry's own Code of Advertising Practice (CAP). The CAP Committee is composed of representatives of various organisations involved in advertising. It is responsible for preparing, amending and enforcing a voluntary code of practice for advertisers. The code, which was first published in 1961, sets guidelines concerning what constitutes a good advertisement. These are stated as follows:

1. All advertisements should be legal, decent, honest and truthful.
2. All advertisements should be prepared with a sense of responsibility both to the consumer and to society.
3. All advertisements should conform to the principles of fair competition generally accepted in business.

The Advertising Standards Authority (ASA) is only responsible for press, poster and cinema advertising. Television and radio advertising is controlled by other institutions (see below). The ASA's function is to protect the public interest and deal with complaints from consumers. It investigates over 8,000 such complaints each year and publishes regular case reports giving details of the results of these investigations. The ASA is financed by a levy paid by the media on advertising expenditure but it remains independent in the sense that it does not consist of members of the industry.

The Regulation of Broadcast Advertising

There is a Code of Advertising Standards and Practice which governs all advertising on independent television and commercial radio. Until recently it has been the **Independent Broadcasting Authority** (IBA) which has had the responsibility for amending this code and ensuring advertisers comply with the code and with the legal controls placed on advertising by the Broadcasting Acts. In January 1991 the IBA was replaced by two new organisations – the **Independent Television Commission** and the **Radio Authority** – which have taken over responsiblity for the Code of Standards and Practice and for receiving complaints from the public concerning broadcast advertising.

QUICK QUESTIONS 2

1. *Does the following price tag on a colour television comply with the Trades Descriptions Act?*
   WAS £350
   NOW £299
2. *Who is responsible for ensuring that traders abide by the provisions of the Trades Descriptions Act?*
3. *What is the function of the Advertising Standards Authority?*
4. *Which organisation deals with complaints from members of the public concerning radio and television advertising?*

The Sale of Goods and Services

Since the 1960s a considerable amount of legislation has been passed aimed at safeguarding the interests of the consumer when purchasing goods and services. The first legislation in this field, the Sale of Goods Act 1893, has already been mentioned. This has since been repealed and replaced by the Sale of Goods Act 1979.

The Sale of Goods Act 1979

This Act is a more thorough attempt than the original legislation to set down regulations governing the quality of goods bought by the consumer. The main provisions of the Act are as follows:

1. Goods must be of merchantable quality in the sense that they must be fit for their normal purpose. They should not be broken, damaged or faulty.
2. Goods must be suitable for the purpose for which they have been purchased, e.g. if you ask for a wristwatch which can be worn under water it must be possible to wear it under water.
3. Goods must conform to the description given by the manufacturer or retailer, e.g. a coat made of synthetic fibre cannot be described as pure wool.

The Act states that when purchasing a good the consumer's contract is with the retailer rather than the manufacturer. This means that it is the retailer who must deal with any customer complaints. If a consumer finds he or she has been sold a product which does not conform to the provisions above, then he or she is entitled to either a proper replacement, a refund or a repair of the item free of charge. Signs displayed in shops such as 'No Refunds' have no validity if the law has been broken. Similarly, the rights of consumers cannot be reduced by any agreement which stipulates that they qualify for less protection.

The Supply of Goods and Services Act 1982

By definition the Sale of Goods Act did not apply to the sale of services. Therefore, the Supply of Goods and Services Act was passed to apply to a whole range of contracts which were not previously covered, e.g. contracts for works and materials, goods that are hired rather than bought, goods obtained by barter, such as trading-in a car in part exchange, and services in general.

The problem specific to services is that if they prove to be unsatisfactory they cannot be returned for a refund, e.g. if a hairdresser is asked to highlight your hair and it turns out to be bright green, the damage has been done and cannot be reversed. Under this Act the consumer is protected if he or she feels the service has not been up to a reasonable standard. Consumers are entitled to a refund of any money spent plus compensation for loss where appropriate. In order to obtain their rights under the Act, consumers often have to make a claim against the business through the County Court, which has the power to decide the appropriate levels of compensation payable.

Here are 3 examples of the Act at work:

1. You collect your car from its annual service and on the way home it begins to make an unusual noise. On investigation you discover that the oil has been drained from the sump but not refilled. In this situation you should have the service completed free of charge and any damage which has been done to the engine should also be rectified at no cost.
2. You employ a builder to replace some broken

tiles on your roof. A few weeks later in a high wind the new tiles become dislodged and smash into your new greenhouse. In this case you can claim a refund for the work done and compensation to cover the cost of repairing the greenhouse.

3. You arrive in Corfu on your honeymoon to discover that your sea-facing room with private bathroom and balcony is not available for the first 3 nights due to overbooking. Instead you have to sleep in a rather small and hot basement room with no windows. Here you can claim a refund on the price you have paid and compensation for the inconvenience and disappointment you have suffered.

Unfair Contract Terms Act 1977

This Act ensures that sellers cannot avoid the provision of the law by placing exclusion clauses in agreements or displaying signs denying any responsibility for loss or damage. Under the Act the seller has to prove that such exclusions are fair. If they are judged not to be so they are totally invalid.

The Weights and Measures Act 1963

This Act makes it an offence for a business to give short weight or short measure of any product for sale. Before the Act was passed it was not uncommon for tradespeople to add other ingredients to products sold in bulk, such as flour, in order to increase the weight. Similarly, beer and spirits could be watered down to increase the publican's profits. Shops used weights and scales which were adjusted to the advantage of the seller. In order to prevent these practices, the Weights and Measures Act stated the following:

1. Certain foods, e.g. milk and sugar, must only be sold in certain prescribed quantities.
2. Other foods must be sold by weight or volume, e.g. vegetables are sold by weight. It is an offence to give the customer less than they have paid for. It is the responsibility of the seller to see scales and other measuring equipment is accurate.
3. Beer and spirits must be sold in standard quantities (although there is no standard measure for wine).
4. Pre-packed foods must be accurately marked

with their weight, and a distinction must be made between gross weight, which includes the packaging, and the net weight of the product itself.

Local councils have **Departments of Weights and Measures** which employ inspectors to check on shops and other retail outlets to ensure that sellers are complying with the Act and that customers are not being sold short measures.

The Food and Drugs Acts 1955

This is a wide-ranging Act which has been amended in recent years. Its main provisions deal with the quality and content of food products in order to protect the consumer in the fields of health and hygiene. The Act brought in the following regulations:

1. It is an offence to sell food, drink and drugs which are unfit for human consumption.
2. Food, drink and drugs should be prepared, processed and handled in hygienic conditions.
3. The ingredients of food and drink packages should be clearly labelled, starting with the most substantial ingredient.

Figure 22.1 Advertising Standards Authority Advertisement

4. Standards of composition of certain foods were specified, e.g. the minimum percentage of meat in sausages and the level of permitted additives.
5. The advertising of food and drugs must not be misleading.
6. Food cannot be repriced upwards unless a genuine mistake has been made.
7. Pre-packed food sold by weight should clearly show the total price and weight of the package and the price per ounce or pound.

Enforcement of the Act is the responsibility of local government **Environmental Health Departments**. These departments employ **Public Analysts** to check the contents of food and drink to ensure they comply with the provisions of the Act.

The Consumer Safety Act 1978

This Act gives the government the power to lay down safety regulations relating to potentially harmful goods in order to reduce the risk of death or harm to the consumer. Regulations cover such products as prams, pushchairs, electrical goods, childrens' toys and nightdresses. Under the Act the government can also instruct firms to issue a warning in the press if they discover a dangerous product has been sold. The Act has since been amended by the **Consumer Protection Act 1987**, which increased the powers of the enforcement authorities.

QUICK QUESTIONS 3

1. *What legal rights do consumers have if they purchase goods which are later found to be faulty?*
2. *You see the following sign in a disco:*

   The management accept no responsibility for loss or damage to person or property under any circumstances.

   Does this mean the owners of the disco are free from all legal liability?
3. *Why must the Manager of a public house be aware of the regulations laid down in the Weights and Measures Act?*
4. *Which local government department is responsible for the enforcement of the Food and Drugs Act?*
5. *What Act was passed to protect consumers from potentially harmful or dangerous goods?*

STUDENT TASK

David and Monica Roberts own a butcher's shop in Dunchester High Street. They recently received a visit from a representative of the local Environmental Health Department, who asked to inspect the premises to see that they were clean and hygienic.

1. What Act should David and Monica be aware of with regard to the conditions in which they prepare and sell their meat?
2. This Act also stipulates the composition of some of the products they sell. If the Environmental Health Department wished to check that the sausages which they make comply with government regulations, how would it do this?
3. David and Monica also have to be familiar with the law relating to the weights and measures of the goods they sell. State 2 ways in which the Weights and Measures Act affects their business.
4. Explain how this Act is enforced and what action could be taken against David and Monica if they are found to be breaking the law.

Paying for Goods and Services

Another area where problems can arise for consumers concerns the financial arrangements adopted for the purchase of goods and services. If something is bought for cash, the contract between buyer and seller is fairly simple and the interests of the consumer are protected by the legislation described above. However, in the last 15 years more and more people have begun to purchase items not for cash but via various forms of credit. There is now a wide range of credit facilities available to consumers. These include:

1. loans and overdrafts provided by banks
2. hire purchase
3. credit cards such as Access and Barclaycard
4. shop cards available from many of the larger stores, e.g. Debenhams, Marks and Spencer.

These forms of credit allow the purchaser either to buy goods and services and pay for them later or to borrow money and pay it back over a period of time. In addition to paying the price for the items bought, it is likely the purchaser will also have to pay interest on the credit they have received. The government considers that the consumer is in a vulnerable position when purchasing goods and services in this way, and has enacted legislation to regulate the terms and conditions of credit transactions. These rules and regulations are laid down in the **Consumer Credit Act 1974**. This Act protects the interests of the consumer in the following ways:

1. All businesses which lend money for interest must be licensed by the Office of Fair Trading.
2. It is an offence to approach someone uninvited and offer to arrange a loan.
3. When goods are being sold on credit the cash price as well as the total cost using credit must be clearly stated so that the purchaser is aware of the cost of the credit facilities.
4. Purchasers must be informed of the true rate of interest they are being charged. This is the **Annual Percentage Rate** (APR), and it must be stated on all agreements.
5. Any person who is refused credit has the right to obtain a copy of any report on their creditworthiness which has been supplied by a Credit Reference Agency. They can ask for any incorrect information to be corrected.
6. If a consumer purchases faulty goods on credit he or she can claim compensation from either the retailer or the institution which has provided the credit. (This does not apply when the finance has been borrowed by consumers to spend as they wish, as in the case of a bank loan or overdraft.)
7. Consumers who are persuaded to sign credit agreements in their own home (rather than in a shop or other retail outlet) are allowed a period of 3 days in which to change their minds.
8. Consumers have the right to seek court action if they feel the rate of interest charged is unfair or extortionate.
9. When goods are bought on a hire purchase (HP) agreement they do not become the property of the purchaser until the complete payment has been made. However, once one third of the total price has been paid the goods cannot be repossessed from the purchaser without a court order.

It can be seen that this is a very comprehensive piece of legislation which aims both to regulate institutions which provide finance for credit sales and to reduce the risk to the consumer of being persuaded to sign credit agreements that they later find they cannot afford.

QUICK QUESTIONS 4

1. *Name 3 ways a consumer can buy goods on credit.*
2. *Which Act of Parliament regulates the purchase of goods on credit?*
3. *What do the initials APR stand for? What is the APR?*
4. *What is the function of a Credit Reference Agency?*
5. *Someone visits your house and persuades you to purchase double glazing. You sign a credit agreement for the goods and installation but later you change your mind. What can you do?*

Figure 22.2 Preparing and Selling Food

All the legislation referred to above concerns the regulation of dealings between the buyer and seller where a decision has been made to purchase a good or service. However, situations can arise when payment is demanded from someone for goods they did not order and do not want. This applies particularly to goods sent through the post which the receiver has not requested. The **Unsolicited Goods and Services Act 1971** was passed to prevent such practices and make it illegal for a business to demand payment for goods which have not been ordered by the customer. Where unordered goods are delivered to a customer they are not bound to accept them or pay any money. The customer can choose one of the following courses of action:

1. Write to the business concerned informing them of where the goods can be collected. If the business does not collect the goods within 30 days they become the property of the recipient.
2. Do nothing, in which case the goods become the property of the recipient if not collected within 6 months.

It can be seen from the Acts listed above that a great deal of consumer law has been passed to regulate the whole process of advertising, purchasing and payment for goods and services. However, consumer protection involves more than just government legislation. In addition there are a number of agencies which provide help and advice on a wide variety of consumer issues. Some of these agencies are government controlled and funded and some are independent bodies. The latter often act as pressure groups on matters related to the interests of consumers.

Government Agencies which Aid the Consumer

The Office of Fair Trading

The OFT was established by the Fair Trading Act of 1973. It is a non-ministerial government department headed by the Director General of Fair Trading. Its broad function is to keep watch on trading matters in the UK and to protect both consumers and businesses against unfair practices. The role of the Office of Fair Trading in cases of restrictive practice agreements has already been referred to in Chapter 20. In addition to these responsibilities, the OFT works closely with local

Figure 22.3 Office of Fair Trading Leaflets

Trading Standards Departments and advice agencies in order to provide help to the public in matters relating to trade. Its principal functions are listed below.

1. It publishes information to help people understand their rights and obligations.
2. It encourages trade organisations to prepare voluntary codes of practice and to abide by them.
3. It reviews existing consumer legislation looking for loopholes, and proposes new legislation to the government where appropriate.
4. It aims to identify persistent offenders who ignore or neglect their responsibilities towards the consumers of their products or services.
5. It monitors the suitability of companies which provide credit facilities or who hire out goods to consumers.
6. It is responsible for the issuing of licences under the Consumer Credit Act 1974 (see above).
7. It can recommend to the appropriate government ministry the prohibition of specific practices if it considers that they contravene the principles of fair trade.

Although the OFT cannot deal with individual complaints or problems from consumers, it is active in a wide variety of areas of interest to consumers.

Central Government Departments

Various government ministries have responsibilities for consumer matters. The Ministry of Agriculture, Fisheries and Food (MAFF) administers the law relating to milk production, fisheries, abattoirs and the meat trade in general, and the labelling and composition of food. Action by the department concerning the 1989 salmonella in eggs publicity is an example of its involvement in consumer issues. The Department of Health has responsibilities related to the manufacture and distribution of medical supplies and the licensing of drugs. In addition there is the Department of Consumer Affairs, which is a sub-department of the Department of Trade and Industry under a Junior Minister. The major responsibilities of this department are to promote legislation relating to consumer protection and administer existing legislation. It also tries to encourage and assist in the establishment of both Consumer Advice Centres and Citizens' Advice Bureaux.

Local Authority Consumer Advice Centres

As already mentioned in the discussion of consumer protection legislation, local authorities have a number of responsibilities concerned with the policing and enforcement of laws relating to the sale of goods and services. These include Trading Standards Departments checking that businesses are complying with the Trades Descriptions Act, Weights and Measures Departments regularly testing weighing and other equipment in shops, and Environmental Health Departments visiting food shops and restaurants to ensure conditions are clean and hygienic. In addition to these responsibilities, some local authorities also provide Consumer Advice Centres, which provide information and advice to shoppers and publish leaflets about consumer rights and the operation of the law concerning consumer protection.

The National Consumer Council

The NCC is a state-funded body which was established in 1975 to advise the government on consumer protection. It acts as a central information-gathering and opinion-monitoring organisation. It also carries out tests on products and publishes the results. Although it is financed by central government, it acts independently and is a channel through which the ideas of a whole range of consumer bodies can be brought together and represented.

QUICK QUESTIONS 5

1. *State 3 ways in which the Office of Fair Trading is involved in consumer protection.*
2. *Which government department is responsible for initiating consumer protection legislation?*
3. *What is the function of the National Consumer Council?*

Non-Government Organisations Concerned with Consumer Protection

As well as the institutions listed above, there are a whole range of private organisations concerned with consumer protection. Although these bodies are independent of the government, many receive state aid in the form of grants to help meet their expenses. The main organisations of this type are described below.

Professional and Trade Associations

It has already been mentioned that the Office of Fair Trading encourages individual trades and professions to establish their own codes of good practice. In order to do this many trades have set up associations which are responsible for preparing a code of practice acceptable to their members and for dealing with customer complaints against members of the industry. Examples of such associations are the Association of British Travel Agents (ABTA), and the Glass and Glazing Federation (GGF). The associations help members of the industry by increasing the customer's confidence in the service they are offering, and they benefit the consumer by investigating complaints against members of the association. Firms found ignoring the code can be excluded from the association.

Figure 22.4 Trade Association Logos

Independent Associations

There are also independent associations which offer help and advice to consumers in a number of areas. These associations generally provide specific services in return for a membership fee. The Automobile Association (AA) and the Royal Automobile Club (RAC), for example, offer a number of breakdown and emergency services to motorists as well as acting as a pressure group on matters affecting road

transport generally. Other organisations make their help available in other ways, e.g. through the publication of information and advice. One of the most important examples of this type of organisation is the Consumers' Association.

The Consumers' Association

The Consumers' Association was founded to provide shoppers with up-to-date information about the quality and value for money of products on the market. It is best known for its monthly consumer magazine *Which?*. Originally modelled on an American publication and launched in 1957, *Which?* proved an instant success. The magazine contains reports on all manner of goods and services, with comparisons of quality, price, after-sales service and so on. *Which?* has been the basis for the development of the Consumers' Association over the last 30 years, and now sells over 700,000 copies each month. The Association also publishes *Holiday Which?* 4 times a year, *Gardening from Which?* 10 times a year, the

Figure 22.5 Consumer Association Publications

Which? Wine Monthly and a fortnightly *Drugs and Therapeutics Bulletin*. The association has also published some 50 books ranging from the *Good Food Guide* to *Understanding Mental Health*.

The Association is a non-profit-making organisation financed in the main by members' subscriptions. Over the years it has grown into the largest consumer organisation in Europe, with a turnover in excess of £22 million and a staff of more than 400. It has specialist testing facilities at its own laboratories in Harpenden, which not only carry out the research work for *Which?* but also work on a commercial basis for government departments and international agencies. The association also directs considerable energy and resources towards active campaigning on behalf of all consumers, not just members. Its first success in this area was the 1971 Unsolicited Goods and Services Act, referred to earlier. It has been successful in ending solicitors' virtual monopoly over house conveyancing and has tackled a wide variety of broader issues relating to the nationalised industries.

The British Standards Institution

BSI was founded in 1901 as a voluntary body financed jointly by industry and the government. It is chiefly concerned with the setting and maintenance of standards with regard to the performance, quality, dimensions and the methods of testing of products. The general acceptance of these standards reduces unnecessary variations and simplifies production. The famous 'Kitemark' symbol of the institution has become an indication of a high standard on a variety of goods, from electrical equipment to motorcycle crash helmets. The institution is governed by a council consisting of representatives from industry, the trade unions, professional bodies and government departments.

Figure 22.6 The BSI Kitemark

The National Viewers' and Listeners' Association

This is a pressure group established to act as a watchdog on standards in broadcasting. It attempts to define and support acceptable standards for radio and television programmes and has become widely known through the work of Mrs Mary Whitehouse, one of its founder members.

The Media

Newspapers, radio and television are very influential in a variety of consumer protection matters. There are specialist consumer programmes, e.g. *That's Life* and *For What it's Worth*, and the media continually assess, compare and recommend various goods and services and offer advice on 'best buys' and consumer affairs in general.

It is clear that consumers are protected by a whole network of legislation and assisted by various organisations and agencies. However, this does not mean that consumers are never cheated or always receive good service. Rogue traders still exist and consumers often receive a poor deal when buying goods and services. The Office of Fair Trading recently called for a new law putting the responsibility firmly on all businesses to trade fairly, and the Consumers' Association believes there is still a long way to go in improving the rights of the consumer. Peter Goldman, a former Chairman of the Association, expressed this in the following way:

> This is an organisation motivated with the desire to rectify an intolerable imbalance in society — between the power of producers and sellers and the relative weakness of buyers. We are an information collective ... providing the information to enable consumers to win the battle in the market place.

QUICK QUESTIONS 6

1. *What are the principal functions of a trade association?*
2. *What is the monthly publication of the Consumers' Association called?*
3. *How does this publication help consumers who are considering buying a particular good or service?*
4. *Why might consumers look for the 'Kitemark' when purchasing a child seat for their car?*

STUDENT TASK

Mary Baker sees a secondhand car in her local garage which is described as 'the car of the month'. She inquires further and the salesman tells her it is in very good condition and a real bargain at the price. Mary decides to buy the car and the garage arranges a hire purchase agreement with a finance company. Unfortunately 2 days after Mary collects the car the clutch fails. The garage maintains that the car was in perfectly good order when it was sold and says she will have to pay to get the car repaired.

1. Mary is convinced that it is the garage's reponsibility to put the fault right. Who can she consult for advice?
2. Is there an organisation to which Mary can make a complaint concerning the attitude of the garage?
3. Explain one Act of Parliament which is designed to protect Mary's rights in a situation like this.

4. How does the fact that Mary bought the car on hire purchase affect her rights in this case?
5. Write a short report explaining what action you think Mary should take.

PROJECT AND ASSIGNMENT SUGGESTIONS

1. Find out more about the role of local government in enforcing consumer-protection legislation. Contact your local authority and collect what information you can about the work of the following:
   (a) Trading Standards Inspectors
   (b) Weights and Measures Inspectors
   (c) Environmental Health Officers
   Where possible include examples from your local area to illustrate your study.
2. Assume you wish to purchase a product on credit. Make a list of the different ways this could be done. Investigate the following:
   (a) How the cost of the credit differs between the various methods. In each case find out the APR.
   (b) What you could do if you believed the cost of a source of credit was unrealistically high.
   (c) What your rights are if you are refused credit without explanation.
   (d) What you could do if the product was to break down a week after you bought it.
   (e) What would happen if you chose to buy the product on hire purchase and after paying half the instalments you fall behind with your payments.
3. Select a product which is available from a number of suppliers and undertake your own *Which?* survey. Draw up a table of all the important information consumers would like to know before they purchased the product and compare different makes against these points. You could undertake this as a group activity with each member of the group concentrating on a different make of the product. If your library has copies of previous issues of *Which?* magazine, investigate whether the Consumers' Association has undertaken a similar report and compare your results.

Index